Behavior and Adaptation in Late Life

Behavior and Adaptation in Late Life

Second Edition

Edited by

Ewald W. Busse, M.D., D.Sc.

J. P. Gibbons Professor of Psychiatry, and
Associate Provost and Dean of Medical
and Allied Health Education, Duke
University School of Medicine;
Chairman, Duke University Council on
Aging and Human Development,
Duke University, Durham, N.C.

Eric Pfeiffer, M.D.

Professor of Psychiatry, Duke University
School of Medicine; Associate Director
for Programs, Center for the Study of
Aging and Human Development,
Duke University, Durham, N.C.

Little, Brown and Company   Boston

Library of Congress Catalog
Card No. 76-4991

ISBN 0-316-11833-8 (C)

ISBN 0-316-11834-6 (P)

Printed in the United States of America

Contents

Contributing Authors

Kurt W. Back, Ph.D.
Professor of Sociology, Department
of Sociology and Anthropology,
Duke University; Professor of Medical
Sociology, Department of Psychiatry,
Duke University School of Medicine,
Durham, N.C.

Ewald W. Busse, M.D., D.Sc.
J. P. Gibbons Professor of Psychiatry,
and Associate Provost and Dean of
Medical and Allied Health Education,
Duke University School of Medicine;
Chairman, Duke University Council
on Aging and Human Development,
Duke University, Durham, N.C.

Carl Eisdorfer, Ph.D., M.D.
Professor and Chairman, Department
of Psychiatry and Behavioral Sciences,
University of Washington School of
Medicine, Seattle

E. Harvey Estes, Jr., M.D.
Professor and Chairman, Department
of Community Health Sciences,
Duke University School of Medicine,
Durham, N.C.

Alvin I. Goldfarb, M.D.
Associate Clinical Professor of Psychiatry,
Mount Sinai School of Medicine of
The City University of New York;
Associate Attending Psychiatrist in
Charge of Geriatrics, Mount Sinai
Hospital, New York City

Dorothy K. Heyman, M.S.W.
Assistant Professor of Psychiatric
Social Work, Department of Psychiatry,
Duke University School of Medicine;
Executive Secretary of the Center for
the Study of Aging and Human
Development and of Duke University
Council on Aging and Human Development,
Duke University, Durham, N.C.

Frances C. Jeffers, M.A.
Research Associate (Retired) and
Executive Secretary (Retired) of the
Center for the Study of Aging and
Human Development, Duke University,
Durham, N.C.

Juanita M. Kreps, Ph.D.
Vice-President and James B. Duke
Professor of Economics, Department
of Economics, Duke University,
Durham, N.C.

George L. Maddox, Ph.D.
Professor of Sociology, Department of
Sociology, and Director, Center for the
Study of Aging and Human Development,
Duke University, Durham, N.C.

Erdman Palmore, Ph.D.
Professor of Medical Sociology,
Department of Psychiatry,
Duke University School of Medicine;
Scientific Associate, Center for the
Study of Aging and Human Development,
Duke University, Durham, N.C.

ix

Eric Pfeiffer, M.D.
Professor of Psychiatry, Duke University
School of Medicine; Associate Director
for Programs, Center for the Study of
Aging and Human Development,
Duke University, Durham, N.C.

†**Grace H. Polansky, M.S.S.A.**
Associate in Psychiatric Social Work,
Department of Psychiatry,
Duke University School of Medicine,
Durham, N.C.

Ethel Shanas, Ph.D.
Professor of Sociology,
University of Illinois at
Chicago Circle, Chicago

Joseph J. Spengler, Ph.D.
James B. Duke Professor of Economics,
Department of Economics,
Duke University, Durham, N.C.

Virginia Stone, R.N., Ph.D.
Professor of Nursing,
Duke University School of Nursing,
Durham, N.C.

Adriaan Verwoerdt, M.D.
Professor of Psychiatry,
Duke University School of Medicine,
Durham, N.C.

F. Stephen Vogel, M.D.
Professor of Pathology,
Duke University School of Medicine,
Durham, N. C.

† Deceased.

H.-S. Wang, M.D.
Professor of Psychiatry,
Duke University School of Medicine,
Durham, N.C.

Preface to the Second Edition

Since its original publication in 1969, *Behavior and Adaptation in Late Life* has enjoyed a degree of use and acceptance that has been extremely gratifying to its editors and publisher alike. Its greatest use has come from two quarters: practitioners dealing with the elderly, and teachers and students of gerontology at the graduate and undergraduate levels. The book, originally published in hard covers, soon had to be made available as a less expensive paperback. It has gone through four printings and been offered by several book clubs in the health care and behavioral science field.

But the field of aging does not stand still. Demographic, social, economic, and political facts about the aging change, and so do scientific findings and theories regarding aging. When it became apparent that a second edition was needed, the task of updating was begun. It is a real credit to the contributors of this volume that all of them accepted the invitation to participate in this work again. In addition, we are extremely gratified that our long-time colleague, Dr. George L. Maddox, out of the country on a sabbatical at the time the first edition was written, has joined us in this edition as the coauthor of the chapter on the sociological aspects of aging.

The reader will note that considerable variation exists in the progress reported in the differing disciplines in gerontology included in this book. These differences reflect in part the rapidity of change of circumstances. But it also reflects to no small degree the variation in support received for new research on different aspects of the overall aging picture. Major progress has been made in some areas of the field. Relatively less progress can be recorded in other areas. This observation is testimony to the need for continued stable support for research into a broad range of aspects of the entire aging experience.

The editors wish to express their thanks to the many readers who have given them encouragement and who, through their highly intelligent questions, have made a real contribution to the shaping of the second edition.

The editors also wish to acknowledge a special debt of gratitude to Mrs. Lin Richter, Editor of the Medical Division of Little, Brown and Company, who originally approached us with the idea for a book on behavior and adaptation in late life and who has given us encouragement, guidance, and counsel over the past eight years during which we have collaborated. Without her skillful efforts, neither the first nor the second edition of this volume would have been possible.

E. W. B.
E. P.

Preface to the First Edition

In this book we have tried to bring together basic information which has a bearing on how people adapt to growing old. We feel that no single discipline, whether it be psychiatry, sociology, biology, or economics, can claim to offer a comprehensive explanation of how aged people act, think, and feel, or what the multiple determinants of their behavior are. Moreover, we feel that a mere collection of unrelated essays by experts from differing fields is not satisfactory, but that instead an integration of the diverse contributions is needed. We have sought to accomplish this integration in several ways. First, we invited as contributors to this volume investigators and clinicians who, as members of a common faculty, or as members of the Duke Center for the Study of Aging and Human Development, or through shared committee and organization work over a period of years, had come to know each other's work and point of view. Second, at the start of the project we made available to all contributors an overall outline of the proposed volume, thus allowing each of them to see how his or her chapter fitted into the entire scheme of the book. Third, we continued to refine the goal and scope of the book in weekly discussion sessions in which drafts of chapters were read and discussed, criticized, rewritten, and discussed again. These sessions were attended by many of the authors; but other staff members of the Duke Center also participated and contributed immeasurably to the final product presented here.

The deluge of new information about the aging process and the rapid obsolescence of present skills and knowledge have, in our opinion, demanded that a determined effort be made to present under a single cover a broad range of material. We further felt that we had to do so succinctly and in understandable terms so that the book might be useful to a wide spectrum of people.

This book is written for those with an interest in any of a number of aspects of aging, with the anticipation that their understanding of their own area of interest will be enhanced by an awareness of other forces also impinging on aged persons. It is our hope that the book will prove useful to psychiatrists who see aged persons in their practice, and to internists and general practitioners who do likewise. We feel the book contains information relevant to health planners, social welfare workers, and state and local health and welfare administrators. We hope this book will also be read by gerontologists from a variety of disciplines—sociologists, anthropologists, economists, psychologists, biologists—in short, all professionals whose topic of investigation is the aging process. College undergraduates or graduate students studying human development or normal or abnormal psychology, as well as their teachers, may find this a useful summary of present knowledge in this field. Furthermore, the book is relatively nontechnical so that it can be read by the general reader who wants to know more about aging, especially if he has aged parents whom he may need to care for or whom he at least wishes to understand. Finally, we feel that the aged themselves may obtain from this book a broader perspective of what they are experiencing.

We are indebted to many persons for their help with this project. In particular, we would like to acknowledge the help of Dr. Carl Eisdorfer, Dr. Walter Obrist, and Dr. Erdman Palmore, who in many ways assisted us in determining editorial policy. We are also extremely grateful to all those who participated in our discussion sessions, including Dr. Kurt Back, Dr. Daniel Gianturco, Mrs. Dorothy Heyman, Miss Frances Jeffers, Dr. Jesse McNiel, Dr. John Nowlin, Dr. Larry Thompson, Dr. Adriaan Verwoerdt, Dr. H.-Shan Wang, Dr. A. D. Whanger, and Mrs. Frances Wilkie.

We are especially appreciative of the two authors not on the Duke faculty who joined our Duke colleagues in this venture and added their highly specialized knowledge. We also wish to express regret that several distinguished members of the Center research staff were unable to collaborate with us on this volume because of previous commitments on their time, and we are sorry that we did not have the total benefit of their combined experience and wisdom. Readers familiar with the structure of the Center will notice, however, the frequency with which reference is made to their work throughout the book.

Special recognition is due Mrs. Rosa Absalom and Mrs. Ann Rimmer for their coordination of the entire editorial and production effort as well as for efficient handling of editorial correspondence. Finally, our gratitude must be expressed to all our contributors who worked diligently to maintain the original writing and production schedule.

Ewald W. Busse
Eric Pfeiffer
Durham, N.C.
June 1969

Behavior and Adaptation in Late Life

1. Introduction

Ewald W. Busse and Eric Pfeiffer

This book is the result of both multidisciplinary and interdisciplinary labor. The terms *multidisciplinary* and *interdisciplinary* are often used interchangeably and, we believe, erroneously [3]. For instance, multidisciplinary research is a type of *group* research involving investigators from several distinct scientific disciplines working in parallel with one another. The investigators are identified as a group because they work in proximity to one another and because their research deals with a common topic. The group usually plans to maximize communication among the various investigators, hoping to increase the breadth and potential of their work.

Interdisciplinary research, on the other hand, is a team effort by two or more persons representing different scientific disciplines. Because of their particular skills and interests, the investigators have accepted responsibility for certain segments of a jointly defined research goal. The meaning of the prefix *inter-* is "mutual," not merely "among" or "between."

A glance at the great variety of scientific disciplines represented by the contributors makes it clear that the entire volume must be viewed as a multidisciplinary product, although many of its sections are of an interdisciplinary nature. All the authors share a common concern with the processes of aging and the problems of the aged. This does not mean, however, that each necessarily agrees with the approach used or the conclusions reached by the other authors. And while the editors hold themselves principally responsible for the selection of topics included in this book, the particular points of view expressed in each chapter are those of the individual contributors.

Estimates of the Older Population

As of 1975, approximately 10.3 percent of the population of the United States are 65 years of age or over. This is an increase of approximately 0.5 percent from 1970, when 20.2 million (9.8 percent) of the 204.8 million persons in the United States were in this age group. This is a remarkable change when one considers that in 1870 the total population of the United States was 40 million, of whom only 1.2 million (less than 3 percent) were 65 years of age or older. According to Brotman [1], the 20 million Americans who in 1970 were 65 years of age or over were equal in numbers to the total population of 21 of the smallest states.

1

Are the Elderly a Minority Group?
Since the elderly constitute such a sizable fraction of the entire population, it may at first be somewhat surprising that the question of the elderly as a minority group should be raised at all. But numbers alone do not determine minority status, as can be seen by comparing the elderly with a more clearly defined minority group in this country, namely, blacks. In 1967 the elderly accounted for 9.9 percent of the population, while blacks accounted for 11.2 percent [6]. Yet the latter clearly constitute a minority group in our society. In any case the question whether or not the elderly are a minority group has been raised, at times only subtly. Sometimes it has been answered in the affirmative; occasionally it has been answered negatively. The status of the aged as a deprived minority group is substantiated by the observations of several of the contributors to this volume. They believe that retired persons rarely share in the advantages enjoyed by the majority of our society and that prejudices restrict opportunities for the elderly to achieve personal satisfaction and participation in the entire range of activities open to other members of the society.

The Nature of Minority Groups
Minority groups will always exist in any sizable group of human beings. How minority groups are defined and recognized is complicated. They can be distinguished by such factors as their expressed beliefs and behavior, their physical appearance, their characteristic dress, eating habits, religious expression, social behavior, or fixed and recognizable patterns of handling such experiences as insecurity, fear, grief, and aggression. At certain points in the history of a nation, minority groups are more easily recognized and are seen as more deviant than at other times. Minority groups often become less visible as they gradually alter their own patterns or effect changes in the majority so that distinctions between the majority and the minority become increasingly blurred. There is still considerable fluctuation in the degree to which the aged are regarded as a minority group in this country. This is reflected in the rapidly changing and often contradictory public policies with regard to many aspects of the lives of the elderly.

Taking the point of view for the moment that any definable group of people who share specific characteristics is in effect a minority group, then the question arises if it is possible for any minority group to have opportunities equal to those of the majority. Equal opportunity is highly unlikely as long as the minority group voluntarily or involuntarily maintains social expectations and behavior that are different from those of the majority. Paradoxically, this may even be true of what might be called affluent minority groups. It is obviously true of retired persons. It is also true that some minority groups elect to bypass the opportunities offered by the majority in order to maintain their own value systems. Minority groups can exist in relatively contented fashion when the advantages offered them by their own group satisfactorily meet their needs or when the opportunities of the majority are also open to them if they so elect.

If one accepts the view that elderly Americans constitute a deprived minority, then it is important to understand how and why they have acquired this status. The elderly differ from many other minority groups in the way in which they have come by their status. They were neither born into it, nor did they achieve it through any action on their part; rather, they had their minority status thrust on them as a result of the accumulation of a certain number of birthdays. Whether lifelong discrimination or recently acquired discrimination is harder to bear is a question that we are hardly prepared to answer, but we do feel that this difference is worthy of note.

The Nature of Prejudice

In primitive societies, social and health problems are often complicated by the existence of folklore, myths, and superstitions. In so-called affluent societies, unexpressed and unrecognized individual prejudices and group biases can be equally troublesome. The complications arising from them are often difficult to recognize, since they are not sufficiently distinct to be classed as myths or superstitions. Nevertheless, they can affect thought and behavior and be manifested by a lack of interest, a misinterpretation of facts, or inappropriate reactions such as overconcern.

The abode of prejudice is largely in the unconscious mind. The conscious recognition that a prejudice exists is usually transient. Prejudices can be acquired throughout life, but the mechanisms that facilitate their development are primarily rooted in childhood fears and in childhood modes of thinking. Consequently, prejudices carry the intense emotionality of childhood, although the "reasons" for them are couched in adult-like terms. Therefore prejudiced adults hold to their convictions with intense feelings that resist reality and logic. They must first recognize that the excessive feelings that accompany their attitude are indeed unreasonable, and they must then be willing to unlearn the faulty learning by actual personal experience, replacing prejudice with a rational approach.

The professional or volunteer worker who is involved with elderly persons brings into his relationships with them predetermined attitudes and patterns of reacting. Many members of the health and welfare professions have difficulty relating effectively to elderly persons. There are several factors contributing to this. We all instinctively fear physical and mental decline. When we observe a patient deteriorating despite our best efforts to the contrary, we are reminded that we, too, are vulnerable and will inevitably experience the changes of the aging process, including death. Also, members of the health disciplines are frequently frustrated because elderly patients often have multiple and chronic physical and psychological complaints that, moreover, are often exacerbated by the patients' life circumstances. The physician is made to feel he is of little value, since he cannot relieve the symptoms, and he has neither the knowledge nor the prerogative to alter the socioeconomic conditions [2]. Comfort [4], considering these same problems, has coined the term *gerontophobia* to refer to the reluctance on the part of some health professionals and others to become involved in the problems of the aged.

The Younger and the Older Aged

As many of the chapters in this volume make it clear, all elderly people share certain problems, but the elderly cannot be considered a homogeneous group. Important differences exist among the younger aged (those between ages 65 and 75) and the older aged (those over age 75). For instance, the incidence of disabling physical conditions is far greater among those over age 75 than in the younger age group, although those between ages 65 and 75 who are disabled may have many more things in common with those age 75 and over than with their nondisabled age mates [1]. That the needs of the extremely old are substantially different from those of the younger group of elderly persons will emerge throughout this book. This differentiation is particularly clearly drawn in Chapters 7 and 18. Elsewhere in the book, age differences are sometimes ex-

5

plicitly stated; at other times they are merely implied. We believe that in the years ahead, gerontologists will become increasingly cognizant of the subgroups that make up our aged population.

The Duke Longitudinal Studies

The reader will quickly notice that in several chapters the authors mention the results obtained from a longitudinal study carried out at Duke University. Some of these authors are co-investigators in that continuing study or in a more recently begun study that also deals with changes observed in individuals over time.* A brief summary of the samples and the methods used in these studies might be useful.

The first longitudinal project, "The Effect of Aging Upon the Central Nervous System," was initiated in 1954. The aim of this long-term study is to identify social, psychological, and physiological factors influencing the behavior of elderly people and to relate these changes to intellectual function, personality, and social competence.

The original sample was composed of volunteers who were 60 years of age or over at the beginning of the study. When initially screened and accepted, they were believed to be relatively free of disease, and they were functioning at an acceptable level in the community. The age range for the group at the onset of the study was 60 to 94 years, with a median age of 70. The sample contained both white and black and male and female subjects in proportions that approximated but did not coincide with the race and sex distribution of the community from which the sample was drawn [5]. Subjects were examined and studied over a two-day period. These studies were then repeated at two- to three-year intervals, and to date five series of studies have been completed. During this time the original sample of 260 subjects has been reduced to 58 (by spring, 1975) because of attrition due to death and other causes.

It is recognized that persons volunteering to participate in a study such as this may possess characteristics that distinguish them from elderly persons who are unwilling to participate. Another limiting factor of the study is the unknown extent of the influence of this long-term research project on the lives of the participating subjects. Only 6 percent of the original sample have been lost over the years because of refusal to

* This research is currently supported by U.S. P.H.S. Grant H.D.–00668, the J. P. Gibbons Fund, and Duke University.

continue to participate. In order to minimize losses, the project has recently acquired a mobile laboratory to permit continuing detailed examination of any subjects who are confined to their homes, to hospitals, or to other institutions.

Masses of data have been acquired. At each full longitudinal examination, over 1,000 variables per subject are coded, recorded, and transferred to magnetic tape for computer uses. The items include 336 medical observations, 109 psychiatric-neurological, 109 routine psychological, 234 social, and a varying number of so-called special items. The investigators have utilized the accumulated data cross-sectionally and longitudinally. Additional data come from so-called satellite projects and are available to the investigators. These projects are conducted independently on the same subjects by an individual investigator with the permission of the interdisciplinary team.

A second longitudinal investigation has recently been initiated and is entitled "Adaptation to Change." Many of the hypotheses and questions, observations, and methodology of this new study have been influenced by the first study. The new study is primarily concerned with the aging process and adaptation to stressful events during middle age and the retirement years.

A sample of slightly more than 500 subjects, ranging in age from 45 through 69, has been drawn. A random selection was employed, and the sample was designed so that there will be approximately 40 persons in each of 10 age-sex cohorts in 1973. This design will make possible basic comparison between age groups, controlling for sex. It is intended to permit the partialing out of the effects of aging from differences between age cohorts by comparing differences over time with differences between adjacent age cohorts at one point in time. Individual differences will be studied after stressful events—such as the death of a spouse or close relative, serious illness, menopause, departure of children, retirement, or economic changes—by comparing differences between age cohorts and time intervals for the same cohort and by time-lag analysis that examines the adaptations likely to follow an identified change. Extensive planning for this study extending over several years resulted in careful definition of terms, the setting up of hypotheses and questions, clear elucidation of the variables to be studied, and the standardization of techniques.

It is one of the ironies of scientific work in the field of aging that many of the contributors to this volume are presently engaged in the gathering of new observations that in all likelihood will make at least portions of this volume obsolete.

References

1. Brotman, H. B. *An Overview for the Delegates to the White House Conference on Aging: Facts and Figures of Older Americans.* DHEW Publication No. (SRS)/72-20005. Washington, D.C.: Government Printing Office, 1971.
2. Busse, E. W. Problems affecting psychiatric care of the aging. *Geriatrics* 15:673, 1960.
3. Busse, E. W. Administration of the interdisciplinary research team. *J. Med. Educ.* 40:832, 1965.
4. Comfort, A. On gerontophobia. *Med. Opinion Rev.* September 1967. Pp. 30–37.
5. Maddox, G. L. A longitudinal multidisciplinary study of human aging: Selected methodological issues. *Proc. Soc. Stat. Sec. Am. Stat. Assoc.* 122:280, 1962.
6. U.S. Department of Commerce, Bureau of the Census. *Statistical Abstracts of the U.S., 1971* (92nd ed.). Topic 22. July 1971. P. 24.

2. Theories of Aging

Ewald W. Busse

The study of aging in all its aspects—biological, psychological, and sociological—is known as the science of gerontology. Gerontologists view attempts to prolong life that do not also improve the lot of the aged as having limited value. In fact, the mere prolongation of life may be more of a detriment than an asset for all concerned. Although the desire to prevent or retard the progress of aging has obsessed human beings for thousands of years, it has been appreciated that to extend life without maintaining vigor has enormous dangers. For example, Swift, in *Gulliver's Travels,* reports how his hero encountered pathetic creatures called Struldbrugs. These unfortunate persons could not die but had all of the gradually increasing incapacities of aging, both physical and mental. Greek mythology teaches a similar lesson. The goddess Aurora (also called Eos) with great effort persuaded Zeus to grant her husband Tithonus immortality. Unfortunately, she did not ask Zeus to give Tithonus eternal youth, and he became more and more disabled, praying fervently for death. In one account, Tithonus escaped his misery by turning into a cicada. The male of this insect produces a shrill sound similar to the voice of a demented person [20].

Alex Comfort [7, 8], a British scientist who has made numerous significant contributions to gerontology, particularly to the biology of aging, has skillfully reviewed past efforts to extend the life span. He points out that over the centuries the hope of delaying aging has been focused on the continuation of sexual vigor and reproductive capacity. In fact, in Darwin's concept of survival of the fittest, reproductive capability plays a central role. This point will be elaborated on shortly.

Perhaps the best known of the attempts to find prolonged youth is the medieval European search for the fountain of youth. Today it seems incredible that this story was taken seriously. It was based on a second-century account by a writer, Pausanias, whose works were revived and popularized by Jean de Mandeville. It is highly likely that this intensive search is particularly remembered because of Ponce de Leon's discovery of the state of Florida, for it is a fact that his 1512 expedition was actually organized and financed specifically to search for the fountain of youth [15].

Comfort also reviews a number of Near and Far Eastern rejuvenation efforts. These efforts to maintain youth were primarily rooted in what is called *gerocomy,* which is the belief and practice that a man absorbs

8

virtue and youth from women, particularly young women. This idea permeated many societies. King David in the Old Testament believed it and practiced accordingly. There is clear evidence also that the Romans held similar views. Further, as Comfort reports, this concept has some support from the modern experimental laboratory. Aged male rats will respond favorably when a young female rat is placed among them. Her presence and activities greatly improve their condition and promote their survival [8, p. 5].

In recent years there has been a recurrence of reports of groups of people that include a significant number of centenarians. One group lives in Vilcabamba, a small village in Ecuador. Two others are in widely separated regions of Asia: the Hunzukuts of the Karakurum Range in Kashmir and the Abkhazians of the Republic of Georgia, U.S.S.R. All live in relatively isolated mountain regions. The cultures are primarily agrarian, physical activity is high, family ties are close, and wine and tobacco are used without negative effects. Longevity is attributed to genetic factors, diet, and work patterns. However, the distinguished Russian scientist Medvedev [22] does not accept the reliability of the advanced years claimed by the elderly of the Caucasus. He cites the lack of birth records, the rapid increase in the number claiming to be centenarians, the greater number of men as compared with women, the discrepancy with the life expectancy of other members of the same group, and the proved falsification by at least one deserter or draft dodger, and so on.

Aging Defined

The biological processes of aging are usually associated with a decline of efficiency and functioning that eventually results in death. Some biologists define aging as a progressive loss of functional capacity after an organism has reached maturity, while others insist that aging begins with the onset of differentiation. Still others contend that a definition of aging is not useful or possible [41]. Many investigators prefer to separate declines in functioning into primary and secondary aging [5].

The biological processes called *primary aging* are apparently rooted in heredity. They are inborn and inevitable detrimental changes that are time-related but independent of stress, trauma, or disease. However, the various aging processes are not recognizable in all people, and those that are present do not progress at the same rate. *Secondary aging* refers to disabilities resulting from trauma and chronic disease.

The designation *aged* is often used arbitrarily to describe or define persons who have achieved a certain chronological age within a given population. The wide variation in who is considered old is evidenced by the fact that a person 40 years of age is old in so-called undeveloped nations, while in an industrialized or advanced society a person must survive many more years before he is considered aged.

Longevity and the Contribution of Benjamin Gompertz
Since 1900 the percentage of the United States population age 65 and over has more than doubled (from 4.1 percent in 1900 to an estimated 10.3 percent in 1975), while the actual number of aged persons has increased sevenfold, from 3 million to over 21 million (8.9 million males and 12.8 million females) [24]. There has also been a clear reversal in life expectancy trends for men and women. In 1900 in the United States there were 98 old women to every 100 old men. Women have had longer life expectancies from 1900 onward [32]. During the period 1900 to 1902, life expectancy for white females below age 20 was lower than for males of a like age but slightly higher for females through the adult years. In 1964 the longevity of the young female had improved remarkably and had considerably surpassed that of the young male. Apparently this was not the result of selective immigration—that is, more men than women coming into the country—but a shift in health as related to sex.

Women are outliving men. In fact, there are about 138.5 older women per 100 older men. Life expectancy for women is still increasing faster than for men. Although it is unlikely that the percentage of older people in the population will increase significantly during the next 20 years, their actual number will go over 27 million [43]. Assuming that the current life expectancy trends continue, by the year 2000 the ratio of elderly women to men will be approximately 149 to 100 [34]. The differences between aging in men and women are clearly presented in a number of chapters in this book.

Human longevity is influenced by a complex of interacting factors, including genetic makeup, environmental and nutritional factors, and psychological, social, and economic influences. The increase in average life expectancy has been largely due to a decrease in deaths attributable to infectious diseases. However, it is highly likely that measures that succeed in improving health and reducing death risk in early life positively affect health in the adult years as well, thereby diminishing the death risk.

Life expectancy is a computed projection, not an observed or estimated phenomenon. The projection is based on the assumption that the death rate experienced in a single year, or the average experienced in a few years, will remain completely unchanged in the future. Obviously, any natural or man-made events that influence future death rates, such as changes in medical knowledge and care, sanitation, nutrition, reduced traffic deaths, and war, automatically affect the accuracy of the prediction.

Primary aging has been described as a time-related process that results in a decline in rate or efficiency of various functions in plants or animals. Obviously, a deterioration in function adversely affects a person's chances of staying alive, increasing the probability of death per unit time. Mortality in human beings, when deaths in early life and deaths from violence are excluded, tends to increase exponentially with age.

Benjamin Gompertz, an English insurance actuary, in 1825 published a description of an empirically derived mathematical equation that is concerned with the probability of dying at any given age. Although this equation is relatively simple, its accuracy has been repeatedly demonstrated. It continues to approximate real systems closely. Gompertz's equation is as follows: $R = R_o e^{at}$, where R is the chance of dying at any age; R_o is a mathematical constant related to the predicted chance of dying at age o; a is a constant that describes the rate of increase of the mortality rate as a function of age; e is the base of natural logarithms; and t is the age in years [14].

Survival and Immortality

"Survival of the fittest" is a biological cliché. In the Darwinian sense, fitness means the ability to contribute a maximum number of live and fertile offspring to assure succeeding generations. Thus evolution is concerned with the perpetuation and improvement of the species but not with the health or longevity of individuals after they have passed the period of reproduction. Further, it is possible that the biological traits that are basic to maximum reproductive capacity may be detrimental to the prolongation of life after cessation of the reproductive life.

An interesting question has been whether or not some animals are immortal, that is, whether they are capable of continuous and total cell replacement. This is far from a settled issue. What is clear is that in animals that are incapable of cell replacement, either initially or for a limited period, a decline in vigor (aging) is seen. The sea anemone, a multicellular invertebrate, apparently is capable of replacing all cells continuously throughout life. The cells making up the sea anemone are in a constant state of turnover and replacement. But even in this system, the notion of immortality is open to some challenge, since the sea anemone divides in two at some point in time. The half that retains the old nervous system ages and dies, while the half that has to grow a new system survives. Consequently, at least one part of the original animal continues indefinitely.

Based on the assumption that immortality exists in the lower, simpler forms of life, it has been held that some animal cells that are capable of dividing are immortal if removed from the body's regulatory mechanisms. This belief in the capacity of animal cells to achieve immortality was given considerable support by the work of the French surgeon Alexis Carrel (1873–1944), who won the Nobel Prize for physiology and medicine in 1912. His contributions included the development of a new technique for end-to-end suturing of blood vessels and work that paved the way for safe blood transfusions. Later, Carrel reported that he had kept fibroblasts from chicks growing and multiplying in glass vessels for more than 30 years. Thus he seemed to have proved that these cells were capable of living far beyond the usual life expectancy of a chicken. Using similar techniques, other experimenters claimed similar success with embryonic cells from laboratory mice. Unfortunately Carrel's success—and apparently that of the other investigators—was the result of errors in techniques. Carrel fed the cell culture with a crude extract taken from chick embryos. This embryo extract actually contained a very few, but a sufficient number of, living chick cells. The introduction of these new fibroblasts permitted the culture to survive. If the extract used for feeding is carefully prepared and the fibroblasts eliminated, the cell colony will die.

Other experiments have suggested that animal and human cells have the capacity to be immortal. It has been demonstrated that all such immortal cell colonies are abnormal in one way or another [45]. At the present time the only human cells that are apparently immortal are transformed or abnormal cells, such as the HeLa cells, which were originally taken from cancerous cervical tissue and grown in glass cultures by George O. Gey in 1951 at the Johns Hopkins University School of Medicine. Normal human cells are diploid, that is, have two sets of 23 chromosomes, or a total of 46. HeLa cells are mixoploid cells and may have anywhere from 50 to 350 chromosomes per cell, with the chromosomes differing considerably in size and shape from the 46 chromosomes found in the normal diploid human cell.

Components of the Body and Aging

The human organism consists of three biological components, two of which are cellular and one noncellular. The first component is made up of cells capable of multiplying throughout the life span. Examples of such cells are epithelial cells (skin) and white blood cells. The second biological component is made up of cells that are incapable of division; these are exemplified by the neurons of the brain. (Some cells, e.g., endothelial cells, rarely divide but are at least capable of doing so.) The third biological component is the noncellular or interstitial material.

The various theories of aging that will be presented often deal with only one of the three components. For example, one theory centers on dividing cells by postulating that new cells in old animals are not as good as new cells in younger animals. A second group of theories focuses on the possibility that irreplaceable cells (i.e., nondividing cells) either are totally lost or decline in function. A third suggested theoretical basis for aging is that damage takes place in the noncellular material of the body, interfering with nutrition, respiration, and excretion (the accumulation of waste products).

It is clear that biological aging can be studied at a number of levels, utilizing differing techniques. Consequently, numerous theories, often overlapping and frequently differing only in semantics, not in substance, can be found in the scientific literature. Only a few of these will be reviewed here.

Selected Biological Theories of Aging

One early biological explanation of aging rested on the assumption that a living organism contained a fixed store of energy, not unlike that contained within a coiled watch spring. When the spring of the watch was unwound, life ended. This is a type of *exhaustion theory*. Although it may have some validity, scientific knowledge has become so extensive that such a simple explanation no longer suffices. Another simple theory relates to the *accumulation of deleterious material*. This particular theory is given some support by the observation that pigments, such as lipofucsin, accumulate in a number of living cells throughout the life span. To date, however, there is no evidence that the accumulation of these pigments actually affects cellular efficiency.

Sinex believes that in attempting to understand the biochemistry of aging one must decide if the aging process constitutes *deliberate biological programming* or if the usual life span of an individual is all that can be expected of an organism as chemically complex as the total human being [37]. Aging in plants and in lower forms of animals often appears to be regulated by deliberate programming that in turn is tied to the seasons of the year. But where the memory for these programmed changes is stored is unclear. It is not necessarily in the nucleus of a cell, the human erythrocyte, for example, has no nucleus but appears to survive in the circulation for 120 days. However, the demise of a circulating cell is not necessarily the result of a lethal process within the cell. The old red cell is recognized and removed by the reticuloendothelial cells. The aging red cell is probably identified by an alteration in the surface electrical charge. At the present time there is no known way to increase the survival of circulating erythrocytes [42].

Similarly, there is considerable controversy over what part of a cell is the most important in cellular renewal. There is evidence that renewal of the nucleus or the cytoplasm may be beneficial. In many protozoa, conjugation (the union of one organism with another for the exchange of nuclear material) initiates a cycle of reproductive activity that gradually decreases [39, 40]. If subsequent conjugation is prevented, the clones die. In other species of protozoa, autogamy, that is, the replacement of the macronucleus by a new macronucleus derived from a micronucleus, restores vigor. Ordinarily, some protozoa contain both a macronucleus and a micronucleus. The macronucleus is considered to be the nucleus that participates in ribonucleic acid (RNA) production and cell metabolism, and the micronucleus is chiefly involved in sexual reproduction [26]. If the deterioration of the clones is due to deterioration of genetic information in the macronucleus, what conditions in the micronucleus would prevent this from occurring? On the other side of the coin, if deterioration is of cytoplasmic origin, how is it corrected by a new nucleus?

Other investigators working with amoebas have reported that they can significantly prolong the life of the amoeba by continuous renewal of cytoplasmic elements. Furthermore, the mating of the paramecium shows that an old cytoplasm has profound adverse effects on an exchanged young nucleus.

As noted, it is highly unlikely that normal human cells are immortal. Only abnormal cells possess this ability. Furthermore, Hayflick [17] has demonstrated that normal human fibroblasts will divide roughly 50 times and then die. Hayflick utilized human fibroblasts from the lung. Cells derived from embryonic tissue achieve approximately 50 population doublings. Cells obtained at about age 20 will double 30 (±10) times, and cells derived at still later ages show progressive declines in their doubling capacities.

In the last few years Hayflick [18] has made additional observations to support his hypothesis that normal cells have a finite capacity for replication and function. He removed cells at regular intervals from his cell cultures and stored them at subzero temperatures under specific conditions. The stored cells, some of which have been preserved for 12 years, are incapable of dividing. When the stored cells are removed from the subzero temperature and returned to a culture medium, they begin to divide again. Hayflick reports that regardless of the number of doublings reached by the population at the time that the cells were preserved, the summated total number of doublings was about 50. The stored cells seem to contain an inherent mechanism for remembering at what doubling level they were stored in the cold. When returned to a suitable environment, their capacity to duplicate takes up at the point where it was interrupted. Hayflick contends that this in vitro demonstration can be repeated in vivo. By marking cells and injecting them into a host animal from which they can be withdrawn later and then reinjected into new host animals, a similar limit to the number of possible doublings can be demonstrated. Cristofalo [9] reports that the number of doublings is not different in male or female cells (female cells are easily identified by the presence of a Barr body, the sex chromatin). If this observation holds up, then it is evident that the difference in life expectancy between the male and female cannot be attributed to intracellular differences [45, p. 492].

The possibility exists that this phenomenon is the result of programmed aging. Although this idea is given some credence by Hayflick [18], he advances another view derived from the engineering concept *mean time to failure*. Engineers contend that every machine has built-in obsolescence and that its lifetime is limited by the durability of its parts. Repair or replacement of parts of the machine extends its life span, but barring total replacement of all of the elements, eventual failure of the machine is inevitable. What determines mean time to failure? Here it appears that one must turn to another theory, the *accumulation of copying errors*. This theory, first introduced by Orgel in 1963 [28], holds that human life is eventually terminated because the cells develop errors in copying, and errors in copying in turn reduce metabolic efficiency and interfere with the capacity for repair [17].

Theories that focus on cell loss or on mutation, both random processes, are termed *stochastic theories*. Stochastic implies "a process or a series of events for which the estimate of the probability of certain outcomes approaches the true probability as the number of events increases." For example, radiation seems to speed up aging by the random hitting of cells, either killing them or inducing mutations in them.

The atomic scientist Leo Szilard advanced a stochastic theory based on what he termed a *hit*. It has been assumed that Szilard implied that such a hit was the result of radiation. However, this apparently was not the case, since he considered any event that would alter a chromosome a hit. In addition, Szilard believed that every animal cell carries a load of what he termed *faults*. A fault is a congenital absence or impairment of one of the genes essential to cell function. A cell is capable of operating as long as one of a pair of genes continues to function; but when both members of a pair of essential genes are incapable of functioning, the cell dies. Therefore, a cell will cease to function if one of the pair carries a fault and the other is the victim of a hit, or if both pairs are the victims of hits. The problem in Szilard's theory is that it is only applicable to irreplaceable cells. But perhaps the greatest objection to the fault-hit approach is that individuals having many pairs of like (homozygous) genes should survive hits much more readily than heterozygous individuals having many dissimilar gene pairs; yet hybrids (i.e., heterozygous individuals with dissimilar genes) are consistently longer-lived than inbreds or homozygous individuals.

Exposure of a living organism to repeated small doses of ionizing radiation or to a larger sublethal dose appreciably reduces the life span of the organism. Consequently, numerous attempts have been made to study the changes brought about by radiation for any possible similarity to the aging process. Radiated animals and aging animals both show an increase in the number of somatic cell mutations. Longevity in an aging animal is inversely proportional to the rate at which mutations develop in the animal. Thus dogs live about six times longer than mice and develop mutations at about one-sixth the rate. It appears that the changes and mutations that are brought about by radiation are not the same as the chromosomal aberrations resulting from aging. When one compares the number of chromosomal aberrations produced by radiation to the life-shortening effect that would be expected proportional to the number of aberrations, there is not nearly the amount of life shortening that would be expected. Aging produces fewer chromosomal aberrations, yet in proportion produces more life shortening. No satisfactory explanation is as yet at hand for this discrepancy.

Howard J. Curtis [12], a radiation biologist, has advanced a theory he elects to call the *composite theory.* In his earlier discussions of the somatic mutations viewpoint, Curtis [11] stressed that somatic cell types differed from one another in frequency of cell division, some dividing frequently, some seldom, and some not at all, as has already been discussed. Defects develop over time in all cells, but in organs that can replace cells, the cell division process allows them to discard aberrant cells. Tissues having nondividing cells do not have this mechanism of rejuvenation and thus are primarily responsible for the aging of the total organism. Consequently, the fundamental aging process is the accumulation of defectively functioning cells in organs whose cells are nondividing. Aberrations occurring in dividing cells produce another serious problem, namely, cancer. This, however, would not be considered an aging event. According to Curtis [12], the composite theory considers aging fundamentally "an increasing probability of developing a degenerative disease." As a person ages, he becomes increasingly susceptible to degenerative diseases. Furthermore, as each person becomes older, he develops virtually all the degenerative diseases but at different rates. The disease that plays the major role in eventual death statistically appears to be a matter of chance.

The composite theory includes the postulate that aging changes take place in the somatic cells and that these changes cause them and their progeny to function to the detriment of the organisms. Although mutation is an important step in this detrimental change, the extent of the change cannot be explained as the result of a single mutation. Curtis [13] believes that for the human being an average of five steps is required to initiate one of the degenerative diseases. The nature of all the steps has not been identified, but the occurrence of each step is a chance occurrence of a certain probability; for example, mutation rate. The probability of occurrence of each step can be expressed in quantitative terms utilizing a mathematical formula devised by Armitage and Doll [1].

The *error theory* of cellular aging previously mentioned proposes that, with senescence, alterations (not necessarily mutations) occur in the structure of the deoxyribonucleic acid (DNA) molecule. These errors are transmitted to messenger RNA and ultimately to newly synthesized enzymes. Such defective enzymes could result in a number of problems. It is conceivable that the enzymes would be inactive and therefore accumulate substrates within the cell. Not only might the accumulation of substrates be detrimental to the cell, but the normal metabolic processes might also be seriously disturbed. To compensate for this deficiency, it is possible that there would be an increase in RNA production and of protein turnover to compensate for the defective enzymes. If the number of defective or inactive enzymes proceeded to a point at which synthesis within the cell was no longer sufficient to compensate for the defective processes, then the death of the cell or its failure to contribute to the organism would result in the death of the organism.

The error theory is linked with the mutation theory in that it has been shown that chromosomal aberrations in the liver cells of normal mice increase linearly with age. Furthermore, these aberrations can be dramatically increased by a dose of x-rays. Following a single radiation dose, however, chromosomal aberrations gradually decrease toward normal.

The defective chromosomes can be traced through a number of cell divisions, but then they disappear. The number of aberrations that occur is roughly proportional to the amount of radiation. Small doses of radiation are not so effective as a large dose. Since chromosome aberrations decline, it would appear that there is an inherent capacity to correct the damage inflicted by x-rays. The picture is further complicated by the fact that neutron exposure produces much more damage than do x-rays. It has been shown that there is a relationship between the amount of chromosome damage and the shortening of life. But the effect of the mutation may take longer to manifest its detrimental influence than might be suspected. A possible explanation is that somatic cells may ordinarily contain a large reserve supply of RNA that permits them to function for a lengthy period without DNA. Actually, several cell divisions may take place before the supply of RNA becomes so low that the cell no longer can function.

The *cross-linkage* or *eversion theory* is primarily applicable to the noncellular material of the body. The investigation substantiating this theory rests on the study of collagen. Collagen is the most abundant protein in the body. It is one of the four major constituents of connective tissue and constitutes 30 to 40 percent of body protein. A collagen molecule is composed of three polypeptide strands. Each polypeptide strand contains four subunits that are held together by pairs of ester bonds. With the passing of time there is a switching of the ester bonds from within to between the individual collagen molecules. Thus a cross-linking between the strands is accomplished, not only altering the structure of the collagen molecule but also changing its characteristics, particularly its elasticity. Although there is little doubt that the cross-linking phenomenon in collagen is an aging process, the change is found only in extracellular collagen and has not been as clearly demonstrated to occur in intracellular proteins.

The Immune System and Aging

The immune system as the primary defense mechanism of the body is essential for the preservation of life. However, with the passage of time, alterations transpire within the immune system. There is a decline in the protective mechanism, impaired surveillance, and a distortion in its functions, resulting in a self-destructive autoaggressive phenomenon. All can shorten life expectancy. It appears that the protective mechanisms of the immune system reach a peak during adolescence and then decline in conjunction with the involution of the thymus. With the passing of the years, there is an increase in susceptibility to infection, and, in general, effective immunization cannot be induced in late life [3].

There is increasing evidence that prolonged survival may be associated with an immunologically elite population. At least two types of serum immunoglobulin concentrate are related to longevity. Early death is likely in subjects over the age of 72 years who have relatively low levels of IgG and high levels of IgM [4]. Such evidence suggests that measures of immunity will serve the clinical purpose of early recognition of vulnerability. The problem of autoimmunity, a series of events in which the immune system attacks or rejects the normal parts of the host, is extremely disrupting to health.

Cells that cannot divide may be particularly vulnerable to alteration in the immune system. Such nondividing cells are gradually lost in the latter part of the life span, and it may be that this loss is attributable to the inability of the immune system to protect these nonreplaceable cells; or they may be lost as a result of autoaggressive processes.

The apparent stimulation of *autoimmune mechanisms* during senescence raises many questions [46, 47]. Is it possible that the gradually increasing amounts of antibody detected in the plasma and the increased incidence of autoimmune disease may be directly or indirectly linked to lifelong accumulated exposure to immunochemical insults? Is it possible that the coding of self-recognition in either DNA or RNA alters with the passage of time, so that cellular antigens are not properly recognized? Do the antibody-producing cells, accidentally or in some programmed manner, contribute to senescence through the release of antibodies to the body's own tissue, thus producing an autoimmune condition [37]? There is much knowledge to be gained regarding the various types of immune responses that begin to deviate with aging from those encountered in the young adult. Investigators are looking for ways of maintaining or rejuvenating a declining immune system and of turning off the mechanism of the immune system bent on self-destruction.

Many attempts have been made to relate life expectancy to the physical characteristics of various species. The so-called *index of cephalization,* that is, the excess of brain weight over the expected amount in relationship to body weight, correlates the most closely with longevity. Since the neurons of the brain are irreplaceable and since they die, it appears that the number of cells that serve as a reserve against continuing loss in some way favorably affects the coordination of the complex body and makes for its longer period of survival.

With regard to the *genetic determinants* of aging, it is frequently stated that there is no known gene responsible for the extension of the life span, but there are genes responsible for defects that result in the shortening of life.

Another destructive theory of aging is the *free radical theory*. Free radicals are molecular entities that contain an unpaired electron. Free radicals are considered to be molecular fragments, and because of the unpaired electron, they are highly reactive. Free radicals exist in the environment, but they are also a product of normal metabolic processes. They are produced by such processes as the auto-oxidation of lipids. Hence they are ubiquitous in living substances but are not essential to normal functioning.

Free radicals have their highest concentration in mitochondria. Mitochondria are very important components of eukaryotic cells, that is, cells that are organized into separated compartments (organelles). Mitochondria are involved in essential metabolic pathways, including the breakdown and synthesis of carbohydrates, fats, and amino acids. If the functions of mitochondria are disrupted by exposure to ultrasonic vibration, metabolic chaos results [26].

It is believed that free radicals are damaging in that they alter, that is, produce a mutation, in DNA, and that they play a role in the cross-linking of collagen. It is also theorized that they are important in the development of aging pigments, especially in neurons and myocardial cells, where, it is held, the aging pigment represents products of molecular membranes and the free radical intermediaries of lipid peroxidation.

Assuming there is validity to the free radical theory of aging, several scientists have proposed that human or animal life spans might be increased by the intake of antioxidants that tie up free radicals and inactivate them. Some antioxidants are butylated hydroxytoluene (BHT), butylated hydroxyanisole (BHA), ethoxyquin, β-mercaptoethylamine, and vitamin E. One study indicates that BHT increases the average life span of a colony of mice but does not extend maximum life span. Some of these antioxidants are already added to foods as preservatives, not for the purpose of increasing human longevity. Both BHT and BHA are carefully regulated by the Food and Drug Administration. The former can be added to animal fats and shortening in maximum concentrations of 0.01 percent. Similarly, an antioxidant compound can be added to dry breakfast cereal at a concentration of no more than 0.005 percent, and another antioxidant can be used in animal feeds. Government regulations permit using some antioxidants in industrial products such as rubber, but the same preservative cannot be utilized in food for human consumption. A great deal of research needs to be done before the government can permit increased use of antioxidants.

The Russian geneticist and gerontologist Zhores A. Medvedev is the chief proponent of the *redundant message theory*. Medvedev, who resides in London after repudiation by his government, is also known for his work that discredits the claimed excessive longevity of the Caucasians in the Soviet Union [23]. The *redundant message theory* is a complicated theory at the molecular level and holds that longer-lived species have the ability to call into activity redundant or reserved message capacities that are utilized when a faulty message system has developed. Errors accumulate in functioning genes or other systems, and reserve sequences containing the same information take over until the redundancy system is exhausted, resulting in biological age changes. Therefore the ordinary life span of a species is directly related to its capacity for gene repetition and other enzyme reserve capacities. At the present time there is limited experimental evidence to support this theory.

Not only genetic but environmental factors as well influence the life span [2]. This is well exemplified by the rotifer, a tiny aquatic animal that has been utilized for research purposes by a number of investigators. About 0.5 mm in length, the rotifer is composed of a rigidly fixed number of cells. No new cells are formed after hatching, and the animal's size is dependent on increasing the size of the individual cell. Rotifers are particularly useful for research because they multiply by parthenogenesis. Consequently, the genetic characteristics of the offspring are theoretically the same as those of the parent.

The rotifer is poikilothermic, that is, its body temperature is always the same as its surroundings. Barrows and Strehler [2] discovered that a substantial increase in the rotifer's life span could be effected by reducing the temperature of its environment or by cutting down on its food supply. That reduction of food intake positively affects the life span had been noted by a number of investigators. In this instance, however, it is of particular interest. Barrows and Strehler reported that the reduced diets result in a gain in life span when applied to younger animals, while the reduction in temperature was effective in animals who had reached full maturity and had ceased to lay eggs.

A recent study indicates that extension of the life span and the reproductive period of the rotifer can be achieved by the reduction of accumulated calcium. This is done by regular brief immersions in a solution containing a chelating agent [36].

Man is not poikilothermic, and thus if one wanted to lengthen the human life span by changing the effect of temperature, one would have to consider utilizing temperature-reducing drugs. This is a very unlikely possibility.

It is an established fact that traumatic life experiences alter the life span. However, that such experience may differentially influence the life span of men as opposed to women has not been given a great deal of attention. One can obtain some evidence for the influence of sex by comparing the age of death in male and female identical twins and male and female fraternal twins. When each of the pair has died of natural causes, there is a much greater variation in the age of death in identical male twins than in identical female twins. It can be assumed, therefore, that at least one of the identical twin males has been exposed to a more hostile environment or to a greater accumulation of traumatic events than the other twin. Further, although the life spans of identical twins are more similar than those of fraternal twins, the discrepancy in age of death is again greater between male than between female fraternal twins [19].

Shock [33] points out that although physiological characteristics differ widely from individual to individual at any specific age, the averages of these values show a gradual but definite decline between the ages of 30 and 90. However, he emphasizes that certain functions in a specific individual at age 80 can be as good as those of the average 50-year-old man.

One of the obvious manifestations of aging is the decline in the ability to exercise and do work. The ability to do work depends on several variables, including the strength of the muscles, coordination involving the nervous system, and a number of other factors, such as the adequacy of the cardiovascular and respiratory system. Shock has made a series of estimates of the remaining function and tissues in the average 75-year-old when compared with the average 30-year-old. He reports that the average 75-year-old man has 90 percent of his original brain weight and 56 percent of his vital capacity. His maximum work rate is 70 percent of his former ability. He retains 63 percent of the original number of nerve trunk fibers and 90 percent of his original nerve conduction velocity.

The effects of aging on swim performance have been carefully studied by Rahe and Arthur [30]. They conclude that swimming performance in aging athletes in excellent condition is primarily affected by pulmonary function and decreases by roughly 1 percent per year from approximately 25 years up to the age of 59 years, the maximum age studied. The authors note that several of the men approaching 60 years of age are breaking a minute for the 100-yard free style, a time that just 15 years ago was a good time for high school swim teams. This is the result of improved training methods.

An intriguing question is often asked: Is it true that space travelers will age at a different rate than earthbound humans? Einstein's theory of relativity includes two suppositions. They are that (1) time actually runs slower for an object as its speed increases (the "time dilation effect"), and (2) time speeds up for an object as it moves away from a body exerting a gravitational force. Thus astronauts engaged in earth orbital missions are primarily influenced by the time dilation effect. Since they are moving much faster than they were on earth, they age more slowly. If an astronaut stays in earth orbit for two weeks, he will be approximately 400 microseconds younger than he would be if he had remained on earth. Moon missions produce a somewhat different problem because here the space travelers virtually escape earth's gravity; therefore time and aging speed up.

Sociological Theories of Aging

Social scientists have developed a number of theories relevant to the aging and elderly and to the structure of society and social change. One of these theories holds that the status of the aged is high in static societies and tends to decline with the acceleration of social change [27]. Another theory is that the status of the aged is inversely related to the proportion of aged in the population: the aged are most highly valued in societies in which they are scarce, and their value and status decrease as they become more numerous. A third theory is that the status and prestige of the aged are high in those societies in which older people, in spite of physical infirmity, are able to continue to perform useful and socially valued functions [35].

It is apparent that we are living in a rapidly changing society and world. In fact, it is viewed by a very prominent sociologist as "the chaotic society" [16]. If the first theory has any validity, it is apparent that the already doubtful status position of elderly persons in the United States will decline even further. As to value being tied to scarcity of the elderly, it does not appear that by the year 2000 the actual percentage of elderly will change, although the number obviously will increase. The third theory has pessimistic overtones. If status is dependent on the performance of socially valued functions, the rapidly accelerating pattern of early retirement will increasingly diminish the status of the elderly person.

A few years ago a group of investigators advanced the so-called *disengagement theory,* which holds that those who accept the inevitability of a reduction in social and personal interactions are usually highly satisfied in old age [10]. This theory has been modified since its original presentation, as new evidence has demonstrated that the degree of disengagement is not a reflection of changing "social" or "psychological vectors" but is proportional to altered "physiological capacities" [44]. The *activity theory* of aging, on the other hand, holds that the maintenance of activities is important to most people as a basis for deriving and sustaining satisfaction, self-esteem, and health. In one study the changes in activities and attitudes of 127 aged subjects were observed over a span of 10 years [21]. It was found that there was no significant overall decrease in activities or alteration in attitudes among men, while there was some decrease among women. The supporters of the disengagement theory base their belief predominantly on cross-sectional surveys. It is possible that this longitudinal study is presenting important contrary evidence. Further, it was found that in these aging persons, reduction in some activities or attitudes resulted in compensating increases in others. In addition, data correlating such measures as mental and physical status and socioeconomic and activity levels all support the activity theory as the basis for the promotion of vigor and satisfactory adjustment in the elderly.

One cannot ignore the fact that there are differences in lifelong patterns of living and that there are some people who tend to maintain relatively high or relatively low levels of activity. It does appear that those who reduce their activities as they age tend to suffer a reduction in overall satisfaction [29].

The pathological consequences of social deprivation and hostile social influences on the infant have been reported by a number of investigators, including Goldfarb, Provence, Bowlby, Kagan, and others. There is reason to think that similar deprivation in old age can have similar pathological effects. Deprivation can take many forms and guises for elderly people. Economic deprivation is a common problem among the elderly, especially for those in voluntary or involuntary retirement, and sometimes has devastating effects. The economically deprived older person must constrict his opportunities for living experience. He cannot buy all the things he immediately needs, much less those for which he supposedly has saved all his life. He does not have the security that comes with a stable financial situation. In addition, he now belongs to a subgroup of society whose values are no longer the same as those of the dominant middle-aged adult society. Furthermore, society has failed to provide learning and recreational opportunities for the elderly to the same degree that it has for the young and middle-aged. Many aged thus lack methods of maintaining self-esteem. A person must feel that he is valued or appreciated by others in order to have reasonable self-esteem [6]. There is little doubt that the elderly American can be identified as belonging to a deprived minority.

Psychological and Combined Theories of Aging

Psychological theories of aging are often the extension of personality and developmental theories into middle and late life. Personality theories usually consider the innate human needs and forces that motivate thought and behavior and the modification of these biologically based energies by the experiences of living in a physical and social environment. Just as the developmental theories of personality in early childhood take into account the physiological changes of the growing child and such factors as interaction with the mother, the study of personality in old age must consider possible alterations in the physiological processes of the elderly person and the interacting relationship that exists between the individual and his environment. To complicate further the problem of understanding personality changes with aging, as human beings pass through their life experiences they become increasingly different rather than similar. Infants at 6 months of age resemble one another more than children at age 12. This divergence continues as a response to the large array of possible learning and living experiences. In extreme old age, people perhaps tend to return to greater similarity in certain characteristics as they share similar declines in biological functioning and as society constricts their opportunities.

A number of investigators have attempted to explore patterns of personality in middle and late life. Neugarten et al. [25] have concluded that 60-year-olds, when compared with 40-year-olds, seem to see the environment as more complex and dangerous. They are less ready to attribute activity and affect to persons in the environment, and they move from an outer- to an inner-world orientation. In addition, older men seem to be more receptive than younger men to their own "affiliative, nurturant, and sensual promptings." Older women become more accepting of their own "aggressive and egocentric impulses" [25].

Reichard and colleagues [31] studied the personalities of older men and were able to classify the men they studied into five major categories according to their patterns of adjustment to aging: the mature, the rocking-chair men, the armored, the angry, and the self-haters. These investigators found that the majority of those adjusting poorly to aging had had a lifelong history of personality problems.

Throughout this book a number of combined approaches to the problems of the aged will be utilized. The *cybernetic theory* is a theoretical approach of the combined type. Cybernetics is a discipline that compares control systems within the central nervous system with computing machines [38, p. 529]. This theory essentially could be called an *activity theory* or an *atrophy-of-disuse theory*. As Smith and Smith [38] state:

To become functional early in life . . . neurons must be activated. To retain their position of control, they must be reactivated repeatedly. We believe that aging involves deterioration of neuronic control which proceeds more rapidly if the cybernetic control systems are not used.

This theory therefore implies that previously established patterns of learning and social activity are the determinants of patterns in late life. As such, it is contrary to the disengagement theory previously discussed.

References

1. Armitage, P., and Doll, R.   The age distribution of cancer and a multi-state theory of carcinogenesis. *Br. J. Cancer* 8:1, 1954.
2. Barrows, C. H., and Strehler, B. L.   Program biological obsolescence. *Johns Hopkins Med. J.* 19:18, 1968.
3. Buckley, C. E.   Aging and Immunity: Clinical Perspectives. In E. W. Busse (Ed.), *Theory and Therapeutics of Aging.* New York: Medcom Press, 1973. P. 89.
4. Buckley, C. E.   Presentation at Symposium, Immunology and Aging. American Geriatrics Society, Miami, Florida, April 1975.
5. Busse, E. W.   Psychopathology. In J. Birren (Ed.), *Handbook of Aging and the Individual.* Chicago: University of Chicago Press, 1959. Pp. 364–399.
6. Busse, E. W.   Social Forces Influencing the Care and Health of the Elderly. In J. C. McKinney and F. T. deVyver (Eds.), *Aging and Social Policy.* New York: Appleton-Century-Crofts, 1966. Pp. 268–280.
7. Comfort, A.   *Ageing. The Biology of Senescence.* London: Routledge & Kegan Paul, 1964.
8. Comfort, A.   *The Process of Ageing.* London: Weidenfeld and Nicolson, 1965.
9. Cristofalo, V.   Personal communication. Wistar Institute, Philadelphia, January 1975.
10. Cummings, E., and Henry, W. E.   *Growing Old.* New York: Basic Books, 1961.
11. Curtis, H. J.   Biological mechanisms underlying the aging process. *Science* 141:686, 1963.
12. Curtis, H. J.   A composite theory of aging. *Gerontologist* 6:143, 1966.
13. Curtis, H. J.   Radiation and Ageing. In *Aspects of the Biology of Ageing* (21st Symposium of the Society for Experimental Biology). Cambridge, Eng.: Cambridge University Press, 1967. Pp. 51–64.
14. Gompertz, B.   On the nature of the function expressive of the law of human morality and on a new model of determining life contingencies. *Philos. Trans. R. Soc. Lond. [Biol.]* 115:513, 1825.
15. Gruman, G. J.   A history of ideas about the prolongation of life. *Trans. Am. Philosoph. Soc.* 56:24, 1966.
16. Hauser, P. M.   The chaotic society: Product of the social morphological revolution. Presidential address at the Annual Meeting, American Sociological Association, Boston, August 1968.
17. Hayflick, L.   Human cells and aging. *Sci. Am.* 218:32, 1968.
18. Hayflick, L.   Biomedical gerontology: Current theories of biological aging. *Gerontologist* 14:454, 1974.
19. Kallmann, F. J., and Jarvik, L. F.   In J. Birren (Ed.), *Handbook of*

Aging and the Individual. Chicago: University of Chicago Press, 1959. Pp. 216–263.

20. Kerēnyi, C. *The Gods of the Greeks.* London: Thames and Hudson, 1974. P. 200.
21. Maddox, G. L. Activity and morale: A longitudinal study of selected elderly subjects. *Soc. Forces* 41:195, 1963.
22. Medvedev, Z. A. Caucasus and Altay longevity: A biological or social problem? *Gerontologist* 14:381, 1974.
23. Medvedev, Z. A. Aging and longevity: New approaches and new perspectives. *Gerontologist* 15:196, 1975.
24. Neugarten, B. L. The Future and the Young-Old. *Gerontologist* 15:9, 1975.
25. Neugarten, B. L., et al. *Personality in Middle and Late Life.* New York: Atherton, 1964. Pp. 189–190.
26. Novikoff, A. V., and Holtzman, E. *Cells* and *Organelles.* New York: Holt, Rinehart and Winston, 1970. P. 184.
27. Ogburn, W. F., and Nimkoff, M. F. *Sociology.* Boston: Houghton Mifflin, 1940.
28. Orgel, L. E. The maintenance of the accuracy of protein synthesis and its relevance to aging. *Proc. Natl. Acad. Sci. U.S.A.* 49:517, 1963.
29. Palmore, E. The effects of aging on activities and attitudes. *Gerontologist* 8:259, 1968.
30. Rahe, R. H., and Arthur, R. J. Effects of aging upon U.S. masters championships swim performance. *J. Sports Med. Phys. Fitness* 14:21, 1974.
31. Reichard, S., Livson, F., and Peterson, P. G. *Aging and Personality.* New York: Wiley, 1962. Pp. 170–171.
32. Riley, M. W., and Foner, A. *Aging and Society.* New York: Russell Sage Foundation, 1968. P. 28.
33. Shock, N. W. The physiology of aging. *Sci. Am.* 206:100, 1962.
34. Siegel, J. S. Demography. In A. M. Ostfeld (Ed.), *Epidemiology of Aging.* DHEW Publication No. 75-711. Washington, D.C.: Department of Health, Education, and Welfare, 1975.
35. Simmons, L. W. *The Role of the Aged in Primitive Society.* New Haven: Yale University Press, 1945.
36. Sincock, A. M. Life extension in the rotifer mytilina brevispina var redunca by the application of chelating agents. *J. Gerontol.* 30:289, 1975.
37. Sinex, F. M. Biochemistry of aging. *Perspect. Biol. Med.* 9:216, 1966.
38. Smith, K. U., and Smith, F. G. *Cybernetic Principles of Learning and Educational Design.* New York: Holt, Rinehart and Winston, 1965. P. 29.
39. Sonneborn, T. M. The relation of autogamy to senescence and rejuvenescence in Paramecium aurelia. *J. Protozool.* 1:38, 1954.
40. Sonneborn, T. M. Breeding Systems Reproductive Methods, and Species Problems in Protozoa. In E. Mayr (Ed.), *The Species Problem.* Washington, D.C.: American Association for the Advancement of Science, 1957. Pp. 155–324.

41. Strehler, B. L.   *The Biology of Aging.* Washington, D.C.: American Institute of Biological Sciences, 1960.
42. Timiras, P. A.   Degenerative Changes in Cells and Cell Death. In *Developmental Physiology and Aging.* New York: Macmillan, 1972. Pp. 442–443.
43. U.S. Department of Labor, Bureau of the Census.   *Statistical Abstracts of the U.S.,* 1971. Table 6, p. 8.
44. Warren, N. D.   Physiological status and disengagement theory: A study on a model population. *Mech. Ageing Dev.* 2:55, 1973.
45. Weiss, A. K.   Biomedical gerontology: The Hayflick hypothesis. *Gerontologist* 14:491, 1974.
46. Wolford, R. L.   Auto-immunity and aging. *J. Gerontol.* 17:281, 1962.
47. Wolford, R. L.   The immunologic theory of aging. *Gerontologist* 4:195, 1964.

3. Sociological Aspects of Aging

Erdman Palmore and George L. Maddox

Students of aging are often so impressed by the obvious physical deterioration and intellectual slowing that may accompany chronological aging that they overlook the central role of culture and society in determining individual and group variations in the aging process. Even when some group differences in the behavior of the aged are noted, it may mistakenly be assumed that these differences are caused by biological differences. For example, the fact that in the United States almost three times as high a proportion of men as compared with women continue to work past age 65 is less related to any biological differences between men and women than it is to our cultural expectations that a man's primary role is to work outside the home, while a woman's primary role is to work inside the home. Similarly, the fact that a majority of Japanese men past age 65 continue to work, while less than a third in the United States do so, is explained by cultural, not by biological, differences [52].

Many people believe that the aged inevitably suffer a steady deterioration in physical and mental abilities and therefore should withdraw from the central arenas of our society. We often forget that in other cultures the aged are the most powerful, the most engaged, and the most respected members of the society. When some aged persons show depression, hopelessness, feelings of inferiority, and paranoia, we may forget that these symptoms may have been caused by deprivation of basic satisfactions, reduction to an inferior status, and discrimination against those with 65 or more birthdays, rather than by any biological process.

To clarify the nature of aging as a social process this discussion will consider the following, in sequence: (1) the differences between cultures in the functions and status of the aged; (2) the differences between various aged groups within our society; (3) the extent to which our aged are treated as a minority group and their reactions to this treatment; (4) the basic controversy and evidence in regard to activity versus disengagement; and (5) some predictions about the aged in our future society.

Cross-cultural Differences in the Status of the Aged

A review of aging in preindustrial societies concluded that "every possible plan for a successful old age has been tried out sometime and somewhere in the world in mankind's attempts to enrich and round off the last years of life" [64]. While this may be an exaggeration, it is clear that an extremely wide variety of plans for successful aging have been tried

31

and with some success. Despite these differences in plans for aging, most of the aged in all societies, developed or undeveloped, seem to share certain basic needs and interests. These basic interests have been summarized by Leo Simmons [64] in five categories:

1. To live as long as possible or at least until life's satisfactions no longer compensate for its privations.
2. To get some release from the necessity of wearisome exertion at humdrum tasks and to have protection from too great exposure to physical hazards.
3. To safeguard or even strengthen any prerogatives acquired in midlife, such as skills, possessions, rights, authority, and prestige.
4. To remain active participants in the affairs of life in either operational or supervisory roles, any sharing in group interests being preferred to idleness and indifference.
5. Finally, to withdraw from life when necessity requires it, as timely, honorably, and comfortably as possible.

Since these are apparently common, if not universal, needs of the aged, any plan for successful aging might be evaluated in terms of how well they meet these needs.

This section outlines the broad trends in the degree to which these needs have been met in the past. The most generally accepted theory of this trend could be represented by a graph of the rise and fall in the security, satisfactions, and status of the aged in the following general form: The baseline or zero point would be represented by animal groups in which there seem to be no instincts or inborn propensities to sustain aged parents or grandparents. The usual pattern among animals is to abandon the aged of the species as soon as their ability to function has seriously declined [64]. It is only through the development of human culture that the aged have been able to achieve any security. Beginning with primitive hunting, fishing, and collecting societies, the status and security of the aged rises until it reaches its peak in highly developed agricultural societies. Simmons and others have argued that the graph would show substantial decline as it moves to our modern industrial societies [18, 65]. Actually, the evidence is not clear as to how much, if any, decline has occurred in industrial societies. Before we argue this point, we will continue with Simmons' theory.

High Status in Agricultural Societies

A few examples from the anthropological literature will illustrate the high status and great satisfactions achieved by the aged in most agricultural societies.

The aged among the Palaung in North Burma were given great prestige and privilege. Long life was considered a great privilege due to virtuous behavior in a previous existence. According to Milne [42], most aged Palaung had happy lives. Everyone was careful to avoid even stepping on the shadow of an older person. The children periodically anointed the chair of the father after his death. A typical prayer of the son was, "Thou are gone, my father, but I still respect these things that belonged to thee. Give me long life and health, oh, my father." As soon as a girl married she was usually eager to appear older than her age because the older woman had more privilege and honor.

The Balinese believe that a child is born close to heaven but moves away from heaven until maturity, when he is at his lowest status. After maturity he rises in status until old age, and the very old person is regarded as being almost in heaven [66].

Aged Kaffir men have both high prestige and access to more creature comforts than any other group in the society. A man is allowed to sing and dance at his pleasure, spear bucks, plot mischief, or make bargains for his daughters. He no longer has responsibilities for hard work. He may take another young wife or concubine because it is believed that as long as he can obtain a youthful bride he will not grow old [34].

The reasons for the rise in status of the aged from the primitive to the stable rural societies involve six factors that may be summarized as follows:

1. Stable agricultural societies were able to develop greater surpluses of food and shelter to share with the aged. As long as the next day's or the next week's meals were uncertain, as long as food storage was inadequate, as long as families had to migrate from one area to another when the local supply of food was exhausted, the aged and infirm were likely to suffer and to be left behind. It is true that in order to counter this tendency the aged in many primitive societies developed food taboos or food preferences that gave them some advantage over the younger tribe members in the competition for scarce food. But when food became more

plentiful and more assured with the development of grain storage and animal husbandry, the security of the aged increased markedly.

2. Stable agricultural societies developed more capital and more personal property, which increasingly came under the control of the aged. Through their ability to dictate who had access to the property, who would inherit it, and so on, the aged were able to exert a strong influence on the society as a whole and thereby maintained their position of power.

3. The growing importance of extended family relations could also be manipulated by the aged to support their status and power. The aged members of the extended family usually were able to influence marriage and birth rates and the economic and social roles that various members of the family assumed, thus assuring the well-being of the clan and of their own position in it.

4. In agricultural societies there are generally more opportunities for auxiliary but useful tasks for the aged than in the more primitive ones. As societies shifted to cultivation of the soil and animal husbandry, the aged could move more easily to lighter tasks, so that they seldom suffered from abrupt retirement and usually found useful functions until near the end of life. Simmons [64] states, "Self-employment or ancillary services in agrarian systems probably have provided the most secure and continuous occupational status that society at large has yet afforded for the majority of its aged."

5. Stable agrarian societies accumulated more and more knowledge and technical skills for adapting to the environment and meeting the needs of its members. The aged tended to be the best authorities on this accumulated knowledge and often the most skilled practitioners of the growing arts and crafts. When most of what was known had to be retrained by memory, the aged were the best source of information and were usually in the best position to make the best judgments. This semi-monopoly on knowledge, wisdom, and skills reinforced the high status of the aged.

6. Similarly, because of their greater experience and knowledge, the aged were usually able to become the main leaders in the growing political, civil, judicial, and religious institutions in the agrarian society. These roles were even more rewarding than their auxiliary tasks. Simmons found that most of the tribes he surveyed had old men as chiefs, council-

men, and advisors. He pointed out that the term *elder* had commonly implied leader, head man, or councilman. Also, as magic and religion developed complex ceremonies and institutions among the sedentary societies, the aged were usually able to control the most important roles in these structures.

Two qualifications of this general picture of the high status of aged in agricultural societies should be kept in mind. First, the aged in some foraging, hunting, and fishing societies had relatively high status, and the aged in some agricultural societies had relatively low status [25]. Second, among all societies, the extremely old and helpless person is viewed as a living liability [63]. Our discussion does not refer primarily to this final pathetic stage.

Decline in Industrial Societies?

There seems to be little question that the status of the aged in most stable agricultural societies tended to be higher than in most primitive societies. However, the assumption that the status and satisfactions of the aged have declined markedly as a result of industrialization is more debatable. Shanas et al. [63], Friedmann [25], and others have challenged the view that today's aged are less socially integrated and are worse off than the aged were a century ago.

Several distinctions need to be made in resolving this issue. First, the different types of status or satisfactions need to be specified, e.g., health, economic, family, political, prestige. For example, there is evidence that the health, education, and income status of the aged as a group is improving as younger and healthier cohorts move into the aged category and as health care improves [53]. Also, the actual standard of living of the aged has probably improved over the past century just as it has for the average younger person. On the other hand, the proportion of the aged living with children or other relatives has declined [27], although the extended kinship network remains strong [63].

Second, trends in the status of the aged differ widely between one industrial country and another. For example, the status and integration of the aged in Japan have remained relatively high when compared with the other industrialized nations [52]. Also, there is some evidence that while the employment, occupational, and educational status of the aged relative to younger people has declined substantially in several industrial societies, this decline may be leveling off or even reversing itself in the most advanced nations, such as the United States and Canada [54].

Finally, trends in the status of the aged vary substantially by race, sex, and socioeconomic status. Therefore it is neither useful nor accurate to make such a broad generalization as "the status of the aged declines as a result of industrialization." Accurate resolution of the issue requires specification of the country, the kind of status meant and how it is measured, and which type of aged person is being referred to.

Social and Economic Differences Among Aged in the United States

Age and Sex Differences

The aged are not a homogeneous group. They are at least as heterogeneous as any other age category spanning 35 or more years. The major differences among the aged are age, sex, class, and race. Furthermore, longitudinal studies have found that variability in most characteristics generally tends to increase among the aged as they grow older [41]. Age and sex grading are probably the most pervasive bases of differentiation in all societies, since they are permanent differences.

A basic difference between the sexes is that women live longer than men—in our society, women live seven years longer than men (see Chap. 6). One consequence of this is that, while two-thirds of the aged men are still married, only one-third of the women are still married [22].

When women become widowed, they are more likely to live with their children or other relatives, while widowed men are more likely to live alone or end up in an institution. In general, men have fewer contacts with their families. They live farther away from their families; they see their children less often; and they exchange services less with their families [63]. (These points are discussed in greater detail in Chap. 7.) The differences described may be related to the general cultural expectation that women should remain closer to their families, and men should be more independent and more interested in things outside their families.

Aged men also claim to be healthier than aged women; they less often say they are housebound, report fewer incapacities and fewer illnesses within the past year, and see a physician less often [63]. It is difficult to tell whether this is due to actual better health among men or to the cultural expectation that men should be "tough" and should not admit illness as readily as women. Since women actually outlive men, it seems likely that the cultural expectation is the major explanation of these differences in reported health.

A clear and fundamental difference between the sexes is that aged men are more often employed than aged women, just as they were in their younger years. Of men over age 65, 38 percent continue some employment, compared with 14 percent of the women [47]. Among those who are retired, more of the men were forced to retire because of compulsive retirement policies, poor health, and the like, while women more often report that they retired voluntarily. These differences are explained by the cultural expectation that man's primary role should be gainful employment, while the married woman's primary role is usually thought to be in the home. Men also are able to earn substantially more than women on the average, even when the number of hours and weeks is controlled [48]. Partly as a result of this difference in earning power, there are about two times as many aged women living in poverty as there are aged men [46].

Differences between age groups also persist among persons over 65. In general, the older aged (those over 75) are in poorer health, are hospitalized more often, are more often widowed and more often live alone, are isolated and lonely, are rarely employed, and have less income than those between ages 65 and 75, [44, 63].

Class Differences
Socioeconomic differences also persist among the aged, although there is some evidence that these differences become somewhat attenuated in comparison with younger groups. For example, income differences become smaller because the income of those on the upper economic level is reduced with retirement, and those in the lower economic groups are supported by Social Security and welfare payments [22]. However, the general stratification patterns remain among the aged: those with less income had less education and came from the blue collar or manual occupations; they have less adequate diets and poorer housing; they see doctors less often, and, as a result, their health is poorer, more are incapacitated, and they have a higher death rate; they are more likely to double up and live with their children; and they have more serious unmet

needs [22, 50, 52, 63]. In general, those in the lower strata have characteristics such as the following: They are less likely than the more affluent to belong to organizations, be church members, travel, and read newspapers. On the other hand, they are more likely to hold fundamentalist views, such as a belief in the existence of the devil, and they are more often anomic, depressed, and unhappy [13]. The same characteristics probably also are present in the aged poor.

Race

An extensive review of research on aged blacks concluded:

> A significantly higher proportion of Negroes than white aged persons occupy the lowest socioeconomic positions of [blacks] and whites. Hence, when judged by the usual objective (demographic) indices of social adjustment to aging, the corresponding rank position of aged [blacks] as compared with aged whites was also lower. Further, the studies definitely demonstrated that aged [blacks], as other aged groups, do not constitute a homogeneous entity. Health status and socioenvironmental conditions, including their previous and present life-styles, also affected and were affected by their adjustment to aging [35].

Beyond these generalizations, there is some scattered evidence that aged blacks have some relative advantage compared with aged whites; e.g., aged blacks do not usually suffer as great a reduction in income as do aged whites [45, 51]. There is also some evidence that aged blacks, as compared with aged whites, feel generally more accepted by their children and receive more assistance from their children [59]. It appears that relative to their previous status and insecurity during youth and middle age, many of the black aged now enjoy somewhat higher status and security because of a more stable income; because surviving to old age is an achievement in itself; because intergenerational family ties are strong; and because some progress toward racial equality has been made.

How Much Social Integration?

A recurrent and controversial issue in social gerontology is the degree to which the aged are integrated in society and whether or not it is useful to view the aged as an emerging minority group. Several gerontologists have argued that minority group concepts and theory help to explain why many of the aged suffer from negative stereotyping, segregation, and discrimination and, as a result, often develop feelings of inferiority and group consciousness [5, 10, 60]. Others argue that the aged are different from racial and ethnic minority groups in several obvious respects, such as not having been "born that way" [68]. In considering this question, the various negative stereotypes about the aged will first be summarized, and then the evidence for or against the stereotypes (such as illness, sexual activity, mental abilities, morale, activities, productivity, and isolation) will be examined. Second, we will discuss the extent of voluntary and involuntary segregation of the aged and third, employment discrimination against the aged. Finally, the reaction of the aged to these forms of prejudice and discrimination will be examined. Despite our use of these concepts, it will become apparent that there are important limitations to the parallel with minority groups.

Negative Stereotypes

ILLNESS. Perhaps the most common stereotypes about the aged have to do with their health status. From one-fifth to two-thirds of various groups, depending on type of group and on the wording, agree with the following statements: Older people "spend much time in bed because of illness," "have many accidents in the home," "have poor coordination," "feel tired most of the time," and "develop infection easily" [71, 72]. Other common stereotypes are that large proportions of the aged are living in hospitals, nursing homes, homes for the aged, or other such institutions, and that the health and abilities of the aged show a steady decline with each passing year.

Most of these stereotypes are not accurate descriptions of the vast majority of aged persons. For instance, it comes as a great surprise to those unfamiliar with study findings that only about 5 percent of persons age 65 and over live in homes for the aged, nursing homes, hospitals, or other institutions [14]. It is true that the aged spend almost two times as many days per year in bed because of illness as do younger persons, but this is still only 5 percent of the total days in the year (10 days per year in bed for men, 13 days for women) [43].

Regarding the belief that the health and physical ability of most aged persons decline steadily, the Duke longitudinal study found that about half of survivors who returned for examinations had *no* decline in physical functioning or actually had some improvement over intervals of 3 to 13 years [51]. Various studies have shown that the aged actually show great variability in patterns of change. A few decline precipitously and quickly become totally disabled. For a majority of aged, health and abilities seem to remain level or go up and down slightly as illnesses are contracted, accidents occur, and recoveries are made. Their health is rated as "good" by 51 percent of the aged; as "fair," by 33 percent and as "poor," by only 16 percent [22]; and 80 percent say they are able to carry out their major activities [43].

Some aged pride themselves on remaining extremely healthy and capable. There are frequent reports of aged persons who run marathons, climb mountains, swim great distances, and carry out other feats demonstrating their high level of physical functioning. A recent study reports that a one-year program of exercise for men 70 and over so improved their health and fitness that their physical performance became similar to those of men 30 years younger [21]. Such evidence suggests that much of the decline in abilities that occurs among the aged may be due more to declining exercise and activity than to any inevitable aging process.

SEXUAL ACTIVITY AND INTEREST. Another generally held belief about the aged is that most no longer have any sexual activity or even sexual desires. Evidence from both the Kinsey survey and the Duke longitudinal study indicates that substantial proportions of the aged continue to engage in sexual activity, and even larger proportions report continuing interest in sexual activity (see Chap. 8). This stereotype often causes resistance on the part of others, especially children, to remarriage and other expressions of normal sexual interest among the aged.

MENTAL ABILITIES. An additional common belief is that mental facilities tend to decline from the twenties onward, especially the ability to learn and remember. Many believe that the aged "cannot learn new things," are "slow," "forgetful," and "become less intelligent" [71, 72]. This subject is discussed in detail in Chapter 11, and it will suffice here to summarize some of the evidence countering or qualifying the idea that there is a general and steady decline in intellectual functioning among the aged.

Longitudinal studies have shown that there is little overall decline in intelligence scores, at least among healthy aged persons up to age 75. Scores on tests of vocabulary and information show less decline than do scores on other parts of intelligence tests [9]. It has been found in several studies that there is more decline in speed of response than in accuracy. It has been the conclusion in seven different studies that subjects with advanced education and superior ability, working without time pressure, show little or no deterioration with age [7, 26]. There is also considerable evidence that many aged continue to be creative in later life [15]. Murphy and Cabrini, quoted by Soddy [66], concluded that the potential peak performance for abstraction and philosophy occurs between the ages of 45 and 83. Dennis [20] found that creativity remained high among inventors and scholars in the humanities, mathematics, and botany through their seventies, while dropping sharply among biologists, chemists, geologists, and artists.

MORALE. Another set of stereotypes about the aged is that they are "grouchy." "feel sorry for themselves," and are "touchy" and "cranky" [71, 72]. The evidence on this stereotype is somewhat mixed. Most studies have found somewhat more depression, neuroticism, and unhappiness among aged persons than in younger groups, although these studies do not show large differences by age [1, 8, 12, 28]. A recent study found more negative affect among the aged, but the majority reported a balance of more positive than negative affect. On the other hand, a detailed item analysis of the Minnesota Multiphasic Personality Inventory found greater amounts of satisfaction and happiness indicated in the young *and in older ages* compared with the middle-aged [56]. Also, older persons are no more likely to express worry than others [28]. A recent review concluded that "the typical older person is not only as likely as a younger person to have a sense of adequacy and self-worth but also as likely to seem content with his occupational and familial roles" [58]. The Duke longitudinal study found little or no significant decline in happiness or life satisfaction over a 10-year period [49].

The discrepancies in the conclusions of these various studies are probably due to the different groups studied, the different aspects of happiness or depression measured, and the different methods used. However, none of the studies would support the stereotype that the majority of aged are extremely depressed or unhappy.

ACTIVITIES. About half of various groups believe that the aged are "un-productive" and "spend most of their time reading or listening to the radio," according to the 1952 and 1958 studies by Tuckman and Lorge [71, 72]. Actually, surveys show that people over 60 spend less time on mass media activities than people in their twenties [57]. Studies also show that interest in hobbies increases after the age of 50 [11, 17]. Two studies have found no marked decrease in role performance with age in the years 40 to 70 [29, 69]. Finally, the Duke longitudinal study also found little or no significant decline in activities among those aged 60 to 90 over a 10-year period [49]. In another study, it was even found that the degree of participation in community activities increased with age after the middle years among those with higher incomes and education [24].

PRODUCTIVITY. Concerning productivity of the aged, 36 percent of men age 65 or over engage in some employment, and earnings from employment are the largest single source of income for persons age 65 or over [48]. A review of most of the extensive studies of productivity has shown that there is either a slight *positive* relationship between productivity and age, or none at all [66]. A 1956 survey by the United States Department of Labor showed that older workers had an attendance record 20 percent better than that of younger workers and that they had fewer disabling and few nondisabling injuries [5]. Other studies of absenteeism show that older workers generally have better attendance records than those under age 35. The frequency of accidents and illnesses tends to decrease with age, though the time off needed for recovery tends to increase [66]. The 1961 White House Conference on Aging concluded that extensive studies reveal no sound basis for the widespread belief that older workers, as an age group, are less productive, less reliable, and more prone to accidents and absenteeism than younger workers.

ISOLATION. The idea that most aged are lonely and isolated from their families and normal social relations is clearly false. About four-fifths of the aged in the United States live with someone else, three-fourths say they are not often alone, and 86 percent say they had seen one or more relatives during the previous week [63] (see Chap. 7). In two studies

it has also been found that there is even more social interaction and less
isolation among aged who live in neighborhoods with a high proportion
of aged like themselves [61, 62]. It is possible to feel lonely even when
not alone, but only 9 percent of the aged report that they are "often"
lonely [63].

WHO BELIEVES THE STEREOTYPES ABOUT THE AGED? In terms of how
similar the aged are to other minority groups, it is significant that persons with more unfavorable attitudes toward the aged also tend to have
more negative attitudes toward ethnic minorities, especially blacks, and
toward the physically and mentally disabled [36]. To put it another way:
those who are prejudiced against other minority groups tend also to be
prejudiced against the aged. It has also been found that those who have
physical or mental symptoms themselves tend to project more symptoms
onto the aged [4, 73].

Segregation

It is known that a sizable and growing proportion of the aged are concentrated in certain states and counties, in certain sections of cities, and
in special residences for the aged [27]. Surveys show that only about one-
fourth of the aged live with their adult children [22, 63]. This is a decline from 1952, when one-third of the aged lived in a household with
two or more generations [67]. The concentration of the aged in certain
counties is dramatically shown in the special Census Bureau map of the
United States that color-codes each county in terms of the proportion
of aged [74]. The urban aged are more and more concentrated in the
central sections of the city, and the rural aged are more and more concentrated in villages [25].

The growing segregation of the aged has been described by Breen [10]
as follows:

Homes for the aged, public housing projects, medical institutions, recreation centers, and communities which are devoted to the exclusive use of the
retired have been increasing in number and size in recent years. Retirement
"villages" have been sponsored by philanthropic organizations, unions, church
groups, and others. Even established communities which are now known as
"retirement centers" have become inundated by older migrants seeking identification and spatial contiguity with "the clan."

The question that cannot be answered at present is how much of this segregation is voluntary or self-segregation and how much of it is subtly or overtly forced on the aged by the younger majority. Probably more of the segregation is voluntary among the aged than among other minority groups. However, regardless of the causes of the segregation, the consequences to the aged and to the rest of society may well be similar to the familiar consequences of segregation of other minority groups. For example, Friedmann [25] warns that the duplication of community facilities and services for segregated aged communities may prove to be as economically unfeasible as attempts to provide "separate but equal" facilities for other groups in our society. He also points out other costs, such as the loss of needed skills in the industrial system and the loss of the potential contribution of this new leisure class in performing nonpaid functions essential in the conduct of political and civil affairs.

Discrimination in Employment

There are many forms of discrimination based on age. Employment discrimination, such as compulsory retirement and failure to hire or promote, is probably the most widespread and the most serious in its consequences for the aged. Not only in our nation but also apparently throughout the world, most employers are generally not eager to retain or hire older workers. As Abrams [2] commented, "Nowhere in the world do employers generally equate the plus factors of age, such as experience, judgment, know-how, with the energy, adaptability, and growth prospects of younger job seekers."

This reluctance to hire older workers is especially intense when the labor supply is high in relation to demand, when the technology is rapidly changing and making older skills obsolete, and when the social status of the aged is low and their political power weak.

It is, of course, difficult to determine how much of the forced retirement and failure to hire and promote is due to discrimination based on age alone and how much of it is due to a realistic and fair appraisal of the aged employees' abilities and efficiency. Undoubtedly, many of the aged who are forced to retire or are not hired are actually no longer capable of doing as good a job as a younger worker. However, an arbitrary compulsory retirement age is, by definition, discrimination against an age group. Also, there is widespread agreement that many employers do discriminate against older workers in general simply because of negative stereotypes and other mistaken or irrational beliefs about older workers. Surveys of employment agencies and employers show that many accept the negative stereotypes discussed in the previous section and believe that the older worker is hard to please, set in his ways, less productive, frequently absent, and involved in more accidents [5].

In addition to these negative stereotypes, employers have several other reasons—or perhaps rationalizations—for discriminating against the aged. For example, they may believe older workers do not stay on the payroll long enough to justify hiring expenses. Yet it has been shown that separation rates for older workers are much lower than for younger employees [5]. Employers may believe it is too costly to provide older workers with adequate pensions or employee group insurance. This generalization may or may not be true, depending on the type of plan, the number of employees, and the average age. In addition, even if there are somewhat higher costs, there may be balancing advantages to offset these costs. Employers may believe that older workers do not have needed job skills. On the contrary, surveys show that older workers are *more* likely to possess skills, training, and know-how than are younger job hunters.

In attempting to combat such discrimination, several states and the federal government in 1967 passed laws that prohibited age discrimination in employment [75]. These laws appear to have been a useful step in the direction of reducing discrimination, but they have several serious limitations. Perhaps the most serious is that most of them do not apply to anyone age 65 or older, which is precisely the age range in which discrimination is most intense. Other limitations of these laws have been summarized as follows:

1. They do not wipe out stereotypes and prejudices against older workers.
2. They do not strike at employer concern with increased costs of pensions and insurance or with personnel policies of promotion from within.
3. Evasion is simple and widespread [5].

Compulsory retirement is a controversial policy and most of the arguments for it are based on false or exaggerated assumptions [5].

Subculture of the Aged?

The usual reaction to discrimination and segregation is for a minority group to form a distinctive subculture. Such subcultures usually are characterized by a sense of group identity, distinctive beliefs and behaviors, protection of members from the dominant majority, and social action to win benefits and reduce discrimination against its members. There is evidence both for and against the emergence of a subculture among the aged.

Rose and Peterson [60] present a number of reasons for their belief in the growth of a subculture of the aged:

1. The growing number of persons who live beyond the age of 65.
2. The growing proportion of the aged in physical vigor and health because of advances in medicine and sanitation.
3. The growing segregation of older people.
4. The increase in compulsory and voluntary retirement and the corresponding decline in employment of older people.
5. The long-run improvement in the standard of living and in educational level, which increases the proportion of aged with the means (in terms of funds, knowledge, and leisure) to do something they consider constructive.
6. The development of special social welfare services for the elderly, particularly group work activities that bring older people together, so that they identify with each other.
7. The decline in the pattern of adult children living in the homes of their aged parents.

Mixed group self-hatred and group pride among the aged, a characteristic of other subcultures, is documented by the finding that aged persons more often accept both the negative and the positive stereotypes about the aged than do younger persons [37, 71, 72]. There is also evidence that the aged tend to associate more with other older persons than with younger persons [60, 62]. Other behaviors of the aged that contrast with those of younger persons are that fewer are employed, they have more leisure activities, their sexual activity is decreased, their crime rates are lower (one-eighth that of those 25 to 29), and they engage in life review and preparations for death. /

Attitudes characteristic of the aged subculture include a diminished emphasis on income and wealth as a basis for status because variations in income are reduced; a lessening of the importance of occupation and positions of power and influence; and an increase in the importance of present health and social activity as a basis for status and prestige [60]. In terms of political attitudes, the aged are likely to be somewhat more conservative, except on issues that would benefit the aged directly, such as Medicare [58].

Finally, there are some signs that the aged are developing more social and political power to reduce discrimination against them and to win benefits to compensate for discrimination. Many groups start out as "golden-age clubs" or "senior citizens clubs," but through sharing common problems, they may develop an awareness that some of these problems occur to them as a group. They begin to talk in terms of taking concerted action, not merely individual action, to correct the situation. To gain benefits for aged persons they may then join or cooperate with larger organizations such as the Townsend movement for pensions for the aged, the McLain movement to eliminate the means test in Old Age Assistance (California Institute of Social Welfare), the American Association of Retired Persons, the National Retired Teachers' Association, the National Council on the Aging, and the National Council of Senior Citizens. Or they may form local pressure groups to achieve local benefits such as reduced bus fares for those past age 65, as in San Francisco and Los Angeles.

On the other hand, there is considerable evidence against the existence of a significantly different subculture among the aged: many of the aged do not even identify themselves as aged; the aged are at least as heterogeneous in their attitudes, behaviors, and life-styles as are younger persons; the aged share the basic values of our culture as much as younger persons; and politically there is little or no aged bloc vote. These points have been summarized by Binstock [6] as follows:

The most important general assertion to be made about the contemporary electoral power of the aged is that there is no "aging vote." The political attitudes and partisan attachments of the aged are diverse and notable for their stability . . . age is not an important variable for explaining voting swings. In short, there is no evidence to indicate that aging-based interest appeals can swing a bloc of older persons' votes from one party or candidate to another.

That presumed old-age interests do not form the basis for a cohesive voting bloc should not be at all surprising. Even to the extent that older persons identify as aging, it is a relatively new identity, negative in effect; and only one among many (usually stronger) competing identities.

Various studies suggest that a substantial proportion of older persons, ranging from 40 to 65 percent, do not perceive themselves as old or aged. Data suggest that most of these persons are relatively well-off, ranking high in socioeconomic status and health. . . .

Even comparatively disadvantaged older persons, who are most likely to identify as aged, do not tend to see their income, health, housing, safety, and transportation problems as primarily aging problems.

In summary: There are ways in which the aged suffer from negative stereotypes, discrimination, and segregation as do other minority groups, but the aged appear to be better integrated into our society and culture than are groups we usually characterize as minorities.

Disengagement Versus Activity

Another controversial issue in social gerontology is the conflict between disengagement and activity theories. In 1961 the theory of disengagement was first systematically introduced, along with some supporting evidence from a cross-sectional study in Kansas City. The basic tenets of disengagement theory are that (1) the process of mutual withdrawal of aging persons and society from each other is modal or typical of most aging persons; (2) this process is biologically and psychologically intrinsic and inevitable; and (3) the disengagement process is not only correlated with successful aging but also is usually necessary for aging [19]. In contrast, activity theory holds that (1) the majority of normal aging persons maintain level amounts of activity and engagements; (2) the amount of engagement or disengagement is more influenced by past life-styles and by socioeconomic forces than by any intrinsic and inevitable process; and (3) maintaining or developing substantial levels of physical, mental, and social activity is usually necessary for successful aging [30, 31, 39, 49]. This summary of the two theories is deliberately stated in an extreme form to contrast the positions. It should be clear that the controversy has far-reaching theoretical and practical implications.

A major reason why this controversy has not yet been finally settled is that cross-sectional data are usually used to support one or another position, even though the theories deal primarily with change over time. This presents various methodological problems that can confuse the issue.

actually work either full time or part time. For instance, in 1962, 40 percent of men between the ages of 65 and 72 who were beneficiaries of Social Security reported some work experience [23]. Persons who work after retirement may be driven to work through economic necessity because the retirement income is not sufficient to satisfy their needs. Alternatively, they may prefer the activity involved in gainful employment to the other possible ways of spending their time. Thus those who work after 65 fall mainly into two income groups: those with the greatest and those with the lowest incomes [10]. Some organizations, such as the military and other governmental units, set the minimum period for reaching retirement so low that the retiree feels easily able to start a second career. In fact, we would hardly have called Dwight D. Eisenhower or Charles de Gaulle "retired officers" while they were serving as presidents of their respective countries. In many of these cases the possibility of early retirement is considered to be purely an economic advantage rather than true retirement. In somewhat the same manner, the short weekly hours specified in construction unions' contracts are often really a vehicle for higher weekly wages through overtime pay.

It seems fruitful, therefore, to make a distinction between economic and social retirement. When studying retirement plans, especially from the point of view of the company from which a person retires, the economist must define retirement as the point at which the worker severs relations with the employer and receives a pension of some kind. However, a person may or may not feel himself to be retired at this point. A social definition of retirement would specify it as that condition in which a person concedes that he is no longer active in the work role or work activity with which he identified his active career. This definition is clearly subjective and may be hard to apply to individual cases. However, it has the advantage of pointing out that the main problem in retirement (apart from the financial loss) is the loss of identification with the work role and separation from the network of relationships the work role involved.

The situation is different for women, both socially and economically. At all ages only a minority of women are gainfully employed, and many of them interrupt their working careers during the childbearing and family-rearing years. Thus, speaking in strictly economic terms, neither retirement nor employment is as widespread in women as in men. In addition, women do not have as much identification with the work role;

many of them enter the labor force late, after children are grown, and their economic and social position is less dependent on their own than on their husbands' work. Although there have been some changes in female labor force participation and career identification in recent years, numerical changes have been small, especially in the age level relevant to retirement (see the preceding section). It may be that for many women the equivalent of retirement is the loss of the mother role, when the last child leaves home, or a bereavement. For all these reasons the impact of retirement on women in today's society is less predictable than it is on men. For some women—career women, for instance—retirement may have the same effect that it does on men. For many other women its importance will depend on individual circumstances. For instance, single women view retirement more as men do than as married women do [32].

Here we shall concentrate on the personal and social implications of retirement as opposed to the economic and financial ones and primarily on men, since for them the work role (and hence separation from it) is universally applicable, and most data have therefore been collected on men [11].

Retirement in Industrial Society

Five kinds of factors have influenced the importance of retirement in industrial society and the conditions under which it takes place. All have tended to make retirement more prominent and more visible in industrial societies than in others.

DEMOGRAPHIC FACTORS. Both the number and proportion of persons in the older age groups have increased during this century. The proportion of people aged 65 and over has increased from 3 percent in 1850, to 4 percent in 1900, and to almost 10 percent in 1970, from which the proportion is expected to decline. However, the proportion does not tell the whole story. With the increase in population the increased proportion means, of course, a vastly larger number of people over age 65. From 3.1 million in 1900, the number of people aged 65 and over has risen to 20.2 million in 1970 and is expected to rise to 27.7 million in 1990 [2, 24]. The aged today, being more numerous, are more visible as a segment of society. Because of this, society's planning for the aged, as evidenced by senior citizen communities, special activities, and general concern with the status of retirees, has also increased.

ECONOMIC FACTORS. Technological advances have led to increased productivity per worker in all industrial countries. In the United States this increase occurred at the rate of 1.5 percent per year before World War I, 0.5 percent per year between world wars I and II, and at a rate of almost 3 percent since World War II [29]. This increased productivity per worker makes it possible to decrease the total working time of the individual worker and still assure a considerable increase in total production and standard of living [19] (see also Chap. 4).

REQUIRED SKILLS. The nature of the skills required in work in modern industry has acted in two ways to increase the pressure to retire the older worker. First, in many industrial jobs, skills, once learned, cannot be improved on. Thus the aged worker does not have any advantage in wisdom, such as the advantage he used to have when jobs were less dependent on specific skills. Therefore, even if there is no actual decrement in performance, the older worker is at no particular advantage. Second, the rapid changes in job requirements, and even in the creation and obsolescence of whole occupations, occurring in a rapidly expanding technological society force the worker to keep learning new skills and ceasing to practice old ones. We may disregard here the question of whether or not an older worker has more trouble than a younger one in acquiring a new skill. Simply because the older worker has to relearn, while the younger worker (especially one just entering the labor force) has to learn only the one skill, he might be expected to be put at a psychological disadvantage. For these reasons a rapidly changing industrial society will tend to put a premium on rapid turnover of the labor force.

SIZE OF ECONOMIC UNIT. Industrial society has in general larger economic units than preindustrial society, even in the agricultural and bureaucratic sectors. In fact, the creation of modern industrial societies is in great part a function of the societies' organizational capacity. One of the by-products of this capacity is the establishment of definite policies that are applied generally, with little regard for individual differences. Thus retirement no longer depends on the individual capacity of the

older worker to hold his job and fend off rivals but on an imposed nego-
tiated policy of retirement at a certain age. In certain positions outside
the organizational pattern, e.g., in the top positions in management, labor, and government, retirement at a certain age is not enforced, and
the aged are able to hold their own. The aged are probably over represented in these power positions. In 1958 Hunter [15] compiled a list of
the 100 most influential Americans. Of these, more than a third were
age 65 or over. However, among the great mass of people in the labor
force, where organizational policies prevail, retirement has been taken
out of the realm of individual decision.

SEGREGATION OF WORK AND LEISURE. Because of the nature of industrial
work, modern society makes a sharp distinction between work and leisure [39]. Special times and places are assigned to work, as opposed to
the preindustrial situation in which work could be performed around the
home and no definite times for work were established. In consequence,
retirement has become abrupt in industrial society. The retired person
does not go to work any more; he does not spend a definite time period
at a working activity. His social contacts are interrupted, and he is suddenly faced with large blocks of free time.

Society Creates the Ambiguity
The Privilege and Obligation to Retire
The foregoing discussion has tried to show the extent and origins of the
retirement status in contemporary society. The next consideration will
be how, from a historical point of view, retirement has come to be an
achievement and a problem at the same time.

Note must first be made of a basic ambiguity inherent in the way retirement plans have developed in modern society. Social legislation
makes it possible for the aged to withdraw from the work force and still
receive income. This has been regarded as a privilege, and political and
economic groups have fought and still fight for an early age limit and
adequate compensation in retirement. However, this right to retirement
shifts subtly to an obligation to retire at the time retirement pay becomes
effective. Retirement is more and more becoming regarded as a role for
the aged. Transition to this role arouses concern in the aged person and

creates problems regarding his adaptation to retirement, his morale, and his ways of spending time.

In a society that is able to support an increasing proportion of non-productive members, we are faced with the fact that all the values of the society are directed at the glorification of economic roles, at work within the society, and in general at the activities related to youth. Here we have the crux of the sociopsychological problem of retirement. Retirement is regarded as an achievement in principle but dreaded as a crisis when it actually occurs.

The prevalence of retirement and society's acceptance of it are still increasing; we cannot at this time tell with certainty how far retirement will become the norm for older people and how completely society will accept the idea of retirement. This transition period is made far more complex by the fact that the provision of reasonably adequate retirement pay, increasing number of years spent in retirement, and social acceptance of the retirement state proceed at an uneven pace. Until the prevalence of retirement becomes constant, we will be faced with these problems of transition.

Development of Retirement Policy
Policymakers may be motivated by any of several different lines of thought in preparing plans for retirement of the aged. They can start from humanitarian motives, using such rationales as: retirement is a right an individual possesses after devoting many years to productive labor, or retirement is a necessity in order to protect the aged who can no longer perform gainful work. They may also be motivated by considerations that have little to do with the aged but are aimed at solving problems affecting society as a whole, such as: retirement is an economic necessity to allow the young to enter the labor force and advance in their occupational career, or if some people have to be eliminated from the labor force, it is best that these be the aged.

The first type of reason for retirement is usually given explicitly in discussions of social insurance schemes and other retirement legislation. The second type is more likely to be present implicitly; however, in times of economic recession, forced retirement is seen clearly as an alternative to layoffs. This second type is important, moreover, in society's transition from permissive to normative attitudes toward retirement, and the eventual social expectation that retirement is a natural stage of life. Both the humanitarian and the economic motives are present in society's thinking and may be simultaneously held by one person. The ambiguity inherent in this double approach underlies the problem retirement poses in dealing with the aged. How did it develop?

The values that originally influenced the acceptance of retirement policies as a social necessity were humanitarian. They were opposed to the extreme individualism of some preindustrial societies that assumed that people should provide for their own old age and that only in extreme cases should society take steps to care for the poor, as expressed in the old English Poor Law. The inadequacy of this policy was demonstrated by the many destitute aged persons who were consigned to poorhouses. As society became industrialized, individualism became completely unrealistic. Workers were unable to put aside substantial savings, nor could the gainfully employed easily support the aged and infirm. Further, the threat of an impoverished old age put pressure on the worker during his younger years, contributing to the precariousness of his existence and his feelings of disaffection. The diverse social insurance schemes that were devised, such as those covering accidents, illnesses, disability, and aging, were probably as much a help to people who were fearful that these calamities would occur as they were a direct aid to those who had suffered them [8].

Europe preceded the United States in the passage of social insurance acts: Germany in 1889 and England in 1910 passed laws that showed genuine concern for the problems of the worker. Bismarck in Germany and Lloyd George and Churchill in Britain, in their speeches proposing these plans, expressed concern for the dignity and security of the working man and dismay at the cruelty of punishing him for not accomplishing what was clearly beyond his means [7, 8]. In the United States, the acceptance of this responsibility on the part of society came in the 1930s. Here, two factors stood in the way of acceptance of a comprehensive insurance scheme: a strong tradition of individualism and an equally strong devotion to the idea of autonomy of communities and states. The depression of the 1930s made the problem of the aged overwhelming, since they were most likely to be unemployed, and the states could not provide for them unassisted. The work of the commissions and committees that eventually led to the Social Security Act showed awareness of this rapid shift in values, and eventually the principle of social insurance was also accepted in the United States [9].

Other, less obvious motives also played a part in this process. Especially in Germany and probably to a lesser extent in the other industrialized nations, one motive of the policymakers was to mitigate industrial unrest and prevent the workers from seeking radical solutions. Bismarck openly campaigned for social legislation on the grounds that it would counteract socialism, and, in fact, the socialist delegates voted against the bill. Soon afterward, however, the socialists became enthusiastic supporters of the system and even of its contributory features (the system was not entirely state-supported, which Bismarck had wanted), which gave the worker dignity and conferred the sense that an old-age payment was a right the worker had earned. The motives of the British Liberal Government were similar, in that they were trying to hold their own against the Labor Party. In the United States, the New Deal measures were partially influenced by similar fears, as well as by a new factor: Because of the high unemployment rate, a regulated way to get the older worker out of the labor force was very appealing. The possibility of obtaining work for the young and middle-aged by encouraging retirement is still instrumental in the efforts of many unions to lower the retirement age.

These historical observations show how much the problem of retirement is linked to the total functioning of the industrial system. It became clear that, as Churchill put it, "It is a great mistake to suppose that thrift is caused only by fear" [6]. For a variety of reasons, the solution was to give the worker a stake in the system by guaranteeing him a pension to which he has usually contributed himself. Even when the premiums are contributed only by the employer, both the employer and the worker can rightly feel that this is a substitute for a payment that the employer would have otherwise given in the form of direct wages. There may be other, incidental effects of retirement on modern society, among them a possible braking effect on the birth rate, since people do not need to have grown children to support them in their old age, but the principal effect of systematic retirement plans on society that concerns us here is the regularizing of passage through the labor force that an old-age insurance system brings about; i.e., the removing of choice from the individual. Retirement benefits are given to the worker for his use when he is no longer able to work.

For a long time it was assumed that every worker would keep working as long as he was able to do so. In line with this point of view, the argument was put forth that the amount of the premium should depend on the hazards of the industry, as is frequently the case with accident insurance. However, under the pressure of circumstance, a subtle inversion of emphasis occurred. From being the provision of aid at a time when the worker was unable to work, the benefits have become a basis for the definition of this disability; i.e., whenever a worker can have the full benefits, he should then retire.

This shift in emphasis has become widespread and has resulted in the age of 65 becoming an almost inviolable borderline between work and retirement. Even legislation against job discrimination because of age does not apply to persons over this age, and the United States Supreme Court decided in 1975 that forced retirement at age 70 does not violate any civil rights legislation. In population statistics the economically active population is defined as being between the ages of 14 and 65, and the ratio of this age group to the total population is defined as the "dependency ratio," assuming that persons outside these age limits are not economically active. Thus retirement has become the social norm for the aged—defined usually as age 65 and older—and this norm is becoming more and more universally enforced. Provision of security for the worker has become a rule to follow that may not be altered to fit individual cases. We can now ask how the individual deals with the problems created by this system.

The Individual Faces the Ambiguity
Kinds of Status Change
Although more and more people expect to retire, and although retirement is becoming a natural stage of life, the step itself represents an important status transition. In many ways contemporary American society identifies the individual by his occupation. Retirement is still, in great part, a giving up of a role and not an acquisition of a new status. There are a number of transitions of this kind in life, some pleasant and some less so. Such transitions all have problems in common. The person has

to give up patterns of behavior and expectations in which he has been trained and acquire new ones, which is difficult both for the person himself and for the group he leaves. Society has developed mechanisms that make this transition easier.

We can distinguish different kinds of status change. One kind is an improvement in status, such as graduation or promotion. In another kind of change a person voluntarily relinquishes a role and takes on another that may be either better or worse, e.g., starting a second career. A third kind of status change takes place when one is deprived involuntarily of a role [12]. The basic ambiguity of retirement is that it is not clearly in the second or in the third category. Retirement may be accepted as a new beginning, similar to the one a woman makes who gives up a career for marriage or motherhood. On the other hand, it can be seen as an involuntary loss of status, which may or may not reflect on a person's worth.

The Retirement Process

We can look at the retirement process as a status change that is only vaguely defined. The tendency of both the individual retiree and of the persons in charge of the process is to make the change look as good as possible; i.e., as a regular status change or, at worst, as an involuntary change that does not reflect on individual worth. The process of preparation for retirement, the change itself, and the person's adjustment to it all influence the success of these attempts to view it optimistically.

In contemporary society, most persons accept the social prescriptions and expect or want to retire. They have some idea of their future financial arrangements and what immediate changes may occur in their way of life. They are less certain about other repercussions, such as the effect on their interpersonal relations with family, community, and former co-workers. In general, however, they seek little information except for the details of their future income.

Looking at the trend of the last two decades, we may presume that retirement will become more accepted by society in future years. In the recent past there is evidence of an increasing acceptance of retirement by people still in the working force. This change has been as rapid as the increase in development of retirement plans. In studies in the 1950s it was found that a substantial proportion of working people opposed retirement [32, 33, 36]; later studies have shown a greater degree of acceptance and favorable expectation of retirement [18, 25]. In fact, many younger respondents would prefer a younger retirement age than they actually expect [14]. Workers in the age group immediately preceding retirement, on the other hand, are less likely to look forward to it. This may be due to either of two factors: (1) the necessity of facing imminent retirement devalues it in the eyes of the workers, or (2) the trend toward greater public approval of retirement is reflected in the younger workers' showing greater enthusiasm for it, whereas the older workers came from a previous generation that did not have such a positive attitude. In the present stage of transition in attitudes toward retirement the latter alternative seems plausible. However, there are some data to suggest that actual retirement is viewed by the older worker as a crisis, lending support to the first, more pessimistic, hypothesis. Further support is given by the finding that younger people tend to anticipate greater happiness in old age in general than older people actually experience.

In spite of people's increasing acceptance of retirement, there is usually little preparation for the change. Financial preparation seems to be the most necessary kind of planning, and Katona [18] found that those who are enrolled in pension plans are most likely to have additional savings. This corresponds to the theory of levels of aspiration, which would predict that people would raise their sights with success. Looking at this question another way, one can say that people will plan for retirement if there is something to plan for. Social provisions will precede individual plans.

The relation between planning for retirement, exposure to information about it, and attitudes toward it are complex. In a study involving people within five years of retirement [26], the majority had been exposed to some material about retirement. Those who had most exposure were also most likely to have some plans for retirement. However, both exposure and planning were related to the degree of favorableness of the subjects' anticipation of retirement.

Taking these findings into consideration, it might be hypothesized that the virtual certainty of being covered by social security and the increasing likelihood of a pension plan at one's place of employment make retirement a state to look forward to. Those increasingly numerous persons who accept the retirement role also seek out more information about retirement and are thus able to plan for retirement [26]. The studies previously cited enable us to understand why, in general, formal preretirement programs have not been effective. Those who are interested will seek out information, while those who dread retirement will not appreciate a reminder of the future. People generally tend to seek information that is consonant with their attitudes.

The worker who finds himself in the process of retiring may experience it either as a crisis that he has done his best to make unexpected or as a normal event, the achievement of a reward due him for his long service to society. It can be said that a minority of workers retire completely voluntarily. In a 1963 study of retirees who had started receiving Social Security benefits during the previous five years, almost half had retired because of poor health, and only a quarter said they had retired voluntarily, because they preferred leisure or for similar reasons. The remaining quarter retired because of company policy, layoff, or similar constraints. However, the proportion of voluntary retirees, although small, had doubled over the past 12 years [23]. It is therefore becoming more acceptable to admit that one wants to retire just because one does not want to work.

Although retirement is such a ubiquitous event, little attention has been given to the actual process. Contemporary society places little ritual emphasis on status change. Thus retirement may pass unnoticed or be marked only in a minor way. One study indicates that the marking of retirement by some ritual act is a portent of favorable adjustment in retirement; somewhat surprisingly, even the kind of retirement gift given is an indication of the retiree's later adjustment. If the gift indicates a new retirement activity (such as golfing), this is a sign that the prognosis for gratification later on is better than if a merely formal gift (such as a gold watch) is given. The more retirement is looked on as a change to a new status, and the less it is perceived as the giving up of a prized status, the better the transition will be [30]. On the other hand, Toffler [35] has suggested that the model of halfway houses is applicable to all transition processes, including retirement.

*Work Status and Retirement**

We have seen that social trends are leading to an increased general acceptance of retirement, but there are still large differences among individuals and among groups in this respect. One important determinant of the person's attitude toward and adjustment to retirement is the nature of the work he has been doing. Two different kinds of work involvement may facilitate adjustment to retirement: One is the feeling of involvement in one's work and the possession of the high prestige work may confer; this gives support to the person and can carry him through the status change involved in retirement. The second is the attitude of separating one's work from one's real life and considering only the extrinsic rewards in work to be important. In this case, retirement is eased because not much had been invested in the work role to begin with.

In accord with the preceding rationale, retirement should be easiest either for people in high-prestige positions—professionals and management men—or for those in low-prestige positions. There is, in fact, some evidence for both alternatives. Both the high-prestige and low-prestige groups show good adjustment to retirement if the conditions that are appropriate for each of them are met. People in high-prestige occupations will be satisfied in retirement if they felt successful and contented with their former work and if they have some chance to continue their former work activities. Among middle-class workers (white-collar and skilled), successful adjustment to retirement depends on factors less related to their occupation; if they are attracted to their work and miss it, they have less of a chance than do the high-prestige workers to recapture in retirement the features of the work they liked. In contradistinction to the high-status occupations, middle-class jobs depend in general on social contacts or intricate tools, neither of which are available in retirement. Thus the factors determining the happiness of the retired middle-class worker are not so easy to pinpoint as those influencing the high-status worker.

Perhaps because the middle-class worker may have more trouble than the upper-class or lower-class worker in making the transition from work to retirement, he reports more of a need for information about retirement than the other two. The upper-class group apparently has

* Unless otherwise stated, the material in this section is based on Section 1, Chapters 2 to 7, in Simpson et al. [25–27].

gained through normal channels all the information it needs about the sort of retirement its members can look forward to, and the low-prestige group is mainly interested in the financial arrangements that are possible. Labor unions, the associations most closely affiliated with the middle-class group, are the organizations that more than any other claim the continued participation of their retired members [34].

Work status differences also play a part in determining attitudes during the retirement process itself. The preretired in high-prestige occupations are least enthusiastic about retirement, while those in low-prestige occupations are most enthusiastic. Thus, unskilled workers are more likely to take advantage of early retirement benefits. The United Auto Workers' experience with an early retirement plan, which allows those who have worked 30 years to retire at age 58, bears this out. Almost twice as many unskilled as skilled workers (16 versus 8 percent) have taken advantage of this provision at General Motors [41]. Later on, this is reversed: The professional men find retirement better than they expected, while the semiskilled workers do not find it so attractive as they had thought they would. This shift probably occurs during the first two years of retirement. Thus the immediate retirement experience represents more of a crisis for the professional, but he recovers over the next few years, whereas the opposite pattern is true for the blue-collar worker [31].

One other difference among occupational groups is that workers in high-prestige positions are less subject to fixed retirement ages than are other workers (it is difficult to find retired physicians and lawyers). This freedom, however, is bought by a corresponding detrimental effect on self-image when they do retire. Professionals, who work as long as they can—as all workers used to do—have to face the fact that in retiring they are giving up a status, and this makes a smooth transition more difficult. Workers who are retired according to a criterion unrelated to their personal worth, such as chronological age, can more easily accept retirement as a transition to a new, equivalent status.

Free Time
One of the major consequences of retirement, in addition to economic and status considerations, is the sheer availability of time. Thus much of the practical concern society has shown for the retiree has been directed toward the problem of the use of leisure time. During the working years,

leisure is a small segment of one's total available time, and activities may therefore be chosen merely to contrast with or to escape from the working activities. This sort of leisure activity may prove to be unsatisfactory when it occupies the major portion of one's life. Thus attempts to expand the working man's leisure-time activities to fill the new-found time of the retiree are frequently useless. The retiree has to work out a meaningful new pattern of life, and this is frequently difficult. Time, which is scarce for the working man, becomes suddenly excessive and can acquire a negative value. As Wilbert Moore [22] has said succinctly, retirees may have "too much time for much too short a future."

There is little consensus on how retirees spend their time, and little systematic research has been done in this area. Most writers merely prescribe how the retired person ought to spend his time, or they classify the various activities he might pursue. Case studies of patterns of successful and unsuccessful retirement show the variety of activities that might be enjoyed. However, the picture that emerges indicates that it is not the activities themselves but the meaning the person is able to give to them that determines his adjustment [17, 20, 28]. Puttering around with toys may be the last resort of a desperate, bored man; but it may be a satisfying activity for a man whose life-style has consisted in general of devotion to others, especially if the toys are for his grandchildren [5].

Retirees spend their time in a variety of ways, just as people in the labor force do. There is no particular reason why people should change their whole style of life merely because they have retired. In effect, people adjust to retirement in a way analogous to that in which they adjusted to their working life. In particular we find the same occupational differences we noticed previously. For retirees from the professional and managerial coterie, continuity of activity from the preretirement period becomes important. This may consist, for instance, of reading in the case of a man whose job activities involved working with symbols. In middle-status jobs, no such relation between previous activities and post-retirement activities is found; there may even be a negative relation [27]. The findings on working among the newly retired are similar. The incidence of working has been reported to be positively related to occupational status and also positively related to morale in high-status groups. Here again, high involvement in his work makes the retiree desire continuity in his life [10]. Of additional importance is the accustomed pattern of the distribution of work and leisure [11, 40].

From these pieces of evidence we can see that provision of meaningful activities for retirees is a difficult and frequently impossible task. The meaning of life in retirement is continuous with the meaning one gives to life over a range of years. If life was not meaningful before, it cannot become suddenly meaningful because one has retired. Many of the morale problems attributed to retirement may be in reality a function of the total life-style of the person.

Retirement in the Future

In *The Human Condition* Hannah Arendt [1] has demonstrated how the meaning of work has changed in the last few centuries. The central figure in today's society is no longer the contemplative, thinking man, nor even the manufacturing man, but the laboring being (*animalis laborans*). Life and values are oriented around activity, the act of working, and all other activities are made subordinate to this central concern. To the degree that high energy levels are prerequisite to this activity, our society can be called youth-centered. The aged person tries to retain his position by showing that he can be as active as the young person. We have seen that the aged can retain power if they are in positions in which they can remain within the competitive world of activity; but even the leisure-time activities of the retiree are defined by the value of leisure to the young [21]. "Eighty years young" is the highest compliment the aged person can be paid.

It may be that the social trend toward early retirement will help inaugurate a new conception of man's relation to work. Taking into consideration the trends toward increasing longevity and decreasing age at retirement, the proportion of a person's life spent in the labor force will soon be less than half. It is difficult to predict from the present trends what form retirement will take under these conditions. Today's retiree has spent most of his working life during a time when retirement pay was not guaranteed, and the status of retirement could not be clearly envisaged. In consequence, he is a victim of change, caught between two patterns of work and retirement. Members of today's labor force, the retirees of the future, can give new meaning to work and leisure and plan for a new pattern of life that includes placing a positive value on retirement.

References

1. Arendt, H.   *The Human Condition.* New York: Doubleday, 1959.
2. Berkner, L. N.   The stem family and the development cycle of the peasant household: An eighteenth century Austrian example. *Am. Hist. Rev.* 77:398, 1972.
3. Bixby, L.   Preliminary Findings, Social Security Survey of the Aged 1968, Report No. 1. *Income of People Aged 65 and Over: Overview from the 1968 Survey of the Aged.* Washington, D.C.: Social Security Administration, Office of Research and Statistics, U.S. Department of HEW, April 1970.
4. Bixby, L.   Income of people aged 65 and older: Overview from 1968 survey of the aged. *Soc. Sec. Bull.* 33:1, 1970.
5. Buhler, C.   Meaningful Living in the Mature Years. In R. W. Kleemeier (Ed.), *Aging and Leisure.* New York: Oxford University Press, 1961.
6. Churchill, W. S.   *Liberalism and the Social Problem.* London: Hodder and Stoughton, 1909.
7. Dawson, W. H.   *Social Insurance in Germany 1883–1911.* London: T. Fisher Unwin, 1912.
8. Donahue, W., Orbach, H. L., and Pollak, O.   Retirement: The Emerging Social Pattern. In C. Tibbitts (Ed.), *Handbook of Social Gerontology.* Chicago: University of Chicago Press, 1961.
9. Douglas, P. H.   *Social Security in the United States.* New York: McGraw-Hill, 1936.
10. Fillenbaum, G.   The working retired. *J. Gerontol.* 26:82, 1971.
11. Freedmann, E. A., and Orbach, H. L.   Adjustment to Retirement. In S. Arieti (Ed.), *American Handbook of Psychology,* Vol. I. New York: Basic Books, 1974.
12. Goffman, E.   On cooling the mark out. *Psychiatry* 15:451, 1952.
13. Goldstein, S.   Socio-economic and migration differentials between the aged in the labor force and in the labor reserve. Presented at the Annual Meeting of the Gerontological Society, New York, 1966.
14. Harris, L.   "Pleasant" retirement expected. *Washington Post,* November 28, 1965. (Reported in Riley and Foner [24].)
15. Hunter, F.   *Top Leadership, U.S.A.* Chapel Hill, N.C.: University of North Carolina Press, 1959.
16. Johnston, D. F.   *The U.S. Labor Force Projections to 1990.* Special Labor Force Report No. 156. *Employment and Earnings,* Vol. 19, No. 7. Washington, D.C.: Bureau of Labor Statistics, 1973.
17. Kaplan, M.   The Uses of Leisure. In C. Tibbitts (Ed.), *Handbook of Social Gerontology.* Chicago: University of Chicago Press, 1961.
18. Katona, G.   *Private Pensions and Individual Saving.* Ann Arbor, Mich.: University of Michigan Press, 1965.

19. Kreps, J. M. The Allocation of Leisure to Retirement. In F. M. Carp (Ed.), *The Retirement Process*. Publication No. 1778. Bethesda, Md.: Public Health Service, 1966.

20. Linder, M. E. Preparation for the Leisure of Later Maturity. In W. Donahue et al. (Eds.), *Free Time: Challenge to Later Maturity*. Ann Arbor, Mich.: University of Michigan Press, 1958.

21. Meyersohn, R. B. Americans Off Duty. In W. Donahue et al. (Eds.), *Free Time: Challenge to Later Maturity*. Ann Arbor, Mich.: University of Michigan Press, 1958.

22. Moore, W. E. *Man, Time, and Society*. New York: Wiley, 1963.

23. Palmore, E. Employment and Retirement. In L. A. Epstein and J. H. Murray (Eds.), *The Aged Population of the United States*. Washington, D.C.: U.S. Government Printing Office, 1967.

24. Riley, M. W., and Foner, A. *An Inventory of Research Findings. Aging and Society,* Vol. I. New York: Russell Sage Foundation, 1968.

25. Simpson, I. H., Back, K. W., and McKinney, J. C. Attributes of Work, Involvement in Society, and Self-Evaluation in Retirement. In I. H. Simpson et al. (Eds.), *Social Aspects of Aging*. Durham, N.C.: Duke University Press, 1966.

26. Simpson, I. H., Back, K. W., and McKinney, J. C. Exposure to Information on, Preparation for, and Self-Evaluation in Retirement. In I. H. Simpson et al. (Eds.), *Social Aspects of Aging*. Durham, N.C.: Duke University Press, 1966.

27. Simpson, I. H., Back, K. W., and McKinney, J. C. Continuity of Work and Retirement Activities, and Self-Evaluation. In I. H. Simpson et al. (Eds.), *Social Aspects of Aging*. Durham, N.C.: Duke University Press, 1966.

28. Soule, G. H. Free Time—Man's New Resource. In W. Donahue et al. (Eds.), *Free Time: Challenge to Later Maturity*. Ann Arbor, Mich.: University of Michigan Press, 1958.

29. Spengler, J. J. Some Economic and Related Determinants Affecting the Older Worker's Occupational Role. In I. H. Simpson et al. (Eds.), *Social Aspects of Aging*. Durham, N.C.: Duke University Press, 1966.

30. Stokes, R. G. *Transition: Factors in the Adaptation to Major Status Transitions*. Unpublished M.A. thesis. Duke University, Durham, N.C., 1967.

31. Stokes, R. G., and Maddox, G. L. Some social factors on retirement adaptation. *J. Gerontol.* 22:329, 1967.

32. Streib, G. F., and Schneider, C. J. *Retirement in American Society*. Ithaca, N.Y.: Cornell University Press, 1971.

33. Streib, G. F., and Thompson, W. E. Adjustment in retirement. *J. Soc. Issues* 14:1, 1968.

34. Tibbitts, C., et al. Panel: Social Attitudes Toward Retirement and Support of Older People. In H. L. Orbach and C. Tibbitts (Eds.), *Aging and the Economy*. Ann Arbor, Mich.: University of Michigan Press, 1963.

35. Toffler, A. *Future Shock*. New York: Random House, 1970.

36. Tuckman, J., and Lorge, I. *Retirement and the Industrial Worker*. New

York: Bureau of Publications, Columbia University Teachers College, 1953.

37. U.S. Department of Commerce, Bureau of the Census.   *1970 Census of Population: Social and Economic Statistics.*

38. U.S. Department of Labor, Bureau of Labor Statistics. *The Employment Problems of Older Workers.* Bulletin No. 174, 1971.

39. Wax, R. H.   Free Time in Other Cultures. In W. Donahue et al. (Eds.), *Free Time: Challenge to Later Maturity.* Ann Arbor, Mich.: University of Michigan Press, 1958.

40. Wilenski, H., and Lebeaux, C.   *Industrial Society and Social Welfare.* New York: Free Press, 1965.

41. *Work in America.*   Report of a Special Task Force to the Secretary of Health, Education, and Welfare. Cambridge, Mass.: MIT Press, 1973.

6. Health Experience in the Elderly

E. Harvey Estes, Jr.

When is a person healthy? When is he ill? These questions are difficult ones at all ages, but for the older person the answers are especially obscure. Many an older person has low back pain, stiff joints, or diminished hearing yet considers himself in the best of health. Experience has taught him that these are common symptoms, that there is little to be done for them in a curative sense, and that life can be pleasant in spite of them, once the anxiety about their potential significance has been put aside.

No attempt will be made here to cover all the illnesses of the elderly. But certain broad areas important to the health care of the elderly, as well as some of the diseases that have an increased incidence in this age group, are discussed.

Illness Patterns in the Elderly

Acute Illnesses

One characteristic of older persons is that they are apparently less often affected by acute illness than are younger people (Table 7). When such illness occurs, however, it usually leads to more days of restricted activity than does illness in younger persons (Table 8). Older women spend about five more days per year in restricted activity due to acute illness than do their male counterparts (13 and 8 days respectively, at age 65 and older). The data in Tables 7 and 8 were obtained by household interviews conducted by the National Center for Health Statistics on a probability sample of the civilian population of the United States. *Restricted activity* was defined in this study as a substantial reduction in activity normal for that day and covered restrictions up to and including complete inactivity.

Why there should be a decreased incidence of acute illness in the elderly is not clear. A greater degree of immunity to common respiratory pathogens, a diminished level of awareness of symptoms, and a diminished concern, leading to less acknowledgment of illness are all possibilities.

As in all other age groups, the group of illnesses consisting of upper respiratory infections, influenza, and other respiratory ailments accounts for the majority of the episodes of acute illness and for most of the days of disability in the elderly. Injuries are the second most common cause of illness and days of disability. Contusions are the most frequent type of injury, followed by fractures, sprains, and dislocations. Digestive dis-

Table 7. Number of Acute Illnesses per 100 Persons per Year, by Age

Age	Number of Illnesses
Under 5	372
5–14	290
15–24	239
25–44	204
45–64	144
65+	109

Source: *Acute Conditions: Incidence and Associated Disability, United States, July 1971–June 1972*. National Center for Health Statistics, Series 10, No. 88, January 1974. Table 11, p. 22.

orders are the third most frequent type of acute illness in the elderly. These three categories alone account for four-fifths of the acute illness problems of the elderly (58, 14, and 7 percent respectively) [9].

Thus the majority of the acute illnesses seen in the elderly are relatively simple in terms of the techniques and professional skills required for diagnosis and treatment. They do not differ substantially from acute illness in other age groups in this respect. However, the superimposition of these illnesses on patients with underlying senility and chronic disease leads to greater disability as measured by days of restricted activity.

Chronic Illnesses

The exact incidence of chronic disease in the elderly is not known due to the inadequacy of methods of obtaining information. The two general types of survey techniques used are (1) a clinical examination of a sample population and (2) a questionnaire given to a sample population. Diseases requiring medical tests or observations (such as hypertension and diabetes mellitus) appear more frequent when a clinical examination is used, whereas those diseases that are largely self-diagnosed (such as chronic sinusitis) appear more frequent when a questionnaire technique is used [8].

On the basis of data from an examination-type survey [1], the chronic illness seen most frequently in the elderly is heart disease. Over half of

Table 8. Days of Restricted Activity Associated with Acute Illnesses per 100 Persons per Year, by Age

Age	Days of Restricted Activity
Under 5	1,151
5–14	896
15–24	833
25–44	883
45–64	928
65+	1,092

Source: *Acute Conditions: Incidence and Associated Disability, United States, July 1971–June 1972*. National Center for Health Statistics, Series 10, No. 88, January 1974. Table 12, p. 23.

persons over age 65 (575 per 1,000) suffer from this disorder, with hypertensive heart disease and coronary artery disease leading the list of specific types. Arthritis is seen only slightly less often, and again over half the persons examined were affected (515 per 1,000). Osteoarthritis was the specific type seen in over 90 percent of these cases. The incidence of other frequently diagnosed chronic disorders per 1,000 is as follows: obesity, 380; abdominal cavity hernias, 212; cataracts, 148; varicose veins, 148; hemorrhoids, 142; hypertension without heart disease, 142; and prostate disease, 135 per 1,000 males.

The incidence of all chronic disease, including relatively mild and non-disabling diseases, rises steadily with advancing years. Under age 15 there are 400 chronic diseases per 1,000 population, and at age 65 there are 4,000 per 1,000 population, a tenfold rise in incidence [1, p. 51]. Thus there are multiple chronic illnesses in many older members of the population.

With respect to the disability caused by these chronic diseases, this is, as expected, more severe in the elderly. In the survey being discussed, about 30 percent of those over age 65 considered themselves to be limited in one or more daily activities (moving about, feeding themselves, climbing stairs) as a result of chronic disease [1, p. 64]. The limitation was usually at the level of inconvenience or discomfort, with a much smaller number requiring assistance from others. Less than 1 percent of persons surveyed were limited in their ability to feed, dress, and bathe themselves or perform toilet functions, but when limitation was present, help was usually required. Locomotion could usually be carried out with help, though with difficulty. Two-thirds of those reporting limitation of ability to move about were still able to function without aid. Three-fifths of those reporting limitation of ability to climb stairs were able to function alone. Of particular importance is the fact that travel on public conveyances was an exception to this trend. Three-fourths of those who reported limitations in this function required help to travel or were unable to travel at all. This fact has obvious implications in planning for delivery of proper medical care to an elderly population.

Mortality and Its Causes in the Elderly

The average length of life in the United States in 1969 was 70 years [10], a figure that has remained essentially the same for 15 years. On the average, the female outlives the male by seven years (74 versus 67 years). This average expectation of life at birth is strongly influenced by infant and childhood mortality and therefore gives little information about the expectation of life at a given age.

At age 60, the average remaining years of life are 18.1; at age 65, 14.8 years; and at age 70, 11.8 years. The same trends exist as in the preceding paragraph. For example, at age 60 the average remaining lifetime for white males is 16.0 years, for white females 20.5 years, for nonwhite males 14.9 years, and for nonwhite females 18.5 years.

The twenty most important causes of death in the elderly are listed in Table 9. Arteriosclerotic heart disease is the most important cause of death in all age ranges, with cerebral and subarachnoid hemorrhage as the second in rank order. Hypertensive heart disease is the third most common cause of death from 65 to 84, and though it remains an important cause of death beyond 85 years, it is outranked by generalized arteriosclerosis and cerebral thrombosis and embolism.

While most of the twenty listed causes of death show an increasing death rate with progressively older age ranges, neoplasm of the lung is a notable exception. The death rate from this cause declines with older age ranges. The death rate from emphysema is also noteworthy in that it is relatively constant with progressively older age ranges.

Table 9. Age-specific Death Rates per 100,000 Population
per Year, by Cause, 1959–1961

Cause	All Ages	65–74	75–84	85+
Neoplasm, stomach	12	67	123	156
Neoplasm, colon	16	87	167	220
Neoplasm, lung	22	123	105	74
Neoplasm, breast[a]	14	55	82	135
Neoplasm, prostate[a]	7	45	116	171
Diabetes mellitus	16	96	167	174
Subarachnoid and cerebral hemorrhage	60	261	749	1,686
Cerebral embolism and thrombosis	32	152	517	1,341
Other CNS vascular diseases	8	34	137	449
Arteriosclerotic heart disease	278	1,433	1,306	6,878
Endocarditis and myocardial degeneration	29	118	438	1,465
Other heart disease	11	47	116	277
Hypertensive heart disease	35	179	446	933
Other hypertensive diseases	7	26	81	221
General arteriosclerosis	18	56	300	1,394
Chronic and unspecific nephritis	6	21	45	101
Influenza and pneumonia	32	102	316	999
Emphysema	5	33	43	46
Senility, ill defined	7	22	49	183
Accidents, falls	11	33	137	513

[a] Incidence per 100,000 males and females. Incidence per 100,000 of the particular sex at risk would be approximately double the reported rate.
Source: Modified from E. A. Duffy, and R. E. Carroll. *United States Metropolitan Mortality 1959–1961*. P.H.S. Publication No. 999-AP-39. Cincinnati: National Center for Air Pollution Control, 1967.

Some Diseases Affecting the Elderly

Arteriosclerotic Heart Disease

There is some evidence that mortality from arteriosclerotic heart disease increased for several decades, reached a peak in the 1960s, and has begun to decline. This raises many questions regarding the influence of external factors on both the incidence of, and the response to, coronary atherosclerosis. There is also a notable variation in mortality in various areas of the United States. The states in the northeast have one and one-half times the incidence seen in the central plains states. These facts serve only to remind us that this disease, though a well-defined entity, still has many unknown facets.

The underlying pathological lesion is coronary artery obstruction, which begins as an intimal lipid deposition early in life and is progressive in nature. The process is spotty in location and affects certain areas preferentially (first portion of the anterior descending branch of the left coronary artery; first part of the right coronary artery; the right coronary artery as it bends at the acute margin). Superimposed on this chronic, progressive process are other related processes that may cause a sudden increase in the degree of obstruction. Subintimal hemorrhage into the hypervascular base of a lipid deposit may cause a thrombosis within the narrowed lumen. Thrombosis may also occur without subintimal hemorrhage.

Potential collateral channels exist at all ages, but channels interconnecting coronary arteries become more frequent and of larger size with advancing years. The interplay between advancing obstructive disease, increasing collateral channels, and the anatomical location of the obstructive disease is an important determinant of acute myocardial infarction. About one-third of cases of acute infarction terminate fatally before medical attention is obtained; in another 20 to 30 percent of cases the patient dies within the period af acute hospitalization, the highest risk being within the first 24 hours. These deaths are of several types. Most are due to acute arrhythmia, and the rest are due to congestive failure or cardiogenic shock. The advent of coronary care areas within community hospitals is a significant development, since continuous monitoring of cardiac rhythm and a staff especially trained for emergency treatment of arrhythmic events have produced a significant reduction in the mortality from arrhythmia. However, the mortality from cardiogenic shock and congestive failure remains essentially unchanged.

PRESBYCARDIA. The existence of a specific disease of the heart related to aging and involutional changes in the heart muscle and independent of the presence of coronary artery disease has been proposed by William Dock [2]. This high incidence of coronary artery lesions in the elderly makes it difficult to judge the independent effect of involutional changes in heart muscle, but rare cases are seen in which no other apparent cause of congestive heart failure can be found.

COMPLETE HEART BLOCK. At one time, the occurrence of complete heart block, particularly in an older person, was considered another manifestation of coronary artery disease. More recent observations have shown that the appearance of stable atrioventricular block in older patients is usually a result of an idiopathic fibrotic change in the upper interventricular septum, extending downward and interrupting the common bundle. Heart block due to coronary artery disease is seen but is usually accompanied by a clear clinical event, such as a myocardial infarction. Thus stable atrioventricular block may represent a form of heart disease related to aging, in that it is caused by an extension of a fibrotic process that is normally present in the upper septum but slowly increases with time, occasionally extending into the conduction system.

Cerebral Thrombosis and Hemorrhage
Table 9 shows the rising incidence of both cerebral thrombosis and hemorrhage with increases in age. Ischemic infarction of the brain and intracerebral hemorrhage are listed as separate entities, in spite of the frequent difficulty in antemortem clinical differentiation between the two. It is also noteworthy that both entities are strongly related to the presence of arterial hypertension.

Ischemic infarction is usually ascribed to progressive vascular narrowing, leading to slowed vascular flow and thrombosis. Intracerebral hemorrhage is a result of arterial rupture, but the events leading to the rupture remain obscure. R. W. R. Russell [7] has suggested that hemorrhage may be caused by a rupture of small microaneurysms that he has found to be present in certain sites in the brain in close correlation with advancing age and arterial hypertension. Such lesions are seen in greatest numbers in older patients with hypertension, and the sites of occurrence are similar to the sites of cerebral hemorrhage. Russell suggests that such lesions are a direct result of damage associated with age and hypertension.

Thrombosis is often seen in the sac of such aneurysms. Hoobler [5] has suggested that the evolution of these aneurysms could produce small nonhemorrhagic strokes related to thrombosis. He thus explains the reduced incidence of both ischemic infarction and intracerebral hemorrhage seen with antihypertensive therapy.

Osteoporosis

Osteoporosis, characterized by a thinning of the cortex of long bones and thinning of the vertebral bodies due to decreased formation of bone matrix, is not usually listed among the most common ailments of the elderly in response to trauma. It has many causes, including immobilization, decrease in estrogen production (postmenopausal osteoporosis), and steroid administration. A specific form related to senility is recognized. Its etiology remains obscure, but diminished androgen production probably plays an important role.

Except for back pain, the condition is usually asymptomatic and is usually an incidental finding or is discovered as a result of a fracture. It is more severe in the spine and pelvis than elsewhere and may lead to vertebral collapse. Normal levels of serum calcium, phosphorus, and alkaline phosphatase usually distinguish it from other bone disorders. However, differentiation from multiple myeloma presents special problems, since alkaline phosphatase levels may not be elevated in multiple myeloma, and the radiological picture may be indistinguishable. For this reason, bone marrow aspiration should be performed in cases of unusual osteoporosis, especially when accompanied by anemia or proteinurea.

Constraints to Proper Health Care in the Elderly

[As discussed in previous sections of this chapter, the elderly patient suffers from relatively few illnesses that are unique to his age group. The special problem of the elderly is that a given illness is usually superimposed on an assortment of preexisting chronic illnesses and on organ systems that have lost their wide margin of reserve capacity. The elderly patient thus represents a delicately balanced mechanism in which even a "minor" illness can lead to major consequences.

This fragile state of affairs poses problems for both elderly patients and their physicians. The patient has multiple problems, and treatment for one may produce adverse effects on the other. Aspirin prescribed for arthritic pains may cause a flare of a peptic ulcer, or a diuretic prescribed for mild congestive failure may cause a painful exacerbation of gout.

"Usual" doses of medications may also cause unusual effects. A sedative dose of a barbiturate may cause mental confusion, for example. The physician (and his patient) may be unprepared to accept the chronic nature of the medical problems, resulting in discouragement, frustration, and even anger.

In treating elderly patients, many physicians wisely follow a general policy of extreme caution in prescribing drugs, changing activity routines, or removing the patient from familiar surroundings. Patience and understanding on the part of physician, family, and patient is highly rewarding.

Manpower and Facilities

The elderly patient faces many problems in seeking assistance for health and illness problems. First, a physician may not be available. Second, the patient usually has several medical problems (e.g., hypertension, prostatic hypertrophy, and glaucoma), and each of these problems may require the services of a different specialist. Third, he has difficulty in obtaining guidance in matters of general hygiene and the application of techniques to prevent illness (e.g., dietary measures, exercise), as well as in obtaining advice for minor day-to-day illnesses, due to the lack of primary care physicians, or the crowding of the physician's schedule, or both.

Many recent publications have noted a growing shortage of physicians [4, 11]. In addition, most (approximately two-thirds) of today's physicians are specialists, and they are therefore less available to the patient as a personal physician than the generalists whom they have replaced.

Maldistribution of physician manpower is also a growing problem and is particularly likely to affect the elderly. The younger physician usually settles in a practice location that is most likely to provide good hospitals, capable colleagues, and good living conditions for his family. These conditions are most often found in areas of economic growth and higher per capita income [3]. The older, declining areas of large cities and the smaller towns and rural areas are the areas that have failed to attract new physicians. These are the same areas in which older persons are found in greater proportion.

Such areas are often dependent on elderly physicians. For example, in North Carolina's rural counties, 40 percent of the physicians are over age 60, and 20 percent are over age 70 [6]. It should be recognized that an ill-defined but very important service of a personal physician is that of providing an interface with, and an input pathway into, the increasingly complex system of medical care. Even though an elderly physician may be unable to provide the special skills required for certain illnesses, he can nevertheless provide the access to these skills. The loss of a physician of many years because of illness, retirement, or death often forces the older patient to seek entry into the health care system with no guidance, and he often has to consult a new, much younger physician who may not transmit the same sense of security as the older man.

Medical facilities are also becoming more complex as they are arranged and equipped to deliver more complex medical treatment. While this is a laudable development, it also creates problems. The physician is much more dependent on the services of these facilities—in clinics, hospitals, and the like—than in the past and has largely abandoned the practice of seeing the patient in the home. The advantage of the available laboratory and radiographic facilities in hospitals and clinics for proper diagnosis and treatment is obvious. However, as noted earlier, the older patient is often limited in his ability to drive and to utilize public transportation, and a high percentage of the elderly require assistance to travel. Even when transportation is arranged, the complexity of the hospital or clinic may deter the older patient from utilizing its services unless compelled to do so.

Another major problem is the lack of a specific cadre of physicians who understand and are able to deal with the health and medical problems of the elderly as a specialty. There are very few training programs in geriatrics and few role models among existing physicians. These physicians are badly needed as medical directors of nursing homes and other facilities responsible for the care of those who are no longer capable of independent living.

Economic Factors

Most older persons face the unknowns of the future (an unknown span of life, an unknown degree of economic inflation, unknown expenses) with a fixed amount of savings or income. Medical care is costly and is becoming more so month by month. It is therefore not difficult to understand why many older persons, with a fixed reserve to cover an unknown period of years, delay or avoid altogether seeking medical care for economic reasons. Medicare has provided a partial answer to the problem, but by uncovering personnel shortages and inadequate facilities, it has undoubtedly forced all medical care costs even higher.

A wider scattering of family members in modern society has heightened the economic threat of illness. Family members who were once available to care for an ill mother or father may now live in distant cities. For many, hospitalization or professional nursing care is now the only alternative—and that one requires considerable financial outlay.

Attitudinal Factors

Most older persons today, perhaps to a greater extent than later generations, have grown up with a conception of themselves as strong, productive, and independent, relying on no one. Hard work and "something for a rainy day" are important components of their value system. Many wish to retain enough of their material goods to pass along an inheritance to their heirs. The acceptance of illness, with its dependency on others, is extremely difficult, and denial of illness is common, particularly in men.

Fear of discovery of a fatal or progressive illness is another common factor leading to delay or avoidance of medical care. A questionable symptom or sign is ignored until pain or other symptoms force a medical consultation, or until concern by other family members leads to the same result. While the consequences of such denial are difficult to quantitate in terms of greater mortality, greater disability, and greater overall cost, these are presumed to result.

Summary

The acute illnesses of the elderly are not unique in type but result in more prolonged disability and probably constitute an increased threat to life because of restricted organ system reserve. Chronic disease is relatively common but usually results in mild limitation in function. Some few illnesses seem directly attributable to aging and its effects. The problems that have led to poor delivery of health care to the population at large have a more profound effect on the elderly.

References

1. Commission on Chronic Illness. *Chronic Illness in a Large City,* Vol. IV. Cambridge, Mass.: Harvard University Press, 1957. P. 539.
2. Dock, W. Presbycardia or aging of the myocardium. *N. Y. State J. Med.* 45:983, 1945.
3. Estes, E. H., Jr. The critical shortage—physicians and supporting personnel. *Ann. Intern. Med.* 69:957, 1968.
4. Fein, R. *The Doctor Shortage: An Economic Diagnosis.* Washington, D.C.: Brookings Institution, 1967.
5. Hoobler, S. W. Cooperative Study on Stroke and Hypertension. In J. F. Toole (Ed.), *Cerebral Vascular Diseases, Sixth Conference.* New York: Grune & Stratton, 1968.
6. Research and Evaluation Division. *General Information for Regional Study Committees.* North Carolina Regional Medical Program, 1968.
7. Russell, R. W. R. Pathogenesis of Primary Intracerebral Hemorrhage. In J. F. Toole (Ed.), *Cerebral Vascular Diseases, Sixth Conference.* New York: Grune & Stratton, 1968.
8. Sanders, B. S. Have Morbidity Surveys Been Oversold? In A. M. Lilienfeld and A. J. Gifford (Eds.), *Chronic Disease and Public Health.* Baltimore: Johns Hopkins Press, 1966.
9. U.S. Bureau of the Census. *Statistical Abstract of the United States, 1967* (88th ed.). Washington, D.C.: U.S. Government Printing Office, 1967. Table III, p. 84.
10. U.S. Department of Health, Education, and Welfare. *Vital Statistics of the United States, 1969,* Vol. II, Sec. 5. National Center for Health Services. Washington, D.C.: U.S. Government Printing Office, 1974.
11. Warren, J. V. The problem of providing health services. *Ann. Intern. Med.* 69:951, 1968.

7. Living Arrangements and Housing of Old People

Ethel Shanas

There are now some 21 million people aged 65 and over in the United States. Who these people live with, that is, their household arrangements, and where they live, that is, their housing or physical environment, have become matters of increasing concern. Are most old people isolated, living apart from family and friends? Or, alternatively, are they part of family networks? Are most old people living in poor housing? Or is the housing of most persons adequate for their needs? It is questions such as these that concern those responsible for social policy and programs of social betterment.

The kind of living arrangements in which old people are found reflects many factors. Most important among these is the sex of the old person; how old he is; whether he is married or unmarried; whether or not he has children; the state of his health; and his income level. Just as household composition varies, the actual housing of the old person also varies. He may live in his own home or apartment, the home of children, a home for the aged, a nursing home, or a hospital. The living arrangements of old people, that is, the composition of the household of the old person, are not the same as his housing, that is, the physical aspects of the old person's environment. It is important to distinguish between the two, since physically adequate housing alone cannot compensate for inadequate or unsatisfactory social relationships.

This chapter deals with both the living arrangements of older people and housing for the aged. It is thus divided into two parts, the first of which is concerned with whom the old person lives with, the second, where he lives.

The first section begins with a general discussion of the living arrangements of older people. It points up some of the differences between the institutional and noninstitutional populations and stresses the small proportion of the aged that are institutionalized. It then discusses the household composition of the noninstitutional aged and the role of children, relatives, neighbors, and friends in maintaining the social integration of the aged. Special attention is then given to the characteristics of old people living in institutions. The second part of the chapter focuses on housing occupied by the elderly and the various types of housing now available to them. The chapter concludes by integrating the two parts in a consideration of the multigeneration family, its increasing importance in the United States, and its effect on future trends in living arrangements and housing for the elderly.

Living Arrangements of Old People

Old people, like younger ones, live in a wide variety of households. Some old people live alone, while others live with family members or with other persons. A person's living arrangements usually reflect his position in the life cycle. As young people become self-sufficient, even before marriage, they may leave the family home and set up households of their own or share households with friends. As they marry, they start their own households. Thus in the United States we find most young and middle-aged adults living in a household with a spouse and children. The households of the elderly, however, differ from the households of middle-aged adults. When the elderly are compared with the middle-aged, there is a substantially lower proportion of elderly households with both husband and wife present.

Not all households of the elderly are the households of widows or widowers, however. Just as those over age 65 differ in their living arrangements from the middle-aged, persons in their sixties are apt to be found in different kinds of households than persons in their nineties. The composition of one's household in old age is a reflection of whether one is a man or a woman, under 75 or over 75, married or unmarried, sick or well, a parent of children or childless, and, finally, whether one's income is large enough to permit a housing choice. All these factors are interrelated.

To illustrate: A man age 65 is apt to be married. He may have unmarried children still living at home. He is likely to be either in good or in fair health, and his income, while reduced from that of his working years, is likely to still be above the poverty level. The chances are about 8 in 10 that he is still the head of a household. A woman of 80, on the contrary, is probably widowed. If she has children, they are all likely to be married. She is likely to be in frail health, and her income is probably below the poverty level. The chances are better than 7 out of 10 that she no longer is either the head of a household or the wife of the head.

Table 10 gives the living arrangements of older men and women in the United States. Because age and sex are the major determinants of living

Table 10. The Older Population: Percentage Distribution
of Living Arrangements, by Sex and Age (1973)

Living Arrangement	Aged 65+		Aged 65–74		Aged 75+	
	Men	Women	Men[a]	Women	Men	Women[a]
Living in families:						
Family head, spouse present	70		76		60	
Wife of head		34		43		19
Family head, no spouse	4	9	3	10	5	9
Relative of head	6	14	4	10	8	20
Total	80	57	83	63	73	48
Living alone or with nonrelatives:						
Alone	14	35	12	32	19	40
With nonrelatives	2	3	2	3	2	3
Total	16	38	14	35	21	43
Living in an institution[b]	4	5	2	2	6	8

[a] Columns do not total 100 percent due to rounding.
[b] Estimated on the basis of 1971 data in U.S. Bureau of the Census [16, Table 2].
Source: U.S. Bureau of the Census [18, Tables 2 and 6].

arrangements, the table divides the elderly into men and women and
those under 75 and those over 75.

There is a widespread belief in this country that most old people live
alone. The facts are contrary to this belief. The majority of both men
and women live not alone but in families, either maintaining their own
households with a spouse or living with relatives either in their own or
the relative's home. Although the census uses the categorical term *relative,* the relatives with whom the elderly share housing are usually adult
children. Among households with a head aged 65 or more, one-fifth have
adult children in the home. In the same way, roughly three-fifths of all
old people who are not household heads and who live in the home of
relatives are the parents or parents-in-law of the household head [3].

Women outlive men, and men tend to marry women younger than

themselves. As a result, widowhood is more usual among older women than among older men. Even at the age of 75 and over, when only 2 of every 10 women are married, 6 of every 10 men are married [19]. With advancing age and increasing widowhood, the proportion of old people living in the homes of relatives increases. Among those over 75, compared with those aged 65 to 74, almost twice as great a proportion of men and women live with relatives. Again as a result of widowhood, the older the person the more likely he is to live alone. Reflecting the higher incidence of the widowhood among aged women, the proportion of old women who live alone is two and one-half times as great as the proportion of old men.

Institutional living is not common among the elderly in the United States or in European countries. Only about 5 of every 100 older men and women in the United States live in institutions. Old people who live in institutions differ markedly from other people. A much higher proportion among the institutionalized have never married or are widowed. The proportion of old people in institutions who are single (17 percent) is about two and one-half times as great as the proportion of single persons in the older population (7 percent). Similarly, widowed and divorced persons are 67 percent of the institutional population but only about 41 percent of the older population [16, 18]. These findings suggest that older persons who have a spouse or children to care for them are far less likely to be found in institutions. This will be discussed later in this chapter.

To summarize the discussion to this point: Most old people live in families; living alone is associated with widowhood and advanced age; more old women than old men live alone; and the elderly in institutions are only a small proportion of the total aged population.

The Role of Children, Relatives, and Neighbors

Living with adult children is not a preferred living arrangement in the United States, nor for that matter in any of the countries of Western Europe in which the situation of the old has been extensively studied [2, 4–6, 11, 13]. In contemporary societies, older parents and adult married or widowed children share a home only under certain well-recognized circumstances.

Housing shortages sometimes make sharing a necessity. In many of the countries of Europe, particularly where there was widespread destruction of housing in World War II, the limited housing supply makes the sharing of quarters inevitable. Historically, economic dependence has been one of the main reasons for parents and adult children to continue to live together. In some rural areas of Europe this type of dependence may still be found, with older parents and adult children working together on the same farm [13, pp. 148–149].

This type of economic dependence is far less common in the United States. In this country, however, economic support of older parents by children often takes the form of providing housing and maintenance for an aged parent in the child's household. The roles of giver and receiver of help may also be reversed. It is sometimes the aged parent who is helping to maintain a dependent adult child; for example, a widowed daughter and her children may share the parent's household. At times, the old parent or the adult child requires services one from the other that cannot be supplied in separate households. Old people may require nursing care; a working mother may need a grandparent in the home to take care of her children. There are as many old people (2 percent) who are totally bedfast at home as live in all nursing homes and hospitals. An additional 5 percent of the elderly are housebound. Many of these bedfast and housebound persons live with their children, who provide nursing care and other services [11, Chap. 2]. Similarly, a woman may only be able to work because another adult is in the household to look after a child, and this adult usually is an aged parent. An example of the exchange of services and help between the generations is the young couple who were both able to complete their work for advanced academic degrees because the husband's 82-year-old grandfather lived with them and looked after their small son when they both had to be away.

Although aged parents and adult children do not commonly share households in this country, this does not mean that older parents and children live at great distances from one another, or that they do not see one another often. Despite the vast physical distances of the United States, most older persons who have children live in close proximity to at least one child. Fewer than 3 old persons in 10 live in the same household with a child, but an additional 5 in 10 live within a half-hour's distance of a child (Table 11). Thus 8 of every 10 old people either live with a child or within a half hour away. Among the aged with living chil-

Table 11. The Proximity of the Nearest Child to Noninstitutionalized
Persons Aged 65 and Over

Proximity of Nearest Child	Percentage Distribution (N = 2012)
Same household	28
Distance away:	
10 minutes or less	33
11–30 minutes	16
31 minutes–1 hour	7
Over 1 hour but less than 1 day	11
1 day or more	5
Total	100

Source: Adapted from Shanas et al. [11, Chap. 2, Table 3].

dren only about 1 in 20 are more than a day's journey from their nearest
child.

Men are less likely to live in the same household with an adult son or
daughter than are women. As has been pointed out, this results from the
fact that a greater proportion of men are married and that a separate independent household is the preferred housing pattern for married couples in the United States irrespective of their age. However, men are
equally as likely as women to live close to their children. Proximity to
children and the opportunity to see them easily may compensate the
widow or widower for the loss of a spouse. Widowed persons with children are more likely to live with their children than are married persons.
Indeed, 43 percent of all widowed persons who have children live in the
same household with their children, and an additional 40 percent live
within a half-hour's distance.

Old people who have children not only live near their children, they
also see their children often. In a national sample study, almost two-
thirds of all persons with children had seen at least one of their children
within a 24-hour period [11, p. 196].

Just as the proximity of children operates to compensate for the loss
of a spouse, the extended family compensates old persons who have no

children. Among widowed and single persons who have no children, 4 of every 10 live with brothers, sisters, and other relatives [10]. In many instances, persons without children are especially attached to some young relative. About one-half of all persons without children (about 10 percent of the total elderly) say that they see a young relative every day or several times a week [9, pp. 99–100]. To all intents and purposes, these relatives assume the responsibilities of a son or daughter.

The extended family, through children and grandchildren, brothers and sisters, and nieces and nephews, operates to maintain the old person in society. In general, social customs and expectations serve to maintain the old person in society. The data indicate that the old people are integrated within a family network whether or not they live with children. The extended kin family system operating along kin lines, and vertically over several generations, serves to expand the immediate living arrangements of the elderly and to integrate them into the community and the larger society [14].

In addition to the supportive roles played by children, siblings, and other relatives, neighbors also play a part in integrating the aged into the larger community. Most old people in the United States are long-time residents of the area in which they live; 25 or more years of residence in a given area is not uncommon. Neighborhood friendships, however, are important for less than half of the aged. Only about two persons in every five interviewed in a national study said that they visited neighbors daily, several times a week, or even once a week. About the same proportion of old people said that they never visited their neighbors or visited them only under special circumstances, when the neighbor needed help, or when there was an illness in the neighbor's family. There was no difference in the proportion of older men and women who visited neighbors. Reviewing these data, we said: "Apparently, whether an older person visits his neighbors or not is a function of the particular neighborhood pattern rather than of the sex of the older person" [9, p. 100].

In a study of 1,200 older people in Cleveland, Ohio, Irving Rosow [8] isolated the factors that determine whether or not neighbors will play a major part in the social relationships of the aged. Rosow showed clearly that the greater the density of other old people in the immediate neighborhood of the old person the greater will be his number of neighborhood friends. Indeed, in areas where there are many old people, when family care in illness may be lacking or insufficient, neighbors will substitute for the family [8].

In keeping with the earlier discussion of the importance of children in the social integration of the aged, Rosow [7] also points out that while neighbors and friends are important in the integration of old people, they cannot take the place of children and family:

Involvement with children and relationships with friends constitute two completely independent systems . . . friends are not functional equivalents of the family . . . whatever intergenerational supports may be built into a system for older people, this particular relationship cannot be duplicated nor can another effectively stand in its place [7].

The Function of the Institution

In contrast to the usual living arrangements of the elderly, the institution as a form of living arrangement stands outside the general pattern of social life. Its residents are physically located in a community but are not part of it. Of all old people in the United States, 4 percent live in institutions. Who are these old people? How do they happen to have this type of living arrangement?

It has already been pointed out that single and widowed persons are more likely than married persons to be residents of institutions. For persons in any marital status the proportion of persons institutionalized is likely to rise with age. Of those aged 75 and over, 7.5 percent are resident in institutions, compared with only 2 percent of those aged 65 to 74.

About half of all people living in institutions are residents of nursing homes and hospitals. These findings suggest that the institution meets the needs of the older frail person and the sick. Not all frail old people are in institutions, however. Of all old people, 7 percent are either totally bedfast or totally housebound at home. Peter Townsend, the British sociologist, has hypothesized that "the likelihood of admission to an institution in old age is partly contingent on family composition, structure and organization, and not only on incapacity, homelessness and lack of socioeconomic resources" [15]. The institution then meets the needs of the frail and sick with certain family characteristics. This means that enfeebled persons who are unlikely to have supportive families are more likely than other feeble old persons to be residents of institutions. This hypothesis is confirmed by British data showing that institutions in Great Britain have disproportionate numbers of single persons, widowed persons with no surviving children or only one child, and persons with no surviving brothers or sisters [11, p. 112].

Old people in the United States are generally opposed to institutional living. The institution continues to be associated in their thinking with the poorhouse, senility, and physical decline. Among every 10 old people queried about possible living arrangements, 6 said that they would least like to live in a home for the aged, even if they needed physical care. The American public, however, is less opposed than the elderly to the idea of institutional living. Among every 10 of a cross section of adults, 4 say a home for the aged is the least desirable living arrangement for old people, while 1 in 8 says it is the best [9, pp. 103–172].

Institutional living for the old, whether in a nursing home or a home for the aged who are well, is disliked by the elderly and only tolerated by their children. As a result, it is suggested that old people with children reach a more advanced stage of illness or dependency than do the single or childless before seeking admission to the institution. The institution serves first frail persons without resources and without family and then enfeebled persons with families.

To this point only the living arrangements of the aged in terms of household arrangements has been discussed. It has been shown that most old people do not live alone but in families. The role of children, relatives, and neighbors in the social environment of the old person have been considered, and the major role played by the extended family has been stressed. Finally, consideration has been given to the institution for the aged and to how differential use is made of the institution by old persons with different kinds of family structures.

Housing of Old People

Housing by itself cannot solve the social or physical problems of the elderly. However, housing may indeed compound or ease these problems.

Where old people live—the physical environment of older people—may be described in different ways. It is possible to concentrate one's description solely on the physical characteristics of housing occupied by old people. Alternatively, one may stress the sociological implications of such physical characteristics. In this discussion we shall consider first where old people live in terms of the population distribution of the elderly; second, the characteristics of the housing of the elderly; and third, the opportunities for independence within different housing environments. Throughout the discussion the emphasis will be on the sociological implications of the physical aspects of housing.

Where Do Older People Live?

POPULATION DISTRIBUTION. Old people in the United States, like the rest of the population, are primarily residents of cities and towns. While children may still sing of going "over the river and through the woods to grandmother's house," some 73 percent of the elderly live in urbanized areas, that is, in places of 2,500 or more persons, and in central cities and their suburbs. Of all old people, 55 percent live either in cities of 50,000 or more persons or in the suburban fringe of such cities [19].

Old people, then, are concentrated in the central city, particularly in its older sections, and in its older suburbs. Few old people can be found in new suburbs unless these have been built as communities for the elderly. The new suburb attracts younger persons with young families.

Some parts of the United States have higher proportions of elderly residents than do others. In Maine, New Hampshire, Vermont, and Massachusetts, among the New England states, old people are more than 10 percent of the population. In Iowa, Missouri, Nebraska, and Kansas, among the north central states, and in Florida, old people make up more than 12 percent of the population. Old people in the New England and west north central states, however, are largely persons who were born in these areas and have chosen to stay there. Others have chosen to migrate; for example, old people in Florida have usually moved to that state after retirement.

In the New England and west north central states, then, most old people continue to live in the same communities and often in the same houses in which they have spent their lives, while in Florida one finds many new types of housing for the elderly. Thus retirement communities, retirement hotels, mobile homes, and other modes of housing are available to Florida residents.

HOUSING CHARACTERISTICS. Old people in the United States are primarily homeowners, not renters. About three of every four old people

Table 12. Characteristics of Housing Units by Age of Head, 1970

Characteristic	Head Aged 65–75			Head Aged 75 and Over		
	All	Owner-occupied	Renter-occupied	All	Owner-occupied	Renter-occupied
Percent lacking some or all plumbing	8	7	12	10	9	12
Percent built 1939 or earlier	56	54	59	64	65	61
Percent moved in since 1950	65	56	85	57	45	82

Source: U.S. Bureau of the Census [17, Tables A–4 and A–5].

who are still household heads own their own homes [17]. This is understandable, since in this country, as Sheldon [12] has stated, "a homeowner is regarded as a stable, responsible and successful member of his community. Sheldon adds that, especially before the Social Security system was established, the "outright ownership of a home provided a kind of insurance against the financial insecurities of old age" [12].

Most of the homes owned by older people were purchased by them at a younger age. As a consequence, the elderly usually own houses that are older than the houses owned by younger persons. Because the older person lives in an older house, it is more likely to be substandard than are houses occupied by younger persons. Rental housing occupied by the elderly, unless it is in housing especially built, for this age group, is particularly likely to be substandard; old people who rent housing are usually unable to compete economically for standard housing with younger persons (see Table 12).

Since older homeowners bought their homes some time in the past, their houses are apt to be in older neighborhoods. Such neighborhoods, particularly in central cities, are often the focus of redevelopment activities, forcing relocation of the residents. The housing unit occupied by the old person may be relatively easy to replace, but the ties of the old person to his familiar surroundings and to his total environment are extremely difficult to replace. Some studies of relocated old persons suggest that for many of them the familiarity of objects in an older home, the accessibility of neighborhood facilities, the long-time patterns of shopping, churchgoing, visiting, and the like are not compensated for by better physical surroundings [1].

Since old people usually purchased their homes when their families were larger, the old person, in comparison with other homeowners, lives in a house that is "underoccupied," that is, too large for him. While older people often cling to familiar surroundings, the situation of the old person in the overlarge house may be equally difficult as that of the old person in an overcrowded single room. The larger the house the more it entails in terms of upkeep, maintenance, and care.

The houses of the elderly, then, are distinguished by their age, their poor condition in comparison with other housing, and their larger-than-usual ratio of number of rooms to number of residents (Table 12).

OPPORTUNITIES FOR INDEPENDENCE. Housing for the elderly may also be evaluated in terms of the degree of independence called for within a given housing setting. From this point of view, housing for the elderly may be arranged along a continuum. At one extreme is the house or apartment in an age-integrated neighborhood, which requires the most independence; at the other extreme is the nursing home or the hospital, which requires the least independence.

Most older people live in housing that requires them to be independent. The forms of this housing vary. An old person may live independently in a house or an apartment in a neighborhood in which his neighbors are persons of various ages. He may also live independently in a community in which most of his neighbors are older people, or in an apartment project for the elderly that provides him no special services.

As physical strength wanes, old people must relinquish some of their independence. Retirement hotels and other living facilities in which meals may be taken in a central dining room serve the needs of many old people who no longer can do their own shopping or who prefer to have fewer housekeeping responsibilities. While some of these facilities are labeled as hotels for the aged, others retain their facade of serving all age groups while they become in effect halfway houses for old people between independent and congregate living.

In congregate living arrangements the old person exchanges independence for dependence. Congregate living arrangements for the elderly vary from homes for the healthy aged who require a sheltered environment to nursing homes and hospitals. Most homes for the well but feeble aged encourage their residents to do things for themselves, but exactly what the old person can do and when he can do it is prescribed for him by the institution. The old woman who before entering a home slept all day and then viewed television all night finds her waking and sleeping hours regulated in the institution so that she will not interfere with the living patterns of the other residents or the work patterns of the staff. In the same way, meals can no longer be catch-as-catch-can affairs but must be eaten at regular hours. Erstwhile favorite foods may never appear on the menu. These changes in the scheduling of time and in matters of taste are sacrifices of independent choice that old people must make in the congregate setting.

Finally, in the nursing home or hospital, the physically decrepit old person becomes totally dependent on other people. These people are not only the providers of physical care but they also comprise the meaningful environment with which the old person interacts insofar as he is able. It should be stressed that only a small proportion of old people come the full circle from active independent living to completely dependent living in a nursing home or hospital. In 1973, between 4 and 5 percent of the elderly population—about 1 million persons, predominantly women (70 percent), of whom the great majority were over 75—were residents in nursing homes [20].

To this point, the housing of old people has been considered in terms of the sociological correlates of population density, housing characteristics, and degree of independence required of the old person. It has been shown that the elderly are primarily urban dwellers; that when they live in their own homes, these houses are likely to be older and more dilapidated than the homes of younger persons; and that, as people become enfeebled, the degree of independent housing they can manage steadily diminishes. Next, we turn to the new types of housing for the aged that have emerged in the United States within the last score of years and that are designed to meet the housing needs of this heterogeneous population.

New Forms of Housing

A variety of types of housing for the aged are now being developed in this country in response to the special requirements of this age group. The motivating force behind this new housing varies. Some developments are sponsored by voluntary organizations such as church and fraternal groups; others are started by private investors, who find a profitable market among the "younger" elderly in particular; and still others are sponsored by the federal government, which, through the Department of Housing and Urban Development (and earlier through the Housing and Home Finance Agency), has taken an active role in stimulating construction for the elderly [21].

These new types of housing include both whole planned communities and individual projects. Among the new styles of housing are the so-called retirement villages. These are communities in which the sale of housing is age-restricted, and they consist of high-rise apartment projects, retirement hotels, mobile homes, and combinations of independent housing units and congregate living facilities.

Housing in retirement villages usually appeals to the younger segment of the aged population. In general, these planned communities offer standard housing at somewhat lower cost than comparable housing in other communities. Some concession is made to the age of the residents in physical planning; for example, electric outlets may be placed higher on the wall, so that they can be reached more easily, bathtubs may be equipped with "grab bars," and so on. The residents in the retirement community are expected to be independent. It is anticipated that they can meet their physical needs. Sometimes, care of lawns and gardens is provided by the developers, but often it is expected that the resident will maintain his property. The planned community often offers its residents special community services such as medical centers or recreation centers, but these features are not its primary appeal. Its primary appeal is that in planned communities one finds standard housing that appears to be good value for the money.

In general, planned communities for the elderly are most successful when they are located in metropolitan areas, least successful when they are located at some distance from existing metropolitan centers. Those in metropolitan areas are usually occupied by former residents of these areas. The older person, then, while he has changed his housing, is still close to his family and friends. Planned communities in nonmetropolitan locations are often difficult to reach by nonresidents, and living in such communities tends to have an isolating effect on the residents. Since retirement communities are usually occupied all at once by persons in their mid-fifties and sixties, these communities face the problem of what will happen as their residents pass from what is essentially late middle age into the older ages of 75 or more. Experience with these communities is still too limited to speculate on their future as the bulk of the settlers who are couples become widowed and more frail.

High-rise apartments for the elderly have been sponsored by local housing authorities, private investors, and voluntary associations. Such apartments may offer amenities to their residents, such as a common dining room, a medical clinic, or an organized recreation program. These high-rise units may be located in central cities or in outlying areas. In urban redevelopment sites they often isolate their residents from the surrounding community and become islands within the total project. On the other hand, the high-rise development, like the retirement community, provides its residents with easy access to their age peers. Such age peers are at once the source of friendships and of various minor services.

Retirement hotels have some of the characteristics of high-rise projects and retirement communities. Like both these environments they bring together a large number of people of the same ages and usually of the same income level. They differ from high-rise projects in that their residents are likely to require more in the way of services. Retirement hotels offer more than meals and maintenance of living quarters to their residents. Often the hotel management serves as a monitoring service that keeps in touch with the residents and ensures them of medical care if it is needed.

Mobile home parks for the elderly are found especially in those states with mild climates: California, Arizona, and Florida. The mobile home is less costly than a fixed home. Rents for sites are apt to be less than taxes for houses, although where spaces are purchased rather than rented, the cost of the site often approximates residential land costs. The mobile home park, like the retirement community and the high-rise project, provides its residents with access to their age peers. Unlike the retirement community, the usual mobile home park makes no effort to provide special amenities for its elderly residents. The responsibilities of the developer are assumed to terminate with the physical maintenance of the site.

The combination of independent housing units and congregate living units is also becoming increasingly visible among housing for the aged.

These developments, unlike the retirement community, appeal to the older segments of the elderly population. In these projects the resident has the privilege of living independently in his own home as long as he is able and then moving to congregate quarters when needed. The residents of independent living units associated with congregate quarters have access to the medical facilities of the institution as needed. Their yard work and often their housework is taken care of by the institution, and they may have their meals in the institution if they wish. This type of development has a special appeal for elderly couples, who may desire the independence and privacy of their own home in combination with the services of the institution.

While the variety of new housing alternatives now being developed for the aged would seem to provide for all segments of this heterogeneous population, participation in new housing is economically determined. Only old people with low incomes can live in certain housing projects, and only old people with better-than-average incomes would appear to be eligible for most retirement communities, privately sponsored high-rise developments, mobile home parks, and many of the new facilities for congregate living. Many imaginative new developments in housing for the aged may be expected in the future. Whether or not these developments will meet the needs of this population is uncertain. At the present time, those who need specific kinds of housing most would appear least able to afford it.

Future Trends
Future trends in living arrangements and housing for the aged will reflect two factors: changes in the income level of the elderly and changes in their family structure. It may be expected that the federal government and voluntary bodies will continue to provide leadership in demonstrations of new sorts of housing. On the basis of past experience, however, the efforts of neither the government nor of voluntary organizations can be expected to meet the needs of old people for adequate housing. In the future, as now, this need will probably be met by private developers. Developers will be interested in this market only to the extent that the income level of old people rises sufficiently for them to compete economically with other segments of the population. Up to now, developers have found a limited but economically viable market among the elderly. With

anticipated rises in real income among this population group, such a market should continue and probably expand.

The revolution in family structure now under way will affect the living arrangements of the elderly and their housing needs. The four-generation family is now emerging as the typical family pattern in old age. As of now, 4 of every 10 people over age 65 who have adult children are great-grandparents. Among the total population of those aged 80 and over, 6 of every 10 men and 7 of every 10 women are great-grandparents [11, p. 151]. What is happening in this country is that both grandparents and great-grandparents are becoming younger. The grandparent generation is likely to be composed of people in their fifties, sixties, and early seventies. Most of the elderly now over 75 are in the great-grandparent generation.

The present grandparent generation is composed mainly of married couples. In the United States the accepted living pattern for couples is to continue to live in their own home as long as possible. With anticipated rises in income level and with earlier retirement, it is the grandparent generation that will increasingly provide a market for single-family retirement homes and for age-segregated apartment dwellings. In many instances the housing of the grandparent generation is not labeled as age-segregated housing but is in effect housing for only the middle-aged or elderly because the housing design discourages the presence of children.

The grandparent generation see themselves as having fulfilled their adult responsibilities. They have raised their children and seen them established. Are they, who are themselves aging, to undertake the responsibility for the elderly? In general, while they assume financial responsibility if necessary, they do not want the responsibility of physical care for the aged parent. This attitude will increasingly affect the housing pattern of the great-grandparent generation, so that there will be an increased demand for congregate facilities to meet the needs of that generation. The increasing popularity of institutional facilities that offer some combination of a small house or apartment and single rooms reflects the pressures and the needs of the great-grandparent generation, which is composed primarily of widowed persons.

Future trends in living arrangements for the elderly will continue to respect the autonomy of married couples and their desire for independent living. At the same time, the desire of older parents and adult children for housing that ensures physical proximity will continue to play a part in housing location. We can anticipate more physically independent housing for the elderly, a lesser proportion of old people living with adult children, and an increase in congregate facilities to meet the needs of the very old.

References

1. Niebanck, P. L.   Knowledge Gained in Studies of Relocation: A Challenge to Housing Policy. In F. M. Carp (Ed.), *Patterns of Living and Housing of Middle Aged and Older People*. Washington, D.C.: U.S. Government Printing Office, 1966. Pp. 107–116.
2. Paillat, P.   Le Degré d'Isolement des Francais Agés. In *Proceedings of the Seventh International Congress of Gerontology,* Vienna, Austria, 1966.
3. Riley, M. W., and Foner, A.   *An Inventory of Research Findings: Aging and Society,* Vol. I. New York: Russell Sage Foundation, 1968. Pp. 174–175.
4. Rosenmayr, L.   Family relations of the elderly. *J. Marriage and the Fam.* 30:672, 1968.
5. Rosenmayr, L., and Köckeis, E.   *Unwelt and Familie Alter Menschen.* Berlin: Luchterland, 1965.
6. Rosenmayr, L., and Köckeis, E.   Housing Conditions and Family Relations of the Elderly. In F. M. Carp (Ed.), *Patterns of Living and Housing of Middle Aged and Older People*. Washington, D.C.: U.S. Government Printing Office, 1966. Pp. 29–46.
7. Rosow, I.   *The Social Integration of the Aged*. New York: Free Press, 1968. P. 317.
8. Rosow, I.   Old people: Their friends and neighbors. In E. Shanas (Ed.), Aging in Contemporary Society. *Am. Behav. Sci.* 14:59, 1970.
9. Shanas, E.   *The Health of Older People: A Social Survey.* Cambridge, Mass.: Harvard University Press, 1962.
10. Shanas, E.   Family and Household Characteristics of Older People in the United States. In P. F. Hansen (Ed.), *Age with a Future*. Copenhagen: Munksgaard, 1964. P. 452.
11. Shanas, E., Townsend, P., Wedderburn, D., Friis, H., Milhøj, P., and Stehouwer, J.   *Old People in Three Industrial Societies*. New York and London: Atherton and Routledge Kegan Paul, 1968.
12. Sheldon, H. D.   Changes in family composition and the housing of the older population of the United States. A paper prepared for the Internation Social Science Research Seminar in Gerontology, Markaryd, Sweden, August 1963, p. 9.
13. Stehouwer, J.   Relations Between Generations and the Three-Generation Household in Denmark. In E. Shanas and G. F. Streib (Eds.), *Social Structure and the Family: Generational Relations*. Englewood Cliffs, N.J.: Prentice-Hall, 1965.
14. Sussman, M.   Relationship of Adult Children with Their Parents in the

United States. In E. Shanas and G. F. Streib (Eds.), *Social Structure and the Family: Generational Relations*. Englewood Cliffs, N.J.: Prentice-Hall, 1965.

15. Townsend, P. On the Likelihood of Admission to an Institution. In E. Shanas and G. F. Streib (Eds.), *Social Structure and the Family: Generational Relations*. Englewood Cliffs, N.J.: Prentice-Hall, 1965.

16. U.S. Bureau of the Census. *Marital Status and Living Arrangements: March, 1971. Current Population Reports,* Series P-20, No. 225. Washington, D.C.: U.S. Government Printing Office, 1971.

17. U.S. Bureau of the Census. *Census of Housing: 1970 Subject Reports. Housing of Senior Citizens.* Final Report HC (7)-2. Washington, D.C.: U.S. Government Printing Office, 1973.

18. U.S. Bureau of the Census. *Marital Status and Living Arrangements: March, 1973. Current Population Reports,* Series P-20, No. 225. Washington, D.C.: U.S. Government Printing Office, 1973.

19. U.S. Bureau of the Census. *Some Demographic Aspects of Aging in the United States. Current Population Reports,* Series P-23, No. 43. Washington, D.C.: U.S. Government Printing Office, 1973.

20. U.S. Department of Health, Education, and Welfare. Nursing homes: An overview of national characteristics for 1973–74. *Mon. Vital Stat. Rep.* 23(6) (Suppl.) September 1974.

21. U.S. Senate Special Committee on Aging. *Housing for the Elderly: A Status Report*. Washington, D.C.: U.S. Government Printing Office, 1973.

8. Sexual Behavior in Old Age

Eric Pfeiffer

As survival into old age has become increasingly more commonplace, the aged themselves and the larger society have become interested in not only the fact of survival but the quality of survival as well. This has led to activity on two fronts. Governmental and private agencies have increasingly concerned themselves with the provision of services to the elderly, particularly in the areas of income continuance, job availability, medical care, and housing. These same institutions have also increasingly encouraged research into basic and applied aspects of aging, and a number of comprehensive reviews of the physiology, psychology, and sociology of old age have appeared [1, 3, 19, 20].

One aspect of old age that until recently has received insufficient consideration by researchers and by clinicians alike has been the sexual life of elderly persons. In fact, until recently, relatively little scientific information with regard to the range and scope of sexual behavior in the elderly has been available, either to the elderly themselves or to those who must care for and counsel them. But the picture has begun to change. With the publication of the pioneering works of Kinsey et al. [4, 5], with the investigations of Masters and Johnson [8, 9] and, still more recently, with the Duke University publications on the natural history of sexual behavior in old age [11, 12, 14–17, 21, 22], a small but significant body of knowledge has now been accumulated. Nevertheless, information about sexual behavior in the aged still lags far behind similar information on adults or adolescents. Our society has to a considerable extent moved toward greater frankness in the study and discussion of many aspects of human sexuality. That is to say, the taboos concerning sex in adolescence and adulthood have largely been laid aside, but not so the taboo against sex in old age.

The Taboo Against Sex in Old Age

There is no doubt that a taboo against sex in old age exists and that it constitutes a serious impediment to systematic, in-depth investigations into patterns of sexual behavior in old age. The taboo operates at several different, if clearly related, levels. First, it is evident among potential subjects and their relatives. A number of investigators have commented on the difficulty of recruiting aged subjects for studies that are clearly labeled sexual in nature [4, 5, 8]. Even when cooperation has been gained, the data that can be collected are generally of a very limited variety. At times the aged themselves may be glad to participate in such studies, but relatives who learn of their participation may become upset and insist that they withdraw from the study. A recent fictional account of a survey type of sex study also depicts the experience as clearly disturbing to some participants [24].

Second, the taboo also operates among some physicians and behavorial scientists. Thus, referring physicians may express concern that such studies may prove upsetting to their patients, or they may contend that such matters are essentially private and should not be studied scientifically. As has been pointed out by Lief [6, 7] in several publications, physicians themselves may not be entirely comfortable with sexual matters, since their training in general has but inadequately prepared them in this regard.

Finally, investigators themselves must learn to overcome a degree of initial hesitancy and embarrassment before they can comfortably inquire into the sexual lives of their elders. For instance, in the Duke longitudinal study, some of the young physician investigators found it difficult to inquire into the sexual lives, past or present, of aged women who had been single all of their lives. There were 14 such women in the study panel; on only 4 of these were any sexual data obtained.

The Nature of the Taboo
What is the explanation of this taboo? One frequently stated opinion is that it is merely a hangover from the Victorian age [18]. But the tenacity with which it persists makes it seem likely that present-day processes are also active in maintaining it. Our society still holds that sexual activity should be engaged in primarily for procreative, only secondarily for re-creative, purposes.* In adolescence and adulthood, when the production of offspring is a possibility, sexual activity can be tolerated. But in old age the fiction that coital activity is being carried on for reproductive purposes can no longer be maintained.

It also seems likely that the taboo against sex in old age is, in part, an extension of the incest taboo. In our society, children of all ages often experience a great deal of anxiety from observing or imagining their

---

* The Catholic Church still teaches that sex should have only one purpose, the production of children.

parents engaged in sexual activity. Since the elderly represent the parent generation, some of the discomfort may be accounted for on this basis.

Finally, the taboo against sex in old age may serve the interests of the regnant generation. By creating and fostering a stereotype of the elderly as an asexual group, the younger group perhaps seeks to eliminate the aged as competitors for sexual objects.

Actually, a series of fictions or cultural stereotypes exist with regard to sexual behavior in old age [2, 18]. The most important ones can be summarized briefly. Many people believe that sexual desire and sexual activity cease to exist with the onset of old age; or that sexual desire and sexual activity should cease to exist with the onset of old age; or that aged persons who say they are still sexually active are either morally perverse or engaged in wish-fulfilling deceptions and self-deceptions.

These stereotypes have only minimal relationship to the actual data and, as is true of stereotypes generally, make little allowance for individual variation. Only the phrase "onset of old age" is variably defined, from the menopause to retirement to extreme old age. Having considered the taboo against sex in old age and the several stereotypes that exist about the topic, the actual data can now be considered. Three series of studies will be reviewed and evaluated: the findings of Kinsey and his associates; those of Masters and Johnson; and the Duke longitudinal data.

From the start it is possible to make one statement that runs as a theme through all the studies to be considered: There are substantial differences in sexual behavior between men and women at any given age, including old age. There are at least two implications of this observation: one is an implication for research, the other for clinical practice. Data concerning any given aspect of sexual behavior should be examined separately for men and women. Second, the sometimes unequal or unmatched sexuality of men and women can at different ages lead to sexual conflicts and frustrations, at least in some individuals.

Kinsey's Findings

Kinsey et al. [4] studied the sexual histories of 14,084 men. Included in this huge group were 106 men over age 60, only 18 of whom were over 70. It is therefore not an exaggeration to say that the aged were underrepresented in the Kinsey et al. sample. For this reason some of the statements Kinsey et al. made must be viewed somewhat cautiously since they were, in a number of instances, based on extrapolations from data on younger age groups. In addition, many of the analyses in their book do not include the aged at all [4, Tables 60–66, Figs. 53–88]. Kinsey et al. nevertheless reached a number of interesting conclusions that they felt were justified on the basis of the data. One of these was that men were most active sexually in late adolescence (ages 16 through 20) and that their activity then gradually declined and that the "rate at which males slow up in these last decades does not exceed the rate at which they have been slowing up and dropping out in the previous age group" [4, p. 235]. This should be contrasted, however, with data on the succeeding page on the rapid increase in the proportion of subjects who are impotent: from 20 percent at age 60 to 75 percent at age 80. Kinsey et al. also noted that married men, when compared with either single men or with men who had been previously married, had frequencies of sexual activity only slightly higher than those of their nonmarried counterparts.

Kinsey et al. also studied some 56 women over age 60 [5]. Their conclusions regarding age-related changes in sexual behavior for the most part represent extrapolations from changes observed at younger ages. They noted a gradual decline in frequency of sexual intercourse between ages 20 and 60 but felt that this "must be the product of aging processes in the male" and that there is "little evidence of any aging in the sexual capacities of the female until late in her life" [5, p. 353]. Kinsey et al. further observed that in contrast to the men, single and postmarital females had rates of sexual activity that ranked far below those of their married counterparts.

Masters and Johnson Report

Masters and Johnson [8] devote a considerably greater portion of their book to geriatric sexual responses than did Kinsey et al. Their data are divided into two categories: (1) findings with respect to sexual anatomy and physiology in old age, based on actual laboratory participation of a small group of aged subjects; and (2) findings with respect to sexual behavior in old age, based on interviews with a somewhat larger group of self-selected aged subjects. Masters and Johnson report that in their sample men past age 60 were slower than younger men to be aroused sexually, slower to develop erection, slower to effect intromission, and slower to achieve ejaculation. Accompanying physiological signs of sexual excitement, such as sexual flush and increased muscle tone, were also less pronounced than in younger subjects. The findings were similar for women. The degree of physiological response to sexual stimulation, as indicated by breast engorgement, nipple erection, sexual flush over the breasts, increased muscle tone, clitoral and labial engorgement, were diminished in women over age 60. However, capacity to reach orgasm was not diminished, especially among those women who had had regular sexual stimulation.

Masters and Johnson [8] interviewed 133 men above age 60, 52 of whom were above age 70. They present their conclusions somewhat dogmatically and often without sharing with the reader the actual data on which these conclusions are based. They state that "there is no question of the fact that the human male's sexual responsiveness wanes as he ages." Great emphasis is placed by them on the role of monotony in sexual activity in determining declining sexual activity. Why monotony should be more important in advanced age than earlier in life is not explained. Vincent [23] has recently pointed out that monotony of sexual expression can be a significant problem in young marriages as well. Masters and Johnson also conclude that men who have had a high sexual "output" during their younger years are likely to continue to be sexually active in old age. This is in congruence with the findings of Newman and Nichols [11], who earlier reported a positive correlation between strong sexual feelings in youth and continued sexual interest in old age.

Masters and Johnson also interviewed 54 women above age 60, 17 of whom were above 70. They conclude on the basis of their sample that capacity for sexual intercourse with orgasmic response is not lacking in older women. Unfortunately, they do not address themselves to the actual incidence of continuing sexual interest or activity in these women. They agree with Kinsey et al. that a sizable portion of the postmenopausal sex drive in women is related to the sexual habits established in earlier years.

Masters and Johnson also asked about masturbation in their sample of women. They conclude, again rather cavalierly, that "masturbation represents no significant problem for the older-age group of women." They further state that "there is no reason why the milestone of the menopause should be expected to blunt the human female's sexual capacity, performance, or drive" and finally, that "there is no time limit drawn by the advancing years to female sexuality." While these statements may be true from a physiological standpoint, they ignore the social and psychological realities involved. Regular or even occasional satisfaction of sexual needs through coital activity is no longer available for many aged women, and considerable conflict may attach to the practice of masturbation; for it is a fact that the majority of aged women will spend a considerable portion of their old age in widowhood, without a sexual partner. Thus time indirectly does set limits on female as well as on male sexuality.

Despite these criticisms, there can be no doubt that Masters and Johnson have ventured into an area of study that has long been closed to scientific investigation and that they have thus made an important contribution to the understanding of human sexual behavior.

The Duke Longitudinal Data

At the Duke University Center for the Study of Aging and Human Development, a longitudinal, interdisciplinary study of older persons has been carried out since 1954 and is still in progress. As part of the study that seeks to elicit somatic, psychological, and social changes associated with old age, data on past and present sexual behavior were also obtained. The subjects of the study were seen repeatedly at approximately three-year intervals. This technique made possible the observation of changes occurring within individual subjects over time, not merely changes in groups of subjects, as is the case in cross-sectional studies. Information was obtained on the degree of enjoyment of sexual intercourse and intensity of sexual feelings, both at the present time and in younger years. Also sought was information on the present frequency of intercourse in those subjects who were still sexually active and on the reasons for and age of cessation of coital activity in those who were no longer sexually active.

Initially, 254 subjects, ranging in age from 60 to 94 years and roughly equally divided between men and women, were studied. At subsequent examinations this number gradually dwindled as subjects died, became seriously disabled, and a few failed to continue in the study for a number of personal and situational reasons. Included in the study panel were 31 intact couples who provided the investigators with a unique opportunity to cross-validate the information provided by each of the two marriage partners. This was important methodologically because the reliability and validity of data on sexual behavior obtained by interview techniques have at times been questioned.

The results of these studies have been presented in a number of related articles and papers [11, 12, 14–17]. Only a brief summary of them can be presented here. From the longitudinal data, two major statements can be made: Sexual interest and coital activity are by no means rare in persons beyond age 60, and patterns of sexual interest and coital activity differ substantially for men and for women of the same age.

About 80 percent of the men whose health, intellectual status, and social functioning were not significantly impaired reported continuing sexual interest at the start of the study. Ten years later the proportion of those still sexually interested had not declined significantly. In contrast, in this same group of men, 70 percent were still regularly sexually active at the start of the study, but 10 years later this proportion had dropped to 25 percent. Thus there was a growing discrepancy with advancing age between the number still sexually interested and those still sexually active.

In the sample of women whose health, intellectual status, and social functioning were good at the start of the study, only about a third reported continuing sexual interest. This proportion did not change significantly over the next 10 years. Only about a fifth of these same healthy women reported at the start of the study that they were still having sexual intercourse regularly. Again, this proportion did not decline over the next 10 years. Obviously and somewhat surprisingly, then, far fewer women than men were still sexually interested or coitally active. How can this phenomenon be explained?

The present author has suggested three tentative explanations. First, women may always have had lower levels of sexual interest than men. Kinsey et al. [5] report a lower frequency of total sexual outlets for women than for men, at all ages. Our own data also lend some support to this notion; most men but only a third of the women in our sample reported strong sexual feelings in their younger years [17]. Whether these differences between the sexes exist as a result of a cultural or of a biological double standard, however, cannot be said at this time. Second, there is reason to believe that the clearly demarcated menopause in women, signaling the end of reproductive capacity, may indeed have a negative influence on sexual interest and activity in at least some women. A new longitudinal study at Duke University of persons between ages 45 and 70 may shed some light on this supposition. Third, decline of sexual interest and activity in women may have occurred before their entry into the study (that is, before age 60). Our data indicated that the median age of cessation of intercourse occurred nearly a decade earlier in women than in men (ages 60 and 68, respectively) [16]. Interestingly enough, the overwhelming majority of women attributed responsibility for the cessation of sexual intercourse in the marriage to their husbands; the men in general agreed, holding themselves responsible.

A number of other important findings also emerged from the study. Among these were the following:

As Kinsey et al. had found for the younger ages, we found that in old age, too, married men did not differ markedly from nonmarried men in degree of reported sexual interest and activity. On the other hand, married women differed substantially from nonmarried women; only a very few of the latter reported any sexual activity, and only 20 percent reported any sexual interest.

While our cross-sectional data indicated a gradual *decline* in sexual interest and activity with increasing age, our longitudinal data revealed that some 20 to 25 percent of the men, but only a small percentage of the women, actually showed patterns of *rising* sexual interest and activity with advancing age. Furthermore, rising patterns were more frequent among nonmarried than among married men.

Among the group of intact couples included in the study panel there was a very high level of agreement between husbands and wives with regard to reported frequency of sexual intercourse and reasons for stopping coital activity.

Another important finding from the Duke studies has been the observation that the likelihood of continued sexual expression in the later years is substantially greater for persons who have been highly interested and highly sexually active in their younger years. Thus there is no basis for the contention that "you can wear it out." Rather, the contrary seems true. Persons who have been very active in their younger years tend to continue their sexual expression into the later decades of their lives [14, 15].

It must be admitted that the Duke longitudinal data on sexual behavior in old age are far from complete. Additional information is obviously needed to answer some of the following questions: What sexual conflicts and problems do the married and the nonmarried aged experience? What are their sexual fantasies, dreams, and concerns? How important is masturbation as a sexual outlet for those aged who no longer have a capable sexual partner available to them, and what conflicts does it arouse? To whom do the aged turn for help with their sexual or marital problems? Full and satisfying answers to these and other questions are not currently available, and more comprehensive studies are needed.

Practical Implications

In the meantime, what are the implications for clinical practice of those areas of ignorance and of knowledge? The practitioner—whether he be a psychiatrist, internist, general or family physician, social worker, or welfare agent—must be aware and accepting of the fact that many aged continue to have or desire an active sex life. Further, he must be able to convey this acceptance to his patient or client. But he must also be aware that not all in the larger society share this view of the legitimacy of the aged person's sexual strivings. He must therefore seek to educate and to temper prejudices where he can.

Chapter 3 of this book addresses itself to the problem of the aged as an underprivileged minority. It is no exaggeration to say that the aged are sexually underprivileged. Their sexual overtures, aspirations, and performances are often ridiculed. Elderly widows and widowers interested in dating or in remarrying are often placed under severe pressure to give up their aims by their "friends" or relatives; they are told "not to make fools of themselves." An openness about sexual matters, availability of counsel for sexual problems, and living arrangements that permit sexual expression to the extent that the aged person is still interested in and capable of it would not appear to be too outrageous a list of demands on behalf of the aged.

In short, we are saying the clinician should be ready to respond to any request for sexual counseling, expressed directly or by innuendo. Any response on the part of the clinician should demonstrate respect for the continuity of the unique life-style of every aged person. We are not suggesting that clinicians exhort older people to engage in uncongenial patterns of sexual expression. Rather, we want to emphasize the desirability of encouraging and assuring continuity of sexual expression in those for whom such expression has constituted an important part of their lives in the past.

A number of intercurrent illnesses, physical or psychological, can *temporarily* lead to a decrease or even a disappearance of sexual expression. Myocardial infarction on the physical side and a depressive reaction on the psychological side are excellent examples of factors that may *interrupt* sexual expression. However, the clinician should be aware that these need be only *temporary* interruptions rather than causes for permanent cessation of sexual expression in all cases. Once a myocardial infarction has healed, there is no reason why the cardiac patient should not return to regular sexual activity, unless he is so severely impaired that he cannot tolerate even modest exercise of any kind. Once a depressive reaction has been treated, whether psychologically or pharmacologically, the patient may need to be informed that his decline in sexual activity was a manifestation of his depressive reaction, not of his advancing age. These points have also been made by Masters and Johnson's [9] more recent studies on sexual inadequacy in aging persons.

We have seen many aging couples who have given great pleasure to each other through continued sexual expression. It is a legitimate and rewarding human activity and its expression should be encouraged as long as possible.

Sexual expression requires *privacy*. For our elderly we often provide adequate physical medical care, good shelter and clothing, and good living arrangements, with this one possible exception. Many living arrangements do not provide for adequate privacy for older persons. This is true whether the older people are living with their adult relatives or whether they are residing in institutions such as nursing homes or homes for the aged. If these facilities are to be homes, privacy must be assured. If privacy is assured, then opportunity for sexual expression is also assured. Because many elderly persons do not have partners, there must be greater acceptance by physicians of solitary sexual expression, and this acceptance should be conveyed to patients and to other caregivers, as well as to family members. We have a great deal of public educating to do in this regard.

There is always the possibility of remarriage. Substantial research has indicated that remarriage in the later years has an excellent chance of being emotionally, socially, and economically satisfying, in addition to extending the likelihood of survival of both participants [10]. Remarriage is especially desirable for elderly persons who have had reasonably satisfactory marriages in their younger years. There is one caution, however: to be successful, remarriage should be between persons who share a common set of values. Thus the widow of a former college president probably should not marry the widowed plumber. However, persons from similar backgrounds make excellent new partners, companions, and lovers for those who have been deprived of their lifelong partners. Sexual expression is one reason for getting married, but it is only one of many reasons.

Sexual expression should be considered in the overall context of successful aging [13]. Examination of all the available data makes it clear that successfully aging persons are those who have made a decision to stay in training in major areas of their lives. In particular, they have decided to stay in training physically, socially, emotionally, and intellectually. We have every reason to believe that staying in training sexually also will help to improve the quality of life in the later years.

References

1. Birren, J. E. (Ed.). *Handbook of Aging and the Individual.* Chicago: University of Chicago Press, 1959.
2. Golde, P., and Kogan, N. A sentence completion procedure for assessing attitudes toward old people. *J. Gerontol.* 14:355, 1959.
3. Group for the Advancement of Psychiatry. *Psychiatry and the Aged: An Introductory Approach.* GAP Report No. 59. New York: Group for the Advancement of Psychiatry, 1965.
4. Kinsey, A. C., Pomeroy, W. B., and Martin, C. R. *Sexual Behavior in the Human Male.* Philadelphia: Saunders, 1948.
5. Kinsey, A. C., Pomeroy, W. B., Martin, C. R., and Gebhard, P. H. *Sexual Behavior in the Human Female.* Philadelphia: Saunders, 1953.
6. Lief, H. I. Sex education of medical students and doctors. *Pac. Med. Surg.* 73:52, 1965.
7. Lief, H. I. Sex and the medical educator. *J. Am. Med. Wom. Assoc.* 23:195, 1968.
8. Masters, W. H., and Johnson, V. E. *Human Sexual Response.* Boston: Little, Brown, 1966.

9. Masters, W. H., and Johnson, V. E. *Human Sexual Inadequacy*. Boston: Little, Brown, 1970. Pp. 316–350.
10. McKain, W. C. *Retirement Marriage*. Storrs, Conn.: University of Connecticut, 1969.
11. Newman, G., and Nichols, C. R. Sexual activities and attitudes in older persons. *J.A.M.A.* 173:33, 1960.
12. Pfeiffer, E. Sexuality in the aging individual. *J. Am. Geriatr. Soc.* 22: 481, 1974.
13. Pfeiffer, E. *Successful Aging*. Durham, N.C.: Duke University Center for the Study of Aging and Human Development, 1974.
14. Pfeiffer, E., and Davis, G. C. Determinants of sexual behavior in middle and old age. *J. Am. Geriatr. Soc.* 20:4, 1972.
15. Pfeiffer, E., Verwoerdt, A., and Davis, G. C. Sexual behavior in middle life. *Am. J. Psychiatry* 128:10, 1972.
16. Pfeiffer, E., Verwoerdt, A., and Wang, H.-S. Sexual behavior in aged men and women. I. Observations on 254 community volunteers. *Arch. Gen. Psychiatry* 19:753, 1968.
17. Pfeiffer, E., Verwoerdt, A., and Wang, H.-S. The natural history of sexual behavior in a biologically advantaged group of aged individuals. *J. Gerontol.* 24:193, 1969.
18. Rubin, I. *Sexual Life After Sixty*. New York: Basic Books, 1965.
19. Simon, A., and Epstein, L. J. (Eds.). *Aging in Modern Society*. Psychiatric Research Report 23. Washington, D.C.: American Psychiatric Association, 1968.
20. Tibbitts, C. *Handbook of Social Gerontology*. Chicago: University of Chicago Press, 1960.
21. Verwoerdt, A., Pfeiffer, E., and Wang, H.-S. Sexual behavior in senescence. I. Changes in sexual activity and interest of aging men and women. *J. Geriatr. Psychiatry* 2:163, 1969.
22. Verwoerdt, A., Pfeiffer, E., and Wang, H.-S. Sexual behavior in senescence. II. Patterns of sexual activity and interest. *Geriatrics* 24:137, 1969.
23. Vincent, C. E. Sex and the young married. *Med. Aspects Hum. Sex.* 3:13, 1969.
24. Wallace, I. *The Chapman Report*. New York: Simon and Schuster, 1960.

9. How the Old Face Death

Frances C. Jeffers and Adriaan Verwoerdt

Professional persons working with older people are concerned that adjustment to the later years of life be as healthy and satisfying as possible, whatever the future may hold for such individuals or however long that future may be. Whatever the circumstances, at this phase of the life span there can be no avoidance of the fact of death. To its approach the older person must either make some type of adjustment or build up defenses that shield him to some extent from facing the necessity that he, too, must die. According to Feifel, "the adaptation of the older person to dying and to death may well be a crucial aspect of the aging process" [6]. To the extent that one agrees with this statement, the aging person's awareness of death, its personal meaning to him, and the effects of these on behavior all become important factors in understanding and managing the problems of late life.

The realization of the inevitability of death, and thus of the extinction of the individual personality, is seen by many therapists as the ultimate threat to a human being. Koestenbaum [18], speaking from an existential point of view, interprets death anxiety as a dread of seeing the world itself disappear. Our modern culture has attempted to alleviate such anxiety by taboos on the topic of death, by increasing the impersonality of memorial services, and by disguising cemeteries as ordinary parks [25, 39]. But from those persons on "the shady side of the hill" of life, death can scarcely be hidden. A realistic acceptance of death as the "appropriate" end of life may well be the hallmark of emotional maturity [40]. If awareness and acceptance of death are characteristics of the emotional maturity of elderly persons, one may also ask to what extent they occur in younger persons and what the effects may be of such factors as age, physical illness, and personality adjustment. At the present time, some research evidence is beginning to accumulate, but much work remains to be done. Kastenbaum [15], in chairing a Gerontological Society symposium in 1965, outlined some of the difficulties and challenges of "death research."

Several problems of research methodology exist in the area of personal attitudes toward death and dying, awareness of death, and means of coping with death anxiety. First, in reading the literature it becomes clear that there are difficulties with regard to the conceptualization of death and in arriving at operational definitions suitable for research purposes. Second, investigations tend to utilize diverse subject groups, methods, questionnaires, and/or interview schedules, so that it is difficult to compare findings from different studies. Third, some of the research methods utilized to date (direct questioning, death attitude scales, sentence completions, projective techniques, and so on) may be inadequate to measure accurately and fully the degrees of death awareness and the meanings death has for different people. In addition, such data are generally obtained at only one point in time. Data obtained from serial interviews over a prolonged period of time might shed additional light on the "deeper" significance of death to the personality. Thus far, reports on this type of material are not available except tangentially (e.g., Lindemann's [22] reports on the effects of grief and bereavement).

Awareness of Death

Awareness of external events, inner physiological processes, or subjective experiences is not an "all-or-none" phenomenon, but rather it can be manifested in varying degrees of consciousness. It follows that awareness of death may be revealed indirectly through the existence of ideas that are related to death. Thus it may be that frequently awareness of one's own death occurs on a preconscious level.

A special instance of preconscious awareness of impending death was described by Verwoerdt and Elmore [37], who studied 30 hospitalized patients (age range 24 to 74) with fatal illness. The data suggested a relationship between actual temporal distance to death, hopelessness, and decreased expectation of futurity. None of the patients could know, or alleged to know, exactly how long they still had to live. Nor was this interval before death known to the investigators at the time of the study; it was obtained instead from a follow-up study one year later. Patients who were closer to death expressed more hopelessness and evidenced a greater reduction of expectation of futurity. This same finding was reported by Lieberman [21] in his study of 22 older persons a year or less distant from death. In illness, especially in fatal illness, the patient may well be aware of the rate of decline in his physical status. By "monitoring" these internal physiological changes, he may be able to "estimate" the rate of his decline from the present to a terminal point [8]. It is possible that to some extent similar mechanisms may also be activated by the much slower biological changes that occur as a result of the aging process.

Studies comparing death awareness in younger and older persons in the general population are few and far between. Investigators appear to be concerned primarily with one group or with the other, and to have done descriptive rather than comparative studies. In a study of 1,500 adults, J. Riley [30] reported that most persons 61 years and older said they think at least occasionally, and 45 percent said they think often, about the uncertainty of their own life or of the death of someone close to them. Such thoughts were somewhat more widespread among people over age 60 than among the younger persons in his sample.

In a Duke study (1966) [13] of frequency of death thoughts among 140 elderly noninstitutionalized persons (60 to 94 years old), 49 percent reported being reminded of death at least once a day, if only by reading the obituaries; 20 percent admitted to death thoughts about once a week and 25 percent, less than once a week; 5 percent denied they ever thought about death; and 1 percent were undecided. It was reported by 7 percent of the subjects that thoughts related to death were constantly on their minds. Several factors differentiated these subjects from the "deniers." The latter tended to believe that such awareness would affect enjoyment of life; they were more active, less "disengaged," and had higher "morale"; their subjective health assessment was higher, although there was no difference with regard to objective health ratings; they had higher IQ scores; and their occupations were primarily in the nonmanual categories. Finally, these subjects were younger than those who always had death thoughts on their mind.

Hence those who shut out thoughts of death presumably felt more distant from it by reason of being chronologically younger and by considering themselves to be in better health. But it is interesting to note that when the two groups were given a sentence completion test in which they were asked to speak directly about personal meanings of death, they differed very little in type of emotional reaction: The incidence of positive (nonthreatened, accepting) reactions in each group was about 50 percent, with neutral or negative reactions making up the other 50 percent.

Richardson and Freeman [29] found that thoughts of death were more common among those in poor than in good health. This is in keeping with the finding at Duke of an inverse relationship between favorable self-health evaluations and frequency of death thoughts and with the findings reported by Shrut [33] and by Rhudick and Dibner [28]. The latter two investigators, using death references from thematic apperception test (TAT) stories, found additionally that neurotic patients showed much more death concern than did psychotic patients. This phenomenon is also mentioned by May [23], who states that whenever *concern* about death arises, it is to be assumed that a neurotic element may be present.

To summarize these findings: Current research evidence suggests that *frequency of death thoughts* may be higher in older age groups and also in conditions of physical illness. *Concerns about death* tend to occur in persons with neurotic conflicts rather than in those who are either normal or psychotic.

Personal Meanings of Death

Closely linked with awareness of death is the meaning of death to the individual. Doubtless the significance of death for the person has a great number of determinants, both personal and sociocultural. "The meaning of death" is not to be equated with the actual experience of the event of dying but is taken to signify the subjective anticipations, interpretations, inferences, or projections of personal feelings onto the fact of death. It is likely that there are as many meanings of death as there are human beings capable of reflection. In spite of such an infinite variety of meanings—with their subtle differences and nuances—a certain degree of classification would seem desirable even on an arbitrary basis. Several possible categories emerge from a scrutiny of the data obtained from sentence completion tests in the Duke study [13] previously referred to. The elderly subjects were asked to complete the following phrases:

1. When a man dies, ——
2. Death is ——
3. I feel that when I die, I ——

It appeared that for the most part the responses could be categorized under one or another of the following headings:

1. *Continuation or cessation of life.* The greater part of the subjects expressed firm religious convictions (it must be remembered that North Carolina lies within the "Bible belt"). For example: "When a man dies,

he lives again," "Death is passing from this life into another world," or, "I feel that when I die, I think my spirit or soul will carry on." The end of life on this earth is seen by these persons as a stepping-stone to another life. Another thought expressed was that "When a man dies, he will keep living on in the minds and hearts of those still here." There were some persons, on the other hand, who thought of death primarily as extinction of the personality and loss of identity. One "ceases to exist," "he's buried," "he's dead all over," "he's soon forgotten." Or, "It's very final." Thus, death was seen as "inevitable" or—more positively—as rest and release: "I will be out of all my troubles," "I'll leave behind me the troubles and worries of life."

2. *Death as the enemy*. Only infrequently was death viewed as an enemy disrupting life patterns and relationships, e.g., "Death is a cruel master." However, more subjects expressed fear of the dependency, disability, or pain that they associated with the act of dying.

3. *Reunion or isolation*. Many persons expressed reunion beliefs, as, for example, "I am going to meet the ones who have gone ahead of me." For some, death involved departure from a known existence and separation from loved ones here with sadness but without the element of decreased self-esteem: "I wouldn't be afraid to die but I dread to leave my children and loved ones."

4. *Reward or punishment*. Most of the subjects viewed death as a transition to a better state of being, a reward for a life well lived: "I will go to heaven, and into the joys of the Lord." This was in keeping with the firm religious beliefs of the study panel members as a whole. Only seldom were there direct expressions that death meant punishment: "He's at rest if he lived right and he's gone if he didn't."

5. *The anticipated or the unknown*. Several subjects expressed uncertainty or curiosity, as follows: "I can't say," or, "I don't know what death is—tell me—what is it?" Or, "I wonder what it is going to be like—who knows?—sort of like going to Egypt." The anticipation of death as an event made familiar through religious rituals was observed in such responses as, "Death is going to my long home," and, "My spirit will go back to God."

In a similar manner Feifel [6] categorized the two dominant outlooks of 40 disabled World War I veterans. One group visualized death as the dissolution of bodily life and the doorway to a new life. The other group, with "philosophic resignation," looked on death as "the end."

Emotional Reactions to Death Awareness

Typically, the older subjects studied at Duke seemed to experience feelings appropriate to the particular ideas about death they had expressed. For example, it was commonly observed that beliefs in reunion after death were associated with feelings of happy expectation [13]. The few subjects who felt threatened by the sentence completion test tended to view death as being cruel or as punishment: "Those questions are very tough. I tell you, they shook me up." There was also some evidence of ambivalent feelings. Several persons stated, for example, "Heaven may be my home, but I'm not homesick yet."

Notably absent were any expressions of angry protest or rage in response to the disruptive or cruel aspects of death. The death-defying mood portrayed by poet Dylan Thomas ("Rage, rage, against the dying of the light") is perhaps more characteristic of the attitude of younger persons.

A number of investigators [6, 12, 35] are in agreement that only a relatively small proportion of older persons—only 10 percent or less in several studies—express fear of death. In the National Institute of Mental Health sample of healthy older persons, overt fear of death was present in 30 percent of the subjects [1]. In a sentence completion test conducted by Kogan and Shelton [19], 200 subjects, aged 49 to 92, thought that death was more frightening to "people in general" than to old people. They also felt that old people were comparatively less likely to regard death as one of their greatest fears but rather thought of it as an escape or as inevitable. Kogan and Wallach [20] found, in comparing older persons with college students, that the responses to the concept of death, utilizing the semantic differential, were less negative among the older subjects than they were among the younger subjects.

In another study at Duke University [12], only 10 percent of the elderly community subjects answered the question "Are you afraid to die?" in the affirmative; 35 percent of the subjects denied being afraid, while 55 percent were hesitant or ambivalent in their answers. The responses admitting fear of death tended to be devoid of religious references. The finding that these particular subjects showed less belief in life after death confirms that in Swenson's study [35]. In addition, it was found at Duke that those persons who admitted fear of death gave fewer responses on the Rorschach test, had fewer leisure activities, and lower IQ scores. Riley [30] reported a similar relationship between negative views of death and lower educational level in his sample of 1,500 adults. Finally, the Duke subjects who expressed fear of death had a higher incidence of feelings of rejection and depression. Rhudick and Dibner [28] suggest that death concern may not necessarily manifest itself as overt anxiety but may be accompanied by somatizing and withdrawal tendencies.

Butler [4] points out that even though many older persons may not show any obvious fear of death, one cannot conclude that the problem of death does not exist for them. Rather, one may need to study the person at a particular stage of his adaptation to the reality of death. As one of the elderly volunteers at Duke put it, "No, I'm not afraid to die—it seems to me to be a perfectly normal process. But you never know how you will feel when it comes to a showdown. I might get panicky."

In summary, it appears from the expressions of older persons that death is feared much less than prolonged illness, dependency, or pain, which may bring the several threats of rejection and isolation, as well as loss of social role, self-determination, and dignity as an individual. To some of the elderly ill who are cared for in their own homes, life may still seem worth living, but even here regret is often expressed for "the bother I am to those I love." Glaser and Strauss [9] point out that terminal geriatric patients often decide to stay in the hospital in order not to be a burden to their families. Experience in nursing homes suggests that, except for an occasional geriatric patient who clings tenaciously to life, death is seen by most of them as preferable to continued illness or chronic disability. These patients may have already become "socially dead"—according to Kalish's concept—in their own eyes as well as to others, and thus they view their impending death as timely and welcome [9, 14]. Kastenbaum [16] quotes staff reports in a geriatric hospital to the effect that, among older persons who were dying, most of their references to death were positively valued, such as calm waiting for death or a desire for the end of all suffering.

There has been such a wide disparity between findings on the one hand of lack of fear of death in older persons and, on the other hand, the assumption of some clinicians of the universality of this fear that Kastenbaum [15, 17], in taking note of the difference in opinion, has challenged the use of this concept altogether in the study of aging.

Coping with the Prospect of Death

It has become a truism that individual variations in adaptive behavior may exist to a greater degree among the elderly than in other age groups because their relative longevity may provide a greater quantity and variety of life experiences. Thus their coping behavior vis-à-vis death may be varied as well. Muriel Spark [34] has written an absorbing piece of fiction, *Memento Mori,* in which she describes in some detail the varied behaviors of several older persons in response to anonymous phone calls of four words only, "Remember you must die."

Certain coping techniques or defense mechanisms may be adaptive for one person but maladaptive for another. Whether or not a particular defense is adaptive depends further on quantitative factors. Some of the determinants for the type of mechanism utilized may be: (1) the temporal factor, i.e., chronological age and distance from death, both of which were found to be of importance in the Duke geriatric studies [13]; (2) physical and mental health; (3) the influence of varying frames of reference, such as religious orientation and socioeconomic and occupational status; (4) community attitudes; (5) family and personal experiences with death; (6) attitudes of persons currently in the immediate environment; and (7) the individual's own psychological integrity and maturity. A major determinant of the adjustment is probably how the person has adjusted to changes and crises in his past life. As an additional determinant to a person's acceptance of his death, Payne [26] cites the nature of the person's emotional commitments during his lifetime to people and to productive endeavors. Wahl [38] hypothesizes that the well-loved child is more likely to retain an unconscious proclivity toward infantile omnipotence, which he is able to put into use in handling the death anxiety, since he has had confidence to face new situations in the past.

In most instances of successful adaptation, an interlocking of several coexisting adaptive approaches may be utilized. By functioning simultaneously, one adaptational technique fosters, or even potentiates, another one.

Many persons have the ability to cross into old age and to face death with a conscious, though perhaps unverbalized, feeling of satisfaction with past achievements and a sense of contentment with life as they have lived it. A decreased energy level may reconcile them to rest from struggle and may facilitate a philosophical attitude toward closure. Wahl [38] quotes Spinoza as having said that the adult who sees death as completion of a pattern and who has spent his time, unfettered by fear, in living richly and productively can accept the thought that his self will one day cease to be.

Mastery and adaptation to the prospect of death may—in addition to the predominantly intrapsychic processes of synthesis and integrity—be achieved in other ways, as through the anchorage point of mature religious beliefs or the securities and satisfactions derived from social relationships.

Feifel's reports [6] and others have confirmed that for many older persons a belief in life after death or a trust in religious support serves as a bolster against the threat of death. The study of the geriatrics panel in North Carolina [12] revealed that there was almost universal belief in a life after death, with only 2 percent of 254 denying such a belief outright; 21 percent compromised by saying they were "not sure" of such afterlife, but 77 percent wished to be counted among those who were sure, with almost as many variations as individuals in imagining what it might be like. On the other hand, for a few in the Duke panel and also for some persons in Feifel's studies, strong belief in religion and in an afterlife can be threatening if the person fears retribution at death for his sins. As Choron [5] notes, belief in "immortality" may generate its own kind of death fear.

One of the most satisfying adaptations to the ending of life is a close but nonambivalent relationship with children and grandchildren. This not only satisfies mutual affectional needs but also reminds the older person of the continuity of life and provides tangible evidence of his own ongoing contribution to mankind. The grandparents can participate, often without overstrained responsibility, in the pleasures of learning, wonder, and companionship of a new generation.

A person's planning the disposition of whatever inheritance he may have to leave to his family and friends is often a tangible mark of his acceptance of the ultimate closure of his life, however near or distant that closure may be. The older a person is the more time he has had for preparation and getting his affairs in proper shape for his death, but in some persons, intervening variables—denial, hostility, fear, or disturbed reactions of family members—may operate to arouse resistance to such planning. Occasionally one can observe the superstitious fear that being prepared for death might actually hasten its coming. In a study at Duke (1965) [11] on the extent of concern and planning for chronic illness, for example, the elderly persons studied expressed relatively little concern and did little actual planning for such an eventuality. Many gave the impression that they did not wish to consider such a possibility.

In a study at Duke based on the Rosow Death-Awareness Scale, the older subjects appeared to be more practical than the younger ones with regard to such financial matters as keeping up their life insurance for funeral costs, making wills, and signing their homes over to their children. One 90-year-old woman had purchased her cemetery lot and tombstone and had even paid in advance for engraving the date of death after her name. More involvement in planning might well be expected by those who also indicated more awareness of death; Rosow and Chellam [31] found this correlation among the 100 community respondents in their study. However, resistance to giving away a few of the most valued keepsakes before death is a hopeful sign, indicating a wish to live as fully as possible until the last; often such treasures are assigned to the appropriate recipients, who will get them "later." These preparations signify a realistic acceptance of personal death and the desire to "set one's house in order" well in advance. But such planning for separation from life is too often upsetting to the older person's family and friends and is viewed as morbid preoccupation with death.

The taboo in Western culture on open discussion of death presents peculiar difficulties both for those who work or live with older persons and for the older persons themselves [7]. Yet the one who is threatened by the prospect of his death has great need to communicate with someone about the problem. Often his own family members are unable to speak with him about it; the prospect of his death and his awareness of it disturbs them too greatly because of their own emotional involvement with him. Riley's [30] findings indicated that older persons may be more comfortable discussing the problems associated with death with clergymen or physicians. But even some of those associated with the medical profession—physicians, nurses, social workers—admit to un-easiness when faced with the care of dying patients or with older persons who seek to discuss their death. As Verwoerdt [36] has pointed out, the physician "sides with health against illness and with life against death." Thus he and others concerned must come to terms with their own anxieties in order to communicate with empathy and to provide supportive therapy for the older person who is threatened by the prospect of dying [10, 27, 32].

In general, in those instances in which the outcome of facing the threat of death has been unsuccessful or maladaptive for the aged person, it may be expected that he has automatically repeated old defenses, that his repertoire of coping techniques is limited, that a few defenses are used rigidly and excessively, and/or that innovative techniques tend to be absent. The essence of maladaptive behavior is that it aggravates the very problem against which it is directed or creates new problems that require additional problem-solving techniques. Keeping in mind the importance of qualitative and quantitative factors, as well as the existence of the individual uniqueness of personality and interindividual variability, it may be well to review various types of coping with the prospect of personal death that we and others have observed.

Denial, which is aimed at avoiding clear awareness of a painful threat, has been considered by many psychiatrists to be a major mechanism for palliating fear of death [41]. Attitudes of denial may manifest themselves in a great variety of ways. For example, an older person may acknowledge that "Death is inevitable," but in the privacy of his mind may add, "For me, however, it's only probable," or, "only in the distant future," or even, "inevitable—except for me." However, persistent denial is difficult to maintain, for the aged are surrounded by death's signposts: the sickness and death of contemporaries, as well as their own decreasing capacities. "Blinders" need to be powerful indeed to block out such ever-present and increasing stimuli. Other defenses that also serve the purpose of exclusion from awareness include suppression, rationalization, and externalization. Frequently these mechanisms occur in clusters rather than singly.

In another group of defenses, the goal of the coping behavior is not so much to exclude the threat from conscious awareness but rather to retreat from the source of anxiety. These defenses include such mechanisms as regression, withdrawal, "disengagement," or even surrender, as in certain cases of suicide. It is well known that direct death-seeking behavior occurs in old age. In fact, the rate of actual suicide increases sharply with advancing age, especially among men, and unsuccessful suicide attempts are of greater significance in old age than in younger years. These points are discussed more fully in Chapter 10. Furthermore, attention should be given to what might be called occult or slow suicide in old age, due to depression, loss of appetite, or lowered vitality. No statistics are available on this point, but the impression of physicians and attendants in hospitals and homes for the aged is that death occurs much more rapidly when there is no will to live.

In cases of withdrawal and disengagement there is a move away from people. This defensive pattern may be aimed at protecting the person against the painful loss, through death, of significant others. In the void of social isolation, the stage is set for hypochondriacal preoccupation with the bodily self. At the same time, hypochondriasis may imply a call for closeness, inasmuch as the physical complaints represent a wish for attention or support.

Among the less socially acceptable mechanisms employed against death fears is that of withdrawal, or escape, or both by way of alcohol and drugs. Because of social disapproval and the need to hide such behavior, it cannot be ascertained to what extent this mechanism is utilized by older persons, but clinical experience and occasional newspaper stories suggest that it is not uncommon.

A third category of coping behavior is characterized by its emphasis on attempts at mastery and resolution. Included here are defenses such as intellectualization, counterphobic mechanisms, hyperactivity, sublimation, acceptance, as well as continued creativity [3].

Butler [4] cites counterphobic behavior as a defensive maneuver in which old persons adopt highly inappropriate dress and ways of behaving in their effort to appear young: "One sees older people who cannot bear to look at themselves in a mirror and whose drawings show signs of dissolution despite intact cognitive and psychologic functions."

Hyperactivity may be observed in certain vigorous older persons and may be vented on hobbies, restless travels, or civic enterprises; it is often accompanied by loquaciousness. This could be interpreted as an almost frenetic hold onto some phase of life that promises an opportunity for continued usefulness and a sense of past achievement, or it may be an anodyne to despair. On the other hand, losing oneself in activity adaptively can be observed in artists, musicians, or professional persons who continue to be absorbed in creative activity, thus keeping death at arm's length, often physically as well as psychologically.

Another important mechanism utilized—for better or worse—by the aged as they face the end of their existence is that of the life review. Butler [2] postulates this as "a universal normal experience, intensifying in the aged, and occurring irrespective of environmental conditions." He views such life review as a primary factor in reminiscence and discusses its contribution to certain disturbances in later life, as well as its probable role in the evolution of more positive characteristics of old people, such as candor, serenity, and wisdom. When a person cannot dodge the fact that time on this earth is running out for him, the nearness of death brings with it almost inevitably, if not a total life review, at least a recall of some of the major events and relationships in his past life. Perhaps this is related to the old belief that a drowning man's life flashes before his eyes before he goes down for the last time.

Thus it is not abnormal that the later years become for many persons a time for introspection and looking back; for creativity in the writing of an autobiography (or for compilation of material toward an autobiography that may actually never be written); for endless recitals of reminiscences often enjoyed only by the central figure himself; or—more unhappily still—for lapses into melancholia and depression triggered by unhappy memories of losses or of regret over misspent years or wrongs done for which it is now too late to atone [24]. Depression tends to sensitize the older person to previous unhappy experiences, so that eventually a bleak perspective may emerge. There are those tragic instances when the review and stocktaking lead to the discovery that one "missed the boat" and that it is now too late to repair previous mistakes. Particularly painful may be the awareness that large or significant areas of human experience have been avoided, that life has not been fully lived.

For those who cannot face the mirror of themselves and the burden of their memories, the life review may be difficult if not shattering. The reminiscences of such persons appear repetitious, shot through with conscious or unconscious misrepresentations, without apparent purpose except to escape the present by filling time. Or they appear to be mere monologues with disturbing themes of old guilt or bitterness, obviating communication with others. Or should they be listened to carefully in an attempt to understand them as the older person's efforts to establish a final identity in his own eyes as well as in those of the listener?

At the time of crisis when a person comes to full realization of the foreshortening of his life span and the approach of death, the self seeks to renew and establish itself before it may be lost. Robert Fulton [7] puts it succinctly: "Death asks us for identity." It is as if Charon, the boatman from Greek mythology, or St. Peter at the gate of heaven, were asking the mortal to present his passport.

From an existential point of view ("the essence of life is its mortality"), Koestenbaum [18] argues that only through awareness of death can a man achieve integrity. Under such pressure, man will attempt to find the meaning and fulfillment of his life. "The vitality of death lies in the fact that it makes almost impossible the repression of unpleasant but important realities . . . and one is able to see all events in life from the perspective of his total existence" [18].

Viewed in this way, the constructive and therapeutic aspects of the life review—whether it be by spoken or silent reminiscing—are apparent when the person can develop a satisfying pattern and meaning out of the conglomerate of events in his past life. Coming to terms with himself—his failures and achievements, his griefs and satisfactions—he seeks to integrate a new identity with a new acceptance of his own humanness, not judging himself too harshly for his limitations. This new crystallization of his self-awareness may affect his relationships with others and may bring increased tolerance, mellowness, and affection as he sees others in a different light as well. The factors that favor constructive reorganization of the personality through life review may include flexibility, resilience, and self-awareness; the reevaluation of the past may facilitate the person's "serene and dignified acceptance of death" [2]. This in turn may facilitate a better acceptance also of whatever life may bring before the final curtain.

References

1. Birren, J. E., et al. (Eds.). *Human Aging: A Biological and Behavioral Study*. Public Health Service Publication No. 986. Washington, D.C.: U.S. Government Printing Office, 1963.

2. Butler, R. N.   The Life Review: An Interpretation of Reminiscence in the Aged. In R. Kastenbaum (Ed.), *New Thoughts on Old Age*. New York: Springer, 1964.
3. Butler, R. N.   The Destiny of Creativity in Later Life: Studies of Creative People and the Creative Process. In S. Levin and R. J. Kahana (Eds.), *Psychodynamic Studies on Aging: Creativity, Reminiscing, and Dying*. New York: International Universities Press, 1967.
4. Butler, R. N.   Toward a Psychiatry of the Life-Cycle. In A. Simon and L. J. Epstein (Eds.), *Aging in Modern Society*. Psychiatric Research Report No. 23. Washington, D.C.: American Psychiatric Association, 1968.
5. Choron, J.   *Death and Western Thought*. New York: Crowell-Collier-Macmillan, 1963.
6. Feifel, H.   Attitudes Toward Death. In H. Feifel (Ed.), *The Meaning of Death*. New York: McGraw-Hill, 1965.
7. Fulton, R.   *Death and Identity*. New York: Wiley, 1965.
8. Glaser, B. G., and Strauss, A. L.   *Awareness of Dying*. Chicago: Aldine, 1965.
9. Glaser, B. G., and Strauss, A. L.   *Time for Dying*. Chicago: Aldine, 1968.
10. Group for the Advancement of Psychiatry.   *Death and Dying: Attitudes of Patient and Doctor*. New York: Mental Health Materials Center, 1967.
11. Heyman, D. K., and Jeffers, F. C.   Observations on the extent of concern and planning by the aged for possible chronic illness. *J. Am. Geriatr. Soc.* 13:152, 1965.
12. Jeffers, F. C., Nichols, C. R., and Eisdorfer, C.   Attitudes of older persons toward death: A preliminary study. *J. Gerontol.* 16:53, 1961.
13. Jeffers, F. C., and Verwoerdt, A.   Factors associated with frequency of death thoughts in elderly community volunteers. *Proc. 7th Int. Cong. Geront.*, Vienna 6:149, 1966.
14. Kalish, R. A.   A continuum of subjectively perceived death. *Gerontologist* 6:73, 1966.
15. Kastenbaum, R.   Death as a research problem in social gerontology: An overview. *Gerontologist* 6:67, 125, 1966.
16. Kastenbaum, R.   The mental life of dying geriatric patients. *Proc. 7th Int. Cong. Geront.*, Vienna 6:153, 1966.
17. Kastenbaum, R., and Aisenberg, R. B.   *The Psychology of Death*. New York: Springer, 1972.
18. Koestenbaum, P.   The vitality of death. *J. Existentialism* 5:139, 1964.
19. Kogan, N., and Shelton, F. C.   Images of "old people" and "people in general" in an older sample. *J. Genet. Psychol.* 100:3, 1962.
20. Kogan, N., and Wallach, M. A.   Age changes in values and attitudes. *J. Gerontol.* 16:272, 1961.
21. Lieberman, M. A.   Psychological correlates of impending death: Some preliminary observations. *J. Gerontol.* 20:182, 1965.
22. Lindemann, E.   Symptomatology and management of acute grief. *Am. J. Psychiatry* 101:141, 1944.
23. May, R.   *The Meaning of Anxiety*. New York: Ronald, 1950.

24. McMahon, A. W., Jr., and Rhudick, P. J. Reminiscing in the Aged: An Adaptational Response. In S. Levin and R. J. Kahana (Eds.), *Psychodynamic Studies on Aging: Creativity, Reminiscing, and Dying.* New York: International Universities Press, 1967.
25. Mitford, J. *The American Way of Death.* London: Hutchinson, 1963.
26. Payne, E. C., Jr. The Physician and His Patient Who is Dying. In S. Levin and R. J. Kahana (Eds.), *Psychodynamic Studies on Aging: Creativity, Reminiscing, and Dying.* New York: International Universities Press, 1967.
27. Quint, J. C. *The Nurse and the Dying Patient.* New York: Macmillan, 1967.
28. Rhudick, P. J., and Dibner, A. S. Age, personality and health correlates of death concerns in normal aged individuals. *J. Gerontol.* 16:44, 1961.
29. Richardson, A. H., and Freeman, H. E. Behavior, Attitudes and Disengagement Among the Very Old. Unpublished manuscript quoted in M. W. Riley and A. Foner (Eds.), *An Inventory of Research Findings.* Aging and Society, Vol. I. New York: Russell Sage Foundation, 1968.
30. Riley, J. Attitudes Toward Death. Unpublished manuscript quoted in M. W. Riley and A. Foner (Eds.), *An Inventory of Research Findings.* Aging and Society, Vol. I. New York: Russell Sage Foundation, 1968.
31. Rosow, I., and Chellam, G. An awareness-of-death scale. *Proc. 7th Int. Cong. Geront.,* Vienna 6:163, 1966.
32. Saunders, C. *Care of the Dying.* London: Macmillan, 1960.
33. Shrut, S. D. Attitudes toward old age and death. *Ment. Hyg.* 42:259, 1958.
34. Spark, M. *Memento Mori.* Time Reading Program No. 17. Chicago: Time-Life Books, 1964.
35. Swenson, W. M. Attitudes toward death in an aged population. *J. Gerontol.* 16:49, 1961.
36. Verwoerdt, A. *Communication with the Fatally Ill.* Springfield, Ill.: Thomas, 1966.
37. Verwoerdt, A., and Elmore, J. L. Psychological reactions in fatal illness. I. The prospect of impending death. *J. Am. Geriatr. Soc.* 15:9, 1967.
38. Wahl, C. W. The fear of death. *Bull. Menninger Clin.* 22:214, 1958.
39. Waugh, E. *The Loved One.* London: Chapman and Hall, 1948.
40. Weisman, A. D., and Hackett, T. P. Predilection to death: Death and dying as psychiatric problem. *Psychosom. Med.* 23:232, 1961.
41. Weisman, A. D., and Hackett, T. P. Denial as a Social Act. In S. Levin and R. J. Kahana (Eds.), *Psychodynamic Studies on Aging: Creativity, Reminiscing, and Dying.* New York: International Universities Press, 1967.

10. Functional Psychiatric Disorders in Old Age

Ewald W. Busse and Eric Pfeiffer

Determinants of Adaptation

It has been customary to say that a person's adaptation at any given point in time is determined by an interplay of the biological, social, and psychological factors impinging on him at that moment and in his recent and distant past. This chapter will treat adaptation in old age as only one special instance of adaptation throughout the life cycle. Erikson [32, 33], who has done pioneer work toward the development of a psychiatry of the life cycle, has rightly pointed out both the uniqueness of each phase of the life cycle and its essential continuity with all other phases.

The unique aspects of old age are easily enumerated. This is the last phase of life, the phase in which a person must come to grips with his own relatively imminent extinction. It is also the phase in which the person's capacities for adaptation are for the first time diminishing, as contrasted with other phases of life, such as adolescence or early adulthood, in which adaptative capacities are either improving or remaining more or less the same. In particular, the brain, the "organ of adaptation," is undergoing involutional changes (see Chap. 12). However, the magnitude of the task of adaptation is not diminished in old age.

Old age is also a phase of continued development. The self-image undergoes its final revision as the person makes a summary assessment of the worth of his life [21, 32, 71]. The sphere of individual concern, which has been expanding throughout the life cycle—including first the mother-child dyad, then the larger family, then the peer group, the community, the nation, and so on—may expand still further to fasten on basic concerns common to all people. Wisdom and judgment (however difficult these may be to define) come to full flower in old age, at least in some persons. Certain qualities, such as statesmanship, seem to be found more often in those of advanced years.

But what, in more concrete terms, determines the balance between the successes and failures of adaptation in old age? On theoretical grounds we might say that the history of adaptation in younger years is probably one of the best predictors of adaptation in old age. A satisfactory adaptation to the stresses of old age will probably be made by those who have been able to develop a basically trusting relationship with others; who have developed a sense of autonomy and a clearly defined, positively valued identity; who have developed satisfying relationships with others in marriage or in a work situation; and who have previously confronted adversity without succumbing to it. There is also some research evidence to support the notion that those in whom emotional disturbances develop in old age have had more emotional disturbances in younger years, while those who adapt well in old age have made good adjustments throughout their lifetime. In short, we can say that the past is prologue [65, 69, 99, 123].

Of course, many factors, biological and experiential, contribute to whether a person in his younger years has been well adapted or maladapted, has been happy or unhappy, productive or unproductive. Good health, intelligence, membership in intact families and in integrated communities, adequate food, shelter, and clothing, good education, and orderly careers can easily be counted on the positive side of the ledger. Extreme poverty, broken families, poorly integrated communities, membership in deprived minority groups, poor education, poor jobs, unavailability of medical care—amounting to what Berkman [7] has called "cumulative deprivations"—all would tend to compromise adequacy of adaptation [49, 60, 81, 86, 123].

We also want to call attention to the importance of chance or adventitious factors, often ignored in psychological writings, in determining adaptation. Accidents of geography, history, politics, or economics may profoundly alter the lives of individuals or groups. For instance, let the reader consider the impact on individual adjustment of such monumental events as the Great Depression of the 1930s, World War II, the passage of Social Security legislation or of Medicare legislation, or the as-yet-unpredictable impact of a developing computer technology.

There is some evidence to suggest that those factors which contribute to good adaptation in younger years also continue to exercise determining influences in old age [81, 86]. This is not to deny individual variation in coping either particularly well or particularly poorly with the unique problem of old age.

Normative Reactions to Old Age
The actual transition from one phase of life to another is never automatic, simple, or quick. But the amount of upheaval or distress that results from a transition depends on whether or not the new phase is welcomed and adequate preparation has been made for it. Throughout earlier periods of life, considerable preparation is made for each suc-

ceeding phase of the life cycle; as a result, the transitions are for the most part reasonably well accomplished by most people. For example, careful planning goes into readying the preschool child for his student career. As he advances through the years of formal education, he is constantly anticipating—or others are anticipating for him—his ultimate economic career. But during the working years very little preparation, formal or informal, is made for the last phase of the life cycle. Consequently, many of the changes that take place in old age come to be viewed as losses pure and simple, in part because substitute ways of utilizing the person's energies have not been planned and alternative ways of maintaining security and self-esteem have not been developed.

But at other phases of life, losses occur, too, and hitherto cherished rights and privileges (e.g., dependency, parental support, parental guidance) must be relinquished. Such losses in childhood, adolescence, and young adulthood are far outweighed by the gains realized (increased independence, prestige, power, sexual gratification). In contrast, the losses experienced in old age are more numerous and more visible, the gains fewer and less apparent.

But losses are already beginning to occur in middle age. In fact, middle age is ushered in by the end of the reproductive period. Sometime during middle age, child-rearing activities cease. Toward the end of middle age or early in old age, cessation of work productivity occurs for the great majority of people in our culture. Unless retirement has been adequately anticipated, the loss of a job may lead to awareness of uselessness, and freedom becomes boredom.

Certain declines and losses are inevitable. It is an inescapable fact that all aged persons experience a decline in physical vigor and stamina [110]. There is a gradual decline in mental agility in all aged persons [8] (Chap. 11). Concomitant with retirement, many of the aged experience significant declines in income, amounting for many to a drop of more than 50 percent from previous income levels (Chap. 4). The loss of loved ones through death becomes a frequent experience of old people and contributes to a growing social isolation and sometimes to intensely-felt loneliness. Last, the death of others may bring forcefully to mind one's own impending and inevitable death.

But loss is only one side of the ledger. With planful anticipation, old age and retirement may bring with it many distinct achievements or gains. Taking events somewhat in the same order as we have before, let us look at this other side of the picture. The loss of reproductive capacity may bring for many a newly won sexual freedom, without fear of pregnancy or unwanted late-life offspring. The fact that the children are grown, that they have been educated and are able to make a life of their own, is for many a source of personal satisfaction. The retirement years, for those who have been able to prepare for them in terms of financial security and through lifelong participation in leisure activity, can indeed be "golden years." While the loss of physical abilities has no compensation as such, the expectations of society in this regard are lowered accordingly, and most older persons can still perform at levels that are in congruence with society's expectations. Much the same is true of the gradual decline in mental capacity. Here, too, the expectations of society are lowered as the age of a person advances. In regard to declines in income on retirement, this is offset in part for many by a decline in work-related expenditures.

It is hardest of all to compensate for the loss of loved ones. This is especially true of the loss of the spouse. This loss is for many aged persons the most grievous assault of all. But even here, new relationships can be established or old ones strengthened, either with other aged persons or with one or another of one's grown children. Finally, even one's own impending death can be dealt with by a philosophical attitude and by a "mannerly" acceptance of its inevitability [10] (Chap. 9).

The Social Pathologies

As a result of the natural losses that accompany old age, a number of social pathologies arise in some older persons. The principle ones are social isolation, loneliness, and family conflicts. If they are not ameliorated by appropriate social or community intervention, they may give rise to more enduring forms of psychopathology, to be discussed subsequently. These social pathologies are a reflection of both intrapersonal factors and the natural losses.

Social Isolation

Living alone is one of the circumstances that foster social isolation but in itself does not account for it. According to Shanas et al. [109], some 24 percent of persons 65 and over live alone. A recent study by Pfeiffer

[88] found this to be true for 28 percent of aged persons living in the community. But in that same study, true social isolation, defined as little or no meaningful contact with relatives, friends, and visitors and no one willing and available as a caretaker, occurred in 9 percent. Moreover, this same percentage obtained for those aged 65 to 74, 75 and over, and even 80 and over.

However, solitary living arrangements and natural loss are not enough to produce social isolation. In general, there has also occurred a failure on the part of the aged person to develop any significant *new* relationships; in fact, vigorous resistance to such new relationships is encountered. Many factors underlie this failure to acquire new relationships. Some are related to the person's previous lack of social skills. Lack of social opportunity, lack of transportation, decreased physical mobility, and sensory losses also contribute. Another determinant may be a philosophical conviction that the older person "should make do" with what he has and not seek to change his life situation. Additional factors are the generally held negative stereotypes about older persons that may make many younger or middle-aged persons, or even older persons themselves, shy away from new contacts with the aging.

Yet, intriguingly, a person's life satisfaction is closely linked to the amount and quality of his social interaction. Intriguingly also, social isolation is an entirely remediable situation. At very low cost in terms of professional personnel, increased social contacts can be organized among elderly persons themselves, utilizing aging persons to effect organizational structures for social contacts, to organize neighborhood visiting programs, and to put isolated elderly persons in contact with persons in other age groups.

Since social isolation has not been seen as a "medical" problem, the current long-term care structures in the United States have not been adequately organized to deal with such social pathology. Recent work at the Duke University Center for the Study of Aging and Human Development, specifically its Older Americans Resources and Services (OARS) Program, has focused on overall functional assessment of aging persons, including assessment of their social resources [90]. As is the case with physical and mental disorder, *assessment* of social isolation must precede ameliorative action.

Loneliness

In view of the ubiquity of loss in old age, it is often thought that the old are also frequently lonely. This is a natural expectation. But loneliness is not merely a matter of being alone. Solitude need not be experienced as loneliness, while loneliness can be felt in the presence of other people. For instance, persons residing in nursing homes often complain of loneliness, even though they are surrounded by people and, at a superficial level, are interacting with them. Loneliness is the awareness of an absence of meaningful integration with other persons or groups, a consciousness of being excluded from the system of opportunities and rewards in which other people participate.

Loneliness is not confined to the old. It is a frequent, though often temporary, experience in adolescence; it is also experienced by many schizophrenic patients who have described feeling utterly and vastly alone while in the presence of others. The late Frieda Fromm-Reichmann [39] devoted her last paper, published posthumously, to a discussion of loneliness, particularly as it is experienced by schizophrenic patients.

Only a few research studies of loneliness have been carried out. Shanas and her associates [109], in their cross-national survey, tried to study the problem by examining the relationship between subjectively experienced loneliness and social isolation in old age. About half of those living alone reported they felt lonely only rarely or not at all. About three-fourths of those living with other people reported they were rarely or never lonely. Particularly vulnerable to feelings of loneliness were persons who had recently lost their spouses. Frequent contacts with their children was a factor that seemed to mitigate somewhat feelings of loneliness among those living alone. Interestingly, persons who had been single all their lives complained of loneliness much less frequently than persons who were either still married or who had been widowed, separated, or divorced. Shanas et al. conclude that it is loss (desolation), not isolation, that has the closer relationship to loneliness. It is also known that persons who have been separated, divorced, or widowed also have higher rates of suicide in old age than those with intact marriages. However, there have been no reported studies of the frequency of subjectively experienced loneliness among persons who have attempted or committed suicide.

Family Conflicts

Up to now we have discussed some social pathologies deriving from diminished social contacts. But problems can also derive from continued contacts with relatives and friends. The vast majority of older adults still have siblings, children, and, more recently, even parents with whom to interact. Lifelong family dramas may of course continue to be played out in late life, but these will not be discussed here.

Some of the conflicts *arising* specifically in this age period relate to the changing relationship between adult parent and adult child. As disability increases, adult children may need to assume increasingly a caretaking or parental role in relation to the older person. Such a change in role is likely to produce anxieties in both parent and child.

Conflicts also arise frequently when some change in living arrangements is contemplated for the older person due to a diminishing ability for self-care. Should the older person come to live with one of the children? If so, with whom? Bitter conflicts can arise in regard to this issue, with the older person sometimes caught in a withering cross fire between the "You take her; I've already done my share" of one sibling and the "You've got her, she likes it there. You know my husband (wife) can't get along with Mother."

Similarly, when increasing disability requires consideration of institutional care, families are plagued with much guilt, conflict, and sometimes bitter strife, with some older persons telling their well-meaning children, "I'll never forgive you for putting me here."

While these illustrate only some of the most common family conflicts involving older persons, they are sufficient to demonstrate the vehemence, intensity, and duration of some of these conflicts.

Skilled assessment of the interactional skills of older persons and their families, knowledge of alternatives and community resources, a thorough knowledge and anticipation of some of the common conflicts in this age and a willingness to share this knowledge with the aging persons and family members are all needed to diffuse explosive situations in the short run and to work out satisfactory long-range solutions. In this regard, general family therapy principles are applicable, with special understanding of the problems and processes of old age [1].

It is obvious from what has been said that, as elsewhere in human affairs, given events in old age may have different meanings for different people. For some the transition into old age will be smooth and gratifying. For others there may be temporary upheavals in response to specific life circumstances, but psychic equilibrium will be reestablished eventually. For still others whose range of adaptive techniques has been narrow, or whose preparation for old age, both psychological and material, has been inadequate, or who have come to experience particularly grave misfortunes in old age, this period of life may lead to the development of overt psychiatric symptomatology requiring professional intervention. Thus some discussion regarding the relationships existing between stress and disease is in order.

The Relationship Between Stress and Disease
It is often assumed that ill health or disease is either caused or exacerbated by a combination of physical causes and social and interpersonal or traumatic events. Distressing psychosocial experiences thus tend to be viewed as causal or aggravating factors in the onset of health problems, and physicians regularly caution patients to avoid social stresses that may prevent or hinder the recovery from physical or mental disease. The family and friends of patients frequently attempt to protect the ill person by isolating him from events that would produce tension or depression.

Stress is often conceived of as an excessive force or overstimulation acting on a system or person so that it temporarily or permanently disrupts the efficiency of the system. It is recognized, however, that stress, that is, a decline in efficiency can also arise from deprivation, which thus is another form of stress. The normal organism that does not receive adequate stimuli or nutrients will also show adverse changes. Unfortunately, human beings differ sufficiently among themselves so that they do not all require the same amount of external sustenance, nor do they respond uniformly to stimuli. It is the responsibility of a physician or an investigator to understand these variations and to attempt to identify the characteristics that permit early recognition of either the vulnerable person or the stress-resistant person.

In recent years, serious attempts have been made to identify and quantify the traumatic social experiences that are most likely to contribute to the onset and prolongation of illness. Considerable progress has been made in identifying specific life-change events and developing severity scalings for each such event [46]. These studies have been largely confined to young and middle-aged adults, but it has been recognized that certain events that are more likely to occur in late life also play a major role in ill health and disease.

One study reported by Swedish investigators [104] included a sample of men 65 years of age and compared them with men aged 62 and 52. These investigators noted that they encountered a problem in that the elderly men did not report recent life changes, since changes such as loss of job and wife- or child-related problems had transpired some time previously. Consequently, the men having jobs, wives, and children may report a maximum possible score of 215 life-change units (LCU), while men lacking these three attributes can answer only 20 out of 43 questions and thus reach a maximum possible score of just 100 LCU [104].

It cannot be claimed that there is a simple and predictable relationship between identifiable psychosocial life events, the exposure to infection or physical trauma, and the precipitation of disease and disability. The interaction is far more complex, since personality types (inherent or acquired) and life-styles or patterns are other dimensions that require attention.

In attempting to correlate the onset of a disease or maladaptive reaction with a stressful event, it is evident that the recency of the event confers a higher stress rating. The passing of time does heal the pain of a traumatic episode. Sex and age influence the perception of events as stress-producing.

Assuming that personality changes are seen throughout the life span, it is important to consider what the common manifestations of personality change are and how habitual patterns of responding to stimuli affect the degree of the stress. Bernice Neugarten [76] says that eccentricity and egocentricity increase with age regardless of social interaction. She also believes that in both men and women there are important differences in the psychiatric processes that are the result of aging. Older men seem to be more receptive than younger men of their affiliative, nurturant, and sensual promptings; older women become more receptive of their aggressive and egocentric impulses than do younger women. Old men appear to cope with their environment in increasingly abstract and cognitive terms; in contrast, older women become increasingly affective and expressive in their terms. Both sexes, however, seem to move toward a more eccentric, self-preoccupied position and to attend increasingly to the control and the satisfaction of personal needs [76]. Meyer [73] believes that stubbornness, mistrust, meanness, and jealousy increase in late life. He also believes that exaggeration of character traits are often found in old age in extroverted personalities.

Lowenthal [66] is concerned with the ambiguities of social stress, particularly the range of responses to what appear to be stressful events that can be found in elderly people. She points out that certain social events usually considered stressful, such as residential moves or retirement, often produce conflicting results and believes that it is necessary to distinguish between these changes as to the voluntary or involuntary nature of the event. Furthermore, the person's characteristic social lifestyle, that is, how he or she copes with life, is essential to the type of response to stress and determines whether or not such a response contributes to mental illness. For example, Lowenthal believes that lifelong isolation is not associated with poor adaptation in late life and does not increase the likelihood of mental illness or, more accurately, the likelihood that treatment for mental illness will be required. In contrast, lifelong marginal social relationships are associated with poor adaptation, including serious mental illness. However, both patterns are associated with a history of parental deprivation in childhood. One style represents a relatively successful protective pattern, while the other produces excessive strain. Persons who have had marginal social adjustment all their lives constitute a population at serious risk in later life.

Lowenthal [66] also contends that some challenging work remains to be done to determine which stressful events produce negative or decremental results as opposed to neutral results (i.e., those that do not seem to alter the person) or positive results (those actually conducive to a better life adjustment). No doubt there is some validity to this concern, since it is evident that people can only learn when they are required to adapt to a new stress or demand but also can be overwhelmed when they lack the capacity to develop coping mechanisms. Lowenthal is also concerned with the issue of physical health status that is the source or result of stress. Obviously, illness can be both a source and a result of stress, and both features can be present simultaneously in the same person.

In what follows, a few epidemiological data in regard to psychiatric illness and psychiatric treatment in old age will be considered. Recent legislation that makes psychiatric treatment more readily available to increased numbers of aged persons than heretofore will also be discussed. Psychiatric disorders in which organic disease of the brain underlies the behavorial disturbance will be dealt with in detail in Chapter 13. The focus here will be principally on psychiatric disorders of functional (psychogenic) origin. I will conclude with a discussion of psychotherapeutic approaches that are especially adapted to the aged.

Epidemiology of Psychopathology

It is difficult to obtain precise data on the incidence and prevalence of psychiatric disorders in old age. As Redick et al. [98] have pointed out, different diagnostic criteria are used in different studies, and the cutoff between what is seen as still within normal limits and what is seen as pathological is by no means uniform. An additional methodological problem exists in that we do not know how the findings from a particular study population in a particular geographical area apply to the aged generally; i.e., we do not know how representative the findings are. Nevertheless, the data that are available deserve examination. They tend to fall into three broad categories: (1) data on aged persons residing in or newly admitted to public and private mental hospitals and psychiatric wards of general hospitals; (2) data on aged persons receiving psychiatric care on an outpatient basis; and (3) data on the proportion of aged living in the community who manifest varying degrees of psychiatric disturbance, as measured most commonly by some type of psychiatric interview schedule. As might be expected, the findings from these three categories of studies diverge, although the data from different studies in any one category show some consistency.

Slightly fewer than 1 percent of persons over age 65 are hospitalized in private or public mental institutions [58]. Of these, roughly half were admitted for psychiatric disorders arising in old age, principally organic brain disease (Chap. 13), while the other half were admitted for functional psychosis, principally schizophrenia, and have grown old in the hospital. An additional 3 percent of old people are residing in nursing homes, homes for the aged, and geriatric or chronic disease hospitals [11], more than half of whom suffer from significant psychiatric disturbances. Combining these data, we can say that between 2 and 3 percent of old people live in institutions as a result of psychiatric illness. Additional information on institutional care of the aged is presented in Chapter 14.

While persons over age 65 make up nearly 30 percent of patients in public mental hospitals and 11 percent of those in private mental hospitals, they account for only 2 percent of the patients seen in psychiatric outpatient clinics [43]. In terms of rates of utilization of outpatient facilities this amounts to only about 0.1 percent of old people receiving outpatient treatment. These figures do not include persons receiving ambulatory care from psychiatrists in private practice, but the number so involved is extremely small. We can conclude from these data that the aged are markedly underrepresented in outpatient or intermediate care facilities. This point will be discussed later. The observation assumes added significance, however, when we look at the findings on prevalence of psychiatric symptoms in community samples.

A number of surveys have also been conducted in this country and abroad to determine what proportion of old people living in the community, in addition to those already in institutions, have psychiatric disorders. Table 13 illustrates the range of findings in different studies. The composite picture that emerges from the several studies is that some 5 percent of old people living in the community are either psychotic or else have severe psychopathological symptoms; when persons with moderate and severe mental illness are considered together, this figure increases to some 15 percent; and when all degrees of psychiatric impairment are included, ranging from the mild to the severe, from 25 to nearly 60 percent of the aged may be affected [67, 102].

It is important to note that the community surveys reported thus far have all been cross-sectional studies, assessing psychiatric disability of a population at only one point in time. Sizable longitudinal studies of the problems of psychiatric disorders in sizable populations of old people are obviously desirable, although the methodological problems are enormous. Further, such survey studies as have been reported do not differentiate psychopathological conditions arising for the first time in old age from disorders continuing into old age from younger years. Nor do most of the studies make a distinction between organically based psychiatric disorders and those of functional origin.

Survey studies, such as the study of Leighton et al. [60] and the mid-

Table 13. Prevalence of Psychopathology in Old Age

Author and Location	Degree of Pathology		
	Severe (%)	Moderate and Severe (%)	Mild, Moderate, and Severe (%)
Pasamanick [84], Baltimore	5	12	. . .
Lowenthal et al. [67], San Francisco	5	15	. . .
Kay [56], Newcastle	8	26	. . .
Nielsen [77], Samsø	7	22	. . .
Leighton [60], Stirling County	. . .	. . .	50–60
Pfeiffer [88], Durham, N.C.	. . .	13	. . .

town Manhattan study of Srole et al. [114], indicate that the proportion of persons who have any degree of mental illness does not increase significantly with age. However, the proportion of persons suffering from psychiatric disorders requiring hospitalization increases dramatically with advancing age. The major cause for this increase is the increasing proportion of cases of organic psychoses in old age rather than an increase in functional psychoses. Organically based psychiatric disorders account for an increasingly larger proportion of the total amount of psychiatric illness as age increases. In the age group 65 to 74, more than half of the persons residing in mental hospitals have a functional disorder, while in the age group 75 and over, this ratio is reversed, with organic psychosis accounting for more than half of those in psychiatric hospitals [102].

It is one of the most interesting aspects of the epidemiological data mentioned thus far that the aged either seek or receive very little psychiatric treatment on an ambulatory basis. They either receive no psychiatric attention at all, or they are hospitalized for lengthy periods, often for life. This lack of intermediate care of aged persons is a puzzling phenomenon. It is not explained by a mere lack of intermediate care facilities, i.e., by a lack of outpatient clinics, although this may be a contributing factor in some locations. Several other factors may also be important. Perhaps a certain amount of mental illness is more easily tolerated by the aged themselves or by those who live with the aged because it is seen as part of "normal aging" [112]. Also, as Estes has pointed out in Chapter 6, there is a general reluctance on the part of the aged to seek medical examination or care; he has emphasized the attitudinal as well as the economic and logistical impediments. There may also be generational differences; psychiatry as a legitimate medical speciality may be much less well accepted in the current generation of aged than among younger people. Finally, there may be a reluctance on the part of some therapists to take old people into treatment because (1) they themselves hold gerontophobic attitudes (see Chap. 1); or (2) they have the mistaken notion that the aged do not respond to therapy; or (3) more simply, because few psychiatrists or therapists have had adequate training in the techniques of treatment that are especially applicable to aged persons (also see Chap. 17).

The Affective Disorders

The affective disorders comprise a heterogeneous group of emotional disturbances that range from transient periods of mild dejection to incapacitating illnesses. It is estimated that in the United States at any given time, 3 to 8 million persons suffer from depression. In recent years a vast amount of new biological and psychological data about affective disorders has accumulated. Of great importance is the development of more accurate diagnostic categories and precise criteria. The new data indicate that recurring episodes of severe depression should be differentiated. The concept of unipolar and bipolar affective illnesses appears to have value. The bipolar disorder, a condition of recurring episodes of both depression and mania, appears to have a genetic determinant. There is a difference in the characteristic time of onset. The age of onset of bipolar illness peaks at 26 years, while that of unipolar illness peaks at 45. Furthermore, it appears that there are at least two general types of unipolar depressions. The typical patient with "pure depressive disease" is a male whose illness starts after the age of 40 and in whose family are equal numbers of male and female relatives who suffer from depression. A typical patient with "depression spectrum disease" is a female whose illness develops before the age of 40 and in whose family more depression is seen in female relatives than in male. However, the males in her family show increased levels of alcoholism and sociopathy. These important types of depression do recur into late life and should be differentiated from the recurrent periods of depression that are common in old age [75].

Depression

Recurrent periods of depression, lasting from a few minutes to a few days, are common in old age. Barnes and his colleagues [4] have made a study of "normal community volunteers" over the age of 60. The study revealed that elderly persons were aware that they were experiencing more frequent and more annoying depressive periods than earlier in life. The subjects reported that during such episodes they felt discouraged, worried, or disgusted with their own uselessness, often to such a degree that they felt there was no reason to continue to live. Only a small number of subjects in the study admitted entertaining thoughts of suicide; but a larger percentage stated that during such depressive periods they would welcome death if it were a painless one [4, 19].

The dynamics of depression are, of course, well known and will be mentioned here only briefly. The most widely held of these is that depression is a pathological response to the loss of a person or object that had been regarded ambivalently [72]. It postulates introjection of the lost object into the self and the directing of hostile impulses toward that object in the form of self-accusations, self-blame, and guilt. However, depressions may also occur in response to the "loss of narcissistic supplies." Here, self-directed hostility and guilt are less of a problem. It would appear that in the depressions of old age, guilt is, in general, a relatively unimportant dynamic force [17]. Such depressions instead seem to be more commonly linked with the loss of narcissistic supplies; the person feels that he has lost everything, that nothing remains. Guilt mechanisms seem to play a more prominent role in the depressions of young people and in the more severe agitated psychotic depressions in old age to the degree that these are not related to biological factors.

First to be discussed is a treatment program applicable to the relatively mild depressive reactions occurring in older persons who are still able to live in their communities and whose depressions are not of sufficient severity to require hospitalization. Precipitating circumstances for the depressive episodes can often be identified. Some of the losses likely to occur in old age have already been detailed.

A treatment approach to the milder depressions of old age is based on the assumptions that they have occurred in response to the loss of dependent or narcissistic supplies. An effort is therefore made to reestablish new or alternate sources of such supplies. In this the physician can be one source. His interest and attention to the patient's problem can instill a renewed feeling of self-worth in the patient. In addition, efforts should be made to see that the patient maintains or regains contacts with other persons in his own environment, that he participates in useful and productive activities. He may also be encouraged to have contact with other persons of his own age. This may initially have a further depressing effect on the elderly person, but with time he may discover common interests and problems in other old people and therefore see himself as less deprived.

As an illustration of the impact of continued activity it may be pointed out that in the study previously mentioned [17], from 44 to 48 percent of persons who were unemployed or retired experienced depressive episodes, as opposed to 25 percent of those who continued to work. One should be cautious in concluding that work alone plays some vital role in preventing or decreasing the number of depressive episodes; it is possible that there are fundamental differences that permit some persons to continue work and to be relatively immune to depressive episodes. Other important defenses against depression would seem to be planned creative and recreational activity if these are a continuation of previous participation in such activities. Clinical experience has shown that the taking up of so-called hobbies on retirement is of little value to elderly persons unless it results in the production of something that is appreciated by others. A hobby that contributes nothing to others but merely occupies the time of an elderly person is in the long run unsatisfactory.

DEPRESSIVE PSYCHOSES. While minor depressive reactions are extremely frequent in old age, major depressive reactions, often of psychotic proportions, also occur. Depressive psychoses may arise for the first time in old age, or they may represent recurring episodes of depression in persons who have previously experienced affective disturbances.

In private psychiatric hospitals, patients with affective psychoses, particularly depressions, make up roughly one-half of newly admitted patients over age 60 or 65 [74, 106, 115]. In public mental hospitals, they constitute a much smaller fraction, somewhere around 10 percent [67].

While the diagnosis of mental disorder is frequently de-emphasized in current psychiatric thinking, correct diagnosis of the type of mental disorder, particularly a differentiation between organically and functionally caused disturbances, is of extreme importance in old age. The outcome of treatment in the affective psychoses is good, while the prognosis of the organically caused psychiatric syndromes is much less favorable (see Chap. 13).

Again, the major signs and symptoms of affective psychosis of the depressed type are well known [45, 85]. There is a pervasively melancholy mood, a drastic reduction in self-esteem, and a pessimistic outlook about the future; there may be frequent crying spells or, more rarely, an inability to cry. These symptoms may be coupled with certain of the biological signs characteristic of depression: loss of appetite, weight loss, constipation, marked sleep disturbances, and sometimes either marked psychomotor agitation or retardation. Sometimes severe depression in old age can mimic an organic brain disease state. Patients who are depressed may be unable to answer questions. They may be so slow in their thinking that they cannot perform simple mathematical problems or correctly produce information about their orientation in time and place. Standardized psychological tests, however, if administered slowly, will demonstrate that no organic impairment exists and that the seeming dementia is a result of an inability to produce answers rather than an inability to formulate them.

TREATMENT OF SEVERE DEPRESSION IN OLD AGE. The treatment of the major depressive psychoses in old age is not markedly different from the treatment of these disorders in younger years [34, 85]. When it is determined that the patient is indeed profoundly depressed, he should be hospitalized, for two reasons. First, the risk of suicide is great in elderly depressed persons (see Suicide in Old Age); second, the depth of depression can be evaluated and treatment can be administered most effectively in a hospital setting.

Psychotherapy may be used as an adjunct to other forms of therapy or, more rarely, it may be sufficient alone. It has several serious limitations, however. (1) Profoundly depressed patients have great difficulty in engaging in ongoing psychotherapy, particularly therapy that depends on a continued dialogue between patient and therapist. (2) Results can be achieved only slowly, if at all, thus leaving the patient exposed to suffering and to suicidal risks for needlessly long periods. (3) Since the psychotherapeutic process is a slow one, and since spontaneous remissions of depressions occur, it is difficult to tell whether improvement has occurred spontaneously or as a result of treatment. Occasionally, profoundly depressed aged persons improve dramatically merely on being hospitalized, responding perhaps to the overall caregiving milieu. In such cases a real danger exists that the improvement is only temporary. If the patient is discharged to the same environment, without making provision for someone to continue to give interested care, relapse may be prompt. For example:

An 80-year-old widow living alone in an apartment was admitted to a psychiatric hospital following a suicide attempt. She said she had become deeply discouraged after the death of her pet parakeet. It was clear from psychiatric interviews that the parakeet had symbolized her remaining involvement with her environment. In the hospital she improved quickly, without specific therapy. She was discharged home in good spirits. Two weeks later she committed suicide by putting a plastic bag over her head.

Depression may also be treated with *drug therapy*. Since 1957 a number of drugs with antidepressant properties have been introduced [55]. These drugs, while somewhat less effective than electroconvulsive therapy (ECT) in terminating depressive episodes, have certain distinct advantages over ECT. Drug therapy is a more flexible and more convenient form of treatment and one that is more readily accepted by patients and by their families. The compounds currently in greatest use are the nonmonamine oxidase inhibitors, such as imipramine (Tofranil), desipramine (Norpramin, Pertofrane), amitriptyline (Elavil), nortriptyline (Aventyl), and doxepin (Sinequan).

Antidepressant drugs, while very useful in the treatment of depressive illness in older persons must be prescribed with caution, and their effect must be monitored very closely. As is well known, antidepressants have multiple side effects in younger patients; but in older patients side effects on the central nervous system and cardiovascular system can be particularly troublesome. At a minimum, the prescribing physician must be familiar with all the common side effects of these drugs and with the overall physical health status of the patient, since these drugs can have effects that exaggerate existing pathological conditions of the cardiovascular or central nervous systems [30, 35, 89].

In general, substantially lower starting doses must be used in patients over 65 than in younger patients. In addition, it has been found useful to give the bulk of the antidepressant medication at bedtime. Thus starting doses of 10 mg three times daily of such drugs as Elavil or Sinequan, plus 50 mg at bedtime, can generally be tolerated by older patients who are free of specific physical disease. A detailed discussion of antidepressant drug regimens is beyond the scope of this chapter, but full information on such regimens is available in a number of publications [30, 35, 89, 92].

When hospitalization alone, supportive psychotherapy, or antidepressant drugs have been ineffective, electroconvulsive therapy should be considered. Research findings are that this mode of treatment is as effective in terminating depressive episodes in old age as it is in younger persons [55]. Before instituting such treatment, however, a thorough evaluation of the patient's overall health status is required, with particular attention to the cardiovascular system. However, apart from acute myocardial disease, few absolute contraindications to its use exist. Age alone is not a contraindication. Details of the procedure and the precautions involved in administering ECT in old age are presented in Kalinowsky and Hoch's [55] standard text on the somatic therapies used in psychiatry.

Mania

Depressive psychoses predominate among the affective disorders in late life as they do in younger years. However, manic psychoses do occur in old age. For instance, in Roth's study of 220 patients hospitalized for affective disorders, 13 percent had predominantly manic symptomatology [105].

Clinically, mania is in many ways a mirror image of depression [85]. The patient feels elated ("like a million bucks"), optimistic, and all-powerful; speech is rapid; hyperactivity may be present; and the patient is euphoric. Joviality is sometimes interrupted by short bursts of anger or paranoid thinking, but the euphoric mood usually returns quickly; there may be short periods of sadness or weeping that suddenly give way to flights into grandiosity. Occasionally, a quiet, transfigured euphoria is observed. While the rate of survival is as good among aged manic patients as among aged depressed patients, continued institutionalization was necessary in over half of Roth's patients [105].

Until the introduction of lithium carbonate, the prognosis for mania in old age was generally regarded as poor. In the last decade, considerable experience has been gained with lithium carbonate in the treatment of manic states [44, 70, 106–108]. It has been found that special precautions must be taken to follow the electrolyte picture and the serum level of lithium in aged patients, since fluid balance may be more easily upset in patients with marginal cardiac or renal status [9, 25]. In general, substantially lower doses of lithium carbonate may be needed for elderly patients than for young or middle-aged adults. If cardiac, renal, or electrolyte status contraindicates the use of lithium carbonate, the phenothiazines may be of some help in controlling the overt symptomatology of manic episodes. However, they are less effective than lithium in bringing about a termination of the manic episode [93, 96].

Suicide in Old Age

In 1970, the latest year for which complete statistics are available, 23,480 persons committed suicide in the United States (16,629 men and 6,851 women). Of these, 7,399, or 31.5 percent, were persons over age 65. Thus the aged account for an inordinately high proportion of the overall suicide problem. Especially among men, there is an almost linear increase in suicide rates with advancing age, as can be seen in Table 14. For the entire population of the United States the suicide rate was 11.6 per 100,000, but among aged white males the rate was four to five times greater than this average. Several investigators have reported slightly different absolute suicide rates in different locations, but the finding of relatively high suicide rates among aged males is uniform in all these studies [119].

Evidence from research studies indicates that the majority of older persons committing suicide have been depressed [41, 103]. A smaller fraction is made up of persons who have used alcohol to excess. A still smaller fraction is made up of persons with organic brain syndrome. A very small percentage of those committing suicide suffer from an untreatable terminal illness.

Table 14. Suicide Rates in the United States (per 100,000)
for 1970 by Age, Sex, and Race

Age Range	White Males	White Females	Nonwhite Males	Nonwhite Females
15–19	9.4	2.9	5.4	2.9
20–24	19.3	5.7	19.4	5.5
25–29	19.8	8.6	20.1	6.0
30–34	20.0	9.5	19.4	5.6
35–39	21.9	12.2	13.9	4.5
40–44	24.6	13.8	11.4	4.1
45–49	28.2	13.5	16.5	4.0
50–54	30.9	13.5	11.3	5.1
55–59	34.9	13.1	12.3	1.8
60–64	35.0	11.5	8.4	2.8
65–69	37.4	9.4	11.5	3.2
70–74	40.4	9.7	8.2	3.9
75–79	42.2	7.3	5.7	3.1
80–84	51.4	7.2	22.9	3.2
85–plus	45.8	5.8	12.6	6.4

Source: *Vital Statistics of the United States, 1970,* Vol. II, Mortality, Part A. Rock-ville, Md.: U.S. Public Health Service, 1974.

While many more young persons attempt than commit suicide (the ratio has been estimated at about 7:1), the number of old people attempting suicide is roughly the same as the number actually committing suicide [5, 6, 27, 78]. Among younger persons, suicide attempts often represent an expression of hostility toward someone or an attempt to bring someone to terms. These are rarely the motivations for attempted suicide in old age. Rather, when an old person attempts suicide, he almost always fully intends to die. Rescue from a suicide attempt in old age is often accidental or due to poor planning of the attempt. Persons attempting suicide in old age should be hospitalized. The psychiatric diagnoses of those attempting suicide are similar to diagnoses of those actually committing suicide, a finding that is in contrast to young would-be suicides who are diagnosed as having neurotic personalities or transient situational reactions.

The most dramatic increase in suicide with advancing age occurs among white men. The suicide rate for white women also increases with age up to about age 50; thereafter, it gradually declines. Nonwhites have lower suicide rates than whites, but the pattern of increased suicide with advancing age is beginning to appear among black men, paralleling the pattern among white men.

Marital status has a significant influence on suicide rates [48]. The highest suicide rates are seen among men who are divorced, followed by the widowed, who are in turn followed by those who have never married; suicide rates are lowest among persons with intact marriages. Other characteristics of persons who commit suicide in old age are lack of employment, solitary living arrangements, and residence in the deteriorating central sections of cities [41].

To date there is no satisfactory explanation of why suicide is more common among men than women. Depression, the psychiatric disorder most frequently associated with successful suicide in old age, is at least as common among women as it is among men. One can speculate that the impact of retirement, of physical decline, or of physical illness is more devastating to the self-esteem of men than of women in modern society. But this does not amount to an explanation. Nor is a truly good explanation available for the increase in suicide with advancing age. Batchelor and Napier [5] quote Swinson (1951) as saying that "suicide in the last 50 years has increasingly become a disorder of elderly people," and he has suggested that "as the present century has advanced, the old may have found their environment more hostile than the young."

Prevention of Suicide
Many suicides in old age can be prevented by early and effective treatment of psychiatric disorders, particularly depression. However, general health and welfare measures aimed at keeping older persons active, useful, and socially involved can undoubtedly also contribute to a reduction of suicide in this age group. As is true in younger years, in old age, too, the suicidal intent is usually temporary. If a person can be helped through a stressful period toward a new and satisfying adjustment, a life will have been saved.

Hypochondriasis
Hypochondriasis is an anxious preoccupation with one's own body or a portion of one's own body that the person believes to be either diseased or functioning improperly. For many years hypochondriasis has been

considered a syndrome rather than a distinct disease entity. But the most recent edition of the *Diagnostic and Statistical Manual of Mental Disorders* of the American Psychiatric Association (DSM-II) has now established hypochondriacal neurosis as a separate neurotic condition [3]. The symptom constellation of hypochondriasis also continues to be described as a feature of other psychiatric disorders, such as some of the psychoses, psychosomatic illnesses, or personality disturbances.

Much of the early work on hypochondriacal patients was carried out by one of us (E. W. B.) in a special clinic for such patients in a large university medical center. In a survey of the patients in this clinic it was found that more than half were over age 60 and the majority were women [13]. Following the survey, efforts were devoted to the elucidation of the dynamics of hypochondriasis and to the development of a therapeutic approach. After considerable experimentation, certain techniques, which will be discussed subsequently, were found to be effective [14].

Dynamics of Hypochondriasis

To understand why some persons develop physical complaints as a way of solving psychological problems, an understanding of the "sick role" in our society is needed. In most Western cultures great emphasis is placed on personal independence, financial success, and social prestige. There is little tolerance for the nonachiever or the person who is a failure. When a person falls ill, however, a different set of rules applies. Talcott Parsons [83] has outlined the sick role in our society as follows: First, the sick person is exempted from his normal social responsibilities if his illness is severe enough. Second, it is assumed that the sick person became sick through no fault of his own and that he therefore has a right to be taken care of. Third, it is assumed that he will desire to get well, in fact, that he is under actual obligation to want to get well. Fourth, it is assumed that he will seek competent medical help and cooperate fully in the process of getting well.

It is fair to say that society regards the person who becomes emotionally ill with much greater ambivalence. While gross psychosis may be acceptable as an excuse for nonperformance, more minor, so-called neurotic complaints are often seen by the society and by many patients themselves as an unacceptable admission of personal failure.

Escape from personal failure into the sick role is available at all ages but seems to be particularly frequently used by the elderly. This can be successful for varying periods of time, but if no organic illness exists, family members and associates ultimately recognize this, and at such a point their attitudes toward the "sick" person begin to change. Recognition that the excuse of illness is physically unjustified makes people feel that they are being exploited. No doubt most people have at times during their lives "played sick" to avoid trouble. Since they have used this defense only to a limited degree, they resent a chronic complainer who does not respect the same limits. As a result, the hypochondriac's problems become greater when friends and relatives become suspicious of the justification for his complaints.

Three psychological mechanisms play a major role in the dynamics of hypochondriasis: (1) a withdrawal of psychic interest from other persons or objects and a centering of this interest on oneself, one's own body, and its functioning; (2) a shift of anxiety from a specific psychic area to a less threatening concern with bodily disease; and (3) the use of physical symptoms as a means of self-punishment and atonement for unacceptable hostile or vengeful feelings toward those close to the person. An awareness of these mechanisms makes the patient's complaints more understandable and contributes to the development of a meaningfully designed treatment program. For instance, it is easy to see why an older worker who has had no other interest except his work is a likely subject for the development of hypochondriasis on retirement. Normal bodily functions—for instance, breathing and elimination—that he ignored in the past may now merit as much attention as did his work before retirement. Or, elderly people who experience anxiety over loss of social prestige, financial security, or marital dissatisfaction because of prolonged serious disability of the spouse may find it more tolerable to shift their anxiety to concern over bodily functioning [16]. More than one of these mechanisms may be active in a given patient.

Treatment of Hypochondriasis
Because treatment approaches to hypochondriasis are rarely presented in textbooks or papers, they will be discussed here in considerable detail. The treatment of hypochondriasis can be frustrating and time-consuming. It can be less so if a few techniques of proved value are used

and if they are used as soon as the physician suspects that he is dealing with hypochondriasis. Delay in recognition can seriously impede effective treatment.

INEFFECTIVE TECHNIQUES. Before going on to a discussion of techniques that have proved useful, a few remarks will be made about techniques that are at best of doubtful value in dealing with this particular group of patients. Ordinarily, giving the patient a full explanation of his medical condition serves as a reassurance. This is not true in hypochondriasis. To explain the patient's physical complaints in psychiatric language is to rob him with one stroke of a carefully designed defense system, thereby undermining his self-esteem. The usual reaction to such explanations is a further increase in the patient's complaints. In addition, the relationship between the patient and the physician is seriously jeopardized. The patient may become extremely hostile or may seek medical help elsewhere. Even less specific explanations of how emotional upsets can sometimes cause physical symptoms are likely to be unsuccessful. The patient may agree that this can happen to some people, but he is sure that such an explanation does not apply to him.

Another technique that has been tried without striking success has been to give the patient a specific organic diagnosis, then treat him for that disorder and suggest that he will get well within a certain period of time. Usually, improvement does occur, to varying degrees and for a varying period of time. But inevitably a reaction sets in, for the patient still requires his illness as a defense. New complaints develop, and old ones return in an exaggerated form. The patient will return to his physician, who in desperation may start the process all over, only to fail again.

A particular caution should be expressed about surgical procedures for the relief of symptoms in hypochondriacal patients. It never helps the patient to have a scar that testifies to the fact that a competent physician believed that he had something wrong with his body. In addition, the operative scar can become the focus of new symptoms, which are then attributed to "complications" or "adhesions" following the surgical procedure.

EFFECTIVE TECHNIQUES. For the hypochondriacal person to continue to live with his family and in society, his psychological defenses must be maintained. The physician must respect this need. He will need to listen attentively to the patient's veritable "organ recital," but until a positive relationship between physician and patient has been established, little can be gained from seeking to direct the patient into a discussion of areas of emotional conflict. A more important point to be made by the physician is that the patient is indeed sick and that the physician is taking care of him.

To make this point more clearly, *medication or a placebo* may be prescribed. In doing so the physician must be careful to avoid utilizing any medication that is likely to produce side effects, since this would only complicate an already confused clinical picture. Particular attention must be given to avoidance of drugs that have been used previously by the patient without success. The drug or placebo must be given with an assured manner, since hypochondriacal patients are alert to any expression of doubt on the part of the physician.

This technique may be criticized in that it implies to the hypochondriacal patient that he actually has an organic illness, however slight. This criticism must be accepted, but in turn it should be pointed out that many hypochondriac patients actually do have changes in their physiological functioning that can respond to medication. The technique is extremely worthwhile in establishing a good physician-patient relationship. It is useful principally because of its symbolic value. A hypochondriacal complaint is a distress signal, and the patient's anxiety may be reduced and his self-esteem increased by knowing that a highly regarded professional person is "taking care" of him. Thus the placebo (Latin for "I will please") can symbolically represent to the patient security and satisfaction. The question may also be raised about the difference between the use of medication and surgical procedures. Very simply, operations leave scars that not only can permanently alter a patient's self-image but also can lead to new complaints of "postoperative" complications. It must be admitted, however, that on very rare occasions placebos, too, may lead to complaints of "side effects" on the part of the patient.

The *handling of relatives* is an important part of treatment. Relatives, particularly those who have begun to suspect that the patient's symptoms are emotional, not physical, in origin may request an interview with the physician to confirm their suspicions. Under these circumstances it is probably best to avoid saying that the patient's symptoms are of psychological origin. A comment to the effect that the patient is ill, worried, and needs help, and that the physician will do what he can for him, is far more helpful. The physician may also seek to involve the relative in the patient's treatment by asking him to be more accepting of, if not more sympathetic toward, the patient's complaints. This will tend to reduce the negative feedback the patient receives from his surroundings and lessen his need to rely on physical complaints. One of the surest ways for the patient to lose confidence in his physician is to be told by a relative that the latter really thinks the patient's complaints are imaginary.

With respect to the *handling of interviews,* generally speaking, it is wise to see a hypochondriacal patient at least once a week for the first several times. Later, the time between appointments can be lengthened. When an appointment is given to hypochondriacal patients, it is interesting how many will respond by saying that the time suggested is inconvenient for them and ask that another time be arranged. This is usually a way of testing the physician to determine the extent of his interest in the patient. Generally, the physician should insist that the patient adhere to the selected time for his appointment and also adhere to the therapeutic regimen. The patient will depart with new confidence, buoyed up by the fact that he has both medicine and another appointment. His anxiety concerning the possibility that his illness would be challenged has been reduced.

The length of the interview is necessarily limited. Although the first contact may require considerable time, return visits can be reduced to 15 to 20 minutes. The patient should be told how long his next appointment will last. This will discourage hypochondriacal patients from making bids for additional time. Not infrequently, when the duration of the interview has not been specified, the patient, sensing that the interview is about to be terminated, may "suddenly" remember something very important, thereby seeking to extend the period of contact with the physician. If the diagnosis has been properly made, the important information can usually be taken up at the next visit.

When the patient returns for his second appointment, he finds that the physician's attitude has not changed. The physician continues to be an interested and understanding listener. When the patient expresses hostility against his previous physicians, the present one must restrain himself from defending his colleagues and must confine his remarks to recognition of the patient's previous experiences as being both upsetting and disappointing to him. No diagnosis or prognosis is ventured by the physician. This restraint is difficult for the average physician because this is foreign to his usual way of handling patients.

As progress from treatment is seen, the physician will become aware of a shift away from the patient's physical complaints to a greater emphasis on psychic conflicts related to family, work, and friends. When this change becomes apparent, treatment can follow two paths: The patient may gradually lose the intensity of his preoccupation with his imaginary illness as a result of the confidence gained in the physician-patient relationship. He may have exacerbations of his symptoms when his life problems increase, but in the meantime he can return to more active and more efficient participation in his social environment. A still brighter outlook can be anticipated if the patient begins to develop some insight into his situation. When he begins to notice that his symptoms become worse after an argument, for instance, he may then be ready to face his problems more directly in counseling interviews or in psychotherapy. As a result, he may be able to abandon his physical complaints altogether.

Especially with older hypochondriacal patients, however, physicians must remain alert to the possibility that true organic illness can develop. Included in the high cost of being neurotic is the distinct possibility that physical illness may be overlooked because all the multiple symptoms previously complained of had been on a functional basis.

Somatic Complaints in Nonmedical Settings
What has been said thus far about chronic complainers applies principally to patients who have sought medical care repeatedly. Studies of community elderly, however, revealed that some 30 percent also had high levels of bodily concern [18, 68]. The term *high bodily concern* as used in the study [18], did not imply anything about the basis of this concern; it might be reality-based, consistent with the presence of organic disease; or it might be of neurotic origin. Of the 30 percent with high bodily concern, one-half had neurotically based concerns, and at least another one-fourth had a physical basis for their concern but with some neurotic overlay. Interestingly, most of these patients did not seek

medical care but used their concern instead as a *social crutch* in an attempt to defend against anxiety and to solicit the sympathy, forgiveness, and help of others.

Paranoid Reactions

Paranoid reactions are also frequent in old age. It is important to distinguish between the mild paranoid reactions that are at times only short-lived, poorly focused, and not at all disabling and those severe and all-encompassing paranoid reactions that are intensely experienced, disruptive of social interaction, and usually lead to hospitalization of the affected person. Intermediate states between these two extremes also exist. Moreover, paranoid phenomena are not entirely outside the range of normal experience. Most people at one time or another have been unjustly suspicious of neighbors, friends, and associates and have at times interpreted essentially neutral stimuli in a personal manner.

Paranoid symptoms occur throughout the life cycle. However, they are more frequent in old age [38]. One may well ask why this should be so. One reason may be that the factors thought to contribute to the development of paranoid reactions at any age tend to be more frequent in old age. Social isolation, general insecurity, solitary living, and sensory defects, particularly hearing loss, tend to increase in the population of older people. One might also be able to say that older persons use projective mechanisms, which underlie paranoid symptom formation, *faute de mieux*. Projective mechanisms are a relatively primitive defense that becomes available to the child at 1 or 2 years of age. They are mechanisms that can be applied instantaneously to any given situation, and more complicated and more highly focused defense operations may no longer be readily available to the aged person. In addition, the use of projection may serve a reconstructive function. Due to declines in vision and hearing, the aged may perceive the external world only imperfectly. Large segments of their surroundings may therefore appear vague to them, and a kind of "filling in the blank spaces" may be necessary for them to exist in this incompletely perceived world. Sensory deprivation experiments or the natural experiments in which a person is isolated in a remote place such as Antarctica or on a long sea voyage have shown clearly that the human mind does not tolerate a lack of sensory stimulation well. In sensory deprivation a new world—to be sure a hallucinated one—is created to fill the void. This mechanism may be operative in the aged as well.

The unknown is often interpreted as hostile and at least threatening. It should thus not be surprising that paranoid projections often have a hostile character. While younger paranoid patients often blame powerful but somewhat remote and esoteric forces for their misfortunes, old people often blame persons either geographically or emotionally close to themselves. Thus paranoid ideas in old age often center on neighbors, on passersby, on the mailman or milkman, or on members of the aged person's own household. For instance, neighbors are accused of laughing or talking about the old person, of maligning his character. Children in the neighborhood are accused of teasing him, or of peering through the windows at him, or spying on him; relatives are accused of trying to push him into a nursing home or other institution, or of trying to poison him. Occasionally, some grandiose idea may be expressed.

A certain amount of suspiciousness may actually be adaptive in the face of a treacherous environment. There is no doubt that the aged encounter more hostility and fewer opportunities in their environment than do young people. Paranoia, like hypochondriasis, can provide an excuse for failure. The person can say that the fault lies not with himself but with "them." "They" are trying to harm him, are taking away his powers, and are trying to make him look ridiculous. Frequent as paranoid symptoms are in old age, it should be made clear that they do not have the same ominous significance that such ideas have in younger persons. In fact, paranoid ideas in old age, while usually indicating hostile intent toward the older person, may sometimes have rather childlike or whimsical qualities attached to them. The following brief case examples may be illustrative:

Mrs. W. was an 80-year-old widow, in good physical health, alert, and well informed about events around her. She was not disoriented, and there was no other evidence of organic brain disease. However, from time to time she became very concerned and upset over the "fact" that her neighbors were putting lint into her washer and dryer. On several occasions she went to the police station to lodge a complaint. She had no good explanation why the neighbors were doing this. Reasoning with her was to no avail. For instance, her daughter tried to prove that this could not be happening because there was nowhere the neighbors could obtain lint to dump into her machine. Apart from this she got along well, but on washdays her complaints and accusations returned.

Mrs. B., age 74, had a happy marriage of 53 years until her husband died. After spending the winter alone in her big house, her son suggested that perhaps she would enjoy going to the spring meeting of the Golden Age Society. This would give her an opportunity to meet new people, see old friends, and have an outing with people her own age. She thought this was an excellent idea, and she looked forward to going.

In the afternoon paper a few days later she saw an article about the meeting to be held the next morning. She noticed that the topic for the meeting was "Correct Way to Prepare Your Will." The article went on to state that questions could be asked, and anyone wishing to make a will could do so that morning. On reading this she "realized" why her son had told her about the meeting and insisted that she go. She became angry, refused to go, and was sure that her son was "in cahoots" with the man making out the wills, and this was his way of seeing to it that she left all her worldly possessions and savings to him.

The Relationship Between Deafness and Paranoid Reactions

A number of investigators have tried to relate sensory defects, particularly deafness, to the development of paranoid ideas [22, 51, 101]. Since some hearing loss is common in old age [120], this may in part account for the frequency of paranoid ideas among old people. Thus Houston and Royse [51] writing in 1954, commented as follows:

Often not knowing what his fellow men are saying the deaf person becomes doubtful about them: losing auditory contact with them he has to rely on an inner-world of auditory memories and images; he misinterprets auditory sense impressions . . . he projects his inner feelings of inferiority caused by his deafness onto his environment and develops ideas of reference. Systematization soon follows, with active delusions of persecution. If the personality is sufficiently unstable a psychotic illness results [51].

In their study, Houston and Royse were able to demonstrate a higher proportion of paranoid symptoms among deaf psychotic patients than among those who were not deaf. Eisdorfer [28], in a Rorschach study of aged persons with sensory impairment, found that deaf aged were more likely to use primitive thought on the Rorschach cards than were aged who had no hearing impairment or who had some visual loss.

Paranoid Psychoses

In addition to the relatively minor paranoid reactions, paranoid psychoses also occur. Post [94], in a monograph on persistent persecutory states of the elderly, reviewed a number of studies in the literature and also reported his own experience with hospitalized paranoid patients. He concluded that in England paranoid psychoses account for nearly 10 percent of all patients admitted to psychiatric hospitals in old age. (He was speaking here of paranoid psychosis in which there is no gross organic brain disease.) Paranoid symptoms are not at all infrequent in the organic brain syndrome. In these paranoid psychoses of old age, females predominate markedly in all of the studies reviewed, with men accounting for only from 5 to 25 percent of the patients with this diagnosis.

The relationship of the paranoid psychoses of late life to the schizophrenias of younger years, particularly to paranoid schizophrenia, is not clear. In Post's study of some 93 patients with paranoid psychoses of late onset, approximately one-third had only paranoid auditory hallucinations without other classic symptoms of schizophrenia. Another third had paranoid delusions that were fairly easily understandable on the basis of adverse living situations and on the basis of social and partial sensory isolation (about a third of his patients were deaf; many lived alone and had little or no social contact). Only about a third had the more or less classic symptoms of schizophrenia, with autistic ideation, disorganized thought processes, and archaic symbolization and delusion formation. In Post's study, as well as in a number of other studies reviewed by him, the typical prehospitalization picture was that of a woman, unmarried (either never married or widowed, divorced, or separated for a number of years), now living alone, with some hearing loss, who had been for much of her past life relatively socially isolated regardless of what the specific living arrangements were. About a third of the patients in Post's study were described as having been suspicious, unduly sensitive, quarrelsome, or hostile throughout most of their lives.

Treatment of Paranoid Patients

The immediate treatment goal with paranoid patients is to reduce the anxiety that leads to the development of paranoid ideas. Basically, this can be accomplished by three differing but related techniques: by psychotherapeutic intervention, by reducing the threat from the external environment, and by anxiety-alleviating drugs. Any or all of these techniques may be used.

In psychotherapy the principal endeavor is aimed at restoring self-esteem through clear communication between the patient and persons in his environment. Empathic understanding of the frightened patient's life situation can be very calming. It is similarly helpful to consider with the patient alternative explanations of what is happening to him.

In terms of environmental manipulation, consideration has to be given to many different types of intervention. It is very important to have the patient in an essentially familiar and relatively uncomplicated environment. For other patients it may be essential to see to it that they have glasses to correct visual defects and hearing aids to correct auditory losses, or that they have adequate lighting in their homes or apartments. Other patients may require financial assistance, medical care, companionship, housekeeping services, or other concrete help. Regardless of the nature of the intervention it is always important to state clearly what steps are to be taken and the purpose of each of these steps.

When these techniques are insufficient or when insufficient personnel exists, tranquilizing drugs are indicated. The introduction of the phenothiazine drugs has wrought a major change in prognosis of the paranoid psychosis in old age. Until about the mid-1950s, the prognosis for most of these patients was seen as bleak, even though they were generally physically well and did not follow the kind of deteriorating course so frequently seen in patients with senile or arteriosclerotic brain disease. In fact, many of these patients survived for many years in institutions, without improvement. With the advent of the major tranquilizers this picture changed dramatically.

Chlorpromazine (Thorazine), thioridazine (Mellaril), and haloperidol (Haldol) have been the drugs most widely used in the treatment of paranoid symptoms and have proved to be effective [50, 94, 116]. As with antidepressant drugs, drug dosages need not be high. Low daytime dosages, with more substantial doses administered at night, are effective and tend to minimize side effects. Doses of 25 mg three times daily, plus 50 to 100 mg at bedtime, are usually sufficient for chlorpromazine or thioridazine; doses of 0.5 to 1.0 mg of haloperidol three times daily, plus 1 to 2 mg at bedtime, usually suffice. Since paranoid patients are paranoid about many things, including medications, these drugs should be administered only in liquid or concentrated form, with ample amounts of fruit juice or other liquid, to assure that the patient in fact receives the prescribed medication [89].

Paranoid Symptoms in Other Psychiatric Disorders
In addition to the syndromes in which paranoid symptomatology is the principal feature, paranoid symptoms may also be present as part of an affective psychosis. In such cases the persecutory ideas are generally in congruence with the dominant affect. Paranoid symptoms may also be seen in the framework of an acute (reversible) or chronic (irreversible) brain syndrome. In such cases, signs of organic brain disease are generally recognizable [24].

The Experience of Anxiety in the Aged
Anxiety plays a central role in most theoretical systems in psychiatry [31, 37, 117]. It is generally viewed as the result of intrapersonal conflict, or interpersonal conflict, or both, or as the result of threatening external circumstances. Anxiety is a complicated psychophysiological response. It may be defined as a subjectively experienced state of dread anticipation in which the object of one's dread is only vaguely defined. The term *anxiety* also includes the bodily manifestation of this uneasy mental state: muscular tenseness, restlessness, rapid heart rate, excessive sweating—all signs of preparedness for fight or flight. The psychophysiological manifestations of anxiety undoubtedly change with advancing age, possibly paralleling the changes in the nervous and endocrine systems. It appears that response to an anxiety-producing stimulus in the elderly is often delayed and may be increased or decreased, depending on which manifestation of anxiety is being measured. Furthermore, the same stimuli that produce anxiety in younger persons may not produce the same reaction in the elderly, and vice versa [29, 95, 111].

Anxiety is a common symptom in old age. It may be present intermittently in response to a specific stress situation; it may be present chronically in some people; or it may be a concomitant of other psychiatric disorders, to be discussed subsequently. Anxiety may be experienced overtly, or, with or without being experienced overtly, it may give rise to a variety of other symptoms or defenses.

When a precipitating circumstance for the anxiety can be determined, an exploration of the possible alternative ways of dealing with the situation need to be explored with the patient. Actually, a certain amount of anxiety in a given situation can improve alertness and efficiency for coping. Even a certain amount of anger can promote readiness for action. However, when fear and anger become extreme or persistent, they tend to have a disorganizing effect on the person's adaptive efforts.

Often, clarification of the nature of the problem, or the discovery that the problem the person is facing is a common one among old people, is enough to reduce the anxiety to manageable levels or to a point at which the person's own coping devices can take over and resolve the difficulty. At other times, practical help may be required. Additional family members may need to be involved, or it may be necessary to refer the patient to other social agencies for help in arranging financial support, rearranging living conditions, securing medical care, or providing for other needs (see Chap. 16).

However, anxiety in old age may also be related not to a specific circumstance but to the more general problem of growing old. Old people are apt to experience increasingly frequent feelings of helplessness vis-à-vis life's circumstances. They can no longer manage on their own. Their dependence on others evokes in many feelings of impotence, worthlessness, abandonment, and rage. The therapist can guide the patient toward a gradual acceptance of this dependency as age-appropriate, while at the same time identifying persons in the older person's environment on whom he can indeed depend—adult children, a still-capable spouse, a trusted paid companion or servant, or, if hospitalized, a familiar, rather than a constantly changing, nursing staff or even a trusted therapist. Dependency can be tolerated more easily if the person can be sure that the support on which he is relying will not be withdrawn at any moment. The provision of a stable physical and psychological environment can reduce anxiety. By a stable environment, however, we do not mean one devoid of stimulation.

It is important that anxiety be relieved relatively promptly whenever possible, since persistent anxiety can have a marked alienating effect on others in the old person's environment. Marked anxiety and the irritability that often goes with it tend to evoke negative rejecting reactions from people around the aged person, thus further increasing his interpersonal estrangement. In addition, such alienation robs him of further sympathetic interest and emotional support.

When ventilation, clarification, and examination of alternative strategies alone are not enough to restore equilibrium, then the use of the so-called minor tranquilizers and sedatives *on a temporary basis* (one to three or four days) as well as the use of nighttime hypnotics, again *on a temporary basis,* is warranted.

These episodes, however, should not become starting points for chronic medication use, since the drugs in question have undesirable characteristics for older patients when they are used continuously. These include tolerance and psychological and physical dependence, as they do in younger patients. But equally or more important, the undesirable effects of the minor tranquilizers when used continuously in older patients can include chronic delirium, with decreased memory capacity and cognitive functioning, drowsiness, and loss of equilibrium, with its attendant increase in accident rate. Used over the short run, however, they are a powerful tool in terminating temporary disturbances in many older people, permitting their greater participation in problem solving and preventing the development of more chronic anxiety states or of one of the other more enduring syndromes already discussed.

Sleep Disturbances
Elderly persons frequently complain of sleep disturbances. Some complain of difficulty going to sleep, some of insufficient sleep, and others of restless sleep, with frequent awakenings. The complaint of sleeping too much is more often the concern of relatives and friends rather than of patients. Many older patients who complain of sleep problems are worried that poor sleep will lead to serious illness. These sleep disturbances may be related to anxiety in some instances, but in others they may reflect age-related changes in the physiology of sleep.

Although variations and disorders of sleep and activities during sleep have always been of considerable importance to physicians, until recently there was very little information of clinical relevance [26, 57]. Most physicians are aware that there are at least four major stages of sleep and that stage one, rapid eye movement (REM) sleep, is the stage of sleep in which dreams are most likely to occur. Further, it is appreciated that there are four to five REM episodes during a night's sleep and that these REM periods become progressively longer during nocturnal sleep.

Sleep patterns and sleep requirements change throughout the life span. A newborn infant sleeps between 16 and 17 hours a day. In most infants there is a gradual decline within the first six months, but at least 12 hours is the usual pattern. By age 3, 10 hours a night is the common rule, and the necessity for daytime naps is decreasing. During adolescence it is not unusual to encounter trouble waking up. This difficulty is probably the result of physiological changes. In young adulthood and, in particular, in middle life and the later years, there are some who claim an increased need for sleep and some a decreased need. However, it is doubtful that any elderly person in reasonably good health regularly requires more than 7½ to 8½ hours of sleep per night. After the age of 70 years, "sleep latency," that is, the time needed to fall asleep, increases considerably to beyond 15 minutes. Time in bed, not necessarily sleeping, also increases with age, but there is considerable individual variation. Many old people spend 8½ to 9 hours in bed but actually sleep only 7 to 8 hours [124]. It has been reported that men between the ages of 50 and 60 who sleep more than 9 hours a day have twice the death rate from stroke as those who sleep only 7 hours. If the men sleep more than 10 hours, they are four times as likely to have a stroke [47].

In elderly subjects there are some important changes in patterns of sleeping. Stage four sleep, that is, deep sleep, virtually disappears, and older people require a longer period to fall asleep [52, 53]. Their sleep is lighter, and more frequent awakenings occur. Feinberg et al. [36] have reported that these changes are still more pronounced in persons with significant organic brain disease. As people pass into the latter part of their life span, it is important that they recognize that the process of going to sleep lengthens and that they, as part of the normal process, will be aware of more frequent awakenings. However, both these phenomena are exacerbated if there is pain or other discomfort. In such cases an analgesic alone or in combination with a hypnotic can help an elderly person have a restful sleep.

Throughout adult life, women sleep differently than men do. Women spend more time in bed, sleep more, and awaken during the night less often than men [111].

Many of the so-called psychotropic drugs, including stimulants, hypnotics, and antidepressants, seem to alter the frequency and duration of REM periods, either during the time that medication is given or after it is withdrawn [79, 80]. These matters require additional elucidation.

Barbiturates produce a sleep much like normal sleep, but unfortunately the elderly person often has a barbiturate hangover the next morning; task performances may be impaired for several hours after awakening. Paraldehyde and chloral hydrate continue to be very reliable medications for assuring a reasonable length of sleep. It also appears that flurazepam (Dalmane) may be particularly useful [54].

Sleep not only serves a normal physiological function but also provides a period of escape from many stresses of life for some persons. Chronic insomnia, on the other hand, is often attributed to unsolved emotional conflict involving feelings of guilt and hostility with fear of retaliation. However, one study of "hard-core" insomnia suggests that the sleep disturbance is a biological defect and that the emotional problems are a symptom rather than the cause [111]. There is a wide variation among people in the amount of sleep required. A few persons can get along on as little as 5 or 6 hours a night. Busse et al. [20] found that in a group of subjects over the age of 60, 7 to 10 percent used sleeping pills habitually (see Patterns of Drug Use and Abuse). In various groups of apparently well-adjusted community subjects over the age of 60, 20 to 40 percent of each series occasionally used sleeping pills. In elderly subjects who were free of physical pain, those who used sleeping pills excessively were found to have many other neurotic complaints and to be poorly adjusted socially. Kutner and his co-workers [59] in the study "Five Hundred Over Sixty" reported that 40 percent complained of chronic insomnia. Nearly one-fourth of their subjects usually awoke tired and exhausted. This is somewhat in contrast to the results of a study by Ginsberg [42], who found that 18.6 percent of elderly non-psychotic residents of a county home complained of insomnia. In fact, sleep problems were the lowest on the list of ten complaints of these elderly county-home residents.

Alcoholism Among the Aged

Alcoholism, both acute and chronic, is not uncommon in old age. It is seen in community mental health centers, psychiatric outpatient clinics, and in psychiatric hospitals generally, but especially in state mental hospitals [40, 98, 113, 122]. For the most part these patients have been chronic abusers of alcohol even in their younger years and are simply continuing the abuse. However, they also include a few new recruits to alcohol abuse. Sometimes there are other underlying psychiatric disturbances, such as depressive illness or chronic anxiety. In such instances the person essentially is trying to treat his basic psychiatric disturbance, using alcohol as an antidepressant or tranquilizer. Chronic alcohol abuse can result in chronic organic brain syndromes of the Korsakoff type.

In general, the symptomatology and other characteristics—and the appropriate treatment—are not substantially different in older chronic alcohol abusers and in younger ones, with the exception that many of the older patients have a number of coexisting physical disorders, such as congestive heart failure, hypertension, emphysema, or other disabling diseases. Alcoholic intoxication and alcohol withdrawal syndromes can have more serious life-threatening effects in such cases.

Schizophrenics Grown Old in the State Hospital

There are currently residing in state mental hospitals—and to a lesser degree in nursing homes—substantial numbers of aged persons who were diagnosed as schizophrenic earlier in life, who have spent much of their lives in institutions, and who have thus grown old in institutions [98]. These patients, while retaining *some* schizophrenic symptomatology, are primarily manifesting the devastating impact of long-term custodial care in institutions. They are not so much manifesting "schizophrenia" in old age as they are symbolizing an era in psychiatry that had few active treatment programs to offer to schizophrenic patients. It is likely that in the future fewer patients will be retained in mental hospitals for such inordinately long periods of time and that active treatment programs earlier in life will restore them to good mental functioning before they reach old age.

Patterns of Drug Use and Abuse

At a number of points in this chapter, we have referred to the use of psychotropic medications with elderly patients and have repeatedly stressed the possible adverse effects of some of these medications. In this section the issue of drug administration and drug taking among older patients will be discussed more generally.

Extent of Drug Use in the Elderly

Studies of physicians' prescribing habits have shown that each hospitalized Medicare patient receives an average of 10 prescription medications and that approximately 200 million prescriptions for psychotropic drugs are written annually by nonpsychiatrists [121]. The high rate of drug utilization by the elderly is understandable if one appreciates their health problems.

The National Health Survey classifies *chronic conditions* as illnesses or impairments that represent a departure from physical or mental well-being and are of a type that persist for more than three months or for a longer or indefinite duration. After the age of 65, more than three of four Americans have one or more chronic conditions. This compares with two of three with chronic conditions between ages 45 and 64 and to less than one in two people during early adulthood. More important than the mere presence of a chronic disease is the degree of pain and visibility that accompanies it. The severity of the symptoms progresses steadily with advancing age, and after 75 years of age, 23.7 percent of people are unable to carry on major activity because of chronic impairment, as opposed to 9.7 percent of those between 65 and 74 years of age. Furthermore, the drain on medical facilities is substantial. Those over the age of 65 years occupy 18 to 20 percent of the beds in general hospitals and 90 percent of the beds in nursing homes and constitute 30 percent of patients in mental hospitals [15].

Drug Metabolism in the Elderly

Drugs are metabolized differently in older people than they are in younger people. The term *metabolism* is employed to designate the sum of all chemical reactions that take place in a living organism [118]. Hence how the drug is handled within the body has a number of metabolic dimensions, including absorption, distribution, destruction, excretion, kinetics of drug binding, and alterations in biological rhythms [100]. All these and other changes seem to decline as the result of the aging processes, as well as from the insults of disease and trauma. Some of the major aging changes are the loss or decline of efficiency of renal function, a redistribution of body content with a decline in protein and an increase in fat, a decline in basic metabolic rate, and the dropping out of nonreplaceable cells. The loss of brain cells probably makes the brain more sensitive to certain drugs, while the increase in fat content is important because drugs are frequently stored in fat. Striated musculature diminishes to about one-half by about 80 years of age. As these muscle cells disappear, they are replaced by fats and fibrous connective tissue; hence the drug storage capacity increases. It is estimated that the basic metabolic rate through the adult years declines 16 percent from age 30 to 70 years, while the caloric requirement drops approximately one-third because of decreased metabolism and exercise.

Age Trends in Drug Use

It is recognized that a significant percentage of the population of the United States use psychoactive drugs at least occasionally. After the age of 65 years, alcoholism is the second most frequent cause for admission to a psychiatric facility, while drug dependency is a very infrequent cause [98]. Alcohol and marihuana, are utilized by many people to cope with the anxieties and problems of living. Others utilize over-the-counter medications purchased at pharmacies, and others depend on their physicians' prescriptions. A national study reported in 1973 [82] concluded that the use of psychotherapeutic drugs is a widespread phenomenon. One-third of the population utilizes "drugs" to varying degrees. The United States data are consonant with reports from other Western industrial nations. The 1973 study included both over-the-counter and prescription drugs; interestingly, less than 4 percent of persons used both these types of drugs. There is widespread consumer satisfaction with prescription drugs, with 75 percent believing that the drugs had helped them in various degrees. Only 40 percent indicated satisfaction with over-the-counter medications [82].

At all ages women use more over-the-counter and prescription drugs than do men. In one year, 22 percent of men and 37 percent of women had taken psychoactive medication. However, it is likely that men made up the difference by the use of alcohol. It is important to note that young men up to the age of 30 and men after the age of 60 show a greater use of drugs than at other ages. The percentage of female users remains level throughout adulthood. In late life, prescription drugs show a clear increase.

Of elderly people, 11 percent use minor tranquilizers or sedatives, 7 percent use hypnotics, and 4 percent use antidepressants. The findings in the national study suggest that these psychotherapeutic drugs are being used as adjunctive therapy to a physical condition rather than for a primary mental disorder [82].

Individual Psychotherapy with Older Patients

In 1959 Rechtschaffen [97] published a thoughtful and well-balanced review of the literature on psychotherapy with geriatric patients. The review contained 72 references and dealt specifically with face-to-face psychotherapy, not with psychiatric treatment generally. Nearly two decades later, the review still stands as an excellent summary.

By beginning with a focus on the "Martin" method, Rechtschaffen sets the tone of the entire discussion. Psychotherapy with old people must differ from psychotherapy with the young, both in aim and method. On the whole the goals are much more highly focused, more specific, though not necessarily more limited—only more limited in the sense that they are more circumscribed. The methods tend to be far more directive, involving the therapist in much greater "activity," where activity sometimes means only greater verbal input but sometimes also refers to greater motor input on the part of the therapist.

Dr. Lillien J. Martin was a psychologist who, after her own retirement, founded the Old Age Counseling Center of San Francisco in 1929. Hers was an active, enthusiastic, inspirational approach to the problems of old age. In a series of short interviews Dr. Martin attempted to instill in her aged clients an attitude of purposeful activity and a "will-to-do" attitude. Clearly, she supported an activity theory of aging, not a disengagement theory. In her own hands this method was apparently successful but gained few adherents outside of her own immediate circle of influence. Rechtschaffen ventures the notion that her approach failed after her death because there was nothing scientific or objective in it that could be transmitted to other therapists.

Rechtschaffen quotes Freud on three points, all of which are of questionable validity in the light of present findings. "Near or above the fifties the elasticity of the mental processes, on which the treatment depends, is as a rule lacking—old people are no longer educable." He is also quoted as saying that "the mass of material to be dealt with would prolong the duration of the treatment indefinitely." Freud also said that when a younger person is cured of a neurosis, he has 30 or 40 or 50 good years of life ahead of him, but that therapy with the aged is less valuable since they have only a few years remaining.

Abraham is quoted as introducing the first note of optimism regarding the analysis of the aged [97], saying that "the age of the neurosis is more important than the patient." S. E. Jelliffee, of Boston, said that "chronological, physiological, and psychological age do not go hand in hand" and proceeded with the analysis of several aged patients. Jelliffee felt that it was important to modify classic psychoanalytical techniques, feeling that many of the aged had arrived at their defensive structure intuitively and that it could not be dismantled without doing a disservice to the patient. Grotjahn, writing in 1940, was the first to give strong emphasis to the real and immediate needs the analyst was called on to fill in the life of the geriatric patient. He wrote:

Not only is the senile person's relationship to reality changed by his psychotic withdrawal, but the reality situation itself is fundamentally changed by the biological and social dependence and helplessness of an old man . . . the analyst is not a more or less unreal image, but a vivid active part of reality engaged in the management of the patient's hospital life.

Rechtschaffen comments that with these remarks Grotjahn seems to have anticipated the development of modified analytical techniques in the treatment of the aged.

Alexander in 1944 delineated two forms of psychotherapy: insight-oriented and supportive. He said that the primary consideration in the treatment of the aged should be the degree of ego strength available. Through the writings of a number of authors also reviewed by Rechtschaffen rings the warning that the established defenses of the aged should not be tampered with unless some modification of the aged person's real life situation is also possible. A rekindling of old conflicts, even though they have not been handled in an entirely satisfactory manner in younger years, is often not indicated. Meerloo has also championed continued therapeutic efforts with the aged. He has called attention to the need for education and environmental modification (especially in conjunction with home visits by social workers), and he has reemphasized the role of the therapist as a real figure in the life of the patient. Meerloo even went so far as to say that the aged might have reduced resistance to therapy and might be more receptive to input from a therapist than younger persons. Meerloo also called attention to the fact that the aged often see their therapist as their child, the reverse of what usually happens in the transference reaction.

Rechtschaffen also reviews the contribution of Goldfarb, who has developed techniques of brief psychotherapy with disturbed aged patients with some brain damage. Goldfarb's experience is extensive. He attributes great importance to the phenomenon of dependency in old age. He feels that acceptance of this dependency is an important goal in therapy, and to some degree he deliberately encourages a limited illusion in which the aged person can see the younger therapist as a child who will take care of the older person. There is obviously the danger that the illusion may go too far and that real disappointment may follow such an approach. Goldfarb's technique, too, runs somewhat counter to the goal of mastery over one's environment. It appears to us that the difference between these two approaches—one seeking acceptance, the other independence and continued activity—may reflect differences in the residual capacities of the particular patients the several therapists have dealt with. It is our impression that with Goldfarb's patients there was relatively little hope of their ever functioning independently again and that his approach was essentially intended for institutional populations.

According to present thinking, psychotherapy with older patients can indeed be effective. One of us (E. P.) [87] has pointed out a number of modifications of psychotherapeutic technique that facilitate therapy of elderly patients. These include: (1) the need for a more active, explorative role on the part of the therapist; (2) greater focus on the here-and-now situation in the patient's life; (3) establishing clear-cut, if somewhat limited, goals for therapy; (4) endowing the therapeutic relationship with symbolic meaning to enhance the impact of relatively modest amounts of actual time spent with the patient; and (5) special emphasis on understanding transference phenomena and countertransference phenomena with aging patients.

What is not changed in psychotherapy with elderly patients is that the therapist must possess and demonstrate certain basic qualities vis-à-vis older patients: (1) a capacity for correct emphatic understanding of the patient's situation; (2) an unconditional positive regard of the patient; and (3) an emotional honesty that is demonstrated in the therapeutic relationship. In psychotherapy with elderly patients it is often very useful to express feelings in general, particularly positive feelings, directly and openly toward the patient. It is beneficial for the therapist to be much more of a "real person" with older patients than he might be with younger patients. Instead of maintaining a professional distance, he should share some of his own concerns and pleasures, by, for example, showing pictures of his own children or looking at pictures of the patient's children or grandchildren. Many older patients welcome the therapist's touch—either a handshake or a hand placed supportively on a shoulder or arm. Since the therapeutic relationship serves as a first step in reinvolving the patient in family and community relationships, this relationship must be construed to be a positive and pleasurable one, thereby encouraging the patient to reacquire or reactivate other real-life interactions and relationships. As was previously pointed out, the person who can make *new* relationships when old ones have been lost is in a better position to maintain or regain mental health than someone who accepts these losses as inevitable and makes no effort to replace them with new relationships.

Group Therapy with Older Patients

The initial efforts utilizing group therapy with aged patients were carried out primarily in institutional settings by a number of clinicians, including Lichtenberg, Linden, and Wolff [61, 63, 125, 126]. These efforts met with considerable success in improving the functioning of hospitalized patients, although usually not to the point of permitting them to return to independent living in the community. More recently, however, group therapy has been offered to older patients with emotional problems on an ambulatory basis. Liederman et al. [62], Altholz [2], and Burnside [12] have reported on their pioneering work in this regard. Actually, group therapy is not only a feasible method of treatment for older patients but also is one that has several distinct advantages over individual psychotherapy [91]. First, it is possible to treat anywhere from 6 to 10 patients at the same time, resulting in a savings of scarce treatment personnel. But this is probably the least of the advantages. More important is the fact that older patients often learn as much from older persons in the group as they do from the group leader. The impact of a fellow group member reporting on how he has adapted to a difficult situation appears to be far greater than the impact of the group leader's having a possible solution to a problem. Interestingly, in such a situation, both the person to whom the solution is suggested and the person who has provided the solution benefit. In other words, the group member has been able to be useful to someone else, resulting in improved self-esteem. An additional advantage is that the older person in the group learns that other persons often encounter problems similar to his own, decreasing the sense of isolation. Finally—and perhaps most important of all—group therapy provides an older person with membership in a real social group. As has been mentioned a number of times, many older persons become socially isolated and lose membership in groups. In group therapy not only do they become members of a social group again, but the social skills they develop often also allow them to reestablish membership in social groups outside of therapy—in other words, in the real world.

The focus of group therapy in general is on two goals: resocialization and problem solving. Given these goals, the process of group psychotherapy differs somewhat with older patients from that usually carried out with younger patients. There is much more emphasis on participating in the group process, with enjoyment of membership in the group as a real goal, rather than on analysis of the group process. Current problems are the focus of problem solving efforts; personality reconstruction and analyses of childhood experiences usually are not the main focus of group therapy.

In general, it is best to select group therapy members with similar social skills and capacities for problem solving. Indiscriminate mixing of persons with, let us say, severe dementia and persons with functional problems such as depression is not productive. However, each category of patient just mentioned may benefit from group therapy.

As a final note, the inclusion of men and women in the same therapy group has proved effective in getting group members to improve appearance, functioning, and problem-solving efforts. It helps the group member to maintain her or his gender identification and sense of integrity.

Preventive Psychiatry in Old Age

From what has been said, it is obvious that many aged persons with psychiatric difficulties receive no psychiatric care until their disorders are far advanced. This raises the question of what preventive steps can be taken to reduce the incidence of severe psychiatric illness in old age.

In the last decade public health concepts of primary, secondary, and tertiary prevention (also defined as prevention, early treatment, and rehabilitation respectively) have been introduced into psychiatric thinking [23]. According to Caplan [23]:

. . . primary prevention is a community concept. It involves lowering the rate of new cases of mental disorders in a population over a certain period by counteracting harmful circumstances before they have had a chance to produce illness. It does not seek to prevent any specific person from becoming sick. Instead, it seeks to reduce the risk of a whole population so that, although some may become ill, their number will be reduced [23].

Caplan goes on to say that preventive psychiatry deals with general influences prevailing in a "population at risk" (such as the aged).

The existence of even severe pathological symptoms alone is generally not sufficient to lead to psychiatric hospitalization; a constellation of a psychiatric disorder and a series of adverse environmental circumstances—e.g., death of a family member, physical illness, social isolation—is necessary before hospitalization is effected [64]. Thus, while efforts to provide early psychiatric care for many more old people would no doubt be valuable, early help along a variety of other lines (the provision of good medical care, good housing, adequate retirement income, continued contact with remaining family members) may be equally significant in reducing at least some forms of psychiatric illness in old age. It has been the experience of medicine over the past 100 years that health measures focused on entire communities have been far more successful in reducing illness and mortality than have measures aimed only at individual patients.

References

1. Altholz, J.   The family and the older person. In D. T. Peak, G. Polansky, and J. Altholz (Eds.), *The Final Report of the Information and Counseling Service for Older Persons*. Durham, N.C.: Center for the Study of Aging and Human Development, 1971.
2. Altholz, J.   Group Therapy with Elderly Patients. In E. Pfeiffer (Ed.), *Alternatives to Institutional Care for Older Americans: Practice and Planning*. Durham, N.C.: Center for the Study of Aging and Human Development, 1973.
3. American Psychiatric Association. *Diagnostic and Statistical Manual of*

Mental Disorders (2d ed.). Washington, D.C.: American Psychiatric Association, 1968.

4. Barnes, R. H., Busse, E. W., and Silverman, A. J. The interrelationships between psychic and physical factors in the production of mental illness in the aged. *N.C. Med. J.* 16:25, 1955.

5. Batchelor, I. R., and Napier, M. B. Attempted suicide in old age. *Br. Med. J.* 2:1186, 1953.

6. Benson, R. A., and Brodie, D. C. Suicide by overdoses of medicines among the aged. *J. Am. Geriatr. Soc.* 23:304, 1975.

7. Berkman, P. L. Cumulative Deprivation and Mental Illness. In M. F. Lowenthal et al. (Eds.), *Aging and Mental Disorder in San Francisco.* San Francisco: Jossey-Bass, 1967. Pp. 52–80.

8. Botwinick, J. *Cognitive Processes in Maturity and Old Age.* New York: Springer, 1967.

9. Bressler, R., and Palmer, J. Drug Interactions in the Aged. In W. E. Fann and G. L. Maddox (Eds.), *Drug Issues in Geropsychiatry.* Baltimore: Williams & Wilkins, 1974. Pp. 49–57.

10. Brosin, H. W. Discussion. *Death and Dying: Attitudes of Patient and Doctor.* New York: Group for the Advancement of Psychiatry, 1965. Pp. 642–643.

11. Brotman, H. B. Who are the aged: A demographic view. *Useful Facts,* No. 42. Washington, D.C.: U.S. Administration on Aging, August 9, 1968. Table 8.

12. Burnside, I. Loss: A constant theme in group work with the aged. *Hosp. Community Psychiatry* 21:173, 1970.

13. Busse, E. W. The treatment of hypochondriasis. *Tri-State Med. J.* 2:7, 1954.

14. Busse, E. W. Hypochondriasis and Its Treatment. In A. Verwoerdt (Ed.), *Introduction to Psychosomatic Medicine.* Mimeographed. Durham, N.C.: Duke University Dept. of Psychiatry, 1963. Chap. 12, pp. 121–130.

15. Busse, E. W. Research on Aging: Some Methods and Findings. In M. A. Berezin and S. H. Cath (Eds.), *Geriatric Psychiatry: Grief, Loss, and Emotional Disorders in the Aging Process.* New York: International Universities Press, 1965. Pp. 73–95.

16. Busse, E. W. The geriatric patient and the nursing home. *N. C. Med. J.* 33:218, 1972.

17. Busse, E. W. Hypochondriasis in the elderly: A reaction to social stress. Paper presented at the Tenth International Congress of Gerontology, Jerusalem, Israel, July 1975.

18. Busse, E. W., Barnes, R. H., and Dovenmuehle, R. H. The incidence and origin of hypochondriacal patterns and psychophysiological reactions in elderly persons. First Pan-American Congress on Gerontology, Mexico City, September 1956.

19. Busse, E. W., et al. Studies of processes of aging: VI. Factors that influence the psyche of elderly persons. *Am. J. Psychiatry* 110:897, 1954.

20. Busse, E. W., et al. Studies of processes of aging: X. The strengths

and weaknesses of psychic functioning in the aged. *Am. J. Psychiatry* 111:896, 1955.

21. Butler, R. N. The life review: An interpretation of reminiscence of the aged. *Psychiatry* 26:65, 1963.
22. Cameron, N. Paranoid Conditions and Paranoia. In S. Arieti (Ed.), *American Handbook of Psychiatry,* Vol. I. New York: Basic Books, 1959.
23. Caplan, G. *Principles of Preventive Psychiatry.* New York: Basic Books, 1964.
24. Davidson, R. Paranoid symptoms in organic disease. *Gerontol. Clin.* (Basel) 6:93, 1964.
25. Davis, J. M., et al. Clinical Problems in Treating the Aged with Psychotropic Drugs. In C. Eisdorfer and W. E. Fann (Eds.), *Psychopharmacology and Aging.* New York: Plenum Press, 1973. Pp. 111–125.
26. Dement, W., and Kleitman, N. The relation of eye movements during sleep to dream activity: An objective method for the study of dreaming. *J. Exp. Psychol.* 53:539, 1957.
27. Dublin, L. I. *Suicide.* New York: Ronald, 1963.
28. Eisdorfer, C. Developmental level and sensory impairment in the aged. *J. Project. Tech.* 24:129, 1960.
29. Eisdorfer, C., et al. The characteristics of lipid mobilization and peripheral disposition in aged individuals. *J. Gerontol.* 20:511, 1965.
30. Eisdorfer, C., and Fann, W. E. *Psychopharmacology and Aging.* New York: Plenum Press, 1973.
31. Engel, G. Anxiety and depression-withdrawal: The primary affects of unpleasure. *Int. J. Psychoanal.* 43:89, 1962.
32. Erikson, E. H. *Identity and the Life Cycle.* Psychological Issues, Vol. I, No. 1. New York: International Universities Press, 1959.
33. Erikson, E. H. *Childhood and Society.* New York: Norton, 1963.
34. Ewalt, J. R., and Farnsworth, D. L. *Textbook of Psychiatry.* New York: McGraw-Hill, 1963.
35. Fann, W. E., and Maddox, G. L. *Drug Issues in Geropsychiatry.* Baltimore: Williams & Wilkins, 1974.
36. Feinberg, I., Braun, M., and Schulman, E. EEG sleep patterns in mental retardation. *Electroencephalogr. Clin. Neurophysiol.* 27:128, 1969.
37. Fenichel, O. *The Psychoanalytic Theory of the Neuroses.* New York: Norton, 1945.
38. Fish, F. J. Senile paranoid states. *Gerontol. Clin.* (Basel) 1:127, 1959.
39. Fromm-Reichmann, F. Loneliness. *Psychiatry* 22:1, 1959.
40. Gaitz, C. M., and Baer, P. E. Characteristics of elderly patients with alcoholism. *Arch. Gen. Psychiatry* 24:372, 1971.
41. Gardner, E., Bahn, A. K., and Mack, M. Suicide and psychiatric care in the aging. *Arch. Gen. Psychiatry* 10:547, 1963.
42. Ginsberg, R. Sleep and sleep disturbances in geriatric psychiatry. *J. Am. Geriatr. Soc.* 3:493, 1955.
43. Goldstein, M. S. Medicare and Care of Mental Illness. *Health Insur-*

ance Statistics HI-4, March 7, 1968. Washington, D.C.: U.S. Department of Health, Education, and Welfare, Social Security Administration, Office of Research and Statistics.

44. Goodwin, F. K., Murphy, D. L., and Bunney, W. E., Jr. Lithium carbonate treatment in depression and mania. *Arch. Gen. Psychiatry* 21: 486, 1969.

45. Grinker, R., Sr., et al. *Phenomena of Depression.* New York: Hoeber, 1961.

46. Gunderson, E. K. E., and Rahe, R. H. *Life Stress and Illness.* Springfield, Ill.: Thomas, 1974.

47. Hammond, E. High risk factors in death of heart disease. (Symposium, Albany Medical College). *Geriatr. Focus* 8:1, April 1969.

48. Hartelius, H. A study of suicides in Sweden 1951–63, including a comparison with 1925–1950. *Acta Psychiatr. Scand.* 43:121, 1967.

49. Hollingshead, A. B., and Redlich, F. C. *Social Class and Mental Illness: A Community Study.* New York: Wiley, 1958.

50. Holstein, A., and Chen, C. Haloperidol—a preliminary clinical study. *Am. J. Psychiatry* 122:462, 1965.

51. Houston, R., and Royse, A. B. Relationship between deafness and psychotic illness. *J. Ment. Sci.* 100:990, 1954.

52. Kahn, E., and Fisher, C. The sleep characteristics of the normal aged male. *J. Nerv. Ment. Dis.* 148:477, 1969.

53. Kales, A., et al. Sleep and dreams—recent research on clinical aspects. *Ann. Intern. Med.* 68:1078, 1968.

54. Kales, A., and Kales, J. In F. Usdin (Ed.), *Sleep Research and Clinical Practice.* New York: Brunner/Mazel, 1973. Pp. 61–94.

55. Kalinowsky, L. B., and Hoch, P. A. *Pharmacological, Convulsive and Other Somatic Treatments in Psychiatry* (2d ed.). New York: Grune & Stratton, 1969.

56. Kay, D. W. K., Beamish, P., and Roth, M. Old age mental disorders in Newcastle-upon-Tyne: I. A study of prevalence. *Br. J. Psychiatry* 465:146, 1964.

57. Kleitman, N. *Sleep and Wakefulness* (rev. ed.). Chicago: University of Chicago Press, 1963.

58. Kramer, M., Taube, C., and Redick, R. Patterns of Use of Psychiatric Facilities by the Aged: Past, Present and Future. In C. Eisdorfer and M. P. Lawton (Eds.), *The Psychology of Adult Development and Aging.* Washington, D.C.: American Psychological Association, 1973.

59. Kutner, B., et al. *Five Hundred Over Sixty: A Community Survey on Aging.* New York: Russell Sage Foundation, 1956.

60. Leighton, D., et al. *The Character of Danger: Psychiatric Symptoms in Selected Communities.* The Stirling County Study of Psychiatric Disorder and Sociocultural Environment, Vol. III. New York: Basic Books, 1963.

61. Lichtenberg, J. D. A study of the changing role of the psychiatrist in the state hospital. *Psychiatr. Q.* 28:428, 1954.

62. Liederman, P. C., Green, R., and Liederman, V. R. Outpatient group therapy with geriatric patients. *Geriatrics* 22:148, 1967.

63. Linden, M. E.   Group psychotherapy with institutionalized senile women: Study in gerontologic human relations. *Int. J. Group Psychother.* 3:150, 1953.

64. Lowenthal, M. F.   Social and related factors leading to psychiatric hospitalization of the aged. *J. Am. Geriatr. Soc.* 13:110, 1965.

65. Lowenthal, M. F.   Antecedents of isolation and mental illness in old age. *Arch. Gen. Psychiatry* 12:245, 1965.

66. Lowenthal, M. F.   Social Stress and Adaptation: Toward a Life-Course Perspective. In C. Eisdorfer and M. P. Lawton (Eds.), *The Psychology of Adult Development and Aging.* Washington, D.C.: American Psychological Association, 1973.

67. Lowenthal, M. F., et al.   *Aging and Mental Disorder in San Francisco.* San Francisco: Jossey-Bass, 1967.

68. Maddox, G. L.   Self-assessment of health status. A longitudinal study of selected elderly subjects. *J. Chronic Dis.* 17:449, 1964.

69. Maddox, G. L.   Retirement as a Social Event in the United States. In J. C. McKinney and F. T. deVyver (Eds.), *Aging and Social Policy.* New York: Appleton-Century-Crofts, 1966.

70. Maggs, R.   Treatment of manic illness with lithium carbonate. *Br. J. Psychiatry* 109:56, 1963.

71. Maugham, W.   *The Summing Up.* Garden City, N.Y.: Doubleday Doran and Co., 1938.

72. Mendelson, M.   *Psychoanalytic Concepts of Depression.* Springfield, Ill.: Thomas, 1960.

73. Meyer, J. E.   Psychoneuroses and neurotic reactions in old age. *J. Am. Geriatr. Soc.* 22:254, 1974.

74. Meyers, J. M., Sheldon, D., and Robinson, S. S.   A study of 138 elderly first admissions. *Am. J. Psychiatry* 120:244, 1963.

75. National Institute of Mental Health.   *Research in the Service of Mental Health.* Report of the Task Force of the National Institute of Mental Health. DHEW Publication No. (ADM) 75-236. Washington, D.C.: U.S. Government Printing Office, 1975. P. 180.

76. Neugarten, B. L.   *Personality in Middle and Late Life.* New York: Atherton, 1964. Pp. 189–190.

77. Nielsen, J.   Geronto-psychiatric period-prevalence investigation in a geographically delimited population. *Acta Psychiatr. Neurol. Scand.* 38:307, 1962.

78. O'Neal, P., Robins, E., and Schmidt, E. H.   A psychiatric study of attempted suicide in persons over sixty years of age. *A.M.A. Arch. Neurol. Psychiatr.* 75:275, 1956.

79. Oswald, I., and Preist, R. G.   Five weeks to escape the sleeping pill habit. *Br. Med. J.* 2:1093, 1965.

80. Oswald, I., and Thacore, V. R.   Amphetamine and phenmetrazine abnormalities in the abstinence syndrome. *Br. Med. J.* 1:5382, 1963.

81. Palmore, E.   Predicting longevity. *Gerontologist* 9:247, 1969.

82. Parry, H., et al.   National patterns of psychotherapeutic drug use. *Arch. Gen. Psychiatry* 28:769, 1973.

83. Parsons, T. *The Social System*. Glencoe, Ill.: Free Press, 1951. Pp. 436–437.

84. Pasamanick, B. A survey of mental disease in an urban population: VI. An approach to total prevalence by age. *Ment. Hyg.* 46:567, 1962.

85. Pfeiffer, E. *Disordered Behavior: Basic Concepts in Clinical Psychiatry*. New York: Oxford University Press, 1968.

86. Pfeiffer, E. Survival in old age: Physical, psychological and social correlates of longevity. *J. Am. Geriatr. Soc.* 18:273, 1970.

87. Pfeiffer, E. Psychotherapy with elderly patients. *Postgrad. Med.* 50: 254, 1971.

88. Pfeiffer, E. Multidimensional quantitative assessment of three populations of elderly: A symposium. Paper presented at Annual Meeting, Gerontological Society, Miami Beach, Florida, 1973.

89. Pfeiffer, E. Use of Drugs Which Influence Behavior in the Elderly. In H. R. Davis (Ed.), *Drugs and the Elderly*. Los Angeles: Andrus Gerontology Center, 1973. Pp. 33–50.

90. Pfeiffer, E. *Multidimensional Functional Assessment: The OARS Methodology. A Manual*. Durham, N.C.: Duke University Center for the Study of Aging and Human Development, 1976.

91. Pfeiffer, E. (Ed.). *Group Psychotherapy* (audiotape). Philadelphia: Borland-Coogan, 1975.

92. Pfeiffer, E. (Ed.). *The Somatic Therapies* (audiotape). Philadelphia: Borland-Coogan, 1975.

93. Platman, S. R. A comparison of lithium carbonate and chlorpromazine in mania. *Am. J. Psychiatry* 127:351, 1970.

94. Post, F. *Persistent Persecutory States of the Elderly*. London: Pergamon, 1966.

95. Powell, A. H., Eisdorfer, C., and Bogdonoff, B. Physiologic response patterns observed in a learning task. *Arch. Gen. Psychiatry* 10:192, 1964.

96. Prien, R. F., Caffey, E. M., Jr., and Keltt, C. J. Comparison of lithium carbonate and chlorpromazine in the treatment of mania. *Arch. Gen. Psychiatry* 26:146, 1972.

97. Rechtschaffen, A. Psychotherapy with geriatric patients: A review of the literature. *J. Gerontol.* 14:73, 1959.

98. Redick, R. W., Kramer, M., and Taube, C. A. Epidemiology of Mental Illness and Utilization of Psychiatric Facilities Among Older Persons. In E. W. Busse and E. Pfeiffer (Eds.), *Mental Illness in Later Life*. Washington, D.C.: American Psychiatric Association, 1973.

99. Reichard, S., Livson, F., and Peterson, P. G. *Aging and Personality*. New York: Wiley, 1962. Pp. 170–171.

100. Reinberg, A. Chronopharmacology in Man. In J. Aschoff, F. Ceresa, and F. Halberg (Eds.), *Chronobiological Aspects of Endocrinology*. Stuttgart and New York: Schattlauer, 1974. Pp. 305–337.

101. Retterstol, N. *Paranoid and Paranoiac Psychoses*. Oslo: Universitetsforlaget, 1966.

102. Riley, M. W., and Foner, A. *An Inventory of Research Findings*.

Vol. I, *Aging and Society*. New York: Russell Sage Foundation, 1968. Pp. 361–406.

103. Robins, E., et al.   The communication of suicidal intent: A study of 134 consecutive cases of successful (completed) suicide. *Am. J. Psychiatry* 115:724, 1959.

104. Rose, A. M., and Peterson, W. A.   *Older People and Their Social World*. Philadelphia: Davis, 1965.

105. Roth, M.   The natural history of mental disorder in old age. *J. Ment. Sci.* 101:281, 1955.

106. Schou, M.   Lithium studies: I. Toxicity. *Acta Pharmacol. Toxicol.* (Kbh.) 15:70, 1958.

107. Schou, M.   Lithium studies: II. Renal elimination. *Acta Pharmacol. Toxicol.* (Kbh.) 15:85, 1958.

108. Schou, M., et al.   The treatment of manic psychoses by the administration of lithium salts. *J. Neurol. Neurosurg. Psychiatry* 17:250, 1954.

109. Shanas, E., et al.   *Old People in Three Industrial Societies*. New York: Atherton, 1968. Pp. 258–287.

110. Shock, N. W.   The physiology of aging. *Sci. Am.* 206:100, 1962.

111. Shmavonian, B. M., and Busse, E. W.   Psychophysiological Techniques in the Study of the Aged. In R. Williams, C. Tibbitts, and W. Donahue (Eds.), *Processes of Aging,* Vol. I. New York: Atherton, 1963. Pp. 168–183.

112. Simon, A.   The geriatric mentally ill. *Gerontologist* 8:7, 1968.

113. Simon, A., Epstein, L. J., and Reynolds, L.   Alcoholism in the geriatric mentally ill. *Geriatrics* 23:125, 1968.

114. Srole, L., et al.   *Mental Health in the Metropolis: The Midtown Manhattan Study*. New York: McGraw-Hill, 1962.

115. Straker, M.   Prognosis for psychiatric illness in the aged. *Am. J. Psychiatry* 119:1069, 1963.

116. Sugerman, A., Williams, B., and Adlerstein, A.   Haloperidol in the psychiatric disorders of old age. *Am. J. Psychiatry* 120:1190, 1964.

117. Sullivan, H. S.   *Conceptions of Modern Psychiatry*. Washington, D.C.: William A. White Foundation, 1947.

118. Timiras, P. S.   *Developmental Physiology and Aging*. New York: Macmillan, 1972.

119. U.S. Public Health Service.   *Vital Statistics of the United States,* Vol. II, *Mortality,* Part A. Rockville, Md.: U.S. Public Health Service, 1968.

120. Weiss, A. D.   Sensory Functions. In J. E. Birren (Ed.), *Handbook of Aging and the Individual*. Chicago: University of Chicago Press, 1959.

121. Whanger. A., Fann, W. E., and Busse, E. W.   *Pharmacology of Geriatric Conditions* (audiotape manuscript). Flushing, N.Y.: Spectrum Publications, 1973.

122. Whittier, J. R.. and Korenyi, C.   Selected characteristics of aged patients: A study of mental hospital admissions. *Compr. Psychiatry* 2:113, 1961.

123. Wilensky, H. L.   Orderly careers and social participation: The impact of work history on social integration in the middle mass. *Am. Sociol. Rev.* 26:521, 1961.

124. Williams, R., Karacan, I., and Hursch, C. *EEG of Human Sleep— Clinical Implications.* New York: Wiley, 1974.
125. Wolff, K. *The Biological, Sociological and Psychological Aspects of Aging.* Springfield, Ill.: Thomas, 1959.
126. Wolff, K. Group psychotherapy with geriatric patients in a psychiatric hospital: Results of a ten year study. *Psychiatric Studies and Projects.* Vol. 3, No. 2. Coatsville, Pa.: Veterans Administration Hospital, 1965.

11. Intelligence and Cognition in the Aged

Carl Eisdorfer

Among the most frequent subjective impressions of the aged is the view that older persons characteristically show a loss of recent memory and impaired learning ability. Indeed, the experience of clinicians who inevitably see large numbers of patients with such memory loss and the other symptoms of senile brain disease reinforces the theme that such decline is an inevitable consequence of the normal aging process past the middle years. Consequently, it is particularly important to appreciate that the empirical data concerning intellectual changes in the aged do not fully support this impression but instead are complex and contradictory.

The findings from a number of long-term longitudinal investigations of middle-aged and aged persons raise doubts about the validity of any simple hypothesis that there is a progressive, generalized loss of intellectual and learning ability in all older persons. Such studies have also highlighted fundamental problems in the study of human aging. Among the more important sets of relationships that require reappraisal is the relationship between initial levels of intellectual ability and age-related decline on the one hand, and the role of physical illness in affecting cognitive behavior on the other hand. Also important are the clarification of present concepts of the nature of intelligence in general.

Intelligence has been a central focus of study not only for research psychologists but also for practitioners of a wide variety of disciplines, including educators, personnel managers, clinical neurologists, and general physicians. For the practitioner, intelligence is a descriptive concept with a variety of meanings, the most salient of which are the ability to communicate and understand and the ability to care for oneself. Educators in particular appear to define it as a person's capacity to acquire and utilize information for the purpose of reaching some "appropriate" goal. Not only is intelligence defined as the capacity to use the environment, but certain other aspects of behavior are also termed intelligence; e.g., "reasonable" or "smart" behavior is highly valued, in contrast to "stupid" or ineffectual behavior. It becomes clear that this latter approach (i.e., focusing on particular activities) has a high social loading, since much adaptive behavior is typically bound to a particular culture. Clinicians and attorneys are often called on to make judgments about the appropriateness of particular actions. Accordingly, poor judgment in interpersonal relationships or in managing personal resources such as money may be seen as implying loss of intelligence and as an indication of inability to continue to be a responsible agent in the community at large.

The Concept of Intelligence

For the psychologist, intelligence is an intervening variable, which is not directly measurable but must be inferred. Thus the criteria for intelligence or intelligent behavior are variable, and a variety of measuring devices have been employed in the search for the most scientifically acceptable ways in which to make meaningful statements concerning the intellectual capacity of a person or group. One should be aware that the accuracy of inferences concerning intelligence is necessarily based on the expectation that the "slice of life" being observed is a relatively typical sample of the person's behavior. This must be constantly reappraised, since there is no question that many factors (e.g., maturation, physical condition at the time of testing, and previous test experience) may affect a person's performance. As will be discussed subsequently, the problem of accurate sampling of behavior may be a particularly acute one with the middle-aged and aged.

According to Hunt [32], psychologists, in their attempts to understand the nature of intelligence, have until recently been guided by two principles: "fixed intelligence" and "predetermined development." These beliefs together lead to the assumption that intelligence is primarily a genetically programmed dimension of human personality that fixes a person's capacity in relation to his peers and is played out during the life span in a predetermined sequence of development and decline. Thus a measurement at any point in time would be predictive of an individual's position throughout life. A convenient leap of faith has also led to the acceptance of data from cross-sectional studies, representing a single time slice at different points in the age span of many persons, to reflect the individual pattern of changes in intelligence with advancing age after maturity has been reached. In view of these factors, the influence of the methodology used to obtain data in this area needs to be examined further.

Another concept that has emerged in recent years involves the definition of intelligence. Operational definitions (i.e., "intelligence is that set of observed abilities measured by intelligence tests") have been proposed with varying degrees of acceptance, but the apparent circularity of such approaches leave most scientists and clinicians uncomfortable. Factorial analyses based on correlational studies of individual subtest variations have yielded some information as to the presence of components of intelligence. Most recently, a concept of intelligence as a multidimensional, multivariate ability has emerged. According to this concept, there is no such entity as general intelligence but rather a large set of cognitive abilities, the pattern of which varies from person to person, as does the level.

Baltes and Labouvie [4] have reviewed many of the conceptual issues in this developing area of interest. They point out that most current tests of intelligence in clinical use suffer from the lack of a conceptual framework. The work of Horn and Cattell [29, 30] provides an example of a conceptual approach. In their analysis of "fluid" versus "crystallized" intellectual ability, they demonstrated that these two separable factors, both important facets of cognitive behavior, decline at different rates with advancing age. Fluid intelligence involves the ability to reorganize one's perceptions. Crystallized ability relates to the organization and utilization of organized information. The fluid abilities are reported to peak earlier and then to decline, while the crystallized abilities peak later and may be more persistent. Although such approaches are controversial [10], they certainly reflect a more sophisticated approach to intellectual functioning than has been suggested heretofore.

Research Strategies

In the examination of intellectual function in adults and in the aged, three different research strategies have been employed: the cross-sectional, longitudinal, and cross-sequential approach. Group tests as well as individually administered tests have been used, each with a built-in bias. Sampling problems have cropped up persistently. Not only is there a selectivity in survivorship into old age, but education, employment status and history, physical health, test experience, and attitude toward examinations are only a few of the relevant variables that require more precise control.

Most of the studies of age-related changes in intelligence have involved the cross-sectional approach. This paradigm, which has the built-in advantages of requiring only a single measurement from each age group and the rapid availability of data, has characteristically not controlled for educational level, cultural differences between age cohorts, and other such factors. Age cohorts thus may differ on a number of variables that have profound effects on intellectual functioning. It is from the results of such cross-sectional studies that the "bow-shaped" curve of intellectual functioning (rising to the late teens or early thirties and dropping after that age) has been derived. The advantage of longitudinal research is that repeated measurements are obtained on the same person. This is time-consuming and cumbersome and involves the added complication of creating a test-wise population. In addition, it is difficult to hold a team of scientists and subjects together for the length of time necessary to complete longer-term studies, and as the years go by, the technology used to perform earlier measures becomes dated or even obsolete.

In 1965 Schaie [47] suggested an alternative model to the traditional cross-sectional and longitudinal designs for studying changes across time. The cross-sequential model involves repeated measurements on a population of subjects of various ages sampled at the same time. It serves to shorten the duration of the longitudinal study, to minimize possible environmental effects, and, it is hoped, to reflect a more valid picture of the aging process. In addition, it enables us to compare cohorts (waves) of persons across the age-time factor.

Measurement of Intelligence

Numerous problems are encountered in the measurement of intellectual changes, not the least of which is the paucity of equivalent test-retest materials and the inappropriateness of many of the tests in the aging condition. Ideally, in studying human development it would be well to proceed through a variety of tests purporting to measure the same phenomenon but shifting focus as one goes from one test to another and from one age to another [35, 42]. As indicated earlier, the changing concept of intelligence from a unitary to multifactor concept adds another dimension of complexity to measurement.

Examining the aged is a specialized problem. Most of the testing materials are geared to the young, not only in that they appeal to the young but also in that they measure knowledge and abilities that are a function of temporal proximity to the academic situation. Many of the tasks on the typical test of intelligence may be seen, therefore, as uninteresting or dull or more typically "silly" by aging persons. The elderly may also be more apprehensive because they lack recent exposure to testing situations and because of an undercurrent of fear that they may be losing intellectual ability.

Older people tend to withhold answers, particularly on timed tests. They respond more frequently and with better results when they are given additional time, although, in fact, they may not need the additional time [20, 21]. Thus in the testing situation it is necessary to give many older persons more time to answer questions and to attempt to control for any anxiety the test situation causes. Familiarizing the older person with the examination situation prior to the actual testing will often help to alleviate heightened arousal levels [53, 54]. Rosenfelt and colleagues [46] have suggested that the investigator must use whatever data possible and develop new ways of looking at the results when there is a minimum output of data. They also suggest that new methods and interpretations must be found for behavior that does not fit the standard, particularly when dealing with physically and mentally handicapped aged persons.

Among the techniques used to appraise individual adult intelligence, the tests designed by Wechsler have been the most widely used in the United States. Wechsler [56], using the 1955 standardization of the Wechsler Adult Intelligence Scale (WAIS) and a cross-sectional design, generated a curve depicting intellectual change with age. The higher level of "mental ability" was found at approximately age 24, with a decline beginning after age 30 and continuing virtually as a straight-line function into old age. A comparison was also made between the standardization curves for the Wechsler Bellevue test of 1939 and the WAIS of 1955. The WAIS scores showed a higher peak, and there was a slight age shift in the ability level, favoring older persons. Wechsler attributes this shift to better sampling, particularly to better control of educational level.

On the basis of his data, Wechsler has also suggested that, with aging, more rapid losses occur on performance-type tests of the WAIS (digit, symbol, picture completion, block design, picture arrangement, and object assembly subtests) than on tests of verbal performance (information, comprehension, arithmetic, similarities, digit span, and vocabulary subtests). Thus, while the ability to manipulate words may seem to hold up moderately well with increasing age, the ability to manipulate symbols on the basis of coordinated perceptual motor skills appears to be somewhat compromised. These data are supported in part by Horn and Cattell [30] and Jones and Conrad [36], using other measures of intelligence in a cross-sectional paradigm.

Jarvik and colleagues [34] performed a nine-year follow-up of subjects past age 60, using the Wechsler Bellevue test, and suggested that intelligence might be stable for the aged across that period. These investigators noted, however, that among persons who died before the end of the nine-year follow-up period, there had been a drop in the similarities and vocabulary subtests, as well as in three of the performance measures.

The writer, in a three- to four-year follow-up study of the Duke longitudinal sample, found no demonstrable decline in a group of subjects aged 60 to 94 and suggested that there was a regression to the mean [17]. This finding has been supported by Rhudick and Gordon [45]. In addition, Eisdorfer and Wilkie [26], in a 10-year follow-up study of the survivors of the original Duke group, found that a group of relatively normal aged persons aged 60 to 69 did not show any systematic intellectual decline over the 10-year period; persons initially evaluated at age 70 to 79 showed intellectual changes, but these were not striking. While it is difficult to evaluate the effects of test repetition, these findings, coupled with the works of others, suggest the need for reappraisal of our concept of a "normal" age-related loss of intellectual function.

The writer, reporting on one of the Berkeley Longitudinal Studies at the Institute on Human Development, noted that mental ability is incremental during adulthood, with an overall increase for both sexes between the ages of 16 and 36, beyond which there is some deceleration [16]. It is interesting to note that the females started out at a higher level but tended to peak by age 26 and subsequently showed only slight improvement in certain subtests (i.e., vocabulary and information). The males continued to improve, achieving equality with the females at age 36. The females past age 36 continued to exceed the males in the vocabulary and information subtests, but the males were superior in arithmetic.

Basing their views on a somewhat different longitudinal approach, Bayley and Oden [5] suggested that intellectual decline in the aging population might be affected by the initial level of intelligence. They contended that brighter persons showed less decline than normal or below-average persons. Owens [39], in a 31-year follow-up study using the Army Alpha score for World War I inductees, found that there was no appreciable difference in the rate of decline between subjects who were initially more mentally able and those who were initially less able. However, his data support the notion that age-related decline is not nearly so dramatic as might have been supposed from Wechsler's [56] curves. Eisdorfer and Service [25] have suggested that persons with a high IQ may have a greater propensity to respond than their average counterparts; this in turn serves to contaminate the interpretation of their test performance. Schaie and Strother [48] studied a stratified random sample of 500 subjects ranging in age from 20 to 70 years and found that, while there were significant age cohort differences cross-sectionally, only performance on the tasks emphasizing speed declined appreciably over time.

A suggestion that emerges from such findings is that age differences in intelligence reported in cross-sectional studies may be a function of a variety of factors that have affected the intelligence of the subject in earlier stages of his development but that may not be consistent from one age group to the next. Numerous variables act on intelligence level: amount of education, recency of education, occupation, character pattern, test responsiveness, familiarity with tests, and a variety of sociological, biological, and health influences that may have affected different age cohorts; e.g., patterns of education in prior years, the possibility of radiation damage or malnutrition in certain groups of children. Schaie's cross-sequential model [47], combining the cross-sectional and the longitudinal methods within the framework of a single design, may give a more valid picture of aging. It seems clear, as he points out, that following a review of the salient research in this field, the members of the American Psychological Association Task Force on Aging [22] proposed that a major portion of the variance attributed to age differences in past cross-sectional studies would be more properly assigned to differences in ability between successive generations.

Health and Intellectual Performance

Botwinick and Birren [11] have reported that among a group of elderly men preselected for good health, those who showed mild and asymptomatic abnormalities performed less well on the WAIS and on a number of other cognitive tasks than did their extremely healthy peers. Birren and Spieth [6] and Spieth [49] have indicated that patients with cardiovascular disease perform poorly on psychomotor and intellectual tasks. In another study, Spieth [50, 51] found that a group of highly intelligent adults who manifested untreated hypertension performed significantly more poorly than did their disease-free peers or a group of medically managed hypertensive patients. The latter did as well as the healthy persons.

In a review of his investigations on decision making in pilots, Szafran [52] reported that cardiac output was related to age and was negatively correlated with speed of decision making, but this was not noticeable until information "overload" was achieved. After this point had been reached, intelligence test performance was significantly impaired among pilots with reduced cardiac output. Short-term memory was particularly affected. Szafran also demonstrated that pilots had greater difficulty in handling information overload material when they showed the early indices of cardiovascular decline. Kedzi and his colleagues [37] found among a group of cardiovascular patients that a significant decrement in performance occurred only when there was a significant history of cardiac failure. Reitan and Shipley [44] showed that reversal of elevated cholesterol levels in the blood could be associated with improved performance on the Halstead-Reitan battery of tests, with this improvement being proportionately greater for the group past the fourth and fifth decades of life.

Apter and colleagues [1], using the Halstead Impairment Index, found that hypertensive persons showed marked signs of organic brain impairment, while Reitan [43] found signs of intellectual impairment on the Rorschach. This writer reported WAIS differences among subjects in the Duke longitudinal project on the basis of cardiovascular functioning [19]. In the Duke sample, Wilkie and Eisdorfer [58] found that hypertensive subjects, as defined by elevated diastolic pressures and associated left ventricular hypertrophy, had lower initial intelligence test scores than did normal or borderline subjects. Perhaps of more striking importance was the finding indicating that diastolic hypertension (105 mm Hg or greater) was associated with a significant decline in the WAIS intelligence test performance over a 10-year period in a group of persons aged 60 to 69. Subjects with mild hypertension showed no such decline, nor did normotensive persons. None of the severe hypertensive subjects first seen at age 70 to 79 survived over the decade of the study, while the normotensive and mildly hypertensive persons who were seen among these older aged did show a decline in functions. The results of the study suggest that, during the 10-year period of the study, intellectual decrement was highly associated with elevated blood pressure levels. The data also support the contention that the intellectual decline among the aged found in many cross-sectional studies may be related to the fact that at older ages more persons with cardiovascular or cerebrovascular disease are included.

The possible influence of genetic factors on intelligence has been a subject of much significance. Even apart from the "nature-nurture" controversy, there have been concerns over the possibility that lifelong patterns of intellectual ability have a genetic loading. The work on identical twins by Blum, Clark, and Jarvik [7] would support this contention, as do the recent indications that women have qualitatively different intellectual and cognitive structures than men [15]. This area, recently reviewed by Jarvik and Cohen [33] and Omenn [38], shows considerable promise in helping understand lifelong patterning of abilities and may be related to the finding that in longitudinal research there may be a positive selection factor, with brighter persons living longer [9, 12, 26, 40]. Whether this is due to higher socioeconomic levels with their concomitant benefits in health, nutrition, and educational and other social supports (measurement error), or whether longevity is in some way related to genetic structure, are questions of far-reaching significance.

Learning

Another approach to the study of cognitive deficits in the aged has been through experimental learning studies. The extensive literature in this area, reaching book-length proportions, has recently been reviewed by Arenberg [3] and Botwinick [9]. Thus a comprehensive review will not be attempted in this chapter, which will instead focus on findings from selected literature.

Serious doubt has been cast on the idea that older persons cannot profit from experience by the work of Canestrari [14], Eisdorfer et al. [23], Hulicka and Weiss [31], Arenberg [2], and others. These studies have also resulted in some new insights into the learning process. Canestrari [14] and Eisdorfer et al. [23], have demonstrated, using the paired associate and the serial rote learning model respectively, that older persons with an average IQ do better at more slowly paced (or self-paced) tasks than in more rapidly paced learning situations. This is reminiscent of Welford's [57] earlier observations that the older worker is less efficient in an assembly line situation than he is at untimed tasks that require a higher degree of craftsmanship. Thus the work of a number of investigators seems to suggest that, with more time available, there is a greater probability that the older person will learn.

Canestrari [14] and Eisdorfer et al. [23] demonstrated that the improvement of learning that resulted when older people were given more time to respond involved an increase in the total number of responses due to their greater willingness to respond. This writer also demonstrated that the time taken by older subjects for making a response was, in fact, short enough so that the response could have been made under the rapidly paced conditions [18]. When the pace was rapid, however, responses were withheld.

In summarizing much of his own work and that of his colleagues, this writer suggested that response inhibition may be a crucial variable in the apparent learning difficulty of older persons [20, 21]. This inhibition of responses, with consequent absence of reinforcement and apparent failure, may be related to a characteristic on the part of older persons that might best be termed *fear of failure*. In a series of investigations this writer and his colleagues found that response inhibition and poor performance among the aged was associated with heightened and persistent autonomic nervous system arousal as measured by plasma free fatty acids, which indicates that the older subjects experienced greater autonomic stress in the learning situation and took longer to recover than did the young [24, 41, 53, 54]. It was further demonstrated that old men responded more and had an improvement in learning at fast pacing when their autonomic arousal levels were pharmacologically reduced using propranolol, a beta-adrenergic blocking agent [24]. Research is continuing in this area, since relatively little is known at this time about the relationship between age-related physiological changes, the older person's reaction to such changes while under stress, and how this in turn might affect performance. Some of the intriguing hypotheses that are being examined include the possibility that poor performance may in part be associated with an apparent dyschrony in activity between the central and autonomic nervous system in old age. Also of interest is the relationship between performance and differential response to arousal by the heart, sweat glands, blood pressure, serum lipid, and so on. As suggested by Frolkis's findings [27, 28], there may also be an age-related increase in organ sensitivity to neurohumoral agents (catecholamines, acetylcholine) that stimulate their activity and thus may affect the older organism's reaction to stress. Attempts are also continuing to find techniques to alter nervous and endocrine activity to modify arousal levels and thus improve performance among the aged.

Response inhibition has also been studied behaviorally in terms of cautiousness. Wallach and Kogan [55] and Botwinick [8] have demonstrated that older people are less prone to risk-taking behavior. This might serve as an appropriate explanation for the failure of older persons to respond in a learning or cognitive task situation. Thus the inhibition on the part of the aged may be seen as a fear of being wrong and, as such, as a fear of failure. The possibility that fear of failure replaces the need to achieve as a motivating force in older persons cannot be ignored. It has dramatic implications for the general behavior patterns of older people. If achievement-oriented motivation characterizes much of middle-class and upper-middle-class behavior in Western society, then it might be expected that in older persons, when positive reinforcement begins to be replaced by negative feedback (e.g., loss of abilities, social change, job displacement by a younger, better-trained person), a shift from a more aggressive to a more defensive posture might result. Thus, in a doubtful situation, the tendency might be to limit the response as a defense against failure rather than to respond in the hope of being successful.

Recent findings of Wilkie and Eisdorfer [59] indicate that aged women perform differently from older men and do not show the same performance deficit during learning. Boyarsky and Eisdorfer [13] reported that forgetting among older women is related to their tendency to associate with too many factors in their environment—an inefficient approach. The value of differential lifelong learning strategies of men and women must also be considered. To the extent that older persons inhibit their responses, they may fail to develop appropriate stimulus-response reinforcers. It seems clear that responsiveness is needed if the appropriate environmental reinforcements are to be obtained that will provide further motivation to continue the learning process. A vicious spiral (involving a change in physiological reactivity to autonomic activation) of withdrawal, negative feedback, and atrophy of function, followed by more withdrawal, might then be postulated. The relationships between initial withdrawal, subsequent withdrawal, and changing physiological conditions are obviously very complex and are currently under study in several laboratories.

Conclusion

An understanding of intellectual and cognitive functioning in aged persons requires as complex an understanding of the array of social, psychological, behavioral, and physiological (including genetic) variables as we pursue among the young. Patterns of response may in large measure be influenced by socially and psychologically mediated interaction with the environment. These in turn may lead to physiological changes that may make the effort of responding to new situations more difficult: It appears to this author that reported declines in intellectual function in advancing age past maturity are based on cross-sectional and cohort-based data. The extent of "normal" intellectual decline among the aged is at this time an open issue. Multifactorial approaches would indicate that even the question will change, becoming "how much of which function"?

However, none of the material presented here should be construed to indicate that there are no age-related changes in intellectual and cognitive functioning. Loss of neuronal tissue, a change in the metabolic rate of the brain, loss of circulatory capacity, and metabolic changes secondary to disease and accumulated stressors all lead to a level of change that is reflected in functioning. The fact remains, however, that we know little about many of these phenomena and how much they would affect behavior in the absence of other complicating social and psychological variables.

References

1. Apter, N. S., Halstead, W. C., and Heimburger, R. F.   Impaired cerebral functions in essential hypertension. *Am. J. Psychiatry* 107:808, 1951.
2. Arenberg, D.   Anticipation interval and age differences in verbal learning. *J. Abnorm. Psychol.* 70:419, 1965.
3. Arenberg, D.   Cognition and Aging: Verbal Learning, Memory, and Problem Solving. In C. Eisdorfer and M. P. Lawton (Eds.), *The Psychology of Adult Development and Aging.* Washington, D.C.: American Psychological Association, 1973. Pp. 74–97.
4. Baltes, P. B., and Labouvie, G. V.   Adult Development of Intellectual Performance: Description, Explanation, and Modification. In C. Eisdorfer and M. P. Lawton (Eds.), *The Psychology of Adult Development and Aging.* Washington, D.C.: American Psychological Association, 1973. Pp. 157–219.
5. Bayley, N., and Oden, M. H.   The maintenance of intellectual ability in gifted adults. *J. Gerontol.* 10:91, 1955.
6. Birren, J. E., and Spieth, W.   Age, response speed, and cardiovascular functions. *J. Gerontol.* 17:390, 1962.
7. Blum, J. E., Clark, E. T., and Jarvik, L. F.   The New York State Psychiatric Institute Study of Aging. In L. F. Jarvik, C. Eisdorfer, and J. E. Blum (Eds.), *Intellectual Functioning in Adults.* New York: Springer, 1973. Pp. 13–20.
8. Botwinick, J.   Cautiousness in advanced age. *J. Gerontol.* 21:347, 1966.
9. Botwinick, J.   *Aging and Behavior.* New York: Springer, 1973.
10. Botwinick, J.   Intellectual Abilities. In J. E. Birren and K. W. Schaie (Eds.), *Handbook of the Psychology of Aging.* New York: Van Nostrand Reinhold, in press.
11. Botwinick, J., and Birren, J. E.   Cognitive Processes: Mental Abilities and Psychomotor Responses in Healthy Aged Men. In J. E. Birren (Ed.), *Human Aging: A Biological and Behavioral Study.* Washington, D.C.: U.S. Government Printing Office, 1963.
12. Botwinick, J., and Storandt, M.   *Memory, Related Functions and Age.* Springfield, Ill.: Thomas, 1974.
13. Boyarsky, R. E., and Eisdorfer, C.   Forgetting in older persons. *J. Gerontol.* 27:254, 1972.
14. Canestrari, R. E.   Paced and self-paced learning in young and elderly adults. *J. Gerontol.* 18:165, 1963.
15. Cohen, D.   *Sex Differences in the Organization of Spatial Abilities in Older Men and Women.* Unpublished doctoral dissertation. University of Southern California, Los Angeles, California, 1975.
16. Eichorn, D. H.   The Institute of Human Development Studies, Berkeley and Oakland. In L. F. Jarvik, C. Eisdorfer, and J. E. Blum (Eds.), *Intellectual Functioning in Adults.* New York: Springer, 1973. Pp. 1–6.

17. Eisdorfer, C.   The WAIS performance of the aged: A retest evaluation. *J. Gerontol.* 18:172, 1963.
18. Eisdorfer, C.   Verbal learning and response time in the aged. *J. Genet. Psychol.* 107:15, 1965.
19. Eisdorfer, C.   Psychologic reaction to cardiovascular change in the aged. *Mayo Clin. Proc.* 42:620, 1967.
20. Eisdorfer, C.   Learning in the aged; New dimensions and a tentative theory. *Gerontologist* 7:14, 1967.
21. Eisdorfer, C.   Discussion of "Age Differences in Verbal Learning and Verbal Behavior," by R. E. Canestrari. In K. Riegel (Ed.), *Interdisciplinary Topics in Gerontology,* Vol. I. New York: Karger, 1968.
22. Eisdorfer, C.   Experimental Studies. In C. Eisdorfer and M. P. Lawton (Eds.), *The Psychology of Adult Development and Aging.* Washington, D.C.: American Psychological Association, 1973. Pp. 71–73.
23. Eisdorfer, C., Axelrod, S., and Wilkie, F.   Stimulus exposure time as a factor in serial learning in an aged sample. *J. Abnorm. Psychol.* 67:594, 1963.
24. Eisdorfer, C., Nowlin, J., and Wilkie, F.   Improvement of learning in the aged by modification of autonomic nervous system activity. *Science* 170:1327, 1970.
25. Eisdorfer, C., and Service, C.   Verbal rote learning and superior intelligence in the aged. *J. Gerontol.* 22:158, 1967.
26. Eisdorfer, C., and Wilkie, F.   Intellectual Changes with Advancing Age. In L. F. Jarvik, C. Eisdorfer, and J. E. Blum (Eds.), *Intellectual Functioning in Adults.* New York: Springer, 1973. Pp. 21–29.
27. Frolkis, V. V.   Neuro-humoral regulations in the aging organism. *J. Gerontol.* 21:161, 1966.
28. Frolkis, V. V.   Autonomic Nervous System and Aging. In J. E. Birren and K. W. Schaie (Eds.), *The Handbook of the Psychology of Aging.* New York: Van Nostrand Reinhold, in press.
29. Horn, J. L., and Cattell, R. B.   Age differences in primary mental ability factors. *J. Gerontol.* 21:210, 1966.
30. Horn, J. L., and Cattell, R. B.   Age differences in fluid and crystallized intelligence. *Acta Psychol.* (Amst.) 26:107, 1967.
31. Hulicka, I. M., and Weiss, R. L.   Age differences in retention as a function of learning. *J. Consult. Clin. Psychol.* 29:125, 1965.
32. Hunt, J. McV.   *Intelligence and Experience.* New York: Ronald, 1961.
33. Jarvik, L. F., and Cohen, D.   A Biobehavioral Approach to Intellectual Changes with Aging. In C. Eisdorfer and M. P. Lawton (Eds.), *The Psychology of Adult Development and Aging.* Washington, D.C.: American Psychological Association, 1973. Pp. 220–280.
34. Jarvik, L. F., Kallman, F. J., and Falek, A.   Intellectual changes in aged twins. *J. Gerontol.* 17:289, 1962.
35. Jones, H. E.   Intelligence and Problem-Solving. In J. E. Birren (Ed.), *Handbook of Aging and the Individual: Psychological and Biological Aspects.* Chicago: University of Chicago Press, 1959. Pp. 700–738.
36. Jones, H. E., and Conrad, H. S.   The growth and decline of intelli-

gence: A study of a homogeneous population between the ages of ten and sixty. *Genet. Psychol. Monogr.* 13:233, 1933.

37. Kedzi, P., et al. The impact of chronic circulatory impairment on functioning of central nervous system. *Ann. Intern. Med.* 62:67, 1965.

38. Omenn, G. Behavior Genetics. In J. E. Birren and K. W. Schaie (Eds.), *The Handbook of the Psychology of Aging*. New York: Van Nostrand Reinhold, in press.

39. Owens, W. A. Is age kinder to the initially more able? *International Symposium on Medical-Social Aspects of Senile Nervous Diseases*, Venice, Italy, July 1957. Pp. 20–21.

40. Pfeiffer, E. Survival in old age. *J. Am. Geriatr. Soc.* 18(4):273, 1970.

41. Powell, A. H., Eisdorfer, C., and Bogdonoff, M. D. Physiologic response patterns observed in a learning task. *Arch. Gen. Psychiatry* 10: 192, 1964.

42. Pressy, S. L. Viewpoint: Not all decline. *Gerontologist* 6:66, 1966.

43. Reitan, R. M. Intellectual and affective changes in essential hypertension. *Am. J. Psychiatry* 110:817, 1954.

44. Reitan, R. M., and Shipley, R. E. The relationship of serum cholesterol changes to psychological abilities. *J. Gerontol.* 18:350, 1963.

45. Rhudick, P. J., and Gordon, C. The Age Center of New England Study. In L. F. Jarvik, C. Eisdorfer, and J. E. Blum (Eds.), *Intellectual Functioning in Adults*. New York: Springer, 1973. Pp. 7–12.

46. Rosenfelt, R. H., Kastenbaum, R., and Kempler, B. The untestables: Methodological problems in drug research with the aged. *Gerontologist* 4:72, 1964.

47. Schaie, K. W. A general model for the study of developmental problems. *Psychol. Bull.* 64:92, 1965.

48. Schaie, K. W., and Strother, C. R. The effects of time and cohort differences on the interpretation of age changes in cognitive behavior. *Multivariate Behav. Res.* 3:259, 1968.

49. Spieth, W. Abnormally slow perceptual motor task performance in individuals with stable mild to moderate heart disease. *Aerosp. Med.* 33: 370, 1962.

50. Spieth, W. Cardiovascular health status, age, and psychological performance. *J. Gerontol.* 19:277, 1964.

51. Spieth, W. Slowness of Task Performance and Cardiovascular Disease. In A. T. Welford and J. E. Birren (Eds.), *Behavior, Aging, and the Nervous System*. Springfield, Ill.: Thomas, 1965. Pp. 366–400.

52. Szafran, J. Psychophysiological Studies of Aging in Pilots. In G. A. Talland (Ed.), *Human Aging and Behavior*. New York: Academic, 1968. Pp. 37–74.

53. Troyer, W. G., et al. Experimental stress and learning in the aged. *J. Abnorm. Psychol.* 72:65, 1967.

54. Troyer, W. G., et al. Free fatty acid responses in the aged individual during performance of learning tasks. *J. Gerontol.* 21:415, 1966.

55. Wallach, M. A., and Kogan, N. *Modes of Thinking in Young Children.* New York: Holt, Rinehart and Winston, 1965.

56. Wechsler, D. *The Measurement and Appraisal of Adult Intelligence* (4th ed.). Baltimore: Williams & Wilkins, 1958.
57. Welford, A. T. *Skill and Age*. London: Oxford University Press, 1951.
58. Wilkie, F., and Eisdorfer, C. Intelligence and blood pressure in the aged. *Science* 172:959, 1971.
59. Wilkie, F., and Eisdorfer, C. Verbal learning performance among old men and women. *J. Gerontol.,* in press.

12. The Brain and Time

F. Stephen Vogel

All somatic cells have a finite life span. The death of most is partially offset by cellular proliferation; but some, notably the neurons, are incapable of division and cannot be replaced. With the passage of time, flaws develop in cellular metabolism and deficiencies occur in cellular turnover that ultimately lead to impaired function and compromised metabolic potential. To the biologist, this is aging. These same phenomena, however, can be viewed as disease. Thus it is not always possible to distinguish between aging and disease; indeed, to make this distinction is often analogous to drawing a line so fine as to have direction but no width.

These biological events occur in time, and thus time is a constituent of all living systems. It is convenient to employ time as a quantitative index or marker of age. But time is not the sole essence of aging, for the aging phenomenon can be accelerated or delayed. Neither aging nor death results from the burden of time alone.

It is the aim of this chapter to identify those biological characteristics of the nervous system that render it prone to irreversible functional and structural decrements, for herein lies its vulnerability to aging. The same characteristics also enhance its susceptibility to disease. Therefore one must approach the difficult task of characterizing aging per se more with concepts than facts—indeed, often deriving these concepts from disease states.

Neural Development

There are several important biological principles that prevail during embryonic development and impart characteristics to the adult brain that bear on the problem of aging. This early stage of neural development is dynamic and is characterized by sequences of structural events that occur in strict chronological order. For example, both the neurons and the glia take origin from a common population of primitive cells. These stem cells occupy the subependymal region about the lateral ventricles in the cerebral hemispheres as well as in the margins of the central canal of the spinal cord. This subependymal region, termed the *germinal mantle,* is truly the breeding ground of the embryonic nervous system [22]. It is here—and only here—during embryonic development that neurons divide. As the neurons differentiate and migrate into the cortex, they acquire certain advantageous functional properties, notably stability of structure and longevity. But at the same time they relinquish a cardinal attribute of other somatic cells: the potential for self-replication. This characteristic is germane to most neurological disorders, and in it is inherent the progressive loss of function that accompanies the neuronal depopulation of the central nervous system. Independent of disease, this loss invariably occurs with time and is therefore a concomitant of age. In addition, neurons experience conditions that are adverse to their metabolism, and these experiences unquestionably hasten depopulation and initiate disease.

Thus any adverse situation, whether it be inborn or an abuse arising out of the environment, such as anoxia or physical injury, can have but one quantitative or numerical influence on the nerve cells. Adverse experiences alter neuronal metabolism, impair function, and potentially hasten cell death. This depopulation of cells occurs at different rates in different individuals, but it is an inescapable phenomenon, which reaches a significant magnitude in the aged brain. The inability of neurons to compensate for this depopulation by replication stands in sharp contrast to other somatic cells; for example, partial hepatectomy is followed promptly by a regeneration of liver mass and a reestablishment of hepatic function; unilateral nephrectomy, when performed early in life, initiates hypertrophy and hyperplasia of the contralateral kidney—again with a restoration of tissue mass and function.

The glial cells, similar to the neurons, are on a well-established timetable of differentiation and cytological activity. They, like neurons, take origin from primitive stem cells in the germinal mantle of the subependymal region, and, as undifferentiated glia, they migrate outward into the white matter during the latter phase of embryonic development and also throughout the first several years of postnatal life [15]. It is the mission of some of these cells, now in the white matter, to participate in a major fashion in myelinogenesis. A structural change occurs in these cells after myelinization is completed. They lose cytoplasm and assume the morphological characteristic of the oligodendroglia. Sibling cells that have not participated in myelinogenesis mature into astrocytes. The oligodendroglia maintain a close anatomical relationship to the myelin sheath and contribute in an unending fashion to the metabolic integrity of these lipid-protein membranes. However, cell maturation has again extracted a decrement in functional capacity, for it is clear that in the adult nervous system oligodendroglia cannot remyelinate to any significant degree. Thus, as the neurons have lost the propensity for mitotic division with differentiation, so, too, the glial cells have lost the capacity for remyelinization.

This is seemingly the price of cell maturation. The phenomenon, as evidenced in the human being, may not be fully manifested in lower animals, for it was demonstrated by Bunge et al. [2] that under very select experimental conditions the glial cells of the spinal cord in the cat can reassume the morphology of primitive glia and can then reconstitute myelin. The precise role of myelin as a contributor to neuronal function is not clear. There is much evidence to indicate that with myelinization the conduction speed through the axon cylinder is accelerated and, in accord, disturbed neuronal function is common to the demyelinating states. Although myelin is clearly sensitive to ischemia, as well as to the many chemical and physical insults that occur throughout life, it has not been possible to equate the waning capacities of the aged brain to structural or functional alterations in these lipid-protein membranes.

Since the peripheral and central nervous systems take origin together from the neural tube and neural crest, the differences in the biological properties of these two portions of the nervous system are of particular interest [10]. For example, wallerian degeneration in the peripheral nervous system is a two-phase phenomenon wherein the axon beyond a point of severe compression first degenerates and then, in the second phase, regenerates as an outgrowth from the cell body and is subsequently remyelinated by Schwann's cells [1]. There is overwhelming evidence to indicate that the neurons in the adult human central nervous system, by contrast, do not manifest the capacity for axon regeneration of any significant degree. A biological limitation has been imposed on these central neurons. Thus a patient with an infarct in the internal capsule does not bridge the defect by regrowth of pyramidal fibers, no matter how slender the line of transection. This is a severe penalty that the host has paid to gain a system of cells with a high degree of structural stability.

The price has not been paid, however, without benefit. For perhaps the most important single feature of the nervous system is the establishment of a complex network of synapses. By these anatomical connections, the central nervous system becomes a confederation of functional units, a concert of activity. The integration acquired through synapses is germane to high cortical function, that is, to intelligence. Synapses are established during the latter period of embryonic life and throughout the first year or so of the postnatal period. It is likely that disturbances in their formation and in their function accompany many metabolic disorders that are manifested as mental retardation. Phenylketonuria exemplifies this type of disorder [4, 8]. Perhaps a less complex example is cretinism. In this condition, until birth, the development of the central nervous system proceeds in a proper manner, since maternal thyroxine is supplied across the placenta. However, during the first year of life, when this hormone becomes deficient, the nervous system does not acquire more than a fraction of its functional potential. Generally, in cretinism, the neurons are normal in number, appearance, and architectonics. However, there is reason to suspect that the development of dendritic processes and synapses is faulty. When these concepts are applied to the other extreme of life, they spawn curiosity about the possible attrition of these delicate dendritic processes and the potential role of their loss in the decrement of cortical function that accompanies aging.

Thus the normal evolution of cortical development and function is dependent in part on factors outside the brain; in the case of cretinism, on thyroxine. Clearly, many metabolites need to reach the central nervous system in an unending flow. This establishes a critical dependency on the integrity of the circulation. Thus, abnormal angiogenesis can lead to severe structural and functional abnormalities. Since this dependency persists throughout life, it is not surprising that cerebrovascular occlusive disorders such as atherosclerosis manifest themselves in cerebral dysfunction. With the advancement of age, they can cut deeper and deeper inroads into the metabolic reserves of neural tissue. A point of no return is reached when the sensitive structures of the nervous system, the neurons and the myelin sheaths, undergo ischemic necrosis. Neither structure nor function is regained. Irreversible vascular problems are frequent in the aged. Indeed, cerebral atherosclerosis has traditionally been a hallmark of this segment of our population. But it must be emphasized that statistically vascular occlusive disorders are by no means the principal cause of dementia [5, 11, 17, 20, 21].

Neuronal Depopulation

The fact seems inescapable that with the passage of time, the accumulation of intraneuronal metabolic errors will diminish the ability of a neuron to survive. The events are individual to each cell. As evidenced by the rate of neuronal depopulation, they reach an end point earlier in cortical neurons than in those of the brain stem or spinal cord. However, the phenomenon is so ubiquitous as to be shared even by the honey bee [16], in which it is most certainly independent of atherosclerosis. It has been estimated that the human central nervous system at age 30 contains approximately 20 billion neurons and that a decrement of about 0.8 percent per year occurs thereafter. Is there a cause and effect relationship between the state of the vasculature and this decrement in neurons? During their transition from embryonic to adult form, nerve cells lose the capability for anaerobic glycolysis; thus they are rendered critically sensitive to anoxia. The phenomenon of neuronal depopulation is unquestionably accelerated by occlusive vascular disease. Cortical atrophy, the gross index of neuronal depopulation, accompanies disorders that affect the cerebral arterioles and capillaries but is not well correlated with obstruction of the major cerebral vessels as by cerebral atherosclerosis [5, 7, 11, 17, 20]. One might logically conclude that the depopulation of neurons is accelerated by occlusive vascular disease but proceeds quite independently of this disorder, and therefore, the "aged brain" is not synonymous with cerebral atherosclerosis.

While the importance of the cerebral circulation to the survival of cortical neurons cannot be denied, other factors are also worthy of consideration. It is a truism that longevity comes to him who carefully selects his ancestors. This is to say that we are physical and functional expressions of our deoxyribonucleic acid (DNA). Clearly, the human species is far from homogeneous in this constituent, since no two individuals are endowed with the same genetic information nor, for this reason, with the same biological potential. One concept suggests that all biological systems are driven as by a mainspring (DNA), which is wound at birth and thus energizes life and establishes its timetable. Such a concept would suggest that longevity is predetermined solely by inherent genetic characteristics. However, it would be unrealistic to forget that the human organism exists in a generally adverse ecology to which neurons are responsive, and that the effects of the ecology are generally detrimental.

In this light, the term *abiotrophy* holds interesting connotations [6]. The concept is best exemplified by Huntington's chorea. This disorder is clearly the result of an inborn genetic error present at birth but generally not manifested by dysfunction until the early adult period. The nerve cells, specifically those of the caudate nuclei and cortex, are of particular interest here, since these are the target of this disease. They may function properly for many years but then degenerate precociously at a disproportionately rapid rate as compared with neurons elsewhere in the same nervous system. An analogy might be drawn between this human biological event and the tree on which an individual branch has died, quite independent of the vigor of the remaining limbs. The genetic background of Huntington's chorea singles out DNA as the prime offender. The pathogenesis has been conceptualized as an exhaustion or depletion of intracellular metabolism occurring insidiously over many years. Thus it is tempting to propose that the structural integrity and the longevity of neurons are dependent in major fashion on the quality of their DNA.

A further documentation of the importance of this constituent to the cell, both functionally and structurally, is to be found in Down's syndrome, in which the disturbance in chromosomal composition is so gross as to be clearly visualized in the abnormal karyotype. Examination of the central nervous system of youthful patients with Down's syndrome rarely discloses cytological abnormalities, although the brain is generally smaller than normal [3]. However, germane to the problem of aging is a phenomenon that occurs with absolute regularity and with notable precociousness in Down's syndrome. Neurofibrillary degeneration, senile plaques, and granulovacuolar degeneration regularly make their appearance before age 35 [3, 9]. The lesions are identical to those that characterize Alzheimer's disease, an entity that occurs rarely in the general population. Alzheimer's disease is most frequent after the age of 50 and by definition occurs before age 65. Identical lesions appear in the general population with increasing incidence as the years accumulate beyond 65, but confusingly, the term *Alzheimer's disease* is no longer applicable; instead, the term *senile dementia* is now employed. Clearly, the morphological triad is precisely the same in all three instances, that is, in Down's syndrome, Alzheimer's disease, and senile dementia. This

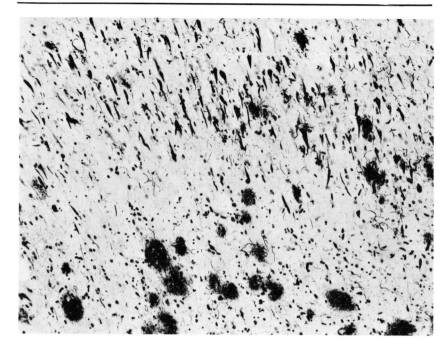

Figure 1. The cerebral cortex of the frontal lobe of a 55-year-old patient with Down's syndrome. Advanced neurofibrillary degeneration has caused most neurons to be strongly argentophilic. In addition, there are numerous senile plaques in various stages of development. (King stain, × 100)

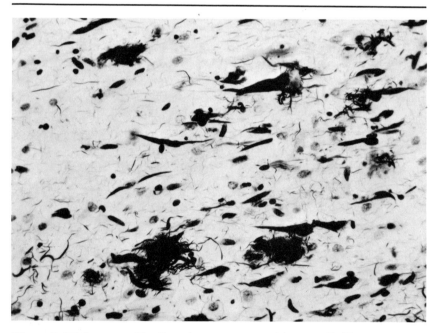

Figure 2. Higher magnification shows neurons with neurofibrillary degeneration and several senile plaques. The senile plaques are composed of a tangle of neuritic processes. Appropriate stains would disclose amyloid, mucopolysaccharide, and glycoproteins within the core of most plaques. (King stain, × 250)

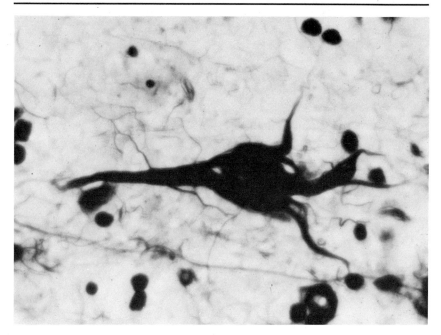

Figure 3. A neuron with advanced neurofibrillary degeneration. (King stain, × 1,000)

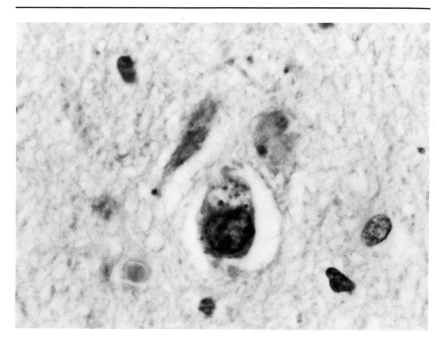

Figure 4. Granulovacuolar degeneration is characterized by a vacuolated appearance of the cytoplasm and by dense particulate granules within the individual vacuoles. The triad of neurofibrillary degeneration, senile plaque, and granulovacuolar degeneration characterizes Alzheimer's disease and senile dementia. They are precocious features in the central nervous system in patients with Down's syndrome. (Luxol fast blue stain, × 1,000)

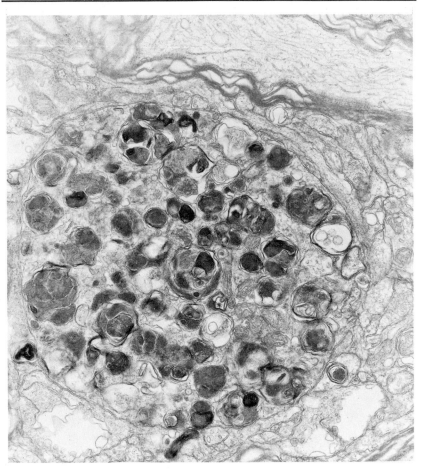

Figure 5. The senile plaque arises in foci that contain closely approximated neurites distended with autophagic vacuoles and abnormal neurofibrils. (Fixed in glutaraldehyde-osmic acid, × 1,700 before 20% reduction)

pathological state constitutes the major cause of dementia [3, 5, 7, 11, 17, 20, 21]. The absence of neurofibrillary tangles, senile plaques, and granulovacuolar degeneration in some persons who have lived well beyond three score and ten years suggests that all central nervous systems are not created alike.

Regularly, the mature senile plaque is structured with a central core of amyloid, with a content of mucopolysaccharides and glycoproteins and with a background structure of abnormal neurites and glial processes [13] (Figs. 1–4). Electron-microscopic observations suggest that the senile plaque takes origin in loci where adjacent neurites show stagnant accumulations of autophagic vacuoles, vesicles, and abnormal neurofibrils [19] (Fig. 5). Is senile dementia, then, a disease or a phenomenon of aging? The pathologist would relegate it to the large category of diseases that increase in incidence through the decades of life.

Inevitably, with the passage of time, lipofuscin pigment accumulates in nerve cells, but at various rates in neurons in different anatomical locations in the brain and spinal cord [14]. This lipoid material is contained within lysosomes. Normally, the lytic enzymes of this organelle degradate this cellular waste and permit it to be reutilized by the cell. The neuron, unlike many cells, is not capable of excretion; thus it either recycles its waste or tolerates its accumulation. It seems unlikely that the physical presence of lipofuscin interferes appreciably with cellular function. However, the accumulation is visible evidence of an imperfection in metabolism, an abatement in metabolic vigor, an index of metabolic senescence. This is aging, essentially without disease.

It is readily apparent that the mechanisms of aging and the distinction between aging and disease are poorly understood. Perhaps, then, we should seek simple information from the lowly planarian. This flatworm is capable, after bisection, of regenerating either a head or a hind part from the respective counterpart. The lesson is embodied in the phenomenon that the life span of the planarian caused to regenerate a new head from a hind part is significantly longer than that of its half-brother, which has regenerated a hind part from a normal head [18]. Thus we are informed that the brain is an impediment to longevity.

References

1. Barton, A. A.   An electron microscopic study of degeneration and regeneration of nerve. *Brain* 85:799, 1962.
2. Bunge, M. B., Bunge, R. T., and Ris, H.   Ultrastructural study of remyelinization in an experimental lesion in adult cat spinal cord. *J. Biophys. Biochem. Cytol.* 10:67, 1961.
3. Burger, P. C., and Vogel, F. S.   The development of the pathologic changes of Alzheimer's disease and senile dementia in patients with Down's syndrome. *Am. J. Pathol.* 73:457, 1973.
4. Chrome, L., and Pare, G. M. B.   Phenylketonuria. A review and report of the pathological findings in four cases. *J. Ment. Sci.* 106:862, 1960.
5. Fisher, C. M.   Dementia and cerebral vascular disease. Dementia in Cerebral Vascular Disease, Sixth Conference on Cerebral Vascular Disease, Princeton, N.J., 1968.
6. Gowers, W. R.   A lecture on abiotrophy. *Lancet* 1:1003, 1902.
7. Hackinski, V. C., Lassen, N. A., and Marshall, J.   Multi-infarct dementia. *Lancet* 2:207, 1974.
8. Jervis, G. A.   Phenylpyruvic oligophrenia. *Arch. Neurol. Psychiatry* 38:944, 1937.
9. Jervis, G. A.   Early senile dementia in mongoloid idiocy. *Am. J. Psychiatry* 105:102, 1948.
10. Johnston, M. C.   A radioautographic study of the migration and fate of cranial neural crest cells in the chick embryo. *Anat. Rec.* 156:143, 1966.
11. Kay, D. W. K., Beamish, P., and Roth, M.   Old age mental disorders in Newcastle upon Tyne. *Br. J. Psychiatry* 110:146, 1964.
12. Mandybur, T. I.   The incidence of cerebral amyloid angiopathy in Alzheimer's disease. *Neurology* 25:120, 1975.
13. Margolis, G.   Observations on senile cerebral deposits using the periodic acid-Schiff's technique. *Am. J. Pathol.* 29:588, 1953.
14. Morrison, L. R. (Ed.).   *Effects of Advancing Age Upon the Human Spinal Cord*. Cambridge, Mass.: Harvard University Press, 1959.
15. Roback, H. U., and Scherer, H. J.   Über die feinere Morphologie des frühkindlichen Gehirns unter besonderer Berücksichtigung der Gliaentwicklung. *Virchows Arch. Pathol. Anat.* 294:365, 1935.
16. Rockstein, M.   The relation of cholinesterase activity to change in cell number with age in the brain of the adult worker honeybee. *J. Cell. Comp. Physiol.* 35:1023, 1950.
17. Roth, M.   Classification and Etiology in Mental Disorders of Old Age: Some Recent Developments. In D. W. K. Kay and A. Walk (Eds.), *Recent Developments in Psychogeriatrics*. Ashford, Kent, England: Headley Brothers, 1971.
18. Sonneborn, T. M.   Genetic studies on *Stenostomum incaudatum*. The nature and origin of differences among individuals formed during vegetative reproduction. *J. Exp. Zool.* 57:57, 1930.
19. Terry, R. D.   The fine structure of neurofibrillary tangles in Alzheimer's disease. *J. Neuropath. Exp. Neurol.* 22:629, 1963.

239

20. Tomlinson, B. E., Blessed, G., and Roth, M.   Observations on the brain of demented old people. *J. Neurol. Sci.* 11:205, 1970.
21. Wells, C. E. (Ed.).   *Dementia.* Contemporary Neurology Series. Philadelphia: Davis, 1971.
22. Yakovlev, P. I.   Pathoarchitectonic studies of cerebral malformations. *J. Neuropath. Exp. Neurol.* 28:22, 1959.

13. Organic Brain Syndromes
Conceptual and Practical Issues

H. -S. Wang

The *Diagnostic and Statistical Manual of Mental Disorders,* published by the American Psychiatric Association, defines organic brain syndrome as a "basic mental condition characteristically resulting from diffuse impairment of brain tissue function from whatever cause" [2]. Although such brain syndromes are known to be very common among old persons, much remains to be learned about the exact dimensions of the clinical problem they present. We do not know just how prevalent they are, and our methods of diagnosing and treating them are far from satisfactory.

Prevalence of Organic Brain Syndromes in Old Age

The fragmentary information that we have concerning the prevalence of organic brain syndromes among the elderly is based largely on statistical data derived from psychiatric hospitals, both public and private [54, 55]. It has been estimated that the number of resident patients in all psychiatric hospitals in the United States at the end of the year 1966 totaled 466,147. During that year, 214,493 patients were admitted to a psychiatric facility for the first time. The proportion of persons 65 years of age or over was 29.5 percent among the resident patients and 16.8 percent among the first admissions (Table 15). It is calculated, according to the estimated population for that year [51], that the incidence of psychiatric disorders requiring psychiatric hospitalization was 941 per 100,000 among the elderly population, or 3.3 times higher than the rate of 284 per 100,000 for those under 65 years old.

The diagnosis made most commonly in these elderly patients was organic brain syndrome. Among the 35,964 geriatric patients admitted to a psychiatric institution for the first time, 77.7 percent were given this diagnosis (Table 16). In contrast, only 47.6 percent of the 137,653 elderly patients already in residence had this diagnosis. The incidence of functional psychoses was only 7.8 percent among the first admissions, as compared with 44.6 percent among the resident patients. This difference was probably due in large part to the fact that many of the resident patients were initially hospitalized with functional psychoses and had grown old in the institution. It is probable that the incidence of organic brain syndrome in these resident patients was underestimated.

In 1964 a survey was made on the prevalence of chronic conditions and impairments among residents of nursing and personal-care homes

240

Table 15. Estimated Number of Patients Living in or Admitted to Psychiatric Hospitals in the United States during 1966

Age	Patients in Residence			First Admissions			Total	Rate*
	Public	Private	Subtotal	Public	Private	Subtotal		
Under 65	317,379	11,115	328,494	131,715	46,814	178,529	507,023	284.2
65 and over	134,710	2,943	137,653	30,771	5,193	35,964	173,617	940.7
Total	452,089	14,058	466,147	162,486	52,007	214,493	680,640	345.8

* Per 100,000 population of corresponding age group.
Source: U.S. National Institute of Mental Health [54, 55].

Table 16. Diagnoses Made in Persons Age 65 and Over Living in or Admitted to Psychiatric Hospitals in the United States in 1966

Diagnoses	Resident Patients	First Ad- missions	Total	Percent	Rate*
Organic brain syndromes	65,449	27,935	93,384	53.8	506.00
Psychoses	61,779	2,793	64,572	37.2	349.90
Neuroses	1,655	1,932	3,587	2.1	19.40
Personality disorders	1,172	962	2,134	1.2	11.60
Psychophysiological disorders	60	19	79	0.1	0.42
Transient situational disturbances	187	227	414	0.2	2.20
Others	7,351	2,096	9,447	5.4	51.20
Subtotal	137,653	35,964	173,617	100.0	940.72

* Per 100,000 elderly population (65 years or over).
Source: U.S. National Institute of Mental Health [54, 55].

in the United States. Of the total number of residents in these homes (estimated at 554,000), 88 percent (487,800) were over 64 [52]. Brain disorders were extremely common among these geriatric residents: 36.0 percent were considered to have vascular lesions affecting the central nervous system and 29.7 percent to have a disorder attributable to senility.

Many old persons with organic brain syndromes are admitted to the psychiatric services of general hospitals or to various types of psychiatric outpatient facilities. According to reports from 650 general hospitals (out of a total of 888 known institutions of this type), 11.7 percent of all psychiatric patients discharged from these hospitals were over 64 [55]. In 46.5 percent of these elderly patients, the discharge diagnosis was an organic brain syndrome; in another 15.4 percent, it was functional psychosis. Only 2 percent of the patients seen in psychiatric outpatient clinics were over 64 [53]. Among all elderly patients discharged from such clinics, a diagnosis of organic brain syndromes was made in 43.9 percent and a diagnosis of functional psychosis in 22.3 percent.

With few exceptions, patients discharged from the psychiatric service of a general hospital or from a psychiatric outpatient clinic can be considered as belonging to one of two possible categories: (1) those having mild or temporary disorders who will probably remain in the community and lead a relatively normal life; (2) those with more chronic and severe disorders who will likely be admitted to one of the institutions that provide long-term and intensive care. Admission to a psychiatric hospital or a facility that provides nursing or personal care usually indicates that the condition of the patient is such that he is no longer capable of leading an independent life or of being cared for in the average family or the average community. When the data from psychiatric hospitals are combined with those from nursing and personal-care homes, it appears that approximately 3,700 out of every 100,000 old persons in the population require such institutional care. Of these geriatric patients, 62.6 percent had organic brain syndromes or conditions in which such brain syndromes are almost invariably present. This percentage suggests that the rate of organic brain syndromes of moderate to severe degree among the elderly population is at least 2,300 per 100,000.

The reliability of this estimate is obviously questionable, since the data from which it is derived were collected through different procedures from diverse sources and were based on a variety of criteria evaluated by persons of diverse training and experience. Another factor that tends to obscure the true incidence of organic brain syndromes is the lack of objective, reliable, and practical means for routine evaluation of cerebral status.

Organic brain syndromes are also prevalent among noninstitutionalized elderly persons. In a survey of a randomized representative sample of residents aged 65 and over in a community, using a mental status questionnaire, Pfeiffer [41] found that about 4 percent of his noninstitutionalized elderly subjects showed moderate to severe mental impairment that warranted the diagnosis of organic brain syndrome. This figure is consistent with those of several epidemiological studies reported in the literature [40].

Concept of Organic Brain Syndromes

Any impairment of the brain tissue is usually accompanied by impairment of the cognitive functions that are directly dependent on the activity of the brain tissue involved. *Disorientation, memory loss,* and *im-*

pairment of intellectual function and *judgment* are therefore considered the primary characteristics of organic brain syndromes [2]. These symptoms may be the only manifestations present, or they may be accompanied by behavioral disturbances or psychotic symptoms that may or may not be related to the brain impairment. When several or all of the primary characteristics of an organic brain syndrome are present, this is the diagnosis usually made, regardless of the presence of other behavioral or psychotic symptoms.

Traditionally, organic brain syndromes are further classified according to their underlying etiology [2]. When the syndrome is temporary, it is called *acute,* and the underlying brain disorder is assumed to be reversible. When the syndrome is permanent, it is called *chronic,* and the underlying brain damage is considered irreversible. This concept of organic brain syndromes clearly reflects the current tendency in psychiatry to divide mental disorders into *organic* and *functional* (or psychogenic) categories. The current diagnostic approach, in fact, overemphasizes the role of the organic factor, while it neglects environmental factors and the patient's underlying personality. The diagnosis of organic brain syndrome implies an understanding of the structural or functional status of the brain and its relationship to clinical manifestations (whether cognitive impairment, behavioral disturbance, or psychotic symptoms). Actually, we have very few reliable means for evaluating the brain in vivo. Most of those available are traumatic, involve considerable risk, and hence are usually reserved for highly selected cases. The clinical diagnosis is usually based on observation and interpretation of the patient's behaviors and responses, both verbal and nonverbal, during an interview or during some simple test designed to reveal the presence of the primary characteristics of an organic brain syndrome. When the brain is moderately or severely impaired, the detection of such characteristics is not too difficult. At this late stage, however, the probability that any therapeutic intervention will be effective is remote.

The prevalence of a fatalistic attitude among psychiatrists working with old persons can, to a great extent, be attributed to the organicistic orientation of the current diagnostic approach, combined with the lack of effective treatment for organic brain syndromes. Consequently, the emphasis has been on the differential diagnosis of organic and functional disorders.

It is well established that the brain undergoes considerable alterations during senescence (see Chap. 12). The structural changes include a loss of neurons and other tissue and an increase in the number of senile plaques and amount of neurofibrillary degeneration. Functionally, there is a reduction in the metabolic activity of the brain tissue involved. Some of these changes are probably associated with chronological aging; others are due to pathological processes in the brain or elsewhere in the body.

The relationship between the status of the brain and the clinical manifestation of organic brain syndromes has long been a matter of controversy. A review of the literature indicates that the cognitive functions of old persons do depend, though not consistently, on the structural and functional status of the brain [56]. It is well known, however, that many variables other than age (sex, race, socioeconomic background, and education, for example) can affect the cognitive function and its assessment [6]. The same variables can also affect such measurements of cerebral activity as the electroencephalogram (EEG) [58]. A relationship between cerebral status and cognitive function is more likely to be demonstrable in elderly people with various brain disorders than in those whose health is good and who show little evidence of mental deterioration. In the latter group, such a relationship can be demonstrated clearly only by controlling the sociocultural factors known to affect the assessment of these parameters and by employing methods that assess a specific psychological or physiological function of one particular region of the brain [61].

The discrepancies observed between brain status and cognitive function, and between these two parameters and the clinical symptoms, suggest that other factors, too, may be involved in determining how well an old person can function or adjust in a particular setting [9, 59].

The adjustment of a person, whether young or old, to a particular environment, can be viewed as the outcome of the ego's functioning—its capability and efficiency in meeting demands from the id or superego in coping with environmental situations and in resolving conflicts that arise from all these demands. Cerebral impairment inevitably has an adverse effect on many functions of the ego (perception, comprehension, learning, reality testing, and the like). The ability of the impaired ego to carry out its functions is, however, relative rather than absolute, being dependent on the types of defensive mechanisms that are available on the one hand, and on the intensity and the nature of the environmental stresses or intrapsychic demands or conflicts on the other hand. Consider, for example, two elderly persons with the same quantity and quality of brain impairment or cognitive deficit—one, a 60-year-old man, compulsive and competitive, who is still active in his business; the other, an easygoing, self-satisfied man of 80 who is retired. The clinical manifestations—that is, the degree of difficulty manifested by these two men in adjusting to their environment and in coping with the problems of their situation—will be quite different.

Evaluation of Elderly Patients with Symptoms
Suggesting an Organic Brain Syndrome

Few, if any, of the psychiatric disorders in old age can be viewed as either exclusively organic or exclusively psychogenic. Even the so-called organic brain syndromes should be regarded as *sociopsychosomatic* in origin, although it is true that one or more components may be more conspicuous in some disorders than in others. Any old person with any psychiatric disorder, particularly if it is of recent onset, should be thoroughly evaluated with respect to the following:

1. Psychological factors (personality traits, defense mechanisms, intrapsychic conflicts).
2. Environmental factors (interpersonal and family relationships, socioeconomic factors).
3. Somatic factors, both cerebral and extracerebral.

The social and psychological evaluations have always been emphasized in the management of patients of all ages with so-called functional or psychogenic psychiatric disorders. These evaluations are equally as important for old persons with varying degrees of brain impairment and will depend on the same standard clinical approaches: interviews, examinations to determine the patient's mental status, social history, and psychological tests. Some of the social and psychological problems commonly associated with old age, as well as their evaluation and treatment, are discussed in other chapters in this book. In the present chapter, some of the methods available for evaluating the status of the brain and some considerations in treating persons with brain impairment will be discussed.

Evaluating the Status of the Brain

Evaluation of Behavioral Manifestations

Although clinical neuropsychiatric examinations have long been the standard procedure for evaluating the behavioral manifestations of cerebral status, the reliability and sensitivity of this approach are open to question. With relatively severe brain damage, the primary characteristics of organic brain syndromes—memory loss, disorientation, and impairment in intellectual functions and judgment—are easily recognized, and it is possible to obtain a rough estimate of the degree of brain impairment on the basis of such a clinical examination. With some exceptions, the clinical diagnosis of dementia and clinical estimates of the degree of dementia correlate well with the postmortem histopathological findings [5, 11]. In certain cases it is even possible to make a differential diagnosis between various types of brain impairment (cerebral degenerative disease and cerebrovascular disease, for example) on the basis of the history and the neuropsychiatric examination [43]. The usefulness and effectiveness of this clinical approach become more uncertain in patients with mild to moderate brain impairment. Such patients usually present no clear-cut neurological signs, and their cognitive function, although impaired, may still remain within the normal range of variation that may be expected in healthy old people. Since the examiner is required to make interpretations and judgments during this clinical procedure, the results of such an examination tend to be biased by his training, experience, and personal interest. Attempts have been made to standardize the interview and mental-status examination [24, 48]. Some of these are too simple or are applicable only to cases of severe dementia; others still need validation.

Many psychological tests have been developed to evaluate various aspects of cognitive behavior [4, 7]. In these tests, clearly defined stimuli, questions, or tasks are presented in a structured manner to the subject in a well-controlled setting. They are usually designed so that responses are simple and unequivocal and therefore can be measured readily. The responses are usually standardized further according to the many factors known to affect the results of testing: age, sex, education, socioeconomic background, and so on.

Psychological testing is generally agreed to be more objective than the clinical examination. In certain cases it is probably more reliable and sensitive in demonstrating evidence of intellectual impairment, whether general or specific (reasoning, problem solving, memory, perception). While these impairments can be considered as evidence of brain damage, they cannot be directly related to the location, intensity, or extent of the cerebral impairment. The relationship between behavioral and cerebral impairment is neither simple nor specific. Impairment in an intellectual function may result from any one of a number of structural or functional abnormalities in the brain [4, 7, 34].

The limitations of psychological testing are the same as those of the clinical neuropsychiatric examination. Both evaluate essentially the person's performance or behavior, which depends not only on the brain but also on many other factors, such as motivation, attention, anxiety, and the person's psychological reaction toward the testing or toward his cognitive deficit. The results of psychological testing must therefore be interpreted in the light of all other findings available from the clinical history, the neuropsychiatric examination, and the laboratory findings [57].

Histopathological Examination
The common features of insults to the brain, from whatever cause, are a loss of neurons and a decline in neuronal function. The only direct method of evaluating the brain is to make a biopsy of brain tissue and examine it by histopathological techniques. Such an approach, even if it were not so obviously impractical, is not as informative as one would expect. Smith and his co-workers [45] encountered considerable difficulty in interpreting cerebral biopsies from patients with presenile dementia. Of 59 biopsies, 17 were classified as nonspecific because they showed only changes due to operative trauma, or mild unclassifiable atrophic change, or no relevant changes at all. The biopsy diagnosis of Pick's disease was particularly difficult because of the artifactual neuronal changes and the inaccessibility of the maximally affected areas.

Measurement of Cerebral Atrophy

An alternative to the histopathological approach is to evaluate the degree of cerebral atrophy resulting from the loss of neurons or other tissues of the brain. Although the presence of cerebral atrophy can be inferred from clinical symptoms and signs, psychological tests, the EEG, or measurements of cerebral metabolic activity or cerebral blood flow, the diagnosis can be confirmed only by pneumoencephalographic demonstration of cortical atrophy or ventricular dilatation. Definite evidence of cerebral atrophy is present in almost all patients with senile or presenile dementia [18, 20]. As the degree of cerebral atrophy increases, impairment of intellectual functioning or adaptive capacity also increases [27, 64]. The intellectual impairment is more closely correlated with cortical atrophy, particularly of the frontal region, than with ventricular dilatation [64].

Intellectual impairment associated with a given degree of cerebral atrophy varies considerably among different people. As a rule, the same degree of atrophy produces greater intellectual impairment in elderly persons than in the young [64]. The explanation may lie in the fact that the cerebral blood flow and the compensatory capacity of the remaining brain tissue are usually reduced in old age. Premorbid personality also contributes to the individual variation; it has been shown that patients who, before their illness, demonstrated a high order of adaptive versatility had less intellectual impairment in relation to loss of brain tissue than those who had for some time exhibited difficulties in overall adaptation, with much anxiety [27]. The individual variations in the degree of impairment were more striking when cerebral tissue loss was small and less evident when it was great.

Because of its traumatic nature and the danger of aggravating the patient's condition, pneumoencephalography is used only in selected cases. *Echoencephalography,* which does not have these disadvantages, has long been used to demonstrate the midline shift resulting from the pressure of a mass lesion in the brain or from marked unilateral cerebral edema. According to recent reports, this technique can also be used to measure the ventricular size [14, 16]. It has been shown [15] that the width of the third ventricle, as measured by echoencephalography, is significantly greater in persons aged 70 or over than in young adults (6 to 11 mm, with a mean of 7.2, as compared with 4 to 7 mm, with a mean of 5.0). The lateral ventricle is more difficult to evaluate because its size varies from one part to another, and echoes from other brain structures are not easily differentiated from those from the wall of the lateral ventricle.

Recently, a tomographic x-ray method utilizing modern electronic and computer technology (so-called computerized transverse axial scanning) [1, 22] has been developed to demonstrate the internal structures of the brain. In this method, the cranium is scanned in successive layers by a narrow beam of x-rays, and the transmission of x-ray photons across a particular layer is measured at a multitude of angles. This procedure is safe and noninvasive and has been found useful in demonstrating cerebral atrophy as well as space-occupying lesions [35].

Measurements of Cerebral Metabolism and Cerebral Blood Flow
The brain derives its energy almost exclusively from the aerobic oxidation of glucose; hence cerebral metabolic activity is represented by the rate at which oxygen and glucose are utilized by the brain. Oxygen consumption is probably a more reliable indicator of cerebral metabolism than the utilization of glucose, for two reasons: (1) the stores of glucose in the brain, though small, are still much greater than those of oxygen; and (2) the analytical method used in the determination of glucose is not specific and includes other reducing substances present in the blood.

The cerebral metabolic rate of oxygen (oxygen consumption) can be calculated by multiplying the cerebral oxygen uptake during a given unit of time by the amount of blood flowing through the brain during this interval (cerebral blood flow) [26, 29, 46]. It has been estimated that, in healthy young adults, each 100 gm of brain tissue consumes about 3.5 ml of oxygen per minute. Because of a unique compensatory mechanism in the brain, the cerebral oxygen consumption, under normal conditions, is more or less independent of the supply of blood to the brain and of the oxygen content of the blood. A reduction in the oxygen content of the blood (hypoxia) is usually compensated for by an increase in blood flow; a reduction of blood flow, by an increase in the brain's uptake of oxygen. Consequently, the cerebral metabolic rate remains constant under a wide range of changes in cerebral blood flow or in the oxygen content of the blood.

The cerebral uptake of oxygen, which is represented by the difference between the amount of oxygen in the blood of any artery and that in blood taken from the superior bulb of the internal jugular vein, is sometimes used as a measurement of cerebral metabolism. Only when the cerebral blood flow is constant, however, is the oxygen *uptake* directly proportional to, and hence useful as an indicator of, the *utilization* of oxygen by the brain.

The cerebral blood flow, under normal circumstances, is unable to affect the cerebral metabolic rate but is dependent on it. This is because the most important metabolites produced by the aerobic oxidation of glucose are water and carbon dioxide; the latter is a potent vasodilator. Any changes in cerebral blood flow, although not always proportional to changes in cerebral metabolic rate, are as a rule in the same direction. The former can therefore be used as an indicator of the latter.

Of the many methods being developed for estimating cerebral blood flow, only a very few are capable of providing quantitative information [19, 33]. All these quantitative methods depend on a diffusible indicator, usually an inert gas, which is administered intra-arterially, intravenously, or by inhalation. The uptake of this indicator by the brain, or its clearance from the brain, is then determined by measuring the amount contained in samples of arterial blood and of blood from the internal jugular vein, or by monitoring extracranially when a radioactive indicator is employed. Some methods, such as the nitrous oxide or [85]krypton inhalation method, give only an estimate of the average blood flow of the whole brain; others, such as the intracarotid injection method using [133]xenon, can also separately estimate blood flow through the gray matter and the white matter in a small region of the brain. All these methods require a puncture of the artery, or internal jugular vein, or both and thus involve considerable trauma and risk. The inhalation method using [133]xenon [38] avoids these hazards but is not as sensitive or reliable as the other methods because of the problems of recirculation and extracerebral loading.

Although the cerebral metabolic rate of oxygen is by far the most reliable and accurate measure of cerebral metabolism, it does not provide any quantitative information regarding the metabolic rates of various components of the brain. These are known to differ considerably under normal conditions, and one would expect them to be affected differently by various pathological processes of the brain. Measurements of the regional cerebral blood flow, such as can be obtained by carotid injection or inhalation of a radioactive inert gas, probably correlate well with the local metabolic rate. However, they provide no morphological information about the brain or the vascular system. The localization of mass lesions in the brain can be helped by brain scans or cerebral angiograms. The latter are particularly valuable in demonstrating vascular lesions.

The decline in the cerebral metabolic rate and cerebral blood flow usually observed in senescent patients is believed to be due principally to pathological conditions rather than to chronological age per se. Dastur and his co-workers [12] showed that in old persons who are in excellent health and have no apparent mental deterioration, cerebral oxygen consumption and blood flow do not differ greatly from those of healthy young adults.

Cerebral atherosclerosis is accompanied by an increase in peripheral vascular resistance and an impairment of the compensatory mechanism by which cerebral blood flow is maintained constant in spite of changes in blood pressure or changes in peripheral vascular resistance. Cerebral atherosclerosis is one possible factor in the reduction of cerebral blood flow that often occurs in senescence. Another possible factor is depression of cerebral metabolic activity secondary to functional or structural impairment of the brain. Such impairment may result from degenerative diseases primarily involving the brain, or from metabolic disorders arising from conditions outside the brain (hypoxemia, ischemia, anemia, uremia, drug effect). The reduction in cerebral blood flow or metabolic rate is therefore not specific for any particular pathological process. It only indicates the presence of functional or structural impairment of the brain.

Among elderly persons with various psychiatric or neurological disorders, it has been repeatedly observed that a reduction of cerebral oxygen consumption and cerebral blood flow is associated with an impairment in intellectual function [10, 21, 28, 30]. In a recent study, the [133]xenon inhalation method was used to measure the cortical blood flow of the left parietal region in a group of aged community volunteers (mean age, 79 years) having relatively good health and in a group of healthy young adults [38, 61]. Values for the elderly subjects were significantly lower than those obtained in the younger ones (33 to 72 ml per 100 gm of brain tissue per minute in the former group, as compared with 57 to 92 ml in the latter). In elderly subjects of comparable educational status and socioeconomic background, there was a significant correlation between cerebral blood flow and intellectual functioning, as indicated by scaled scores on the WAIS test, administered both at the time of the blood flow study and prior to the blood flow study [61].

Electroencephalographic Study
The electroencephalograph has long been employed to study electrocortical activity of the brain in vivo. A review of the literature [8] shows that EEG abnormalities are extremely common among hospitalized psychiatric patients over 60 years of age. The incidence of abnormal EEGs is significantly higher (75 percent or more) in elderly persons with brain disorders of various types than in old people with so-called functional or psychogenic disorders. These abnormalities are not specific for any type of brain disorder; they consist almost exclusively of *diffuse slow activity in the theta or delta range,* whether the brain impairment is caused by cerebral degenerative disease or by a metabolic disturbance secondary to systemic disease. Several studies [23, 37] have shown a good correlation between the dominant frequency in the EEG and cerebral oxygen consumption or cerebral blood flow. It is very likely that the slowing of the dominant frequency so often observed in old persons is due to depression of cerebral metabolic activity—a common feature of almost all brain disorders associated with old age.

As a rule, the EEG abnormalities, particularly the degree of slowing, correlate well with the degree of intellectual deterioration or with the clinical evidence of organicity found on psychiatric examinations or psychological tests [8, 56]. It is also possible to demonstrate a relationship between the EEG findings and the prognosis. Patients with diffuse slowing in their EEG tracings are more likely to remain hospitalized and have a shorter life expectancy than those with normal EEG tracings [8]. Exceptions do occur, however. The EEG may be negative or unremarkable even in the presence of definite brain disease or severe dementia, while psychologically well-preserved persons may have abnormal tracings.

The interpretation of the senescent EEG is made more difficult by the fact that similar, though less marked, slowing of the dominant rhythm is frequently observed in elderly persons with excellent health. A longitudinal study on a group of elderly community volunteers whose good health was maintained for at least three years after they entered the study showed an inverse relationship between age and the frequency of the dominant rhythm [58]. The mean frequency declined, at an almost steady rate of 0.08 cycles per second (cps) per year, from 10.3 cps at age 60 to 9.5 at 70 and 8.7 at 80. Subjects with the slowest dominant frequencies on the first examination functioned initially at an intellectual level that was not much different from that of volunteers with faster frequencies; but the decline in their performance ability during the next three to four years was significantly greater than that in the subjects whose dominant frequencies were initially higher [61].

Other EEG findings that are common in senescence are *focal disturbances* and *diffuse fast activities in the beta range*. The clinical significance of these patterns is not clear [8]. Focal disturbances seem to appear first in middle age and to increase in incidence with advancing age. They usually consist of slow activity of the theta or delta frequency and less often of marked amplitude asymmetry and localized sharp waves or spikes. In almost all cases these foci occur predominantly or exclusively over the left anterior temporal region. Although similar focal disturbances are also not uncommon in patients with cerebrovascular insufficiency or with intratentorial or deep subcortical neoplasms, longitudinal studies have shown that such foci may be present for several years without the development of clinical symptoms. The EEG finding has not been correlated with any particular psychological or physical factors [8], although there is evidence suggesting that subjects with such foci showed a significantly greater decline in verbal ability over three to four years than did those without such foci [61].

In about half the elderly population, fast activity in the beta range is present in one or more EEG tracings; this finding is inversely related to the occurrence of diffuse slowing. These fast waves appear to be related to age and mental status; they become less common after the age of 80 and in the presence of mental deterioration [8]. It has also been shown that elderly subjects who did well in verbal learning had significantly more beta waves during eye opening and photic stimulation than those who did poorly in such learning [49].

Because the EEG changes associated with various conditions common in senescence are neither specific nor pathognomonic, and because of the wide variations found among old persons of compatible age and health status, the diagnostic value of single EEG tracings is somewhat limited, especially in cases in which the findings deviate only slightly or moderately from the standards for healthy young adults. Serial EEG tracings, on the other hand, are of great value, particularly in following the course of a patient suspected of having a brain disorder.

The Brain Scan and Other Diagnostic Procedures
In brain scanning, a sophisticated radiation-detection system is used to map out the distribution within the brain of an intravenously administered radioisotope compound. Abnormal intensity of radioactivity may result from a lesion that leads to an impairment of the blood-brain barrier. The brain scan remains normal in most slowly progressive degenerative or metabolic diseases of the brain. Brain scanning is a noninvasive procedure and is of great value in detecting or ruling out certain localized brain diseases such as neoplasms, acute cerebrovascular disease, and arteriovenous malformation [31].

Other useful diagnostic procedures include angiography and intrathecal cisternography, although both involve relatively more trauma and risk than does brain scanning. Angiography is particularly useful in determining the exact location and extent of a vascular lesion. Intrathecal cisternography using a radioiodinated human serum albumin helps in the diagnosis of normal-pressure hydrocephalus [3].

Therapeutic Considerations
The ultimate goal of evaluating the brain is to uncover any conditions in which causative or contributory factors can be corrected or at least alleviated before the brain tissue is permanently damaged. The many conditions included in this category [13, 32] can be divided into two groups.

The first group consists of conditions in which there is an insufficient *supply* of the two nutrients that are essential for normal brain function: oxygen and glucose. The brain's supply of *oxygen* may be decreased by low ambient oxygen or by respiratory depression or various pulmonary diseases that lower the oxygen content of the blood (hypoxic hypoxia);

by anemia of various types (anemic hypoxia); or by ischemia secondary to hypotension or to cerebrovascular insufficiency (ischemic hypoxia). The amount of *glucose* available to the brain may be decreased in essential hypoglycemia or by certain drugs such as insulin.

In the second group there is inefficient *utilization* of the nutrients that are essential for normal brain function. The brain's consumption of oxygen and glucose may be impaired or depressed by certain drugs such as barbiturates; by a deficiency of vitamins such as B_{12}; or by various metabolic and electrolyte disturbances, such as diabetes mellitus, uremia, hyperammonemia, hypothyroidism, dehydration, and acidosis.

Unfortunately, the causative or contributory factors in many brain disorders—for example, senile or presenile dementia—are not yet recognized. Other types of cerebral impairment are due to factors that are recognized but cannot be effectively controlled or treated—for example, cerebral atherosclerosis. Several drugs are capable of increasing the cerebral blood flow under normal conditions but have little or no effect on the blood flow or brain function when cerebral atherosclerosis is present.

Brain tissue, once damaged, cannot be restored. In many cases, therefore, the most important part of treatment is to prevent any complication or aggravating factors that may cause further impairment of cerebral function. Drugs that are known to depress the cerebral function (barbiturates, for example) should be avoided if possible. Drugs that may reduce the blood pressure, such as the phenothiazines, should be used with the utmost caution. A fall in blood pressure that would hardly be noticeable in persons with normal vessels may significantly affect the cerebral hemodynamics in persons with cerebral atherosclerosis. Because this condition increases the peripheral vascular resistance and impairs the compensatory mechanism of the cerebrovascular system, a relatively high blood pressure is required to maintain the normal supply of blood to the brain.

The tendency to cerebral hypoxia is also greater in old persons than in young adults [36, 44, 47]. Conditions that cause hypoxia—for example, low ambient oxygen and certain anesthetics, surgical procedures, medications, or postures [36, 39, 63]—should be avoided if possible. If hypoxia occurs, it should be corrected as soon as possible in order to avoid further insult to the already impaired brain.

Among the positive steps that can be taken to help old people with brain impairment are any measures—drugs, activities, psychotherapy, environmental manipulation—that can alleviate the social and psychological stresses contributing to their problems of adjustment.

Prognosis

It is generally agreed that psychiatric disorders of later life have a particularly poor prognosis when evidence of brain impairment is present [60, 62]. Because of the high mortality and long periods of institutionalization that are characteristic of elderly psychiatric patients who show evidence of dementia or organic brain disease on clinical examination [25, 42, 50], the differential diagnosis between organic and psychogenic disorders has been emphasized. All too frequently, aggressive therapeutic approaches are reserved for patients with disorders of the latter type.

From the clinical point of view, such a categorical differentiation and the fatalistic attitude often adopted toward elderly persons with organic disorders are unjustified, particularly in the treatment of an *individual* patient. First of all, the clinical differentiation between these two diagnostic categories is not reliable. Second, most psychiatric disorders in old age are neither exclusively organic nor exclusively psychogenic. Third, even if it were possible to differentiate clinically between these two groups, the belief that organic disorders have a poor prognosis is true only when they are viewed as a *group* and are compared with psychogenic disorders as a *group*. There are considerable individual variations within each diagnostic category and hence overlapping between them. Two separate studies made on elderly patients two years after their admission to a psychiatric institution [42, 50] showed that almost 10 percent of those having so-called organic disorders were living in the community, and an even larger proportion (11 to 33 percent) were still alive in the institution. Among those having so-called psychogenic disorders, more than 25 percent were dead and another 25 percent had remained institutionalized during these two years.

To predict the outcome of a psychiatric illness for an individual patient on the basis of the clinical diagnosis is extremely difficult and unreliable [21]. It has been demonstrated that, among aged institutionalized patients, predictions by psychiatrists or internists that death would occur within a specified period after admission were correct in only one-third of the cases; usually the prediction was more pessimistic than the actual outcome [17]. The prognosis for each individual elderly patient, whatever the psychiatric disorder, cannot safely be based on age, diagnostic classification, or any single variable. It must be based on the person's *total* condition, including his sociocultural background and premorbid personality, current environmental and psychological stresses to which he is subject, his physical health, and the structural and functional status of his brain. Another factor in the prognosis—perhaps the most important of all—is the result of vigorous intervention and treatment designed to alleviate or improve all the factors that are contributing to his illness.

Summary and Conclusion

Senescence is commonly associated with many adaptational or behavioral problems and even with psychotic symptoms. These conditions may or may not be related directly to the structural or functional impairments that are expected to develop sooner or later in all senile brains.

The primary characteristics of a diffuse brain disorder are impairments of cognitive functions that depend directly on the activity of the brain tissue involved. These impairments are readily recognized when the disorder is severe. When the disorder is mild, however, its manifestations may be completely masked by other clinical problems resulting from environmental stresses, intrapsychic conflicts, or both. For this reason, a thorough evaluation of the brain is as important for old persons with so-called functional or psychogenic psychiatric disorders as for those in whom a brain syndrome is obvious. Such an evaluation, in addition to determining whether or not a brain disorder is present, should ideally also be able to reveal its severity and its relationship to other concurrent clinical manifestations.

Unfortunately, there are very few safe, effective, and practical clinical procedures that throw much light on the status of the brain. Electroencephalography, the xenon-inhalation method of measuring cerebral blood flow, and echoencephalography are the only methods that are completely nontraumatic and safe enough to be used for routine screening of the brain. Electroencephalography is by far the most practical diagnostic procedure; the value of serial electroencephalograms is well recognized. The xenon-inhalation method and echoencephalography are still under development and need further validation.

In some cases it seems wise to employ more specific evaluative procedures, in spite of the trauma and risk involved. Although biopsy is the only procedure that offers an opportunity to study the brain tissue directly, the pneumoencephalogram may provide considerable morphological information about the brain and is the only sure method of determining the presence and degree of cerebral atrophy. The cerebral metabolic rate can be determined by measuring both the oxygen uptake of the brain and the cerebral blood flow. Brain scans and cerebral angiograms help to localize mass lesions in the brain; the latter are particularly valuable in demonstrating vascular lesions.

It is obvious that no single procedure can provide complete information regarding the status of the brain. To evaluate even a limited aspect of the brain, more than one use of a particular procedure will be necessary. Because of the considerable variation found among individuals with much the same condition, the *change* observed in a variable over a period of time is much more informative than a single reading. This is particularly true of brain disorders in their early stages.

When a complete evaluation of an elderly person with slight, moderate, or marked brain disorder uncovers any causative or contributory factor that is amenable to treatment, everything possible should be done to eliminate, or at least alleviate, the underlying problem. Where the brain disorder is due to factors that cannot be controlled, the therapeutic effort should be directed toward preventing further insults to the impaired brain and alleviating environmental and intrapsychic stresses that may be contributing to the patient's problem.

References

1. Ambrose, J. Computerized transverse axial scanning (tomography): Part 2. Clinical application. *Br. J. Radiol.* 46:1023, 1973.
2. American Psychiatric Association. *Diagnostic and Statistical Manual of Mental Disorders* (2d ed.). Washington, D.C.: American Psychiatric Association, 1968.
3. Benson, D. F., LeMay, M., Patten, D. H., and Rubens, A. B. Diagnosis of normal pressure hydrocephalus. *N. Engl. J. Med.* 283:609, 1970.

4. Benton, A. Psychological Tests for Brain Damage. In A. M. Freedman and H. I. Kaplan (Eds.), *Comprehensive Textbook of Psychiatry*. Baltimore: Williams & Wilkins, 1967.

5. Blessed, G., Tomlinson, B. E., and Roth, M. The association between quantitative measures of dementia and of senile change in the cerebral grey matter of elderly subjects. *Br. J. Psychiatry* 114:797, 1968.

6. Botwinick, J. *Cognitive Processes in Maturity and Old Age*. New York: Springer, 1967.

7. Burgemeister, B. B. *Psychological Techniques in Neurological Diagnosis*. New York: Harper & Row, 1962.

8. Busse, E. W., and Wang, H. -S. The value of electroencephalography in geriatrics. *Geriatrics* 20:906, 1965.

9. Busse, E. W., and Wang, H. -S. The Multiple Factors Contributing to Dementia in Old Age. In E. Palmore (Ed.), *Normal Aging II*. Durham, N.C.: Duke University Press, 1974, Pp. 151–160.

10. Butler, R. H., Dastur, D. K., and Perlin, S. Relationships of senile manifestations and chronic brain syndromes to cerebral circulation and metabolism. *J. Psychiatr. Res.* 3:229, 1965.

11. Corsellis, J. A. N. *Mental Illness and the Aging Brain*. London: Oxford University Press, 1962.

12. Dastur, D. K., et al. Effects of Aging on Cerebral Circulation and Metabolism in Man. In J. E. Birren et al. (Eds.), *Human Aging: A Biological and Behavioral Study*. Washington, D.C.: U.S. Government Printing Office, 1963.

13. Dewan, J. G., and Spaulding, W. B. *The Organic Psychoses: A Guide to Diagnosis*. Toronto: University of Toronto Press, 1958.

14. Erba, G., and Lombroso, C. T. Detection of ventricular landmarks by two dimensional ultrasonography. *J. Neurol. Neurosurg. Psychiatry* 31:232, 1968.

15. Feuerlein, W., and Dillin, H. The Echo-encephalogram of the Third Ventricle in Different Age Groups. In E. Kazner, W. Schiefer, and K. J. Zulch (Eds.), *Proceedings in Echo-encephalography*. New York: Springer, 1968.

16. Garg, A. G., and Taylor, A. R. A-scan echoencephalography in measurement of the cerebral ventricles. *J. Neurol. Neurosurg. Psychiatry* 31:245, 1968.

17. Goldfarb, A. I., Fisch, M., and Gerber, I. E. Predictors of mortality in the institutionalized aged. *Dis. Nerv. Syst.* 27:21, 1966.

18. Gosling, R. H. The association of dementia with radiologically demonstrated cerebral atrophy. *J. Neurol. Neurosurg. Psychiatry* 18:129, 1955.

19. Harper, A. M. Measurement of cerebral blood flow in man. *Scott. Med. J.* 12:349, 1967.

20. Haug, J. O. Pneumoencephalographic studies in mental disease. *Acta Psychiatr. Scand.* [Suppl. 38] 165:1, 1962.

21. Hedland, S., et al. Cerebral blood circulation in dementia. *Acta Psychiatr. Scand.* 40:77, 1964.

22. Hounsfield, G. N. Computerized transverse axial scanning (tomography): Part 1. Description of system. *Br. J. Radiol.* 46:1016, 1973.

261

23. Ingvar, D. H., et al. Regional cerebral blood flow related to EEG. *Acta Neurol. Scand.* [Suppl. 14] 179, 1965.
24. Kahn, R. L., et al. Brief objective measures for the determinations of mental status in the aged. *Am. J. Psychiatry* 117:326, 1960.
25. Kay, D. W. K., Norris, V., and Post, F. Prognosis in psychiatric disorders of the elderly. An attempt to define indicators of early death and early recovery. *J. Ment. Sci.* 102:129, 1956.
26. Kety, S. S. The Cerebral Circulation. In J. Field (Ed.), *Handbook of Physiology,* Section I, *Neurophysiology,* Vol. III. Washington, D.C.: American Physiological Society, 1960.
27. Kiev, A., et al. The highest integrative functions and diffuse cerebral atrophy. *Neurology* (Minneap.) 12:363, 1962.
28. Klee, A. The relationship between clinical evaluation of mental deterioration, psychological test results, and the cerebral metabolic rate of oxygen. *Acta Neurol. Scand.* 40:337, 1964.
29. Lassen, N. A. Cerebral blood flow and oxygen consumption in man. *Physiol. Rev.* 39:183, 1959.
30. Lassen, N. A., Munck, O., and Tottey, E. R. Mental function and cerebral oxygen consumption in organic dementia. *Arch. Neurol. Psychiatry* 77:126, 1957.
31. Maynard, C. D., and Janeway, R. Radioisotope Studies in Neuro-Diagnosis. In J. F. Toole (Ed.), *Special Techniques for Neurologic Diagnosis.* Philadelphia: Davis, 1969. Pp. 71–91.
32. McCarron, M. M., and McCormick, R. A. *Acute Organic Disorder Accompanied by Mental Symptoms.* Sacramento, Calif.: California Department of Mental Hygiene, 1967.
33. McHenry, L. C., Jr. Cerebral blood flow. *N. Engl. J. Med.* 274:82, 1966.
34. Meyer, V. Critique of psychological approaches to brain damage. *J. Ment. Sci.* 103:80, 1957.
35. New, P. F. J., et al. Computerized axial tomography with EMI Scanner. *Neuroradiology* 110:109, 1974.
36. Nunn, J. F. Influence of age and other factors on hypoxemia in the postoperative period. *Lancet* 2:466, 1965.
37. Obrist, W. D., et al. Relation of EEG to cerebral blood flow and metabolism in old age. *Electroencephalogr. Clin. Neurophysiol.* 15:610, 1963.
38. Obrist, W. D., et al. Determination of regional cerebral blood flow by inhalation by 133-xenon. *Circ. Res.* 20:124, 1967.
39. Payne, J. P., and Conway, C. M. Hypoxemia after surgery and anesthesia. *Postgrad. Med. J.* 42:341, 1966.
40. Pearce, J., and Miller, E. *Clinical Aspects of Dementia.* Baltimore: Williams & Wilkins, 1973.
41. Pfeiffer, E. A short portable mental status questionnaire for the assessment of organic brain deficit in elderly patients. *J. Am. Geriatr. Soc.* 23:433, 1975.
42. Roth, M. The natural history of mental disorder in old age. *J. Ment. Sci.* 101:281, 1955.

43. Rothschild, D.   The clinical differentiation of senile and arteriosclerotic psychosis. *Am. J. Psychiatry* 98:324, 1941.
44. Simonson, E.   Experimental hypoxemia in older and younger healthy men. *J. Appl. Physiol.* 16:639, 1961.
45. Smith, W. T., Turner, E., and Sim, M.   Cerebral biopsy in the investigation of presenile dementia: II. *Br. J. Psychiatry* 112:127, 1966.
46. Sokoloff, L.   Metabolism of the Central Nervous System in Vivo. In J. Field (Ed.), *Handbook of Physiology,* Section I, *Neurophysiology,* Vol. III. Washington, D.C.: American Physiological Society, 1960.
47. Sorbini, C. A., et al.   Arterial oxygen tension in relation to age in healthy subjects. *Respiration* 25:1, 1968.
48. Spitzer, R. L., et al.   Mental status schedule. *Arch. Gen. Psychiatry* 16:479, 1967.
49. Thompson, L. W., and Wilson, S.   Electrocortical reactivity and learning in the elderly. *J. Gerontol.* 21:45, 1966.
50. Trier, T. R.   Characteristics of mentally ill aged: A comparison of patients with psychogenic disorders and patients with organic brain syndromes. *J. Gerontol.* 21:354, 1966.
51. U.S. Bureau of the Census. *Current Population Reports.* Series P-25, No. 352. Washington, D.C.: U.S. Government Printing Office, 1966.
52. U.S. National Center for Health Statistics. *Prevalence of Chronic Conditions and Impairments Among Residents of Nursing and Personal Care Homes—United States, May–June, 1964.* P.H.S. Publication No. 1000, Series 12, No. 8. Washington, D.C.: U.S. Government Printing Office, 1967.
53. U.S. National Institute of Mental Health. *Outpatient Psychiatric Clinics, Special Statistical Report, Old Adult Patient, 1964, State and Total United States.* P.H.S. Publication No. 1553. Washington, D.C.: U.S. Government Printing Office, 1967.
54. U.S. National Institute of Mental Health. *Patients in Mental Institutions, 1966, Part II. State and County Hospitals.* P.H.S. Publication No. 1818. Washington, D.C.: U.S. Government Printing Office, 1968.
55. U.S. National Institute of Mental Health. *Patients in Mental Institutions, 1966, Part III. Private Mental Hospitals and General Hospitals with Psychiatric Service.* P.H.S. Publication No. 1818. Washington, D.C.: U.S. Government Printing Office, 1968.
56. Wang, H. -S.   Cerebral Correlates of Intellectual Function in Senescence. In L. F. Jarvik, C. Eisdorfer, and J. E. Blum (Eds.), *Intellectual Function in Adults Psychological and Biological Influences.* New York: Springer, 1973. Pp. 95–106.
57. Wang, H. -S.   Special Diagnostic Procedures—The Evaluation of Brain Impairment. In E. W. Busse and E. Pfeiffer (Eds.), *Mental Illness in Late Life.* Washington, D.C.: American Psychiatric Association, 1973. Pp. 75–88.
58. Wang, H. -S., and Busse, E. W.   EEG of healthy old persons—a longitudinal study: I. Dominant background activity and occipital rhythm. *J. Gerontol.* 24:419, 1969.

59. Wang, H. -S., and Busse, E. W.   Dementia in Old Age. In C. E. Wells (Ed.), *Dementia.* Philadelphia: Davis, 1971. Pp. 151–162.
60. Wang, H. -S., and Busse, E. W.   Brain Impairment and Longevity. In E. Palmore (Ed.), *Normal Aging II.* Durham, N.C.: Duke University Press, 1974. Pp. 263–268.
61. Wang, H. -S., Obrist, W. D., and Busse, E. W.   Neurophysiological correlates of the intellectual function of elderly persons living in the community. *Am. J. Psychiatry* 126:1205, 1970.
62. Wang, H. -S., and Whanger, A.   Brain Impairment and Longevity. In E. Palmore and F. Jeffers (Eds.), *Prediction of Life Span: Recent Findings.* Lexington, Mass.: Heath, 1971. Pp. 95–105.
63. Ward, R. J., et al.   Effect of posture on normal arterial blood gas tensions in the aged. *Geriatrics* 21:139, 1966.
64. Willanger, R., et al.   Intellectual impairment and cerebral atrophy—a psychological, neurological, and radiological investigation. *Dan. Med. Bull.* 15:65, 1968.

14. Institutional Care of the Aged

Alvin I. Goldfarb

Our purposes here are to define some types of services and programs included in the term *institutional care,* to identify the characteristics of the aged population for whom this care is the treatment of choice, and to list briefly the range and types of services such institutions should provide for this special group of aged persons.

The chronologically old and the truly aged persons—those who have suffered a serious decline in physical or mental functional status—are in need of a wide range of social and health services. Response to their many problems is now in a state of change greatly influenced by economic and political factors. Who is entitled to what, for what reason, to be given by whom, where, under what auspices, at what cost, and at whose expense is, in 1976, under embattled consideration [1, 18, 22, 23].

There has been much discussion about how the needs of the heterogeneous population of old and aged persons should be met. Personal prejudices, the bias of vested interests, public misconceptions about social responsibility, and underestimation of the number of afflicted persons and their needs for comprehensive care, joined with widespread reluctance to finance expensive services, have influenced planning for the development of long-term care facilities and the rational integration of patterns of care. Health care delivery has remained fragmented. Probably the chief reason for poor planning is ignorance or intentional disregard of the fact that 70 to 80 percent of persons who reach facilities for long-term protective and supportive care in their old age have a relatively severe degree of irreversible mental impairment. To this group has recently been added, by transfer or "discharge," persons who have aged in state psychiatric hospitals because of disorders of thinking, perception, or mood that have been resistant to the treatment offered, or who, when relatively improved, had no place in the community to which they could return.

Thus a wide variety of old persons need protective care in a congregate living arrangement that provides a therapeutic milieu. Included are persons from 65 to over 95 years of age, of varied ethnic, religious, cultural, occupational, and socioeconomic backgrounds, who differ in terms of the availability of supportive family members, friends, and other personal resources, as well as in energy, interests, type of illness, and physical and mental functional status.

At present there are few, if any, well-organized agencies or institutions for the provision of comprehensive care for the old and aged; there is now no coherent plan for the organization of a system of health care—not to speak of comprehensive care delivery. Current planning and propaganda place emphasis on nonmedical, antimedical, and anti-institutional concepts. This appears to be largely economically motivated and a result of jockeying between governmental agencies about who should bear the costs. Consequently, there have been revolutionary changes in the actions of state and local departments of health and welfare in their attempts to pass the expense of care on to the federal government.

Institutional Facilities

Contraction of services in the once-promising state hospital systems of health care delivery has occurred in most states. The government's sub-contracting of long-term institutional care to proprietary management has encouraged the evolution of the nursing home industry. This industry has followed business practices, recruiting consumers for the purposes of profitable expansion rather than as an answer to needs for service [12, 14, 23]. In effect, this probably increased the cost to the states and localities and certainly has done so for the taxpayer. Also, because of state psychiatric hospital discharge "to the community" of old persons who have been long-term hospital residents and the exclusion of old persons who may need lifelong care, an indiscriminate mixing of incompatible populations within inadequately designed institutions has resulted. These institutions are poorly staffed in terms of numbers of personnel, the adequacy of their training, and the strength of their motivation and purpose. Moreover, the responsibility for regulation and supervision of these institutions is fragmented among the various levels of government and among departments at each level, so that in many localities effective regulation does not exist.

Obviously, old persons should be helped to remain in their own homes or in the homes of family members for as long as this can meet their needs without senseless destruction of family and social patterns. However, for the physically and mentally ill old, attempts to keep them at home or in a relative's home are often overenthusiastic and exceed what is physically, emotionally, or financially practical for the patient, family, and community. Well-intentioned advocates of keeping old people out of congregate residential settings are often unaware of, or ignore, the high proportion of the elderly ill, impaired, or disabled who have no protective family; family members may be dead, ill, alienated, or emotionally incapable of providing protective care. Studies of the pathways to institutions show that the very old, the very ill, and the severely impaired are not "dumped" by families but find their way into institutions as a last resort after heroic efforts have been made to keep them in their own or a relative's home. At the policy and planning level, home health care programs for the aged are "sold" to the public as an inexpensive way of maintaining the old in their own homes, thus making institutional care unnecessary. Unfortunately, therefore, many old persons who could profit from protective, supportive care do not find their way into institutional settings or do so late because of ignorance, socially determined prejudices, or because of the very mental incompetence that calls for it.

All too often, the individual and family group facing the declining physical and mental health of their aged relatives are confronted by professionals who either explicitly or by implication question their decision to seek and make use of institutional care. Experience has shown that, except for the very rich, home care of the mentally impaired, chronically ill, or severely disabled old person in most instances can be provided by the family only at the cost of subverting the abilities of the family unit to perform its other essential tasks and at the risk of individual, family, and community stress.

Institutions are not easily defined because of the variations of application of the term. The term *institutional care* usually refers to the inpatient services rendered by long-term care facilities known as psychiatric hospitals, homes for aged persons or skilled nursing homes, intermediate care facilities, and health-related facilities. Foster homes, retirement homes, personal-care homes, and senior citizen hotels may at times also be counted as places of "institutional care" in that they attempt to handle persons whose needs and problems are similar to those who reach "institutions." In the past, residents of nursing homes were, by some definitions, considered to be "in the community"; now this fiction appears to have been abandoned. The fiction that persons in senior citizen hotels or personal-care boarding houses are "in the community" is still prevalent, and day-care-center populations that overlap in characteristics with the populations of some 24-hour-care centers are also usually not considered to be institutions because the person cared for returns home at night to be looked after by a relative.

State Hospitals

Prior to 1950 the burden of care of old persons with combined psychiatric and physical illness was carried in large part by state hospitals and was shared to some extent by homes for the aged and chronic disease hospitals. Overcrowding in state hospitals and the medical demands made by a large number of patients who were acutely ill on first admission and whose death rate soon after admission was extremely high led to protests, surveys, and claims that state hospitals were being used as dumping grounds for the incurably ill aged and poor, that medically ill were being misdirected, and that large numbers of relatively well, aged persons were kept in state hospitals simply because they had no place to go. In the 1940s there was much talk about excluding aged homeless persons from state hospitals. Among other efforts to decrease the state hospital burden was the passage, in one state, of a law forbidding state hospital admission or retention of dotards; this was soon rescinded.

The claims that state hospitals were being abused as a site of care for aged persons were actually exaggerated. For example, the examination of patients in Connecticut state hospitals by Schindell and Cornfield [21] at the time the furor about "mistaken admissions" was at its height revealed that very few could justifiably be transferred to other types of facilities—to say nothing of private homes. Furthermore, examinations of the categories of hospitalized old persons revealed that first admissions in old age constituted only 12 percent of the total hospital population. Further, although they might have constituted 30 to 40 percent of all first admissions in a given year, they were only one-fourth to one-third of the hospital geriatric population. It was patients who aged in the hospital, chiefly those with schizophrenia, who constituted by far the largest number of old persons in state hospitals. A relatively small proportion had entered with an affective disorder, drug dependence, or organic mental syndromes of relatively early occurrence. Many proved resistant to therapy or became withdrawn examples of the "hospitalization syndrome" or "social breakdown" syndrome that emerges with relative neglect. Others were relatively well adjusted within the protective hospital setting [36].

Following on the expansion of welfare benefits, especially with the advent of Medicaid in the late sixties, there was an effective effort to reduce the number of old persons in state hospitals [13]. This was achieved in several ways: (1) by transfer of chronologically old persons—predominantly the well-adjusted, chemically restrained, or relatively meek and submissive members of the aged-in-the-hospital group—to nursing homes, boarding homes, lodgings, or foster homes; and (2) by "exclusion at the gate" of chronologically old persons who appeared to be physically acutely ill, likely to become permanent residents, or apparently free from gross affective disorders. For example, from 1965 to 1974 there was a 40 percent decrease in patients 65 and over in the New York State hospital system. Nevertheless, their proportion of the total population in 1974 rose to 45 percent as compared with 39 percent in 1968 because of greater reductions in the number of younger patients. Only 8 percent of the old persons in the New York State hospitals were there for less than two years; 82 percent were residents for five or more years, and 42 percent had been hospitalized for 30 years or more.

In the 1950s the growth of proprietary nursing homes burgeoned; regional overbuilding and empty beds led, in part, to the recruitment of so-called improved or well, or well-adjusted, state hospital patients to fill them. This was accepted as a solution to hospital overcrowding and was welcomed as a means of decreasing direct financial responsibility by many state hospital systems. Also, it was heralded as a humane "return of aged patients to the community." The wholesale transfer of patients to nursing homes was advocated as the preferred alternative to state hospital care. In fact, the majority of transferred patients consisted of those who had aged in the hospital, not of those first admitted in their old age. Through the use of preadmission screening teams prior to state hospital admission, nursing homes were recommended as alternatives to the state hospital for patients who might have been first admissions in their old age, and the recommendations were implemented. The responsibility and accountability for medical supervision present in a hospital were absent in nursing homes, although many plans for medical consultation were devised. The change of institutions was the equivalent of exchanging one inadequate, poorly staffed back ward for another where space, medical and general care, helpful personnel, and community life either within or outside the institution were less rather than more available.

Recently, investigations of nursing homes to which old persons were transferred or encouraged to use as alternatives to the psychiatric hospital have made it very clear that these do not in any sense constitute adequate alternatives. Usually, they do not offer as good care as the state hospitals (bad as they were) did in the past. Mortality is as high or higher than in state hospitals, as is morbidity of all types. They have in no sense constituted a real return to or a use of the community. This has led to much clamor to provide alternatives to these institutions, and the problem is now being passed to day centers, home care agencies, and other methods of delivering care. The results of these efforts remain to be evaluated.

Nursing Homes and Homes for the Aged
Even well before efforts to use alternatives to state hospitals, old persons with psychiatric disorders were found in a variety of institutions called nursing homes, personal-care homes, or homes for the aged. Two general types in addition to the state hospital were more or less clearly identifiable: homes for the aged and nursing homes. Each of these types of facilities continues to be in an accelerated transitional state because of changes in Medicare and Medicaid financing and changes that may take place in the use of proprietary nursing homes because of recent revelations about profiteering, fraud, and patient neglect. At best, the type and quality of functioning of institutions of the same general type, whether commercial or noncommercial, have tended to vary from place to place and from time to time. There are wide variations in the selection and retention of patients and in size, staffing, programs, and quality of care, as well as in cost to the consumer. At present, all appear to be moving toward providing "skilled nursing care," general care, and residential care by way of the development of differently staffed areas within one facility, as determined by federally set reimbursement formulas.

It is convenient to distinguish the characteristics of two nonhospital categories, namely, old-age homes and nursing homes. Small (for example, 8 to 15 beds) old-age homes as well as lodging houses, senior citizen hotels, residential hotels, housing projects for the old, or foster homes that are not clearly affiliated with homes for the aged are not considered to be institutions in the sense of this discussion. Unfortunately, there are many miscellaneous types of residence and fragmented programs now emerging for the aged that care for many persons who actually need and would benefit from the use of the more formally organized institutions [20]. Despite their claims and current public acceptance of them, these facilities are makeshifts that have arisen because of social attitudes that discourage the rational use of more formally organized protective care settings such as long-term hospitals and homes for the aged. Furthermore, these efforts do not cost less; when all the facts are known, they cost far more. Their actual costs are usually hidden because the government's share is supplemented by the private funds of the resident and his family.

Because Medicare provides money to old persons for three to four months of posthospital care in specified nursing homes that could prove themselves worthy of categorization as extended care facilities (ECFs), there were changes in the selection of patients by many of the homes so classified and a move away from long-term care. The attempt to raise and maintain standards of nursing home care for the long-term as well as the short-term patient, which lay behind the creation of extended care facilities, has now given way to the concept of "skilled nursing care" areas (SKFs). Patients in these sections are entitled to reimbursement by Medicare. Patients who need less skilled nursing care are assigned to "intermediate care" areas (ICFs), with a smaller and less skilled staff. Skilled nursing care, however, is very difficult to define, whether in terms of staff member, type, or duty, just as is the need for such care. Medicare reimbursement has been predicated on a nursing home's rehabilitative, restorative efforts and based on outmoded concepts of the need for staff and facilities to accomplish these purposes, thus giving rise to the extended care facility as a "halfway house" or place for convalescence after acute hospital care. While praiseworthy in their intent to elevate standards of care, these rulings had a considerable—and not entirely desirable—influence on patient selection and care without leading to true upgrading of services. In general, truly convalescent patients after acute illness need a less skilled staff and fewer numbers of caregivers than do patients who require a protective or therapeutic milieu continuously for the last years of their lives.

Another problem arising from the creation of the extended care facility, skilled nursing home concept of classification has been its effect on nonprofit homes, especially the large, urban, well-staffed quasihospitals, which contain the highest proportion of beds. These homes, for purposes of reimbursement, are reclassified as skilled nursing care facilities and accredited as such rather than as hospitals. In actuality, such homes receive few or no patients on a Medicare reimbursement basis because such admissions must be within a 10-day period after discharge from a general hospital, and old-age home waiting periods usually exceed this because of their low turnover, which is about 18 percent (in a 500-bed facility, this would be 90 possible admissions a year). Their residents are now relegated to the lower Medicaid or welfare reimbursement category on the same basis as commercial homes, even though they may provide far more facilities, staff, and restorative programs. This has resulted in a steady deterioration of services.

The differences between noncommercial old-age homes and proprietary nursing homes, somewhat dogmatically stated below and in the tables on the following pages, are not well known and have led to misunderstandings. These misunderstandings tend to be reinforced by the misleading names that confuse the types of facilities. Physicians and nurses in general hospitals, for example, often overrate the functional and caretaking potential of residences whose names include the term *nursing,* and they underestimate the severity of impairment found in residents of facilities called old-age homes or retirement hotels. Also, there is inadequate understanding of the complex admission procedures and the variety of plans for financing care. Mistaken ideas may lead to unreasonable demands on families to make complicated arrangements for a patient's care.

Comparison of Old-Age Homes and Nursing Homes

Old-age homes are as a rule nonprofit, voluntary, and sectarian. The private (nonsubsidized) old-age home may resemble the nursing home in such things as admissions policy and patient population, depending on the level of care provided, the size of the home, and financing. Most nursing homes are commercial (proprietary), and tend to provide lower levels of care than do old-age homes. A few nonprofit voluntary nursing homes are comparable to old-age homes, as some "homestead" wards of general hospitals are comparable to proprietary nursing homes. Because of reimbursement formulas, old-age homes and nursing homes are now coming to resemble each other closely in all respects.

Supervision and Licensure
The supervision and licensure of old-age homes are by social service departments (in residential areas), or by state departments of health (in hospital or infirmary areas). Nursing homes are overseen by state and municipal departments of social welfare, hospitals, or health. Because 50 to 80 percent of the residents in old-age and nursing homes are welfare-supported, it is usually the case that welfare departments have some supervision over both types of home.

Care and Services
Medical care varies, in old-age homes, from minimal to almost complete, except for major surgery and radiotherapy. When care in outside hospitals is required, it is paid for by Medicare in most instances. In nursing homes no medical care is provided; it must be obtained from private physicians or from physicians assigned by welfare agencies through group, hospital, panel, or team; or in acute illness, by transfer to a local hospital. Old-age homes are permitted to employ physicians, and nursing homes are not (except that since January 1975 nursing homes have been required to have a physician medical director on staff to coordinate and monitor medical services).

In both types of home the nursing care varies from fair to excellent. Patients may be required to have special nurses and/or aides if the family wishes, or if the patient requires care beyond the norm of the institution, or if the patient or family can afford the care; in the majority of old-age homes and nursing homes, however, nursing care is very limited and often exists on paper but not in fact. Special duty nurses are frequently required. Since care is thought of as custodial, the need for psychodynamically sophisticated personnel is ignored, aides are poorly chosen, staff turnover is high, and abuses are common. Skilled nursing care facilities are presumed to provide adequate nursing, but the definition of adequacy of such care is vague. Exclusion of psychiatric patients is actual exclusion of those who need nursing care most.

Social services vary, but in old-age homes they are often considerable. Applicant screening and continuing liaison work with family are customary. In nursing homes social services are rare, in fact usually nonexistent. Nursing homes may encourage family counseling, but at times this practice is a means of increasing reimbursement otherwise restricted by law.

Duration of Stay

Patients usually stay in one type of home or another for the remainder of their lives. In old-age homes the death rate ranges from about 20 percent in homes that select the healthy to about 40 percent in those that are more like chronic disease hospitals. Transfers of nursing home patients from home to home and from home to hospital are frequent, though transfers are rare from nursing homes to old-age homes. The length of stay in some nursing homes is decreasing with conversion to skilled nursing facilities, and increasing in those that add intermediate care facilities. SKFs allow for greater selectivity in admissions (see below), and ICFs permit continued maintenance of patients who would otherwise be transferred.

Size of Homes

The number of beds in old-age homes ranges from 20 to 500 or more, and a great variety of services may be provided, including: occupational and recreational therapy, sheltered workshops, physiatrics, podiatry, barbers and hairdressers, shops, chapel, clinics, dentistry, clubs, activities, libraries, music rooms. In contrast, the size of nursing homes ranges from 15 to 300 or more beds, and services are usually severely limited. It is still unusual to find in nursing homes libraries, shops, hairdressers; podiatry and other services are by special arrangement only, but nursing homes are beginning to add such services as ICFs are added. In small homes of either type (under 100 beds), the range of services is rarely adequate. Services for which Medicare reimburses are often given priority by extended care facilities (ECFs).

Admissions Policies
In the past the admissions policies of old-age homes, while not uniform, were usually very selective. Patients in crisis, or who were acutely ill or mentally ill, were excluded. Preference was given the relatively healthy. Donations from the patient's family might be invited. Waiting periods varied from 3 to 6 months for the relatively well to periods of 2 to 3 years for the ill, impaired, or disabled. "List hopping" for various reasons was not uncommon (e.g., donations, suitability as roommates in vacancy areas, connections with important persons). Of late, as the age of applicants and residents has increased, admissions policies have been relaxed, and older, sicker, more confused persons are more readily and rapidly admitted than was common in the past.

In nursing homes until recently the admissions policies have been "anything goes." If adjustment was not made, the patient was transferred, often to a state hospital. In the past, there was usually no waiting period. The availability of patients with Medicare money has resulted in occasional variation in waiting periods, and has permitted the selection of residents in nursing homes to emphasize the home's image as an SKF. As ICFs are added, admissions policies of nursing homes come to resemble those of old-age homes. Recently with ECF labels many nursing homes are converting to the type of facility that will permit the selection of those patients who can profit from rehabilitation. Small selective homes are likely to have the shortest waiting periods because there are too few eligible persons for the small range of services offered.

In old-age homes the population is usually homogeneous with regard to socioeconomic, cultural, and religious background; in nursing homes it is more heterogeneous. One hundred-day Medicare policy encourages the admission to SKFs of rich and sick, or poor and well, in preference to the poor and sick. Other homes, preferring low turnover, place emphasis on evaluation as ICFs, which again tends to exclude the poor. Few old-age homes exist for the black population, and in nursing homes the black population is over-represented.

Finances
Contributions to institutions must be from families, not out of patient's funds, and are for capital, not maintenance, costs. In both types of home

the patient's own funds (savings and income from Social Security and/or other pensions) are used for maintenance. Since 1965 amendments to the Social Security act are making filial responsibility unnecessary, maintenance is seldom paid for by families. Referral is made to department of social services for Old Age Assistance or Medical Aid for the Aged on exhaustion of the patient's own funds or to make up the difference between the patient's monthly income and the monthly rate (set by state department of health and/or department of social services). Rates for domiciliary care are much lower than for infirmary care.

Sixty to eighty percent of patients are recipients of Old Age Assistance; proprietary homes are, in effect, subcontractors to the government for the care of sick or impaired aged poor. Changes stemming from Medicare, and restrictions in Medicaid money, now press many old-age homes to become skilled nursing facilities or intermediate care facilities with decreased medical services and generally lowered standards of care, rather than to remain relatively autonomous, innovative, and creative designers of facilities, programs, and concepts of care.

Characteristics of the Institutionalized Population

Over one million of the approximately 21 million elderly persons in the United States are now in institutions [15]. Many more need protective care in hospitals, homes, and well-regulated congregate living quarters. This actual and potential institutional population is heterogeneous with respect to the characteristics previously enumerated. Most are poor and have had difficult lives with few advantages. The average age at application to long-term protective care settings is now about 80 years, and the average age of residents of long-term protective and nursing care facilities is now well over 80 years.

Old persons now in congregate protective settings or therapeutic milieus require *comprehensive* care, including basic and special medical services as well as psychiatric and social services.

The psychiatric conditions of chronologically old persons who find their way into institutions for care span a wide range. The largest group of persons who need institutional comprehensive care are those with mental impairment, that is, organic brain syndrome, whether or not this is accompanied by clear-cut functional mental disorder or physical illness or physical functional impairment. In some persons, disorders are brought into old age from youth and are complicated by, or complicate, the age-related changes in health and socioeconomic status. In others, depressive disorders or disturbances of thinking processes develop or first emerge as significant in old age and may be complicated by brain changes that result in the loss of memory and mental impairment psychiatrically known as organic brain syndromes. The major psychiatric conditions commonly present in old institutionalized patients have already been reviewed in Chapters 10 and 13.

Studies reveal that in the variety of institutions providing long-term care for the old, from 30 to over 60 percent are nonambulatory, and as few as 6 to 10 percent may be fully ambulatory. Confusional states are common. From 30 to 70 or 80 percent suffer from organic brain syndrome of some degree; i.e., the majority are constantly disoriented regarding time, place, and person, have gross memory defects both remote and recent, cannot do even simple calculations, and have a dearth of usable general information. In most homes, in over 30 percent of the elderly the confusional state is severe. From 25 to over 40 percent are incontinent. Depressions and paranoid thinking and behavior are commonly associated with poor physical functional status and active disease of the cardiovascular-renal, pulmonary, musculoskeletal, or central nervous systems. Even when disorders of affect or content of thought are not obvious, either episodically or continuously, the aged with brain syndromes of even minimal degree are vulnerable to acute confusional states in which agitation, behavioral disorganization, and alterations of mood and thinking call for psychiatrically oriented care. There has been an increase in the number of persons with needs for care on account of mental impairment and its associated disturbed and disturbing behavior in those with physical impairment, disease, and debility with associated depression. There is also an increased need for care of chronologically old persons with relatively good physical and mental functional status who may require care for varying degrees of time because of a so-called functional psychiatric disorder.

Contrary to popular belief, old persons have not tended to reach old-age homes for social reasons, nursing homes for medical reasons, and state hospitals for psychiatric reasons alone. A number of factors contribute to overlapping characteristics in these groups [4, 5, 16]. Table 17 presents some of the characteristics of persons at the time of their

Table 17. Socioeconomic Factors Related to Admission to Three Major
Types of Institutions, by Percentage of Persons Sampled 1957–1958

Factor	Percent in Old-Age Homes	Percent in Nursing Homes[a]	Percent in State Hospitals[a]	Percent in All Institutions[a]
Age at admission:				
65–74	44	33	44	40
75–84	47	48	44	37
84+	9	18	11	13
Average age at admission	(76)	(79)	(76)	...
Marital state:				
Married	12	9	22	12
Widowed	67	60	60	64
Divorced/separated	6	2	5	4
Single	15	23	12	18
Number of living children:				
None	35	43	34	36
One	14	22	26	18
Two	16	14	12	15
Three+	35	11	23	26
Sources of income at admission:[b]				
Welfare	28	73	22	43
Family aid	32	18	21	27
Personal income	72	29	9	58
Admitted from:				
Own home	61	25	41	45
Relative's home	26	8	31	19
Nursing home	8	8	7	8
General hospital	3	56	15	21
Other	4	3	4	2
Years of schooling:				
0–7	33	70	54	55
8+	67	30	46	45

[a] Where categories add to less than 100 percent, the remainder represents "unknown."
[b] Adds to over 100 percent because some had multiple sources of support.

admission to the three types of institutions in 1958. The figures in Table 17, gathered in 1958 and representative of the New York metropolitan area, are a fairly accurate reflection of the present situation throughout the urban United States, except that patients (or residents), both on admission and on a sampling of the population at any given time, are older and more impaired physically and mentally, and except that all institutions are now in a transitional state. In the past 10 years admissions of the very sick elderly to state hospitals have decreased, and the old-age homes and various types of nursing homes—skilled nursing, intermediate care facilities, personal-care homes—have became more alike in population. Also, many homes have become repositories for patients, young and old, transferred from state hospitals.

A comparison of the findings obtained in 1957–1958 with a similar study performed in selected homes of the northeast United States by the Council of Jewish Federation and Welfare Funds in cooperation with the National Institute of Mental Health in 1966 indicates that for old-age homes the age at admission and the age of residents are slightly more advanced. More recent information indicates that the average age of application is now close to 80 years and the average age of residents is about 85 years. The prevalence of organic brain syndrome is now somewhat greater, and the proportion of severely impaired persons in the old-age homes is higher. There is no significant change with respect to marital state at the time of admission, or to number of living children. A higher proportion of those in the more recent sample were dependent on welfare aid at admission and at the time of the study [11, 24]. This appears to reflect primarily a change in the law, which now relieves children of legal responsibility for the support of aged parents. While there are still many private patients in commercial and nonprofit homes, about 80 percent of the payment for the care of old persons in institutions is from government funds.

From these data and from other studies it can be seen that the majority of those who come to live in institutions as first admissions in their old age do so when in their late seventies or eighties [17, 19]. The presence of protective, caretaking persons, such as a mate or children, favors the chances of the aged person's admission to the more selective, better-equipped old-age home, as does the existence of a good personal or family income. Many aged persons, even if extremely incapacitated or disturbed, can wait out the time required. Years of schooling are a fair index of socioeconomic status and are illustrative of the same point: the better off one is socioeconomically, the less one is apt to use the commercial nursing home or state hospital. This is now changing as nursing homes that have moved toward skilled nursing care facility and ICF status are developing areas of care of the long-term, old-age-home type that compare favorably with those of the best nonprofit homes.

While immediate factors leading to institutional care include advanced age and debility or multiple impairments—of sight, hearing, ambulation, mentation, and self-care ability—together with a need for care, these are usually joined by an absence of available resources, such as money or family, sufficient to provide a "one-bed nursing home" (or hospital) in their own home.

The proportion of men and women may vary greatly from one institution to another. In general, women tend to outnumber men by at least two to one; in some homes for the aged the ratio is as high as seven to one. This is probably because women live longer than do men and outlive their usually older spouses, thus providing a large population at risk of institutionalization on account of age, impairment, and the absence of a protective mate. Conversely, men of considerable disability may be maintained at home by younger and functionally more capable wives.

It is of interest that the burden of care of an aged, ill person is such that the well spouse, especially if male, often dies before the sick one. The death of the latter, who is now left without a protector, quickly follows. It is also worthy of note that after years of caring for the sick mate who dies, the well person, having become exhausted, debilitated, and ill, may die soon after. It appears to be to the advantage of the survivor to have had a short preparation for the death of the mate.

Persons of either sex—more often women—are frequently maintained outside of institutions by children who thus provide protection against institutionalization. Nursing homes and old-age homes have been, almost invariably, permanent residences. For state hospital patients the existence of a spouse or children increases the chances of leaving the hospital—at times for home, at others for an alternative institution. The better-educated and socioeconomically advantaged aged tend to reach an institution later than their poorer counterparts. It is then more likely to be a home for the aged, except for the very old who, because of a severely disturbed mental state, find their way to a state hospital. Men who have never married appear to make use of institutional protection earlier than equally disabled married men or widowers. The youngest and oldest of old people are admitted to state hospitals. These ends of the age spectrum are represented respectively by functional disorders and by severe organic brain syndrome in the presence of a relatively sound body. Admission to old-age homes and state hospitals is usually directly from home, whereas admission to nursing homes is most frequently from general hospitals.

Symptoms of disturbed behavior, such as suicidal attempts, attacks on others, dangerous wandering, or confused and dangerous misuse of household appliances, frequently lead to psychiatric hospitalization. The loss of protective persons by death, or the loss of accommodations or changes in neighborhoods, as well as needs for protective care, often lead to application to old-age homes on the part of persons who can foresee waiting the three months to three years required. Crises such as accentuation of preexisting impairment by acute illness, accidents, or a sudden shift in social circumstances frequently lead to nursing home care by way of the general hospital or, less frequently, directly from home. Who needs an institution, and what kind is needed, cannot be determined merely by looking at who is now in which type of institution.

Thus as is shown in Table 18, old-age homes do not necessarily serve only social and retirement needs. Over 50 percent of their beds are of the infirmary type, caring for grossly impaired and disabled aged persons. Nursing homes serve a large number of relatively ambulatory, energetic, and physically well but moderately to severely mentally impaired aged. State hospital populations of persons first admitted in old age include the following: a few relatively "young-old" persons (60 to 70) with functional disorders and some with organic mental syndromes (organic brain syndromes [OBS]) related to cerebral arteriosclerosis (presenile brain disease); a very large number of "middle-aged" old (70 to 80), most of whom have OBS of the senium, often in association with disorders of affect or thought content; and a substantial number of the very old with relatively uncomplicated severe OBS.

Persons with OBS are found in each setting. The proportion of the severely afflicted, however, is less in old-age homes than in nursing homes and is highest in state hospitals. Also, persons with disorders of

281

Table 18. Selected Characteristics in Three Types of Institution by Percentage of Persons, 1957–1958

Characteristic	Percent in Old-Age Homes	Percent in Nursing Homes	Percent in State Hospitals	Percent in All Institutions
Age distribution of residents:				
65–74	23	21	44	25
75–84	49	43	43	46
85+	24	24	13	23
All mental disorders	90	93	100	90
Chronic brain syndrome:				
Mild	37	24	9	27
Moderate	28	35	32	31
Severe	15	29	53	27
Total	80	88	94	85
Physical functional status:				
Fair	51	21	30	36
Poor	37	36	38	36
Very poor	13	43	32	27
Bedfast	10	33	27	. . .
Incontinent	10	37	29	. . .
Physical dependency:				
Cannot				
Bathe self	33	77	57	50
Dress self	13	40	36	24
Walk alone	11	37	28	22
Mobility poor	7	26	13	14

mood and content associated with brain syndromes are found in all, but there are fewest in old-age homes and more in state hospitals than in nursing homes. Also, persons with poor physical functional status and multiple impairments or chronic illnesses are found in each type of institution, with the highest proportion being found in nursing homes and the fewest in state hospitals. It should be noted that until recently less than 10 percent of persons coming to state hospitals in their old age

Table 19. Persons with Organic Brain Syndrome and Differing Combinations of Disability: Acceptability According to Type of Institution

Functional Mental and Physical Status[a]	Acceptability[b]			
	Old-Age Home	Nursing Home	State Hospital	Home Care
Both good	4+	4+	4+	4+
Mental—good, physical—poor	2+	4+	0	4+
Physical—good, mental—poor	1+	2+	1+	0
Both poor	1+	2+	0	0

[a] Physical status evaluation is based on capacity for self-care, ability to ambulate, and vigor. Mental status is based on severity of OBS.
[b] Numbers indicate increasing degree of acceptability: 0 is not acceptable or least acceptable; 4 is most acceptable.

had a disorder of affect or thought content in the absence of OBS. On the other hand, in private psychiatric hospitals prior to Medicare, the majority of persons admitted in old age suffered from disorders of affect (depressive reactions), a few were paranoid, and the rest had OBS. Now that general hospital psychiatric wards have been developed, the largest number of old persons with affective disorders will go (admission policies permitting) to such units, although the state hospitals, because of their commitment to developing as intensive care centers, would welcome them. A further reason for state hospital competition for these patients is their value as payers via Medicare.

What kind of persons tend to gravitate (and be acceptable to) what type of institution is indicated in Table 19. This illustrates that persons who have the poorest mental functional status are the most difficult to place at the present time because of the unwillingness of state hospital systems to undertake long-term care of patients in the old age group.

Mortality
Mortality is higher in institutional populations than in the general population [10]. Taken as a group and excluding acutely ill persons who die in the first three months after admission to a psychiatric hospital, about 25 percent are dead within the first year, over 40 percent by the end of the second year, and over 50 percent by the end of the third year. Comparable figures for four, five, six, and seven years are 65, 73, 79, and 82

Table 20. Comparative Percentages of Deaths by Year in Old-Age Homes, Nursing Homes, and State Hospitals

	Total		Percent Died Within:						
			Years						
	Number	%	1	2	3	4	5	6	7
OAH	454	100	17	32	46	58	69	74	78
NH	396	100	26	45	58	71	79	86	89
SH*	166	100	35	48	63	69	75	80	83
Total	1016	100	24	40	53	65	74	80	83

* Survivors of at least three months in the hospital.

percent respectively. The death rate is higher for males than for females and is exceptionally high for persons who have severe CBS as determined by psychiatric or psychological tests or by observation of a high degree of physical functional impairment or incontinence [8] (see Table 20).

The high mortality of state hospital patients—a group now going to other facilities in many states—in the first year and especially in the first few months after admission is undoubtedly due to their moribund or preterminal condition. Many aged persons in their last few months of life become extremely difficult to manage. They may be noisy, destructive, impulsive, assaultive, or self-destructive to degrees that endanger others as well as themselves. When medicated, they may become more disorganized or comatose. Their nursing needs tend to exceed the available facilities in general hospitals, and, in desperation, family or physicians send them to the psychiatric hospital. The latter, unfortunately, has not always been well enough equipped or staffed to manage the multiple medical problems of these patients. Despite the likelihood that the best of medical care would make little difference to most of these patients, prolonging the lives of a few only for a short time—and of an exceptional patient for a longer period—state hospitals have been severely criticized for their high death rate.

Perhaps it is partly in reaction to this criticism that state hospital systems have declared themselves out of bounds to the medically acutely ill aged patient, whatever his mental status. But studies have demonstrated that mortality is high even for aged persons who are not acutely ill and who have reached nonhospital institutions. The course of transferred patients and longitudinal studies of institutionalized persons suggest that mortality is related to the basic condition of the patient rather than to the facility, program, or transfer. In general, the data suggest that, given adequate shelter, food, and general medical care, the life span of severely impaired and disabled aged persons in any type of institution is related to their individual physical condition or viability. It seems doubtful that the provision of extra services greatly prolongs life in the very ill, although it may add immeasurably to comfort. Conversely, the relatively well may live somewhat longer in shelters that have programs and services that contribute to pleasure and the maintenance of dignity. The relatively robust also may react favorably to a shift or change in domicile, whereas for the severely functionally impaired, shifts appear to make demands or lead to relative neglect, which may shorten life.

Therapeutic Efforts
Ideally, if it is to be properly and flexibly utilized, the inpatient care of persons who need help from social institutions because of physical decline, mental impairment, and disturbed or disturbing behavior should be part of a larger, integrated comprehensive care system. Residential care facilities can respond episodically or for the long term to the needs for bed and board, social integration, recreation and relaxation, basic medical care, and special medical services within a community type of organization. In them, a small proportion of old impaired persons can be at least temporarily restored for continued life at home, i.e., "rehabilitated"; others can be housed and cared for temporarily to give their caretakers a vacation and rest, but the majority will need the facility for the remainder of their lives. For all, the milieu should be protective and emotionally and psychologically supportive. Enfeebled or mentally impaired persons are protected from the demands and challenges of society and the specific community from which they come. The ideal institution is one whose protective services, reassuring and supportive environment, general medical care, and special medical services cover a wide spectrum.

The essential services in any residential facility are food, lodging, and basic medical care. Only some of the special points of importance can be touched on.

The goals of basic services, like those of psychotherapy, are as follows: to decrease fear and anger; to increase the sense that one is self-sufficient and capable and to foster actual self-sufficiency, where possible; to induce pleasure, or at least contribute to comfort; to ease the relationship of staff to patients; and to promote social integration and good social relations while permitting privacy and a sense of independence. Good general medical services, food, lodging, good counseling and support or casework, and activities therapy are needed by all institutionalized persons. Most (about 90 percent) need special medical care, foot care, dentistry, occupational or recreational therapy, and group therapy. Some (about 30 to 40 percent) need physiatric treatment and aid in ambulation or "lifters," special nursing, or psychotherapy (group, dyadic, or both). A smaller number (about 10 to 40 percent) require intensive care for cardiovascular disease, infections, neoplasms, intercurrent diseases, and the acute complications of chronic illness, and there are always a number of persons who need terminal care. These proportions in institutions must vary because the factors of selection determine the differing types of population in residence. For all institutions the range of services must be large, or there must be liaison with other providers.

In addition to opportunities for fuller use of the self within a helpful setting there must be medical care that monitors the relatively unstable health state of a high proportion of the aged. Prompt and often elaborate attention is required for such conditions as diabetes, hypertension, arteriosclerotic cardiovascular disease, emphysema, anemia, and arthritis, which fluctuate in severity. Such patients need medication, an appropriate diet, exercise or rest, and treatment for the accidents and infections that complicate chronic disease. The "multiplicity, chronicity, and duplicity" of their disease states call for alertness, quick response, much medical skill, and abundant medical supplies.

Within a home, many old persons can be assisted toward special flowering as active persons and competent citizens who can aid their fellows. A few can be so restored to health that they may expand their activities and once again work or play within the larger community and—if there are safe places to live that are economically practical—can consider leaving the home. An institutional home for old persons is thus a community in which there are many overlapping levels of caretaking for persons who have different combinations of disease, impairment, and physical, emotional, psychological, and basic mental functioning. A home may even include as its charges for care volunteers from the outside, persons who themselves are lonely, disabled, and impaired in function to a degree yet are capable of being helpers and motivated to do so. For example, in Beth Abraham Hospital, New York, about 7 percent of a volunteer group of about 300 are retired senior volunteer program (RSVP) persons.

Patients generally do better if they have opportunities for privacy. For sufficiently well persons, social interaction and good interpersonal relationships are favored by residential accommodation in private, unshared rooms. Cultural differences, however, exist, and many old persons prefer to share rooms because they have never lived alone. Other reasons for a desire or need to share living space are extremely severe impairment and fear of becoming ill and not being able to signal for help; or simply fear of being alone, which may be continuation of a lifelong anxiety. Eating facilities, however, should not be in the patient's room but in a common dining room. The atmosphere should be homelike and it should not be clinical, even in units where medical care is intensive, because this is the patient's home. Rugs are useful and should be wall-to-wall, nonskid, washable, and not so soft as to impede walking or interfere with balance. Rugs of any type, however, prove to be unsatisfactory where incontinence is uncontrollable. Lamps, homelike fixtures, and individual, easily accessible, yet personally safeguarded storage places are essential.

The beds should be low for the sake of the patient, although this may mean some extra effort for the nurse. Side rails generally cause more falls and fractures than they prevent, in addition to being personally humiliating. Furthermore, in the absence of additional restraints, they are rarely effective in limitation of wandering. The best restraints for confused and agitated patients are properly motivated alert personnel, minimum amounts of the proper medications, and seduction into activity. A useful way to restrain wandering patients is to build in the round, so that, no matter how far he walks, the wanderer is never farther from the centrally stationed nurse than he is when in his own room. Necessary in all institutions that care for the aged is psychiatrically oriented supervision of residents based on the recognition that most behavior can be understood.

Basically, the establishment of relationships with personnel, not physical or chemical restraints, is a patient's greatest safeguard and reassurance. However, optimal care of the frightened and confused aged person is consequently expensive under the best of conditions.

Encouraging social interests in old persons with OBS requires leadership. As in military groups, relationships are established first with the leader and later, if at all, with peers through this common bond.

Staff morale, in turn, is favorably influenced by vertical and horizontal staff conferences about patient problems, in which a framework for the selection and collection of information is provided and guidelines for care and management are offered and freely discussed. Such conferences are best led by psychiatrists or psychologists experienced in the care of the aged. In general, institutional staffs have too little an appreciation of their importance as psychotherapists and of the importance of their nonpsychiatric skills and duties as vehicles for psychotherapy. They need psychiatric consultations and conferences to educate them to these factors, to maintain morale, and for periodic reinforcement. They respond with optimism to the interest of a psychiatrist and react favorably to his policing function with respect to human transactions. Staff attitude toward, interest in, and care of aged, mentally impaired persons, the severely physically disabled, and the slowly dying or terminally ill are improved by the introduction of psychiatric assistance.

Aged institutional residents tend to respond favorably to a structured but flexible program that leads them to exploitation of their assets without unduly subjecting them to failure or confrontation of their deficits, physical or mental. In this, even skilled staff may need considerable aid, so that patients may not be wrongly assessed. For example, a behavioral disturbance should not be mistaken for dementia, or mild and cooperative behavior be taken as evidence of cerebral competence. In a recent survey, staffs of unsophisticated old-age homes grossly underestimated the number of persons in their charge who had OBS; the disorder was recognized only if severe.

Staff members often need assistance in reaching decisions about the specific types of activity that can have maximal restorative or remotivational influence. The fear that patients will lose self-sufficiency if permitted to become emotionally dependent, or that they may be vulnerable to grief at the loss of personnel by staff turnover, must be vigorously countered. Personnel on all levels need much instruction about the value of transference, rapport, "parentification," or the interest of the "significant other," found in the guise of a staff member, in promoting self-sufficiency or optimal function. The nuclear importance of a dependency relationship as a means of helping the patient toward optimal functioning and minimal vulnerability to personal losses is a paradox with which an institutional staff must become well acquainted.

The importance of sheltered workshops, music rooms and music therapy, and—most of all—physiotherapy as vehicles for psychotherapy cannot be overrated. Like the provision of good basic medical care and the establishment of a relationship with the physician or the medical department of the institution, each of these has an extremely important reassuring and supportive influence on the patient. However, individual differences must be grasped and their implications heeded. For example, many old persons gain a sense of worth and confidence from working for pay. To others, this is objectionable, since they feel they have worked long enough. For some, any such work for pay is felt to be humiliatingly childlike, especially if patronizingly led by rich volunteers [2].

Attitudes Toward Institutional Use

Old persons in general are opposed to the use of institutions; this is more the rule than the exception and is most obvious in the clearly mentally ill, the subtly mentally disturbed, and in the oldest and the most impaired. Thus those who need protective care the most want it the least and may oppose it the most vigorously, whereas those who may need it the least are less resistant to accepting the change in residence. This makes it obvious that one reason aged persons who need protective institutions also need psychiatric assistance is the intensity of their feelings that institutional use constitutes rejection by family and friends and a loss of independence.

Unfortunately, the low quality of institutional care in the past, however attractive the physical plant, has tended to reinforce such beliefs and attitudes. Institutions are for the most part so poorly equipped, staffed, and organized that the resistance of families of aged persons to making use of them is more frequently related to realistic appraisal of the site of care and anger against "the system" than to guilt based on giving the care of the parent over to others; or, as is so often asserted, on unconscious hostility.

Institutional care is usually regarded as a prelude to death by applicants and their families rather than as a new, useful experience in community living. It can be such an experience in the best old-age homes and could be in many state hospitals that attempt to become communities in themselves as well as to remain related to the outside world. Unfortunately, most institutions are not self-contained communities and are by no means a part of the larger community. Therefore, they become places in which old persons with little or nothing to do and with their senses, minds, and emotions blunted by drugs simply wait for death.

Entrance into residences of such poor quality tends to downgrade the person's image of himself. His disability may become greater, and there may be development or exaggeration of psychological and emotional disorder. Institutional deterioration can be counteracted by the provision of community-type activities: sheltered workshops in hospitals or homes, recreational therapy, hotel-type accommodations, and the contagion of high morale in a well-motivated staff. These improve self-concepts and behavior and help decrease objections to entrance into homes as well as to continued residence in them.

Conclusion

There are a number of commonly held beliefs about persons who have reached, or appear to need, institutional care in their old age. Some of these incorrect ideas can be summarized as follows:

Aged persons in our society are rejected and neglected and discriminated against. They are discarded by selfish, callous families and are relegated to loneliness and discomfort, which affect their mental and emotional well-being. When they become ill, they are quickly dumped into state hospitals, nursing homes, or old-age homes, where many of them die from the shock of transfer or from humiliation. Large numbers of them are forced to remain in institutions simply because they have no place to go, and this is largely because their place in the community has been permitted to close in behind them. The children of this generation lack estimable character and virtue. They make one wonder how it is that "while one parent can take care of twelve children, twelve children cannot take care of one parent."

Such seemingly compassionate remarks appear to be exhortative toward improving the sorry lot of the aged. They are actually misstatements that tend to confuse thought and to block social action. They tend to turn one away from social organizations aimed at ameliorating a major public health and welfare problem [7].

Thoughtful review of the actual state of affairs supports the contention that only persons with great need for institutional aid reach such points of care. There is no evidence that families "dump" troublesome old persons into an institution, whether it be a state hospital or some other facility. On the contrary, the presence of family tends to be a major protection against institutional care, often to the disadvantage of the patient and contrary to his needs. It is more the rule that families wait too long for and fight against the use of institutions than that they make unnecessary use of them. A capacity for self-maintenance or the availability of personal and familiar resources helps impaired persons avoid institutionalization; an absence of family and the presence of excessive disability fostered by ignorance, a psychological or emotional disorder, or alcoholism increase a person's chances of institutionalization. The question whether institutionalization is really necessary for those found in these facilities can best be answered by research findings that have demonstrated that it is usually a last resort—and a late solution—on the part of persons helping the aged, rather than the result of a properly timed search for assistance [9].

References

1. Davis, B. H. A.   A descriptive exploratory study of the dimensions of institutional totality and its correlates in proprietary nursing homes of New York City. Doctoral thesis. Teachers College, Columbia University, New York, N.Y., 1974.
2. Goldfarb, A. I.   Contributions of psychiatry to the institutional care of aged and chronically ill persons. *J. Chronic Dis.* 6:438, 1957.
3. Goldfarb, A. I.   Current Trends in the Management of Psychiatrically Ill Aged. In P. Hoch and J. Zubin (Eds.), *Psychopathology of Aging.* New York: Grune & Stratton, 1961. Pp. 248–265.

4. Goldfarb, A. I.   Mental health in the institution. *Gerontologist* 1:178, 1961.
5. Goldfarb, A. I.   Prevalence of psychiatric disorder in metropolitan old age and nursing homes. *J. Am. Geriatr. Soc.* 10:77, 1962.
6. Goldfarb, A. I.   An exploration of research findings. In *Research Utilization in Aging,* P.H.S. Publication No. 1211. Washington, D.C.: U.S. Department of Health, Education, and Welfare, 1964. Pp. 24–38.
7. Goldfarb, A. I.   Responsibilities to our aged. *Am. J. Nurs.* 11:78, 1964.
8. Goldfarb, A. I.   Predicting mortality in the institutionalized aged. *Arch. Gen. Psychiatry* 21:172, 1969.
9. Goldfarb, A. I.   Intimacy, loneliness and boredom in the older patient. Paper presented at the annual meeting of the American Psychiatric Association, Miami Beach, Florida, May 1969.
10. Goldfarb, A. I., Fisch, M., and Gerber, I.   Predictions of mortality in the institutionalized aged. *Dis. Nerv. Syst.* 27:21, 1966.
11. Goldfarb, A. I., Zelditch, M., and Burr, H.   *Mental Impairment in Homes for the Aged.* New York: Council of Jewish Federations and Welfare Funds, 1969.
12. Hess, J. L.   How referrals to nursing homes are made. *New York Times,* May 12, 1975. P. 18.
13. Kobrynski, B., and Miller, A. D.   The role of the state hospitals in the care of the elderly. *J. Am. Geriatr. Soc.* 18:210, 1970.
14. Kosberg, J. I.   Differences in proprietary institutions caring for affluent and non-affluent elderly. *Gerontologist* 13:299, 1973.
15. Kramer, M., Taube, A., and Redick, R. W.   Patterns of Use of Psychiatric Facilities by the Aged: Past, Present and Future. In C. Eisdorfer and M. P. Lawton (Eds.), *Psychology of Adult Development and Aging.* Washington, D.C.: American Psychological Association, 1973.
16. Pollack, M., Kahn, R., Gerber, I., and Goldfarb, A. I.   The relationship of mental and physical status in institutionalized aged persons. *Am. J. Psychiatry* 117:120, 1960.
17. Pollack, E., Locke, B., and Kramer, M.   Trends in Hospitalization and Patterns of Care of the Aged Mentally Ill. In P. Hock and J. Zubin (Eds.), *Psychopathology of Aging.* New York: Grune & Stratton, 1961. Pp. 21–56.
18. Reich, R.   Care of the chronically mentally ill—a national disgrace. *Am. J. Psychiatry* 130:8, 1973.
19. Riley, M., et al.   *An Inventory of Research Findings.* Vol. I, Aging and Society. New York: Russell Sage Foundation, 1968.
20. Rogin, M., Goldfarb, A. I., and Turner, H.   Institutional care facilities of older people in New York City. *J. Mount Sinai Hosp.* 35:358, 1968.
21. Shindell, S., and Cornfield, E.   Aged in Connecticut state mental hospitals. *J.A.M.A.* 160:1121, 1956.
22. U.S. Senate, Special Committee on Aging.   *Mental Health Care and the Elderly: Shortcomings in Public Policy.* Report by the U.S. Senate Special Committee on Aging, 1971.
23. U.S. Senate, Special Committee on Aging.   *Nursing Home Care in the*

United States: Failure in Public Policy. Report of the Sub-Committee on Long-Term Care of the Senate Special Committee on Aging, 1975.

24. Wolk, R., Karp, E., and Goldfarb, A. I. Mental impairment in residents of homes for the aged. Research project on mental impairment in the aged. Council of Jewish Federation and Welfare Funds and Office of the Consultant for the Aged, New York State Department of Mental Hygiene. Abstract in *Gerontologist* 7:24, 1967.

15. Nursing of Older People

Virginia Stone

A recent innovation is the assumption by the professional nurse of a leadership role in the delivery of health care to older people. Within the profession, gerontological nursing has become a specialized area of practice, built on specific knowledge transmittable through various types of educational programs.

The person prepared as gerontological nurse functions in such a way as to assist the aged person to regain or maintain his functional capacities, both physical and mental. She must therefore have knowledge of the psychosocial and physiological changes related to the process of aging.

Psychological Knowledge Influencing Nursing Practice

Research findings, as well as clinical experience, strongly suggest that the nursing approach to the aged needs to be different from that directed toward other age groups. The slowing-down processes accompanying aging demand that the nurse adjust her own behavior to that of her patient. It is difficult for a young, energetic person to move at a rate less than her usual speed. Yet if a correct response to a stimulus is desired, timing on the part of both the sender and the receiver of the message must be considered.

To determine an effective nursing approach, the nurse has a responsibility to assess the older person's capacities. This includes an assessment of thought processes as well as of physical capacity. Speed of perception is considered an important factor in the thought processes of the aged. Two important areas of perception that the nurse can aid to some extent are vision and hearing. These can be grossly evaluated on initial contact. Because of the prevalence of hearing loss in old age, the nurse should assume that the patient may have difficulty in hearing. By altering the pitch and loudness of her voice when addressing the older person, she determines the level of hearing for meaningful dialogue. This is done by asking questions that require a declarative sentence in response. In her evaluation the nurse also determines if there is a problem in speech discrimination. Various patterns of speech spacing are presented and responses evaluated to determine the most effective pattern for the individual patient. Allowances should be made for some background sounds, for as Busse [2] has indicated, the older person is often unaware that he is missing background noises, but is aware of a feeling of loss and a sensation that the world is silent. Thus, hearing ability, speech discrimination, and background noise in relation to the strength of communication stimuli all influence the effectiveness of the reception of these stimuli.

To determine the correct nursing approach, visual acuity needs to be similarly assessed. Because of changes in the visual pathway, lighting intensity needs to be increased with age. As the nurse considers the changes in dark adaptation, side vision, color matching, and contrast discrimination, she can assess the vision potential. She can then make environmental adjustments as necessary, such as the use of light bulbs with high wattage and the use of contrasting colors. In generally dark areas, such as bathrooms, there should be constant low-intensity night-lights for safety.

Aged persons often have difficulty perceiving the outlines of objects, especially if they are small and lack color contrast. Therefore they may require the assistance of another person in handling such things as a glass of water. Because of the translucence of both water and many drinking glasses, the perception of the object is difficult. Therefore the patient needs assistance and time to identify the glass of water and the rim as separate from the whole. Otherwise, he may spill the contents, to his embarrassment. Adaptations to visual difficulties can be made when the nurse realizes their influences on patient behavior.

Though efforts are made to improve the distinctness of the input in the nursing approach, the processing of information has some influence on the response. The stage of research in this area gives limited direction to nursing the older person. However, it is known that processing seems to be influenced by the number of message units presented at one time. It is believed that when the nurse is interacting with an aged person, she should present one thought at a time, with a time allowance between each thought for a response. This is of major importance when teaching the older person about self-care or instructing him about a procedure such as using a walker.

The nurse, more than any other professional health worker, has a more intimate and sustained relationship with the older person. Because of her assessment and evaluation of her own nursing action, she may have a better understanding of the patient's behavior. Acting as interpreter to members of the health team, she can assist in the diagnosing and understanding of the patient by others. Correct interpretation of behavior can sometimes prevent false classifications of patients as "uncooperative," "disoriented," or even "senile." When a fast-moving entourage of a health team approaches an elderly person, its pace and numbers are such that the older person often behaves inappropriately at the moment. It is in this situation that the gerontological nurse has the obligation to be a clarifier of patient behavior.

Summarizing what has been said thus far, the nurse, using research findings from other disciplines, realizes the need to pace her behavior to match that of the older patient so that the patient has an opportunity to perform at his level. As Welford [10] has stated in relation to performance:

. . . pacing, in relation to age, illustrates an important general point about the relation between environmental demand and individual capacity. If the pace is slow enough, the effects of age, or any other factor which slows performance, will make little or no difference at first; all the necessary decisions will be made in the available time. . . .

Physiological Knowledge Influencing Nursing Practice

The foregoing has emphasized psychological factors, especially as they affect communication processes. But the nurse must also consider physiological changes as they influence physical care.

In providing care for patients of any age, the nurse needs to assist in the maintenance of homeostasis. This becomes difficult when caring for older people because they show differences in physiological reactions as compared with younger people. As an example, it may be more difficult to stabilize temperature in old people in that their bodily response to changes in environmental temperature is less effective than that of younger people. Hypothermia is not uncommon. Protection from extreme temperatures becomes an important nursing responsibility.

Decreases in oxygen utilization and the amount of blood pumped by the heart under resting conditions occur in aging. Cerebral anoxia or hypoxia is a common occurrence in the aged, caused by such conditions as pneumonia or chronic emphysema. Because of the relationship between anoxia and confusion, the nurse is aware of those factors that may contribute to the lowering of blood pressure, such as rapid movement from a reclining position to a standing position, or a sudden neck movement, which may cause a kinking and occlusion of the vertebral arteries.

Another common nursing responsibility, bathing the patient, needs special attention in the older person. If the water is too hot, the blood vessels in the skin and muscles dilate and may cause temporary slowing of blood to the brain, which may cause a temporary confusional state.

Difficulty in physical movement is influenced by muscular wasting and weakness as well as by joint discomfort from arthritis and rheumatism. Sensory changes, such as sensitivity to temperature changes, the lowering of pain threshold with age, and olfactory changes, are physiological alterations that require modification of nursing intervention.

This limited enumeration of physiological changes indicates that the nurse needs to use a more protective approach when dealing with the aged. She must rely many times on covert rather than overt behavior to determine the older patient's needs. Some older persons can fracture a bone without being aware of such an accident. The alert nurse may discover this fracture when bathing the patient. It is not uncommon for the aged patient to have a distended bladder without feeling discomfort. Therefore the nurse has to depend on her observations rather than on expressions of discomfort by the patient.

As the nurse intervenes, regardless of the simplicity of the act, she uses the psychophysiological knowledge available to determine her nursing approach. This is illustrated in the simple act of assisting the patient to sit on the side of the bed. The nurse has to consider muscular weakness; she has to time the movement, and then evaluate the patient's behavior as to its appropriateness. The task could be simplified if there were color contrast between the sheets and the furniture. Should the patient become confused while carrying out the act, this could have been caused by faulty communicational input, or the rapidity of movement from the reclining to the sitting position, or both.

Other Influences

In the care of older people, the nurse has to consider not only the psychological and physiological influences on the patient but also his physical environment. The environmental needs of older patients can be determined by examination of life-style, life space, and functional capacity from the physical and psychological point of view. If one is to understand the needs, motivations, and anxieties of the patient, understanding of his life space is of paramount importance, keeping in mind that his psychological present is influenced by his past and future. Illness, especially if of a debilitating nature, tends to narrow life space. Therefore, the nurse attempts to prevent the shrinking of the space and seeks ways to enlarge it. Institutionalization causes some isolation. Isolation can produce physiological and psychological disturbances. By finding ways of maintaining life space, the nurse is assisting in the prevention of such disturbances.

Since it is stated that "each life-style has its characteristic structural properties, especially in relation to orientation to interaction and types of social relationships" [11], the life-style needs to be identified and support provided to maintain the style, even in an institutional setting. The correlation of life space, life-style, and functional capacity provides the nurse with a broad frame of reference for determining the sociological, psychological, and physiological needs of the elderly patient.

Gerontological Nursing Research

Although gerontological nursing practice has been based on knowledge from other fields, nurse researchers are beginning to test such knowledge in clinical settings to determine its applicability to nursing and to study the effects of certain types of nursing intervention on patient behavior. Several nurse investigators have examined the influences of nursing intervention on orientation status. Thomas [7], exploring the effects of individualized nursing intervention on senile status, found that when individualized care was administered, positive trends were observed in the achievement of self-care and in the alteration of senile status. Tyler [8], in studying the effects of individualized nursing intervention on orientation status, found that the state of orientation did not change, but that functional capacity improved. Both studies indicate a change in behavior, in that elderly persons improved in the area of self-care when nursing intervention took into account psychophysiological alterations in old age.

A group of nurses, realizing the need for communication with the elderly, conducted a study on the use of expanded speech and self-pacing in communication with the aged. They concluded [6]: "The comfort and reassurance that the elderly person derives by the slowing of the pace of the situation and by communication at a slower rate of speed is invaluable."

Still another research project dealt with the environment. It was hypothesized that the psychosocial atrophy common to institutionalized older patients might be reversible through the medium of skilled nursing intervention. It was found that it was possible for older people to be involved in meaningful human relationships. For the purpose of the study, nurse-patient dyads were organized, with special emphasis on continuing verbal communication. It was found that enriched environments generally fostered positive physical and psychosocial change, whereas deprived environments inhibited such change. The introduction of skilled nursing care produced the greatest impact in those environments in which the prior level of active interactional involvement of patients was lowest [9].

Lowery [4] studied the relationship of patient life-style and gerontological nursing in a nursing home and concluded that: (1) patients adjust differently to confinement, and, as they adjust, they alter their life-styles; (2) nursing intervention should vary for each patient because of the different adjustment patterns, the alterations in life-style, and the person's uniqueness; and (3) nursing intervention can be planned so that life-style is partially restored.

One nurse, using the operant conditioning theory, attempted to modify incontinence in neuropsychiatric geriatric patients using an experimental and a control group [3]. The hypothesis that incontinence could be significantly decreased by the introduction of social or material reinforcement or both was not confirmed in her study.

Through studies such as these, nurses are attempting to build a body of knowledge concerning the nursing practice relating to the care of older people.

The Gerontological Nurse Practitioner

The depth and scope of practice in the delivery of care is influenced by the educational preparation of the nurse [5]. The emphasis in the education of a gerontological nurse practitioner is to prepare a registered nurse to assume responsibility for an expanding practice in the field of gerontological nursing. The practitioner has been prepared in a baccalaureate program or in a continuing education program under the auspices of an educational institution. Persons who have successfully completed such a preparatory program in gerontological nursing may use the title Gerontological Nurse Practitioner.

The gerontological nurse practitioner is concerned with all stages of health and illness and utilizes knowledge of the aging process in giving or directing care. The gerontological nurse practitioner works collaboratively with the physician and with other health professionals, making independent decisions about the nursing care needs of patients and collaborating with other health professionals in other aspects of the patient's care. The services to be provided include the delivery of primary, acute, and long-term care to the chronically ill aged. The focus of the care is on the achievement, maintenance, or restoration of optimal functioning or on maintaining dignity until death.

In the practitioner role, the nurse gives care and supervises other nursing personnel who participate in the provision of care to aging persons, individually or in groups, in a variety of settings. The gerontological nurse practitioner is concerned for, and aware of, the families or the significant helping persons in the aging person's life, or both, and involves the aging person in decisions about his life and death.

The functions of the practitioner, as recognized by the American Nurses' Association [1], are:

1. In addition to giving direct care to patients and supervising nursing assistants, the nurse in current gerontological nursing practice may carry out the following nursing functions and activities:
   a. Secure a health history.
   b. Perform a physical appraisal.
   c. Advise and counsel older persons and their families.
   d. Help in the management of economic social aspects affecting the health of older persons.
   e. Meet the health needs of aged persons in cooperation with physicians and other members of the health team.
   f. Utilize community resources.
2. On completion of a formal course of study the gerontological nurse practitioner is able to perform the nursing functions in greater depth and with broader applicability. In addition, this practitioner will be capable of performing some of the activities that traditionally had been within the domain of the physician.
   The gerontological nurse practitioner will be prepared with increased knowledge and skills to perform the following nursing functions:

a. Act as an advocate and/or significant other for patient when this is needed.
b. Sustain and support patients during diagnosis and treatment.
c. Obtain a comprehensive health history.
d. Work collaboratively with physicians and others in identifying and meeting health needs of gerontological patients.
e. Coordinate health care and/or coordinate other health resources.
f. Teach and counsel patients and families about aging, health, and illness.
g. Make appropriate community referrals.
h. Evaluate the nursing process and the milieu in which care is given.

The geronotological nurse practitioner will likewise be prepared to function in the following areas that have usually been designated as medical activities.

a. Perform a physical examination.
b. Assess and manage acute and chronically ill aged patients within established parameters; this includes providing preventive aspects of care as well as direct patient care.
c. Prescribe or manage selected medications within established protocols.

The gerontological nurse practitioners assume responsibility for the performance of their acts and are accountable to the aging person for the quality of nursing care the patient receives [1].

The loci of practice may be in senior citizens centers, day care centers, clients' homes, and/or institutions. Her role in providing quality health care has grown in relation to increase in the older population and legislative action concerning the delivery of quality health care to the aged.

References

1. American Nurses' Association. *Guidelines for Short-Term Continuing Education Programs: Preparing the Geriatric Nurse Practitioner.* Kansas City, Missouri, 1974.
2. Busse, E. W. Geriatrics today—an overview. *Am. J. Psychiatry* 123: 1231, 1967.
3. Grosick, J. Effect of operant conditioning on modification of incontinence in neuropsychiatric geriatric patients. *Nurs. Res.* 17:304, 1968.
4. Lowery, P. Patient life style and gerontological nursing. Unpublished master's thesis. Duke University, Durham, N.C., 1968.
5. Moses, D. V., and Lake, C. S. Geriatrics in the baccalaureate nursing curriculum. *Nurs. Outlook* 16:41, 1968.
6. Panicucci, C. L., et al. Expanded Speech and Self-Pacing in Communication with the Aged. In *A.N.A. Regional Clinical Conferences.* New York: Appleton-Century-Crofts, 1968. Pp. 95–101.
7. Thomas, F. J. Effects of Individualized Nursing Intervention on Senile Status and Self Care Achievement on Institutionalized Senile Patient. In

A.N.A. Regional Clinical Conferences. New York: Appleton-Century-Crofts, 1968. Pp. 152–162.

8. Tyler, C.   The effect of individualized nursing upon the orientation status of the elderly patient in a long-term setting. Unpublished master's thesis. Duke University, Durham, N.C., 1968.

9. Weiss, J. M.   *Nurses, Patients, and Social Systems.* Columbia, Mo.: University of Missouri Press, 1968.

10. Welford, A. T.   Social, Psychological, and Physiological Gerontology— An Experimental Psychologist's Approach. In R. H. Williams et al. (Eds.), *Processes of Aging,* Vol. 1. New York: Atherton, 1968. P. 119.

11. Williams, R. H., and Wirths, C. G.   *Lives Through the Years.* New York: Atherton, 1965. P. 13.

16. Social Casework and Community Services for the Aged

Dorothy K. Heyman and Grace H. Polansky

In many communities there is a growing awareness of the needs of the elderly and a new willingness to take responsibility for more adequate services to these citizens. Welfare agencies provide basic financial assistance to those in need in all areas of the country. In addition, other social services in local communities as well as on state and national levels are expanding.

While the medical needs of the elderly have been properly emphasized, it must also be made clear that their needs are far more extensive than for medical assistance alone. The bedridden are only a small fraction of the total older population [32], and most older people continue to live active and independent lives [22]. They continue to function in their accustomed ways until a crisis or change occurs profound enough to challenge their equilibrium. The crises of old age may take various forms, and they are usually multiple in nature. At such times of distress, older persons are turning increasingly to social workers for help.

This chapter will be concerned first with social casework as it attempts to help people and their families (1) with problems of social functioning and maintenance of optimum emotional and physical health in the older person's usual setting as long as this is possible, and (2) with the same problems in a new setting when this becomes necessary. Second, a variety of other community services will be discussed that also seek to maintain or improve the level of adaptation in older people.

Social Casework with Older Persons

The basic problems of the aged are in the areas of emotional and physical health, retirement and finances, physical living arrangements, marital and family relationships, relationships between generations, and problems connected with the use of leisure time—all of which relate to a sense of worth and belonging. Many older persons struggling with these problems, singly or in combination, can use social casework help. Interestingly, some of these problems do not require intensive intervention but respond to assistance of a superficial nature. Unfortunately, the aged are often unaware of the resources available to them. For this reason it is extremely important that information about such resources be widely disseminated to the aged themselves and to those in contact with them. Applications for help may be received by agencies from older persons themselves, from immediate family or other relatives, or from friends and neighbors. Referrals are frequently made by physicians, clergymen, nurses, and other professional persons. Usually only a simple telephone call is needed to initiate the process of obtaining assistance for a troubled elderly person.

Although it is obvious that social workers in public and private agencies must be familiar with community resources, it is equally important that the full range of community supportive social, home, health, and financial assistance be known to the social worker based in an institution. These resources can make a critical difference in the quality of the client's adjustment to an institution or in his transition back to the community [10].

Goals

Social casework has as its goals helping the older person in his adaptation, in his social functioning, and in maintaining or reestablishing psychic equilibrium. Old age is a time when crises involving losses and changes coincide with diminishing strength and energy. The impact of multiple losses may result in a depletion of personal resources, and a supportive relationship and other restitutive measures may be needed. Casework tries to aid the person in adapting his environment to his diminishing functional abilities, or in lessening external stress. If these adjustments are not possible or sufficient, he is then assisted in moving to a new setting in which physical, emotional, and social needs can be met more adequately [36]. At all points the older person is helped to maintain or regain his self-image, to maintain a sense of mastery and control over his environment, and to be relieved of immobilizing fears and anxieties.

Casework frequently involves not only the older person but also the spouse, adult children, grandchildren, and other relatives, as well as interested friends. Professionals such as the physician, nurse, attorney, clergyman, banker, and other social workers may participate in planning and treatment. Landlords, neighbors, staffs of institutions and home care facilities, paramedical personnel, and others are additional resources. The person may need the help of an increasing variety of people. At the same time the emotional involvements of some of these people, particularly of family and friends, need to be taken into account.

Settings

The setting for social casework may be in a counseling service for older persons, a sectarian or nonsectarian family agency, a public welfare department, an institution for the aged, or a general, geriatric, or psychiatric hospital. Other settings are senior centers, community centers, and housing projects or other locations easily accessible to older persons. Agencies such as public welfare departments that perform many supportive functions also use casework concepts and techniques. Here, at the frequently painful point of applying for help, dignity and a sense of self-worth can be maintained or increased while a determination is made as to what services are needed. Continued individualized interest in the person and the experience of a positive relationship can be as helpful as the concrete financial or other assistance provided.

Problems

The specific focus of counseling and the specific services to be provided are generally determined by multiple, interrelated needs. For example, personal adjustment to actual and threatened changes and losses, as well as marital and extended-family relationships, are areas in which help is frequently requested. These problems are often accompanied by inadequate income and by the necessity to change physical living arrangements. At other times, physical and mental disability or retirement, with its possible loss of social and economic roles, may necessitate treatment intervention by a caseworker. A brief case history may serve to illustrate the problem:

Mr. B., age 82, and his wife, who was six years younger, each were experiencing difficulties because of Mr. B.'s progressive brain disease. He was showing memory loss, increasing suspiciousness, disorientation, and lack of judgment. His increasing dependence on Mrs. B. was becoming intolerable to her, especially as it represented a reversal of their previous roles. She herself was feeling vigorous and full of plans and activities but was prevented from carrying them out because of Mr. B.'s unwillingness or inability to participate. Although depressed with her "babysitting" role, Mrs. B. felt guilty about her thoughts of placing her husband in a home for the aged. Friends, too, reinforced her guilt by hinting that he would die sooner if placed in an institution. Her husband clearly opposed any discussion of such placement, and their son obviously was uneasy with the idea of having his father in a home for the aged. Mrs. B. was clearly conflicted in her feelings about the problem. She and her husband had gotten along well during 53 years of marriage. She was afraid she would miss him greatly if he were to leave. In fact, she hardly knew whether the present situation was not better than the guilt she might feel if she placed him in an institution.

A caseworker met with Mrs. B. and her son over a period of time. On one occasion the psychiatrist who had evaluated Mr. B. joined them. In these sessions Mrs. B. and her son were given emotional support and guided toward realistic planning. The caseworker suggested the possibility of hiring an attendant who could relieve Mrs. B. from time to time, thus freeing her for her own activities and interests and for an occasional vacation. This plan was more acceptable than the institutional solution, and the caseworker told them of the resources for such help.

For his part, Mr. B. was experiencing fears of abandonment, which he expressed through concerns that his wife might die before he did. He said that he regretted being such a "burden" to her. His past occupational success and his previous sexual prowess became important elements in his conversation. At one point he made a sudden attempt to have sexual relations with his wife, after 15 years of inactivity. This proved upsetting to Mrs. B., and she retaliated at first with threats of proceeding to institutionalize him. In casework, Mrs. B. was helped to see the meaning of these developments and to be more understanding. She was also helped to anticipate her own emotional reactions to having someone else caring for her husband for periods of time, and she also grew somewhat more comfortable with the idea of temporary or permanent placement of her husband if the present plan did not work out. She was able to make good use of professional support. The son, too, became freer to look at the needs of each parent without overidentifying with his father's wishes.

Clients

A study of the whole person, with concern for his individual physical, emotional, and social needs, is the basis for treatment. The older person may be identified as the primary client, or he may be seen as part of a family unit that can then be considered "the client," with the needs of each family member taken into account. Thus, treatment can be either client-centered or family-centered.

Casework Treatment

Identification of the problem is followed by treatment planning. The goals of treatment may be limited to helping the person deal with the immediately stressful situation. On the other hand, increased self-awareness and self-understanding, with consequent behavior modification, may be sought [36]. Treatment is basically ego-supportive, with the caseworker sustaining and developing the healthy personality aspects and useful defenses of the client. The essential ingredient is the relationship between caseworker and client. Past achievements and present strengths are given recognition. Physical and emotional supports within the family and the community are utilized to promote self-mobilization and independence. Depending on the ego strength of the client, confrontation, clarification, and interpretation may also be used on a selective basis. Sometimes role shifts occur in old age that require the establishment of new or changed relationships and a redefinition of social identity.

Casework continues as long as it is needed. It may be resumed at any time when a new crisis arises. For the elderly, need, rather than motivation for behavioral change, is the primary indication for intervention. A prompt response to requests for service is essential for the older person whose self-esteem may be depleted. Caseworkers cannot expect to see all their elderly clients in the customary office settings; many will have to be visited in their own homes or in hospitals and nursing homes. Interviews cannot be hurried, and repeated contacts may be needed to accomplish what might be accomplished in a single sitting with a young person. Personal warmth and positive affect are essential [36].

Among specific problems often referred for treatment are marital problems. Possible causes for disruption in the marriage are many; for instance, retirement and new uses of leisure, or changing financial and health situations. Primary family roles often shift from a focus on child care to mutual nurturance between the two marriage partners. If the marriage has been essentially sound, it can become even more satisfying in old age. If there have been deficiencies in closeness, perhaps camouflaged by the presence of children in the household, these tend to increase when children move out and family roles change. Casework assistance may then be needed to reestablish a satisfying balance [36].

A second area for casework help is the relationship between the aged parent and his adult child. Old problems between parents and children may be reactivated as help from adult children is needed. Because disabilities in old age often progress at an uneven pace, the adult children may themselves become confused and require help in modifying their own roles and changing relationships to their parents. Alternating feelings of dependency and hostility are not uncommon responses on the part of the older person.

A poignant and possibly traumatic situation requiring casework intervention occurs when a decision must be made about a change in living arrangements or placement of an older person in a rest home, nursing home, or other institutions. Careful evaluation is made of the desirability and necessity of placement, along with its meaning to the older person and those close to him. Caseworkers must be aware of all the alternative placement possibilities in a given community for the best matching of the specific services required by the aged person to the services available in specific institutions. Sometimes a seemingly intolerable home situation can be ameliorated and the aged person maintained in his own home, with the provision of added supports, such as skilled home nursing care.

The most common reason for relocating an older person is the development of mental deterioration in the absence of adequate supervision in his own home. Organic brain changes may result in severe memory loss and disorientation; the older person may wander away from home, or forget to turn off the stove, thereby creating a fire hazard; or he may become offensive in his personal hygiene. Dramatic personality changes may take place, with loss of inhibitions, irritability, or paranoid ideation. A rest home may provide adequate care in some instances; in others, admission to a psychiatric hospital may be required.

A second common reason for considering placement is the presence of a physical disability requiring extensive care. The individual who has suffered a stroke or is for some other reason bedridden, who may require special medication or is in need of physical assistance that cannot be provided at home, may need to be admitted to a nursing home or extended care facility. There are some elderly who are not significantly deteriorated either mentally or physically but who are socially isolated and require an environment in which social interaction is again possible. A day care center or a rest home may provide enough satisfaction to prevent or reverse emotional problems. As of this writing, not all of the types of facilities mentioned are available in all communities. But it is hoped that eventually each community will be able to provide a full range of coordinated alternatives to serve the elderly.

Older persons often find the change to completely new settings very disturbing. The older person, as well as members of his family, may experience feelings of ambivalence, anger, rejection, depression, and guilt.

A caseworker can often be of help with these feelings, not only in the planning of the move but also after the aged person has moved to a new setting.

Thus casework helps the older person and his family to handle as comfortably and effectively as possible changes resulting from those internal aging processes that effect each one at different rates and in different areas of functioning. For those elderly persons who are not in need of the kinds of services that have been described, there exist many valuable supportive structures in the community that may be used as tools to bolster the drive to remain independent and to maintain a continuing role in society.

Community Services for the Aged

As Shanas et al. [33] have pointed out, it is often assumed that the community, through the provision of social services and voluntary organizations, has supplanted the family and its functions, providing the elderly with a "kind of comfortable seclusion." However, these investigators go on to state that the evidence suggests "that the social services tend to complement rather than replace informal community and family associations and that they tend to reach those in genuine need" [33]. Through gerontological research, new concepts of aging have become accepted and have brought about the establishment of a different type of agency for the elderly, integrating new and traditional services.

Comprehensive Services by a Single Agency

Probably the most important element in a community program for older persons is to have available resources that enable older people to remain independent with a maximum degree of self-determination. A central referral service, with caseworkers able to work with the older person on his own terms, going into the home if necessary, is of great importance [23, 28].

The Older Americans Resources and Services Program (OARS), sponsored by the Duke Center for the Study of Aging and Human Development and funded by the Administration on Aging, is an information, referral, and counseling service designed to provide assistance to persons over 50 years of age or their families when faced with problems associated with growing older. The multiple nature of an older person's problems often requires an interdisciplinary approach to a solution. The OARS staff and services, therefore, are unusually comprehensive. The staff includes professional personnel in psychiatry, psychology, social work, pastoral counseling, law, and related fields. A unique feature of the OARS is the training opportunity afforded professional persons to work with the elderly within a multidisciplinary setting.

In addition to offering individual and group counseling, discussion groups are held to explore such areas of concern as preretirement and postretirement, coping with losses, and other topics. The emphasis in the OARS program is on providing the help and related social services that can postpone or prevent placement in long-term care facilities.

While most referrals to the OARS clinic are made by physicians on the hospital staff and in community private practice, many other referrals are initiated by adult children, grandchildren, or siblings rather than by the spouse of an older person. There are few self-referrals, perhaps because in this age group there is either little awareness of the service, or there is resistance to applying for professional help. Social workers have found that they need to be somewhat more aggressive in offering help to older persons than has been traditional in this field.

To supercede the Information and Counseling Service for Older Persons, which was an earlier service-oriented program [23], the Duke University OARS project, while continuing to offer service, has added a major research component. One recent development is a multidimensional functional assessment questionnaire that measures five dimensions, namely, social resources, economic resources, mental health, physical health, and capacity to cope with the activities of daily living. The instrument is applicable to all ages and to all degress of impairment. This versatile tool is as useful to the clinician assessing the functional state of a single person as it is to an agency planning services for groups.

Nutrition Programs for the Elderly

In 1972, federal funds were authorized for the establishment and operation of nutrition projects that would provide low-cost, nutritionally sound meals in congregate settings to persons over 60 years of age and their spouses, regardless of age. Several goals are thus achieved simultaneously: provision of nutritious meals to elderly persons who are malnourished as a result of poverty or physical or mental incapacity; social interaction and the breaking of barriers for the lonely and isolated older person; and facilitation of the delivery of supportive services.

Federal funds are provided to local programs through designated state agencies, and specific regulations are defined in the federal guidelines. In addition to providing at least one hot meal per day that meets the nutritional criteria established by the Food and Nutrition Board of the National Academy of Science–National Research Council, the grantee agency must provide the following supportive services: transportation, information and referral, health and welfare counseling services, nutrition education, shopping assistance, and recreational activities.

Another aspect of providing proper nutrition is the training of personnel who understand the biological nutritional requirements of the elderly, the importance of ethnic and cultural food patterns, and the socioeconomic constraints facing this population. An eight-session minicourse has been developed cooperatively by Vincennes University and the Duke Center for the Study of Aging and Human Development to be used to train persons who are responsible for the care and feeding of the elderly in senior citizens centers, nursing homes, hospitals, and other institutions [19].

Legal Services
The services of a lawyer are too infrequently called on by the elderly [29]. Transportation difficulties and marginal income undoubtedly inhibit some elderly from consulting a lawyer, but ignorance of legal rights and lack of knowledge on how a lawyer may be able to help may be more important inhibiting factors. Paul Nathanson, Executive Director of the National Citizens Law Center, Los Angeles, California, believes that the services that a lawyer can offer to the elderly are barely tapped [20].

In addition to information and referral and drawing up of wills and contracts, lawyers can be invaluable in assisting the elderly in contacts with the Social Security Administration and the Supplemental Security Income program, in providing information on federal and state benefits programs, and in advising on consumer contracts and pension problems. Groups as well as individuals may find the advice of lawyers valuable in assisting in the organization of cooperative stores, group housing, tax exemptions, and other concerns.

Providing legal assistance to persons who are not able to go to the lawyer's office is a challenge that St. Louis, for example, has met by equipping a mobile law office. In another area, a rural "circuit rider" travels in an especially equipped van. People trained as paralegal aides can serve in senior centers, but such centers should have a lawyer in attendance at least once a month. A lawyer or paralegal aide could ride on a regular schedule with a meals-on-wheels driver. His schedule could also include visits and counseling in nursing homes and with the men and women in institutions.

The government presently supports legal services through the National Senior Citizens Law Center (Los Angeles, California, and Washington, D.C.), the Council of Elders (Roxbury, Massachusetts), and the Presbyterian Senior Citizens Center in New York City. Neighborhood legal service offices, established by the Office of Economic Opportunity, need to be expanded into a larger network.

Law schools have heretofore been negligent in teaching law students about the special problems of the elderly. In 1974, the Duke Law School, in cooperation with the Duke Center for the Study of Aging and Human Development, instituted a course on legal problems of older Americans. Funding was provided by the American Association for Retired Persons and the National Retired Teachers Association. Designed for third-year law students who are permitted by North Carolina law to represent clients in litigation, this clinical course concentrates on areas of special concern to the elderly: Social Security, Supplemental Security Income, Medicare, Medicaid, welfare, commitment, and competency. In addition, the students study administrative law, constitutional law, evidence, and tax and estate planning. Training in interviewing skills, counseling, negotiations, and the handling of other interpersonal relationships are also emphasized. Readings in the psychology and sociology of aging, gerontology, economics, and other materials are required to be studied concurrently, since these areas of knowledge are basic to an understanding of the problems of older persons.

The Duke Center and Law School have also provided training to community college faculty and state governmental personnel in the divisons of social service, mental health, health services, and others. These short-term training courses provide basic legal information on matters related to the Older Americans Act, Social Security, Supplemental Security Income, commitment and competency, delivery of protective services, and state and federal legislation affecting the elderly. The training emphasizes the interrelationships of federal and state legislation as it affects delivery of services to the elderly [26].

Protective Services

Older persons without close and interested relatives or friends are often in need of protective services, since they are not capable, physically or mentally, of either planning or caring for themselves or of protecting whatever resources they may have. Serious legal and financial problems may be involved and require the services of experts [17].

The nature of protective services for the elderly is not generally understood, and responsibility for protecting those in need of such services has not as yet been clearly allocated. To date, it is generally considered that the elderly person who needs protective services from some agency is one who is so mentally ill that he cannot make rational decisions; who is scarcely able, or is unable, to care for himself physically and financially; who may harm himself or others; or who manifests seriously disturbed behavior [36].

The most comprehensive project undertaken to develop a program of intervention on behalf of older persons requiring protective services was assumed by the Benjamin Rose Institute. This was a controlled demonstration project in which the determining factor throughout was the research aim, which was "to test the effectiveness of a program of protective services representing the 'best' social work thinking and practice." The project has been described in detail in a series of progress reports [3–7].

In many states the department of public welfare assumes legal responsibilities. Professional persons working with older people recognize the deficiencies in this field [37]. There is also a need to establish protective devices for the elderly person who may not be irrational or totally incompetent but is nevertheless helpless in the face of complex problems.

A study of a group of cases of persons requiring protective services [18] revealed that: (1) old persons in need of such services often do not or cannot seek the help of an agency; (2) service must continue for a long time, possibly the balance of the client's lifetime; and (3) the client's helplessness, demands, and needs may require that the caseworker assume a preponderant amount of responsibility. It was concluded from the study that, to meet the needs of these elderly, resources of many kinds must be readily available to be dispensed as needed: medical and psychiatric care, legal services, nursing care, hospital and nursing home care, family home care, housekeeper and homemaker services, drugs, ambulance service, and money for rent, clothing, food and the like [18].

Retirement Planning

Services for the aging are concerned in a major way with the problems of retirees, i.e., those facing a readjustment that "involves filling the gap in social relations, the day-to-day or hour-by-hour contact with other persons which was provided by the work situation" [15]. In recognition of the fact that retirement can be problematical, widespread efforts are being made by industry, labor, and communities to prepare the preretiree to accept and enjoy the years after 65. Classes are held, sometimes years before a man is scheduled to retire, to help him face the implications of retirement with its possible financial, social, personal, and family problems. Typical preretirement courses may include management of financial resources, budgeting, and health information, along with adult education classes, hobby shops, and a variety of other subjects.

The role of the wife of a retiree is often overlooked. Although retirement is a different experience for the wife than for the husband, and although she may feel herself less deeply involved [24], her attitudes undoubtedly will affect the satisfactions both derive from the retirement years [21]. Thus wives must be included in planning for retirement.

Centers for Older Persons

It has been amply shown that social interaction and activity improve the morale of the elderly. As Maddox [27] has expressed it: "Social structure constraints which limit or deny contacts with the environment tend to be demoralizing and alienating and to be associated with withdrawal of various forms of aggressive behavior."

Organized activity for the elderly exists in many places and in many forms. Experience in working with older people has demonstrated that to be successful the programs offered to older people must meet their needs and interests and must be sufficiently varied to satisfy differences.

It is also important that some of the older people participate in the planning of these programs [11]. Too often, activities are planned for the elderly by the middle-aged and are consequently poorly attended since they do not relate to the needs and interests of the group.

As Wickenden [39] has pointed out, the social programs that are most successful are those that seem to meet all needs, or at least a combination of certain needs: a sense of usefulness, the opportunity to learn, as well as to create something, the desire for recognition, an environment in which to establish social relationships with others, as well as to find oneself in relaxing preoccupations.

Community centers for the aging, with their varied and well-planned programs, offer these opportunities. Such centers usually provide recreational activities and entertainment, are often equipped with game rooms, craft shops, sheltered workshops, and cooking and dining facilities. The staffing of centers varies, but many have professional group workers, a public health nurse, a social caseworker, and a part-time physician.

Programs reflect the interests of the members. Films, lectures, discussion groups, and other intellectual activities are available. Summer camp and vacation programs are occasionally sponsored. A few centers contain such auxiliary services as a barbershop, mending shop, swap shop, and mimeographed newspaper published by center members.

Groups interested in establishing or improving adult day care centers will find Helen Padula's *Developing Day Care for Older People* [31] extremely helpful. It is a well-organized book that contains valuable basic information on how to start a program and target the population and on program planning, minimum services, transportation problems, space needs, staffing, record keeping, evaluation, and other techniques for successful continuance of the program. It contains a section on financing adult day care centers with suggestions for possible funding sources and examples of established day care centers. There is also a section suggesting specific community services for the aged. Among them are the following: the establishment of neighborhood health centers; a registry of day sitters or night sitters for ill patients; escort services to health facilities; light medical equipment, such as canes and walkers, for use in homes; a home repair service; assistance in moving; rental of television, radio, and talking books; the maintenance of sheltered workshops; burial funds; vacation trips; multipurpose vans; provision of transportation for shopping; and advocates for the aging.

It cannot be assumed that the establishment of a center will automatically attract older people. Lifelong characteristics persist into old age, and while the gregarious will probably turn up promptly, those who are shy, timid, or feel themselves handicapped by inadequate education or by social awkwardness will need to be encouraged to participate.

In many communities, public welfare workers who have frequent contact with the elderly have made a special effort to stimulate the interest of their clients, especially the isolated ones, by preparing mimeographed lists of social organizations, giving their neighborhood locations, interests, and meeting times, and places; or they prepare lists of specific projects, such as hobby shows or lectures. Volunteer groups have printed directories containing information on community resources that may be of particular interest to the elderly.

The housebound elderly are, of course, more limited in their opportunities for organizational participation but need not be forgotten. Regular visits by a bookmobile are provided in some communities, as are visits by church, fraternal, and social groups.

Involvement of the Community in Program Planning

At one meeting, organizational leaders concerned with programs for the aging were asked which activities sponsored by their organizations had been considered most successful by their members. Listed as successful were the following:

1. Classes on information pertaining to wills, property, Social Security benefits, and similar matters.
2. Classes on personal grooming as well as volunteer services of hairdressers to the bedridden.
3. Transportation to meetings, clinics, church, and Sunday school.
4. Red Cross–sponsored courses on "Fitness for the Future," which emphasized exercises appropriate for the elderly.
5. Classes dealing with diet, health care, and health problems.
6. Bird-watching groups and nature walks.
7. Parties, suppers, and picnics in which three generations participated.
8. Classes in which members not only make items to take to hospitals or

to shut-ins but also teach each other skills in knitting, woodworking, or some other craft.

In addition to the community organizations that are usually associated with planning programs for the elderly, such as churches, community centers, and service clubs, some new groups are becoming involved. For example, in Washington, D.C., law students at the George Washington University School of Law, supported by funds from radio station WMAL, have established a program called "P-E-P," or "Protection for Elderly People," which accepts complaints by mail or telephone and supplies information and referral as well as acting as intermediary in appropriate instances. Single individuals and ad hoc and grass-roots groups can become spokesmen on behalf of older persons through letters to newspaper editors and approaches to community leaders and influential people.

A few banks have begun to cater to the special needs of the elderly. The Marquette National Bank in Minneapolis has an elaborate program that includes a senior citizens information center, a hobby fair, a directory of organizations offering activities and services to senior citizens, a sing-along manual published by the bank, a speaker's bureau on subjects of particular interest to senior adults, a travel club, and seminars for club treasurers to help them manage club funds [34].

An interesting example of another effort to assist the aged is Project Outreach, established by the Central Utah Resource Development Association [12]. Because applicants often "become lost in the process of referrals and re-referrals" and despair of being helped, an expediter has been appointed whose chief responsibility is to locate the service needed by his client. The expediter is "employed to represent the client's interests against all the tendencies in all the agencies that may delay or deprive the client of the agencies' services." He may act in a variety of roles: negotiator, advocate, teacher, and helper.

Adult Education

In planning ahead, it should be recognized that the elderly of the future not only may expect to live longer but also to maintain reasonably good health for a longer period of time, be better educated, and have more intellectual interests. Too often the activities of older persons are thought of purely in terms of leisure, recreation, or entertainment. As Anderson

[2] has pointed out, "Work substitutes should do psychologically for the person what work did for him in his period of maturity. . . ." Anderson further suggests that what is needed is interaction between the person and the task of the kind that draws on the person's resources, thus giving him the sense that he is growing or developing [2].

Adult education programs, although not new, will need to expand if the interests of the elderly are to be met. The impetus for this movement will undoubtedly be provided by the Community Schools Act (August 1974), which authorizes the Commissioner of Education to make grants to state and local educational agencies "to plan, establish, expand, and operate community education programs" [1].

A number of universities have already established extension courses and special programs geared to the interest of the elderly. The Institute for Retired Professionals at the New School for Social Research in New York has a program designed specifically to meet the interests of the re- tired professional person. According to Hyman Hirsh, founder and di- rector of the Institute, the courses are intellectually of a high caliber and attract about 3,000 students each year. Second-career programs are be- coming widely available as continuing education courses under the aegis of universities. Some traditional four-year colleges and universities are permitting retired people to attend classes on a minimum cost or tuition- free basis as in the Donovan Scholar's Program at the University of Ken- tucky. Junior and community colleges welcome opportunities to teach courses of special interest to older people and, in addition, have insti- tuted courses for training younger people who serve the elderly [25]. The American Association of Community and Junior Colleges in Wash- ington, D.C., has considerable information on these programs.

The open university system, based on the British model, is taking hold in this country and should appeal particularly to older people, since the academic requirements are flexible, and regular classroom attendance is not required. Home study materials, television courses, and cassettes form the core of the study program.

The educational challenge has been accepted on the state and local level by the many churches, clubs, and schools that already sponsor afternoon or evening courses. Planning can be simplified, since the necessary equipment is usually already in the buildings, and staff are not difficult to recruit.

Interesting examples of such activity are the Institutes of Lifetime Learning, sponsored jointly by chapters of the American Association of Retired Persons, local teachers' associations, universities, and colleges. The pilot project in Washington, D.C., offers classes at the college level for a 10-week period in over 51 different subjects, including refresher courses in commercial subjects, painting, lipreading, music, and many others [14].

A considerable number of films have been produced dealing with various aspects of aging that would lend themselves well to workshops, extension courses, and informal seminars. Lists of available films may be secured from the University of Michigan Film Library at Ann Arbor, Michigan, the Ethel Percy Andrus Gerontology Center at the University of Southern California, Los Angeles, and from the Duke University Center for the Study of Aging and Human Development in Durham, N.C.

A useful book for those considering establishing educational programs for older persons is *Never Too Old to Learn* [30], which considers the problems, opportunities, guidelines for program development, and other matters related to such programs. *Learning for Aging* [16] focuses on the older adult as *learner,* describing opportunities for learning in a variety of settings and discussing governmental resources in education.

Volunteer Services

A central volunteer bureau staffed by older persons is needed in many communities. Elderly persons who are in good health should be encouraged to serve as volunteers: as visitors to other elderly people at home or in institutions; as Girl Scout or Boy Scout leaders or assistant leaders; or as hospital auxiliary or ward aides, helping to write letters and passing out books.

Programs designed specifically to encourage intergenerational contacts have been established. Children's wards in hospitals or custodial institutions have volunteer programs in which elderly people regularly visit the wards to read to and play with the children, thus providing love and individual attention.

Young people on some college campuses have established programs in which visits are made to homes for the aged or to elderly persons in their own homes at regular intervals. Often a grandparent is "adopted."

Birthday parties are held, entertainment provided, and trips outside the home arranged. Both these programs appear to provide mutually shared satisfactions.

The Friendly Visitors is another volunteer program open to persons of all ages; this activity offers opportunities for healthy older persons to be of service. It can provide much satisfaction to both the visitor and to the persons visited. A friendly visit with a contemporary may be especially enjoyable. Activities should be mutually satisfying and may include table games, gardening, sewing, knitting, reading, crafts, going for rides, shopping, movies, lectures, or any interests that appeal to both.

Friendly Visitors, either to institutions or to people in their own homes, should operate under the supervision of a social agency for the protection of both the person visited and the Friendly Visitor. Although the volunteer is anxious to be helpful, this quality is not necessarily innate, and the volunteer should be carefully selected, trained, and supervised. Perhaps the most satisfying results are obtained when there is not too great a difference between the volunteer and the person visited in educational or intellectual level, socioeconomic status, and interests.

Friendly Visitors assume certain minimum responsibilities. They obligate themselves to serve clients' needs rather than their own, to be dependable in making regular visits, to be good listeners and interested in the client as a person, to refrain from comments that may be upsetting or depressing, and in general to be welcomed with pleasure in another's home. The goal is very worthwhile, and together with social workers and other professionals, such volunteers can help to bring satisfaction and meaning to an isolated or unhappy older person.

Telephone reassurance programs are widespread. Volunteers check on regular "clients" to be sure they are managing as usual. Arrangements are generally made beforehand to alert someone to assist the client should there be no satisfactory response to the telephone call.

Following the recommendations of the 1971 White House Conference on Aging, a program was organized under the Administration on Aging to provide opportunities specifically for older persons to volunteer their services in community projects. ACTION, the sponsoring agency, has developed a variety of programs jointly supported by federal and local funds. Older persons are presently involved in the Retired Senior Volunteer Program (RSVP), which serves many community needs; in Foster

Grandparents, who give "tender loving care" to children in institutional settings; and in Senior Companions, who "sit" with the ill or disabled. Senior Corps of Retired Executives (SCORE) and Active Corps of Executives (ACE) offer the services of volunteers to businessmen for advice, and Vista Volunteers join a variety of programs, usually educational in nature.*

Employment Opportunities

Although many older people retire from work with a sense of relief, others in good health would, if given the choice, enjoy continuing to work, for many reasons: financial needs, a continued sense of usefulness, and participation in the mainstream of life. Older people cannot easily find jobs in the open market, but employment opportunities can be located or even created by a skilled employment counselor matching the job opportunity to a selected individual.

Employers often have openings that do not appeal to younger people and yet are suited to the capacities or interests of the older man or woman. Jobs offering only part-time or seasonal work or unusual hours may be more appealing or more acceptable to an older person than to a younger one, particularly because of the Social Security limitations on yearly earnings. Employers must often be convinced of the value of hiring older persons in appropriate positions, and the importance of experience, stability, and reliability must be emphasized to them. Vocational guidance is a helpful adjunct to job placement, even with older persons.

The Comprehensive Employment and Training Act (1973) provides funds to state or local governments for manpower recruitment and for the training, placement, and counseling of mature workers [1].

Vocational Rehabilitation

The Vocational Rehabilitation Agency, while geared primarily to the needs of the handicapped "of working age," may be of assistance in re-

* Guidance and assistance in planning and developing projects are available from the Administration on Aging, Department of Health, Education, and Welfare, Washington, D.C. 20201, and from designated agencies of the state. Information on successful established programs can also be secured by writing to the National Center for Voluntary Action, which publishes a newsletter, *Voluntary Action News*. The address is 1735 Eye Street, N.W., Washington, D.C. 20006.

habilitating older persons. Disabled housewives have been accepted for help and assisted in learning better ways of managing a household [35]. Older persons who cannot be retrained for employment in the open market may find employment in the sheltered workshops utilized by this agency.

Extended Care Facilities

In spite of strenuous efforts to maintain independence, many elderly face the necessity of giving up their homes. The available choices may be limited by lack of money, family problems, or poor health. While for some the only possible resource is a nursing home or chronic disease hospital, for others, suitable arrangements may be made in a boarding or a family care home where membership in a "family" provides some protection and concern on the part of interested nonrelatives yet permits some degree of independent living. This arrangement would benefit the isolated man or woman who is not able or willing to prepare adequate meals or is in need of some assistance with medications.

Intermediate care, between a boarding home and a nursing home, is provided by the rest home that accepts ambulatory persons who need a protected environment and some supervision, including minor nursing care. Nursing homes will accept bed-care patients and offer a full range of nursing and medical care.

Homemaker Services

Although most older people continue to live in environments that allow them to be independent [32], some of the aged, particularly the widowed, single, and divorced, live in isolated and lonely circumstances. Provision of specialized services to these elderly, as well as to elderly couples, may enable them to live independently in the community. To keep the elderly functioning in their own homes, homemaker services are available in some communities, supported by public welfare or private social agencies.

The trained homemaker assigned by the caseworker as the need arises is usually responsible for the general housework, shopping, and cooking. She also gives some personal care, such as helping with bathing, shampoos, and dressing. This is an expensive service and is therefore generally used only on a part-time basis. When necessary, this service may be supplemented with visits by a public health nurse.

Meals-on-Wheels

Many of the elderly living and eating alone lack motivation for proper meal planning and preparation. They soon deteriorate in energy and in interest, and continued poor nutrition often leads to illness. Some communities have therefore established programs in which appetizing and balanced meals are delivered to the homes of elderly persons at modest cost. The program must be subsidized, even though much of the food preparation and delivery is done by volunteers. Arrangements are sometimes made to have meals prepared in the kitchen of an institution, such as an old-age home or a church, with delivery before noon. Two meals are provided, one of which is to be eaten hot and one cold.

Home Nursing Care

County health departments in many areas maintain a staff of registered nurses to make home visits and evaluations, to perform nursing duties, and to educate the patient and family in nursing care procedures. There are also private organizations, religious and secular, which provide visiting nurse services at modest fees, including The Visiting Nurse Association of America, the nursing services of Metropolitan Life and other insurance companies, and Catholic nursing orders. In some large cities, all of these organizations provide nursing services.

Physical Therapy

Many hospitals now have physical therapy departments with extensive exercise and retraining programs, but these services are not often available to the homebound elderly. However, county health departments often have graduate physical therapists on their staffs who will make regular visits for evaluation and treatment. There are also a number of therapists in private practice who accept patients on referral by a physician.

The physical therapist, after an evaluation of the facilities of the home, devises an individualized program to help the handicapped person adapt to his setting and to maintain or regain maximal functioning.

Often, equipment is improvised with whatever resources the home setting provides. All the prescribed exercises and planned activities are oriented toward achieving physical independence. The physical therapy program that is designed to prevent chronic invalidism may begin with simple instructions on transferring from bed to chair, the use of a walker, or techniques for self-care.

The aged confined to the home can be helped to move out into the community by learning simple methods of managing steps and curbs and entering a taxi or a bus. Progress in self-help, even when measured by small achievements, leads to a sense of independence and is valuable in combating depression and self-devaluation.

Occupational Therapy

Although there are not enough trained occupational therapists to maintain a home visiting program, the skills of this discipline are appropriate to services in the home. Self-maintenance can be taught to the partially disabled, so that they can prepare meals and carry out other chores satisfactorily. The goals are not to teach arts and crafts per se, or to provide entertainment, although these are often pleasurable by-products. Through individually designed occupational therapy programs, the aged may be assisted in regaining physical and emotional strength while learning to adjust to their limitations and disabilities.

Conclusions

Although the services that have been described are many and varied, few communities now provide all of them to their elderly populations. Funding new programs and accommodating the demand are always difficult. Accessibility to the facilities is also a problem in that some of the elderly dislike traveling to various centers or offices or are not physically able to do so. As have a few other states, Pennsylvania has established a rural transportation system.* However, such programs are scarce in some locations, perhaps because of community inertia or lack of awareness—not, it is hoped, because of lack of interest. When communities

* Information on this system may be secured by writing to the Office for the Aging, Department of Public Welfare, P. O. Box 2675, Harrisburg, Pennsylvania 17120.

are small or unable to provide sufficient financial support, strong volunteer efforts are needed; or else the resource of several communities should be combined into regional programs.

Recognizing that the government may not be as responsive to the needs of the elderly as professionals might desire, maximum advantage should be taken of new and existing programs. The Older Americans Comprehensive Services amendments of 1973 modifies the Older Americans Act in important ways. For example, a new model projects program was established to develop innovative solutions to such common problems as housing, preretirement counseling, continuing education, and social services for handicapped elderly Americans. Changes in the Title III program provided for comprehensive and coordinated social services delivery systems through the establishment of planning and service areas. Opportunities for training for careers are expanded by these amendments and include the encouragement of "artists, craftsmen, scientists, and homemakers to undertake assignments on a part-time basis or for temporary periods in the field of aging." Funds are also available for preparing and distributing materials, for recruitment and training, and for research and training "for the establishment of a national senior service core to provide new job opportunities and for other new programs" [1].

The more recently enacted Title XX adds to and improves the opportunities for services and programs for the elderly. The following are some of the services for the elderly to be permitted to be funded under Title XX.

1. Chore services: personal care services that do not require the services of a trained homemaker or a specialist
2. Companionship services
3. Day care services
4. Educational services
5. Foster care services
6. Health support services
7. Homemaker and aides services
8. Home management and maintenance services
9. Housing and home improvement services
10. Legal services
11. Personal and family counseling

12. Preparation and delivery of meals
13. Protective services for adults
14. Recreation services
15. Transportation services

All these services may be provided if they meet one of the five objectives of the federal law: achieving or maintaining economic self-support; self-sufficiency; preventing neglect or exploitation; preventing or reducing institutional care or securing referral or admission for institutional care when other forms of service are not appropriate or available.

Programs for the aged exist on all levels: local, state, regional, and national. States have taken increasingly more active roles in programming for the aged; indeed, there is a trend for states to establish separate state departments in aging, as in Connecticut, Massachusetts, and Illinois. A valuable report on recent activities at the state government level in the field of aging and on the as yet unmet needs of the elderly can be found in *Developments and Trends in State Programs and Services for the Elderly* [13].

Future planning for the needs of older persons should envision the extension of comprehensive and coordinated services to ever-increasing numbers. It is important to help not only those whose needs are critical but also those in somewhat less difficult financial circumstances. For them, the availability of these programs would serve to enhance the quality of life and help to reintegrate them into the larger society, thus avoiding a painful sense of marginality.

References

1. *Action on Aging Legislation in 93rd Congress.* Washington, D.C.: U.S. Government Printing Office, 1975.
2. Anderson, J. E. Psychological Aspects of the Use of Free Time. In W. Donahue et al. (Eds.), *Free Time: Challenge to Later Maturity.* Ann Arbor, Mich.: University of Michigan Press, 1958.
3. Blenkner, M., et al. *Protective Services for Older People, Progress Report for 1964–1965.* Cleveland: Benjamin Rose Institute, March 1965.
4. Blenkner, M., et al. *Protective Services for Older People, Progress Report for 1965–1966.* Cleveland: Benjamin Rose Institute, March 1966.
5. Blenkner, M., et al. *Protective Services for Older People, Progress Report for 1966–1967.* Cleveland: Benjamin Rose Institute, March 1967.
6. Blenkner, M., Bloom, M., and Nielsen, M. A research and demonstration project of protective service. *Soc. Casework* 52:483, 1971.

7. Blenkner, M., et al. *Final Report Protective Services for Older People.* Cleveland: Benjamin Rose Institute, 1974.
8. Bloom, M., and Nielsen, M. The older person in need of protective services. *Soc. Casework* 52:500, 1971.
9. Bottenfield, J. L. A Nutrition Package: An Example of Short-Term Training. In D. Heyman (Ed.), *Community and Junior Colleges: Education and Training for Work with the Elderly.* Durham, N.C.: Duke University Center for the Study of Aging and Human Development, 1975.
10. Brody, E. M., et al. *A Social Work Guide for Long-Term Care Facilities.* National Institute of Mental Health. Washington, D.C.: U.S. Government Printing Office, 1975.
11. Burgess, E. W. The Retired Person and Organizational Activities. In W. Donahue et al. (Eds.), *Free Time: Challenge to Later Maturity.* Ann Arbor, Mich.: University of Michigan Press, 1958.
12. Central Utah Resources Board. Personal communication, March 1968.
13. *Developments and Trends in State Programs and Services for the Elderly. Survey of Activities at the State Government Level in the Field of Aging, 1972 and 1973.* Washington, D.C.: U.S. Government Printing Office, November 1974.
14. Fitch, W. C. The new look in aging. *Wilson Library Bull.,* May 1966.
15. Friedman, E. A., and Havighurst, R. J. *Meanings of Work and Retirement.* Chicago: University of Chicago Press, 1954.
16. Grabowski, S., and Mason, W. D. *Learning for Aging.* Adult Education Association of U.S.A. Washington, D.C.: ERIC Clearinghouse on Adult Education, 1974. (Alternative title in ERIC system: *Living with a Purpose, as Older Adults, Through Education.*)
17. Hall, G., and Mathiesen, G. *Guide to Development of Protective Services for Older People.* Springfield, Ill.: Thomas, 1973.
18. Hemmy, M., and Farrar, M. Protective services for older people. *Soc. Casework* 42:16, 1961.
19. Heyman, D. *Community and Junior Colleges: Education and Training for Work with the Elderly.* Durham, N.C.: Duke University Center for the Study of Aging and Human Development, 1975.
20. Heyman, D. *Legal Problems of Older Americans.* Durham, N.C.: Duke University Center for the Study of Aging and Human Development, 1975.
21. Heyman, D. K., and Jeffers, F. C. Wives and retirement: A pilot study. *J. Gerontol.* 23:488, 1968.
22. Hobson, W., and Pemberton, J. *Health of the Elderly at Home.* Toronto: Butterworth, 1955.
23. Jeffers, F. C., and Polansky, G. H. Initiation in a university medical center of an information and counselling program for older people. Paper presented to the annual meeting of the Gerontological Society, Denver, Colorado, November 1968.
24. Kerckhoff, A. C. Husband-Wife Expectations and Reactions to Retirement. In I. H. Simpson and J. C. McKinney (Eds.), *Social Aspects of Aging.* Durham, N.C.: Duke University Press, 1966.

25. Korim, A. Service Centered Training of Manpower for the Field of Aging. In D. Heyman (Ed.), *Community and Junior Colleges: Education and Training for Work with the Elderly*. Durham, N.C.: Duke University Center for the Study of Aging and Human Development, 1975.
26. Lewis, J. A. *Law and Aging: A Conference Report*. Raleigh, N.C.: North Carolina Governor's Council on Aging, 1975.
27. Maddox, G. L. Activity and morale. Paper presented to annual meeting of the Gerontological Society, Washington, D.C., 1962.
28. Mathiesen, G. Current Status of Services to the Aging. In J. L. Gorn (Ed.), *Social Work Education for Better Services to the Aging*. Proceedings of a seminar on the aging, Aspen, Colorado, 1958. New York: Council on Social Work Education, 1959.
29. Nathanson, P. Legal Services for the Elderly. In D. Heyman (Ed.), *Legal Problems of the Elderly*. Durham, N.C.: Duke University Center for the Study of Aging and Human Development, 1975.
30. *Never Too Old to Learn*. New York: Academy for Educational Development, June 1974.
31. Padula, H. *Developing Day Care for Older People*. Washington, D.C.: National Council on the Aging, 1972.
32. Shanas, E. *Family Relationships of Older People*. Health Information Foundation Research Series, No. 20. New York: Health Information Foundation, 1961.
33. Shanas, E., et al. *Old People in Three Industrial Societies*. New York: Atherton, 1968.
34. Sloan, S. The Role of Banks: Helping Senior Citizens Manage Money. In D. Heyman (Ed.), *Legal Problems of the Elderly*. Durham, N.C.: Duke University Center for the Study of Aging and Human Development, 1975.
35. U.S. Department of Health, Education, and Welfare, Vocational Rehabilitation Department. *For the Disabled: Help Through Vocational Rehabilitation*. Washington, D.C.: Department of Health, Education, and Welfare, 1967.
36. Wasser, E. *Creative Approaches in Casework with the Aging*. New York: Family Service Association of America, 1966.
37. Wasser, E. Protective practice in serving the mentally impaired aged. *Soc. Casework* 52:510, 1971.
38. Wasser, E. *Protective Casework Practice with Older People*. Cleveland: Benjamin Rose Institute, 1974.
39. Wickenden, E. *The Needs of Older People*. Chicago: American Public Welfare Association, 1953.

17. Training in Geropsychiatry

Adrian Verwoerdt

Conceptual Considerations

Concerning education in the various fields of aging, there is the question: "Who should teach what to whom?" The answer is related to the concept of discipline and specialty [2, 18, 25].

The term *geriatrics* usually denotes medical practice in the care of the aged that yet remains within the purview of a given medical or surgical specialty. Similarly, gerontologists tend to identify themselves primarily as biologists, psychologists, or sociologists who happen to be studying the aging process [24]. Since geriatrics is not clearly defined with regard to its position in medicine, the question has been raised whether or not something can be gained from organizing geriatrics into a structured specialty [3, 13, 15, 20]. The general impression is that the proponents and opponents are approximately equal in number, the proponents being more likely to be professionals with a clinical background (*-iatry*) than a basic science orientation (*-ology*). Those who are inclined to oppose geriatrics as a separate entity prefer to see it become an integral part of other disciplines and specialties [13, 24]. Those who favor the idea of a separate specialty (subspecialty) frequently do so because of practical considerations, such as facilitation of professional identity, a higher degree of "visibility" in society, and the opportunity to consolidate resources and develop high-caliber clinical facilities [1, 20, 28].

Cogent arguments are made either way, but few, if any, discussions are aimed at the question what a discipline or specialty is, from a conceptual point of view. At the root of the issue is the very concept of "aging." Aging is a biological process; gerontology involves the study of time-related biological changes in living organisms. On this level, concepts such as aging, growth, development, change, becoming, and so on, tend to become indistinguishable. Inasmuch as gerontology studies a time-related biological *process,* it would be only logical that it represent a specific dimension of various biological disciplines.

The Concept of a Discipline

In the field of medicine, a discipline or specialty can be defined and conceptualized by way of two parameters: (1) the systematized study and accumulated knowledge with reference to clearly delineated interest areas and specific target phenomena; and (2) the type of professional activity directed toward these specific objects.

The *target phenomena* or *interest areas* that provide a basis for a given medical discipline usually represent components of the human organism. Thus, the specialty of hematology is primarily aimed at cellular phenomena; cardiology, at a specific organ system; psychiatry, at the organism as a whole; and public health, at society. In some cases the interest area pertains to a specific dimension of human life (e.g., industrial-occupational medicine, marital or family therapy).

There are no sharp boundaries in biology, which is reflected in the multiple interactions between disciplines. Thus, the boundary of a medical specialty is never static or absolute but always semipermeable. Inasmuch as a medical specialty or discipline is only a nodal point in a larger framework, interdisciplinary contact is not a matter of choice but a necessity. In the course of time, a body of scientific knowledge is accumulated with regard to the principal target of a discipline.

The second set of parameters pertains to the *methods of practice,* or *types of professional activity,* within a given discipline. These include:

1. *Production* of information: e.g., doing a physical examination; laboratory tests; making a diagnosis; basic research; clinical research.
2. *Application* of information: e.g., clinical treatment; cancer detection programs; community service programs; policy making.
3. *Transmission* of information: e.g., teaching, consultation; explaining a treatment plan to members of the therapeutic team; public relations.
4. *Organization* of information: e.g., the administration of research, training, and clinical programs; recording, storing, and retrieving clinical data or research data; management of resources, talents, and personnel.

All medical professionals are involved in these four activities in varying proportions. One's primary professional identity may be based on one type of activity, the other three being subsidiary or complementary professional activities. Since the varying amounts of time and effort allocated to these activities add up to an infinite number of possibilities, no two professional career patterns will be the same.

Geropsychiatry: Scope and Practice

Geropsychiatry, the psychiatry of late life, encompasses the behavioral sciences, psychodynamic concepts, and psychiatric practice with reference to the aging personality and the mental disorders of late life.

The Scope of Geropsychiatry

AGING AND HUMAN DEVELOPMENT. When we speak of psychodynamics of the last phase of life, the emphasis is on the word *last*. The movement toward a final end distinguishes old age from foregoing life phases. The latter have a beginning and an end, which at the same time is a new beginning. If old age is viewed as a developmental phase, then what are its goals?

Human aging cannot be understood in the framework of biological aging in general. The latter can be conceptualized as a lifelong process, which is genetically programmed, begins at conception, and ends in the death of an organism. What makes human aging different is that a human being is aware that he must grow old and die. From a developmental point of view, there are three dimensions of human aging: cognitive, experiential, and adaptational. These dimensions correspond with three developmental milestones: the cognitive one in early life; the experiential one in mid-life; and the adaptational one in late life.

The *cognitive* dimension refers to the intellectual comprehension of the concept of a personal death and of aging as a process that progressively increases the probability of death. This knowledge about the facts of death is learned about the same time as the facts of life, i.e., in early adolescence. The full comprehension of the concept of a life span and a personal death depends on the attainment of specific psychological capacities, including the completion of the body image, a mature time perspective, and the capacity for abstract thinking. Through the abstract capacity it becomes possible to imagine one's own death (i.e., to apply the fact of the death of others to oneself). The mature time perspective enables one to envision a life span and to place the end of the self at the horizon of one's existence. And, finally, the concepts of aging and death are meaningful only to the extent that there is a self-concept and body image to begin with.

That point in life when the sum total of a person's biological, psychological, and social capacities are in an optimal configuration constitutes the peak or prime of life (*climacter,* a Greek term for "rung of the ladder"). Most people perceive the period of life before the peak as one of evolution, growth, or ascendance, and the time following the peak, as a period of involution, decline, or descendance. The perception of these age-related changes and the subjective experiences associated with being aware of them (and realizing their implications) constitute part of the *mid-life crisis* [17]. This phenomenon is often lucidly apparent in the lives of persons with creative genius. Examples are Nietzsche's *Thus Spake Zarathustra* and Dante's *Divine Comedy*. The opening stanza of Dante's *Divine Comedy,* written at the age of 35, are as follows:

Midway through life's journey I was made aware
That I had strayed into a dark forest,
And the right path appeared not anywhere.
Ah, tongue cannot describe how it oppressed,
This wood, so harsh, dismal and wild, that fear
At thought of it strikes now into my breast.
So bitter it is, death is scarce bitterer.

The *adaptational* dimension refers to the psychological processes of working through of involutional losses and taking a final position vis-à-vis one's past life and the necessity of death. (The term *adaptational* is bland, considering the dramatic proportions of this task.) The developmental task, then, is the resolution of involutional grief and the acceptance of losses. These processes are not in the nature of a "one-time thing," but are ongoing. Successful completion of this developmental phase brings about a state of being described by Erikson [10] as *integrity*. Failure in resolving involutional losses (i.e., failure to accommodate oneself to the realities of aging) produces varying degrees of psychological decompensation. The latter may eventually become specific dimensions of *despair*, the term used by Erikson [10] to designate failure in achieving integrity.

Integrity, the final developmental task, is described as the acceptance of one's life and the significant people in it as something that had to be and that, by necessity, permitted no substitutions. In addition, there is the requirement of accepting one's life and what happened in it as one's own responsibility [10]. It would appear that the integrating processes are aimed at three phenomena. First, there is the integration of one's past life. Through the mental activities of reminiscing, sorting out, and evaluation (which come under the heading of the life review), a concept of oneself emerges as a historically unique being [4, 7]. Second, one is faced with the task of integrating life and death. The synthesis of these seemingly antithetical concepts requires a perspective from which death is viewed as an integral part of life. The attainment of this perspective places one beyond anxiety, into a realm of serenity. Finally, there is the need to integrate the paradox (implied in Erikson's description) of accepting the inevitability of one's life and yet being responsible for it. The only way in which the antithetical notions, necessity versus responsibility rooted in freedom, can be synthesized is the creation of a larger framework that encompasses both. From a scientific point of view, little can be said about this phenomenon, because of its apparently transcendental nature.

In many respects the senium is still a terra incognita. We need to · know a great deal more than we do about the psychosocial and intrapsychic processes involved in attaining a sense of integrity; the causes and mechanisms of failure to do so; the clinical expressions of such failure and, most important, about therapeutic modalities. An understanding of the final phase in human development can provide additional insights into earlier developmental periods and contribute toward a comprehensive theory of human behavior.

DYNAMIC PSYCHOPATHOLOGY. The focus of geropsychiatry is on the *process* of becoming old and the *outcome* of this process in specific individuals. The processes we are interested in studying are organic as well as psychodynamic in nature. The former pertain especially to the central nervous system; the latter, to the experience of loss, the vicissitudes of grief, and the various forms of decompensation that are the outcome of inadequate coping and restitution.

The psychopathology of senescence is either *specific* or *nonspecific* with respect to age. Nonspecific psychopathology is that which can be found among persons of any age. When present in the senium, it may be a carry-over from earlier life phases. A schizophrenic person, for example, who reaches the senium is not suffering from a specifically senescent pathological condition. From a process point of view, our interest is how aging can affect (in terms of amelioration or further decompensation) these nonspecific disorders. Aging frequently has certain *pathoplastic* effects on psychopathology. Some schizophrenic patients, for example, show a lessening of psychotic symptoms with aging; on the other hand, certain involutional depressions gradually decompensate toward hypochondriasis or a paranoid position.

In psychopathology that is specific to senescence, aging is the *patho-*

genetic factor. On the organic level, this usually involves age-related central nervous system changes. On the psychological level, the patho-genetic effects of aging include the awareness of, and need to cope with, the stress of physical, social, and economic losses, as well as the unique situation of facing the end of life. Specific psychopathological entities may develop, depending on the various ways in which the involutional grief reactions decompensate. A depression may become chronic when ambivalence interferes with resolution of grief. Through withdrawal, hypochondriasis and self-absorption come about, reflecting a disturb-ance in intimacy as well as generativity. Persisting hypochondriasis leads to progressive de-cathexis of object relations and impoverishment of the self, predisposing to further decompensation. A variety of misan-thropic depressions may occur at the end of the line, including bitter resignation, vindictive depressions, and depressive cynicism.

In some respects the psychopathology of senescence may be intrinsi-cally different from that of the younger years. For example, it has been observed that classic depressions with feelings of guilt are relatively rare in late life. But when we do encounter guilt feelings in elderly patients, they may have a special significance. When, for example, an elderly pa-tient expresses guilt about past autoerotic activities (a fairly typical de-pressive symptom), the real issue may be a sense of hopelessness that so much opportunity for genuine intimacy has been irrevocably lost. It is more comfortable to feel guilt (and to imagine that one can correct things by doing penance) than to face the fact that one has "missed the boat." The nature of anxiety in aging persons is also different than in the young. While anxiety often is a danger signal in response to ego-alien impulses in younger people, in older people it pertains to the fear of losing external supplies. In addition, anxiety will arise when, for what-ever reasons, the older person's perspective changes from a sense of integrity to the direction of despair.

Geropsychiatric Practice
CLINICAL ASPECTS. The characteristics of the *physician-patient relation-ship* include problems of communication, transference, and counter-transference. Communication with psychiatrically ill elderly persons may be difficult due to age-related central nervous system slowing, organic brain syndrome, or functional psychiatric disorders. Aged patients with

a decrement in cognitive and abstract capacity present unique problems. In senile regression, for example, ideational phenomena dominated by primary process thinking frequently occur. The resulting thought disorder closely resembles that of schizophrenia.

When the older patient lives in the past, the physician may not be recognized at all, or he may become one of the persons in the patient's past. By and large, elderly patients appear less able to distinguish the therapist as a real person from the therapist as a transference figure. Typically, transference phenomena are not interpreted or analyzed, in contrast to what occurs in therapy with younger adults.

Countertransferences may present serious problems, too. For the clinician who has gerophobic attitudes or unresolved fears of aging and death, it will be difficult to approach disorders in the aged with enlightened detachment and rational compassion. Often one may feel frustrated by his inability to modify lifelong behavior patterns in aged patients and the need to accept limited treatment goals. Our cultural emphasis on youth and attractiveness may be a further burden to the therapist dealing with the aged or chronically ill. Finally, early emotional conflicts between the physician and his own parents may be reactivated, causing specific countertransference.

Many problems are related to the patient's dependency on other family members and the multigenerational aspects of family conflict. The frequent need for *contact with relatives* makes it imperative for the geropsychiatrist to be skilled in the diagnosis of disturbed family interactions and in family therapy. Such approaches can be compared with those in child psychiatry. However, the nature of the transference and of the identifications observed between the child patient and his parents is the reverse of that observed between the child and the parent patient. The problems of role reversal that may develop in the aged parent and in the adult child are frequently sources of pathological disturbances in the family. The aged parent may be the one who clings to an obsolete role in the family; or the child who is chronologically adult but emotionally immature may not permit his parent to become appropriately dependent. Without corrective intervention, such family disturbances may be passed on from one generation to the next.

Geropsychiatric diagnosis always involves a complex formulation and never a simple description. The diagnostic formulation integrates multiple etiological factors (e.g., premorbid personality, past experiences, current stresses, nature of coping behavior) in such a way that the disturbed mental functions can be understood as the outcome of the interaction of all these factors. In the etiology, organic, psychogenic, and social factors usually coexist, and their interaction leads to vicious circles that tax the patient's homeostatic capacity to the breaking point. Organic brain syndrome, for example, has been described in terms of a sociopsychosomatic syndrome (see Chap. 13). The diagnostic formulation at the same time points the way toward the essentials of the treatment plan.

Geropsychiatric therapy never consists of a single treatment modality but is always a treatment program. The composition of a treatment program is determined by the significant elements making up the diagnostic formulation. By and large, an effective treatment program, which is an individualized package of specific treatment modalities, contains medical, psychotherapeutic, and social measures. Other measures, such as legal aid and financial assistance, are often included as well.

Another characteristic of geropsychiatric therapy is that it involves adjusting the environment to the patient rather than adjusting the patient to the environment, as with the younger age groups. This principle follows from the age-related decline in homeostatic capacity. Therefore, environmental planning, protective services, and protective intervention are important aspects of geropsychiatric practice.

A major therapeutic goal is to assist the aged patient in actualizing his potential, freeing him sufficiently from illness so that he will be able to attain specific goals: a sense of integrity, the maintenance of personal dignity, and the creative capacity to experience the last years as the consummation of life.

Complex as the diagnostic formulation and the treatment plan may be, the implementation of the latter is even more difficult. This touches on another facet of geropsychiatric work, i.e., providing leadership in planning and developing service programs for the elderly.

SOCIAL ASPECTS. The lack of meaningful communication between researchers, practitioners, and planners has come into progressively sharper focus. Related to this is the realization that research findings must be translated, applied, and attuned to social issues and problems [9, 16, 19, 26, 29].

Social geropsychiatry involves cooperation with community agencies, consultation with nursing homes, environmental planning, and programs of releasing hospitalized patients into the community. It also includes retirement counseling. Since the psychopathology of retirement often reflects the psychopathology of work, the geropsychiatrist needs to be acquainted with the meaning of work, leisure, and recreation.

RESEARCH ASPECTS. Major areas where additional research is needed include: etiology and treatment of organic brain syndrome and senile dementia; the psychodynamics of coping with involutional losses, and the psychopathology of "despair"; psychopharmacology and geriatric prosthetics; development of adequate service programs and optimal environments; and ways and means to enhance the quality of life (e.g., marital, sexual, recreational).

Trainee Categories and Characteristics

Trainee Categories and Occupational Groupings

Trainees can be categorized according to their discipline, principal type of professional activity (research, clinical work, teaching, administration), and level of professionality (semiprofessional or paraprofessional, master's degree level, graduate, postgraduate). Occupational groupings to which training activities can be directed would include:

1. *Health and medical services:* e.g., clinical psychology, dietetics, dentistry, health education, nursing home management, nursing, nutrition, occupational therapy, medicine, surgery, podiatry, rehabilitation counseling, social work, and speech therapy.
2. *Social services:* e.g., financial planning with older people, social casework; family counseling; intake services and assisting in adjustment in institutions and hospital discharges; arranging for guardianships; organizing and administering home services; providing information; referral and placement services; conducting group programs for older persons; planning for community agencies.
3. *Educational, religious, and recreational services:* e.g., program planners, arts and crafts, vocational and avocational counselors, librari-

ans, club leaders, senior activity centers, group workers, pastoral counseling.

4. *Environmental planning:* e.g., architecture, community organization, federal and state planning, institutional administration, and housing for older people.

To these may be added *paraprofessional* and *semiprofessional* personnel (e.g., hospital attendants, Friendly Visitors).

Geropsychiatry can make contributions to the training of many of these professional service fields, as illustrated by the following examples: The rehabilitation counselor needs to know how psychological factors influence motivation, and how mental impairment affects performance. The nursing home manager can be more effective when he is aware of the high incidence of psychiatric symptomatology among nursing home residents and has a working knowledge with regard to the implications for treatment programs and an optimal physical and social environment. The family counselor needs to be well informed about the psychopathology of senescence and the possible effects of the presence of an aging person on other family members. Specialists in architecture and human engineering are best equipped to create optimal environments (retirement villages, recreation centers) when their basic expertise is supplemented by comprehension of the particular needs of elderly persons. Such complicated tasks as balancing the need for privacy against the risk of psychological withdrawal and social isolation, the need for stimulation and activity against the risk of undue passivity, and the need for peer contact against the risk of alienation from younger people can be more easily carried out if the persons assigned these tasks have had some appropriate exposure to information from relevant areas of aging.

Quantitative Aspects: The Personnel Shortage

On all levels there is a shortage of professional personnel working with elderly patients, and the field of aging is not attracting enough scientists and practitioners [13, 23, 29]. Lack of adequate leadership is perceived to be critical in almost every area, in particular, in policymaking, program planning, education, and bridging interdisciplinary gaps [9, 11]. And there is a need to increase the skills of those already active in the field of aging.

An accurate assessment of the manpower shortage is not possible because most workers in the field of aging spend only part of their time with the aged, and their basic professional identity remains rooted in other disciplines. This partial commitment to the field of aging does not negate the need for a core group of professionals who spend *most* of their time in this area. Without a minimal number of such specialists, little effective training could take place in various branches of aging. Thus, generally speaking, two types of training activities are needed: (1) staff development and teacher training, productive of specialists with a major commitment both to education and to the field of aging, and (2) training of personnel whose work involves the rendering of services and care to aged patients.

The lack of personnel is sometimes ascribed to gerontophobia, which is perceived by some authors as a serious problem [5]. It is often stated that students or physicians are not interested in working with elderly patients. A few authors, however, go beyond this by observing that the amount of interest generated by students depends on the extent to which they have opportunities to work closely with aged patients in a clinical setting and on the caliber of such a geriatric facility [1, 2, 21].

There is reason to believe that gerontophobia and the alleged lack of interest among students and physicians are manageable problems. Other subspecialties have their own prejudices to contend with (e.g., mental retardation, alcoholism). Furthermore, as long as most professionals in the field of aging are only part-time gerontologists, it would not be proper to place responsibility for lack of progress on outsiders. Although there is little question about the existence of gerontophobia and the lack of interest among students, these obstacles are not static impediments but are capable of dynamic transformation, depending on our own efforts. Probably the best way to overcome lack of interest is to have excellent geriatric facilities that provide opportunities for clinical learning experiences. There is general agreement that there are not enough clinical facilities capable of providing optimal care and high-caliber training in geriatrics or geropsychiatry. Related to this is the question of the extent to which elderly patients themselves would use geriatric facilities. It has been observed, however, that when geriatric facilities are available, offering high-caliber services, elderly people do make use of them [12, 14, 27]. This suggests that elderly patients themselves do not object to being identified as "geriatric."

Methods of Training

Teaching methods depend on the training *objectives,* the curriculum *contents,* and on the *type and level of professionality* of the trainees. For example, the training may focus on clinical skills, on principles of research, or on teaching techniques. These objectives are further modified by the nature of the setting in which the trainee ultimately expects to work (e.g., academic, private practice, institutional). Teaching methods should be closely attuned to the subject matter to be taught. For example, it is not possible to master the science and art of psychotherapy without doing psychotherapy under close supervision. Nor can one learn to teach without the actual experience of instructing different types of students, or without proper feedback from an experienced teacher. Such a matching of course contents to practical experience is feasible, however, only in training programs of reasonable duration. It is a drawback of conferences, workshops, and short courses that they do not provide the time-consuming but crucial element of *experience.*

Finally, methods of training are also determined by the type of professional to be trained and by the level of his education (e.g., physicians, clergymen, social workers, nurses, physical therapists, hospital aides, community volunteers). The differences in characteristics between these groups and levels require corresponding differences in focus and depth of content. The process of transmitting to others one's own knowledge requires that it be transformed into objective information that can be received and assimilated by others. The greater the professional distance between teacher and trainee, the greater are the potential difficulties in communication. It is then essential that the teacher has thoroughly understood and clearly conceptualized for himself what he is about to teach, and that he find the appropriate language for transmitting the information to his audience. One important advantage of relative closeness of the professional levels of teachers and trainees is the opportunity of the former to serve as a professional role model for the latter.

Specific methods of teaching include conferences, workshops, or institutes; regular consultations; formal courses; or full-time professional training programs.

Conferences, Workshops, and Institutes

Conferences, workshops, and institutes are a popular means of disseminating information. This format usually involves a series of presentations by authorities in the field, the use of discussion groups, and panel discussions. The program may last from one to several days and usually has a substantial attendance. The advantages of this approach are strategic (e.g., alerting a relatively large group of professionals to particular aspects of aging; creating enthusiasm); economic (e.g., little expenditure of time and money on the part of the participants); and social (e.g., the fringe benefits of conventioneering). The disadvantages include the risk of superficiality of the learning experience and the difficulty in evaluating accurately the impact of the training effort. Institutes and workshops are most effective when participants are carefully selected, the number of participants is small enough to permit group discussions, the conference lasts long enough to allow for assimilation and integration of the information presented, and the proceedings are later made available to the participants.

Consultation Programs

Consultation programs represent a format less clearly defined than other training programs. Consultation may take the form of problem-centered seminars or of individual and group supervision. The consultant, who may be of a different professional background than the consultee, usually functions in an advisory role and tends to avoid recommending personal solutions based on his own experiences.

Because of the relatively unstructured nature of the consultation process, special difficulties may arise, such as disillusionment when the consultees discover that the consultations do not answer all their questions. This points up the need for clearly defining the roles and expectations of consultant and consultees.

There is a variety of formats from which the consultant and consultees can select one that is suitable for their particular objectives. The components that can be used to put a consultation program together include:

Didactic presentations, which can be given by the consultant, usually at the beginning of the consultation session, to delineate the subject matter for the day, stimulate the audience for later discussion, or set the stage for a case presentation.

Case presentations, which can be given by the consultees. They have a greater chance of being effective if a case summary is made available ahead of time to the participants, including the consultant. The case discussion involves two phases. During the first phase the consultant essentially raises questions and stimulates the consultees toward greater intellectual effort. At the end of the first phase there are numerous isolated bits of observation, but there is little closure. During the second phase the consultant sees to it that the bits of information are integrated into a cohesive framework. This usually necessitates the providing of additional theoretical knowledge to the trainees to enable them to see the whole forest rather than the single tree.

Group discussions, which may be periodically scheduled to talk informally about topics about which the consultant has some expertise; for example, ward management techniques, the structure and function of the treatment team, contact with the patient's relatives, and professional frustrations.

Audiovisual presentations, which can be used as a teaching device in an ongoing consultation program (or any type of training program, for that matter). Some points to keep in mind, with regard to audiovisual presentations are the following: (1) Usually, the audiovisual presentation is no better than the instructor who uses it; in fact, audiovisual techniques simply represent a method by which an experienced instructor enhances his effectiveness in communication. (2) Most instructors prefer to use videotapes that they themselves have produced. (3) No audiovisual presentation (film or videotape) should run uninterruptedly for more than 20 to 30 minutes, or the audience will get sleepy. (4) Technical perfection of both the audio and video aspects is an absolute must. (5) The preparation and utilization of audiovisual materials is expensive and time-consuming. This investment is justified if there is sustained utilization of the hardware and the software in such a manner that teaching effectiveness is significantly enhanced.

Courses

Courses are usually offered as a part of a larger curriculum, such as continuing education programs, or as part of in-service training programs.

Courses in geriatric subjects are not currently a regular feature of medical school curricula or residency training programs, but attempts are being made in several places and in several ways to tackle this problem [2, 6, 8, 20, 22, 23]. The general impression is that lectures, reading assignments, and larger conferences are not effective in stimulating interest among students. On the other hand, when students have access to clinical work with elderly patients, this serves as an eye-opener. Thus, if a student is going to be interested in the field of aging, he is likely to do so by way of developing an interest in aged *persons*.

To go on with the medical student: Although he may take certain courses in aging, these are not sufficient for geriatric clinical work later on. Rather, he should learn how the "being old" of his patient can cause age-related impairments; how these determine the patient's reactions to therapy; and how they influence the physician-patient relationship. He should have opportunities to apply this knowledge in clinical situations under supervision and to observe his instructor perform clinically with geriatric patients.

Similar considerations apply to other disciplines. In the area of occupational therapy, it is clear that elderly patients with mental disorders require therapeutic activities that are different from those for other age groups. In the field of nutrition the need for specialized knowledge is underscored by the fact that many elderly patients have a host of peculiarities related to loss of teeth, diminution of the sense of taste and smell, and altered gastrointestinal functioning, as well as many related to psychological, social, and economic factors. Thus geriatric medicine, geriatric occupational therapy, and geriatric dietetics are sufficiently unique and complex to require special training experience organized by experts in these respective areas. The same applies to many other areas, such as geriatric dentistry, recreation, and social work.

Courses in the medical and psychiatric aspects of aging have special relevance for persons already working with elderly patients. Among these groups there is usually substantial interest in additional training opportunities. The largest number of persons engaged in the care of geriatric patients are probably the nursing aides and practical nurses in extended care facilities. These persons appear to receive little in the way of formal training in geriatric topics. For example, mental hospital aides usually receive a general course orienting them to work with psychiatric patients, and topics related to aging constitute only a small part of the curriculum. When these aides are placed on a geriatric unit, on-the-job training is expected to supplement their limited knowledge. It is questionable, however, that these circumstances foster an optimal degree of clinical know-how.

In-service training programs for this type of personnel are not without problems. First, there is the problem of finding instructors with competence in specific content areas as well as in teaching methods who are willing to teach and who have sufficient time. Second, additional personnel must be available to carry on with patient care while the trainees are in class. Third, mental hospital aides represent a heterogeneous group with respect to age, intelligence, and motivation. By and large, they are more interested in learning practical know-how than in theoretical concepts.

A few comments on the *evaluation* of training programs may be in order here. Several methodological problems exist. (1) The accuracy and usefulness of the assessment data depend on determining the pretraining level of trainee knowledge and skills. (2) Knowledge and information can be more easily and accurately tested than the level of clinical skills. (3) Improved morale, self-confidence, and job satisfaction in the trainees, which can be a definite fringe benefit of training, are even more difficult to measure. These subjective phenomena may be evaluated on the basis of personal reports given by the trainees. (4) Occasionally, a paradoxical phenomenon occurs: some trainees seem to know less on completion of training than at the start. One possible explanation is that, as a result of the training, they have begun to ask themselves questions about phenomena previously taken for granted. The evaluation test catches them at a time when they have more questions than answers.

In-service training staffs tend to develop their own *course materials:* texts, reprints, bibliographies, edited lectures, illustrative clinical case write-ups, and so on. These materials can eventually be put together in the form of a compendium or manual. Once such course materials are available, they can facilitate extension of the training program to other institutions.

As previously mentioned above, audiovisual methods can add a unique dimension to educational programs. Closed-circuit television enables an audience to follow an actual interview closely and permits the instructor to make ongoing comments on the patient's behavior and the communication in the physician-patient relationship. A playback of previously recorded videotapes offers the advantage that the videotape can be stopped at any time to discuss specific behavioral phenomena or to replay parts of particular importance. Another use of videotape materials is the development of a library of videotapes on such topics as the psychopathology of senescence, techniques of interviewing, family dynamics, and intergenerational conflict. From the videotapes, instructional films can be made.

Formal Training Programs

Formal training programs in aging require full-time participation on the part of the trainee. They are usually oriented more toward training in research than in applied gerontology or geriatrics. This trend is not surprising, because a professional orientation toward research in aging promises the rewards of prestige. Further, the intellectual detachment needed in scientific research may be preferable to the personal anxieties and professional frustrations with which the clinician has to come to grips. But this trend does suggest that, to recruit bright and well-motivated persons for clinical work with the aged, part-time research needs to be emphasized. In fact, diversification generally is wise: the investigator may get new hunches from clinical work, and the clinician may improve his professional effectiveness by participation in research.

The Duke Geropsychiatry Training Program

The Duke Geropsychiatry Training Program, in existence since 1966, is aimed primarily at physicians who have completed two or three years of psychiatric residency. Its primary objectives are to increase skills in the clinical practice of geropsychiatry. In addition, it aims to stimulate geropsychiatric research and to develop administrative and teaching skills with reference to geropsychiatry. The two-year program includes training in geropsychiatry proper, as well as selected learning experiences in geriatric medicine, social gerontology, neuropsychological gerontology, and biological gerontology (Table 21). The contents of the curriculum are covered by way of didactic seminars, case conferences, research seminars, and visiting lecturers. Clinical training includes case studies and supervised therapy of ambulatory aged patients in the Duke Older Amer-

Table 21. Duke Geropsychiatry Training Program: Curriculum

Geropsychiatry:

Psychodynamics of senescence (patterns of successful aging, coping with involutional losses)

Psychopathology and psychiatric syndromes of senescence

Psychotherapy (individual and group therapy, family therapy, etc.)

Psychopharmacology and other somatic therapies

Environmental planning (milieu therapy, reality orientation, etc.)

Geriatrics:

Geriatric medicine and neurology

Somatopsychology (changes in body image, psychological reactions to chronic illness and disability, etc.)

Psychosomatic approach (the sick role, psychosocial factors in organic brain syndrome, rehabilitation techniques, management of hypochondriasis and regression, etc.)

Psychosocial gerontology:

The human life cycle

Ecology of senescence; sociocultural determinants

Social attitudes toward aging and mental illness

Work and retirement (career patterns, psychopathology of work and retirement, leisure and recreation, etc.)

Family dynamics and conflict

Programs of care for the aged and chronically ill

Psychological gerontology:

Age-related changes and measurement techniques of intelligence, perception, psychomotor skills, learning and memory

Neuropsychological deficits of senium (clinical and laboratory techniques)

Biological gerontology:

Psychophysiology

Neurophysiology (senescent EEG, cerebral blood flow studies)

Neurochemistry and neuropharmacology

Genetics and biology of aging

icans Resources and Services (OARS) Program, of patients admitted to the Duke Geriatric Psychiatry Inpatient Service, and of patients in the geropsychiatry units of two nearby state mental hospitals. Research experiences are available by way of participation in ongoing basic or clinical research projects of the Duke Center for the Study of Aging and Human Development. The activities and resources of the program are summarized in Table 22.

Table 22. Duke Geropsychiatry Training Program: Activities and Resources

Training Activities	Resources
Geropsychiatry:	
Diagnostic studies	Duke Cerebral Diagnostic Unit
Individual and group therapy	Duke Geriatric Psychiatry Inpatient
Drug therapy	Service
Ward milieu techniques	Duke OARS Program
Clinical research projects	Geropsychiatry units of North
Management and administration	Carolina state mental hospitals
Geriatrics:	
Psychosomatic aspects	Duke Psychosomatic Service
Neurological aspects	Duke Department of Neurology
Rehabilitative techniques	Geropsychiatry units of North
Therapy in chronic illness	Carolina state mental hospitals
	Nursing homes
Social gerontology:	
Retirement counseling	Duke Department of Medical
Family counseling	Sociology
Agency consultations	Duke OARS Program
Environmental planning	Community mental health centers
Research projects	Duke Center for Study of Aging and
	Human Development
Psychological gerontology:	
Neuropsychological tests for CNS deficits	Duke Gerontology Research Laboratories
Measurement of cognitive, perceptual, learning and memory, and psychomotor functions	Duke Gerontology Research Training Program
Research projects	Duke Center for Study of Aging and Human Development
Biological gerontology:	
Electrophysiology, bioelectric techniques in clinical diagnosis	Duke Psychophysiology Laboratory
EEG, cerebral blood flow	Duke Gerontology Research University Courses

Since it is impossible to become well versed in all phases of the program, the trainee is encouraged to select those training experiences that will best fit his career plans. Because the program is designed for the training of psychiatrists, primary emphasis is placed on geropsychiatry proper, including the psychodynamics and psychopathology of senescence, relevant therapeutic techniques, and the like. Next in importance is the area of geriatrics, with special focus on the psychosomatic approach, which involves an understanding of psychophysiological and somatopsychic reactions. A thorough acquaintance with geriatric pathophysiology and an understanding of general psychodynamics must be supplemented by, and integrated with, clinical experience.

Important elements of this program are learning experiences aimed at developing skills in administration and management, communication, teaching, consultation, and program planning. An example of a learning experience that combines all of these skills is the planning and implementation of local or regional workshops. Experience in consultation is gained in various settings, such as nursing homes and community mental health centers. Administrative skills are learned by way of assuming specific management responsibilities under close supervision in the geropsychiatry unit of a mental hospital.

References

1. Arie, T. Morale and the planning of psychogeriatric services. *Br. Med. J.* 3:166, 1971.
2. Bayne, J. R. D. Geriatrics and gerontology in medical education. *J. Am. Geriatr. Soc.* 22:198, 1974.
3. Beattie, W. M., Jr. Gerontology curricula: Multidisciplinary frameworks, interdisciplinary structures, and disciplinary depth (Symposium: The Real World and the Ivory Tower). *Gerontologist* 14:545, 1974.
4. Birren, J. E. Life Review, Reconciliation and Termination. In *The Psychology of Aging.* Englewood Cliffs, N.J.: Prentice-Hall, 1964. Chap. 12.
5. Bunzel, J. H. Recognition, relevance and deactivation of gerontophobia: Theoretical essay. *J. Am. Geriatr. Soc.* 21:77, 1973.
6. Busse, E. W. One medical school's approach to teaching problems of the aging. *J. Am. Geriatr. Soc.* 17:299, 1969.
7. Butler, R. N. The life review: An interpretation of reminiscence in the aged. *Psychiatry* 26:109, 1963.
8. Committee on Undergraduate and Continuing Medical Education of the Clinical Medicine Section of the Gerontological Society (Manuel Rodstein, Chairman). A model curriculum for an elective course in geriatrics. *Gerontologist* 13:231, 1973.

9. Elias, M. F. Dialectics of professional training, education, and delivery of services to elderly persons (introduction to the Symposium: The Real World and the Ivory Tower). *Gerontologist* 14:525, 1974.
10. Erikson, E. H. Identity and the Life Cycle. In *Psychological Issues*. New York: International Universities Press, 1959.
11. Fauri, D. P. Educating for gerontological leadership roles (guest editorial). *Gerontologist* 14:466, 1974.
12. Feigenbaum, E. M. Geriatric psychopathology—internal or external? *J. Am. Geriatr. Soc.* 22:49, 1974.
13. Freeman, J. T. A survey of geriatric education: Catalogues of United States medical schools. *J. Am. Geriatr. Soc.* 19:746, 1971.
14. Furstenberg, F. F. Should your hospital have an aging center? *Hosp. Pract.* August 1968. Pp. 48–53.
15. Goldman, R. Geriatrics as a specialty—problems and prospects. *Gerontologist* 14:468, 1974.
16. Hickey, T., and Spinetta, J. J. Bridging research and application (Symposium: The Real World and the Ivory Tower). *Gerontologist* 14:526, 1974.
17. Jacques, E. Death and the mid-life crisis. *Int. J. Psychoanal.* 46:502, 1965.
18. Lawton, A. H. The role of medical education in gerontology. *J. Am. Geriatr. Soc.* 17:230, 1969.
19. Lawton, A. H. Continuing postgraduate medical education in geriatrics. *J. Am. Geriatr. Soc.* 19:97, 1971.
20. Libow, L. S. A fellowship in geriatric medicine. *J. Am. Geriatr. Soc.* 20:580, 1972.
21. Libow, L. S., Viola, R. M., and Stein, M. F., Jr. The extended care facility at Mount Sinai City Hospital Center, Elmhurst, New York: Three-year experience. *J. Am. Geriatr. Soc.* 16:1164, 1968.
22. Miller, M. B. Restructuring medical education for management of the chronically ill aged. *J. Am. Geriatr. Soc.* 22:501, 1974.
23. Rao, D. B. Fellowships in geriatric medicine. *J. Am. Geriatr. Soc.* 21:169, 1973.
24. Schaie, K. W. Training of trainers to train trainers (Symposium: The Real World and the Ivory Tower). *Gerontologist* 14:533, 1974.
25. Sinex, F. M. A view of training from within the medical school: Attitudes, status, and structure (Symposium: The Real World and the Ivory Tower). *Gerontologist* 14:538, 1974.
26. Urban, H. B., and Watson, W. Alternative approaches (Symposium: The Real World and the Ivory Tower). *Gerontologist* 14:530, 1974.
27. Varner, R. V., and Clavert, W. R. Psychiatric assessment of the aged: A differential model for diagnosis. *J. Am. Geriatr. Soc.* 22:273, 1974.
28. Weg, R. B. A view from curricula for gerontology (Symposium: The Real World and the Ivory Tower). *Gerontologist* 14:549, 1974.
29. Wright, I. S. A look into the future of geriatric medicine. *J. Am. Geriatr. Soc.* 21:55, 1973.

18. The Aged and Public Policy

Joseph J. Spengler

Seventy is not a sin.
—Golda Meir, *Time,* March 14, 1969

Let's take the instant by the forward top;
For we are old, and on our quick'st decrees
Th' inaudible and noiseless foot of Time
Steals ere we can effect them.
—Shakespeare, *All's Well That Ends Well*

Nothing 'gainst Time's scythe can make defence.
—Shakespeare, "Sonnet XII"

To live is to struggle.
—René Dubos, *So Human an Animal*

Over the past 40 years, increasing public provision has been made for the aged. The concern in this last chapter is with some of the forces giving rise to this increase in public provision and with prospective future trends.

The prospect for increase in longevity will not be considered.* Note may be taken in passing, however, of recent gains in longevity and of the effect of eliminating the leading causes of mortality after age 45. Between 1950 and 1972, the expectation of life at age 45 has increased about 0.7 years for white men and 2.7 years for white women. Mainly responsible for post-45 mortality are cardiovascular-renal diseases and malignant neoplasms. If mortality from these two sets of diseases were reduced by 30 percent, expectation of life at ages 45 and 65 would increase only about 3 and 2.4 years respectively, for males; the corresponding gains for females would be about 2.9 and 2.45 years. If mortality from all causes were reduced by 30 percent, expectation of life at age 65 would increase by 2.94 years for males and 2.88 years for females. These extensions would raise life expectancy at age 65 to about 15.9 years for males and 19 years for females [6, 18, 40].

---

* While man may complete a larger fraction of his life span, the life span itself is limited by the deterioration and loss of cells and physiological function [12, 22, 35, 41]. Prehoda [32] believes, however, that man's life span may approximate 200 years within three to four decades and eventually 1,000 years. In time, of course, an increase in our understanding of the aging process may make possible both some extension of life expectancy at higher years and some deferment of senescence.

Forces Operative in the Recent Past

When one seeks to identify the forces giving rise to legislation economically favorable to the aged, one may look at immediate antecedents or at long-run forces. It is the latter, however, that are overriding in the long run. It is these, therefore, that we shall discuss.*

The long-run forces are divisible into the ideological and the real. At least three somewhat distinct *ideological* forces are recognizable. First, already in the early part of this century, a kind of collectivistic, redistributive ideology was coming into being, only to be smothered during World War I and its immediate aftermath. Yet, like the fabled phoenix, it began again to take on life in the 1920s and lent passive support to actual demands for various kinds of public assistance for the aged (as well as for others). After 1929 the havoc-spreading Great Depression triggered off this support into something more active and gave it manifold organizational forms (e.g., the Townsend movement).

Second, with the secularization of values and the dissipation of conduct-determining religious belief, the ancient religious obligation to be charitable gradually metamorphosed into a politically and economically oriented poverty ideology. This ideology is now current among those (many of whom are economically untutored) presently in charge of critical and strategic channels of communication and engaged in the dissemination of information to college students and other well-meaning receivers of information, most of whom are also economically untutored. These opinion-dispensers have helped propagate a distorted, value-ridden picture of the poor (among them the aged) that, as Walter Miller observes, is at variance with both the judgments of the poor themselves and that subculture of poverty that affords the relatively poor a "coherent way of life geared to the circumstances of lower-class labor."† Poverty, in other words, has two dimensions, one objective and the other subjective and reflective of the interpretation and self-image that one who is objectively defined to be poor puts on his own status and condition. The image that a person defined to be poor forms of his objective poverty, even though self-protective, may be modified by exposing him

---

* On relatively recent aspects of the genesis of the so-called war on poverty, including poverty of the aged, see the symposium, Antipoverty Programs [1].
† See summary of Seminar on Poverty [34], Valentine [47], and Canham [8]. See also footnote on p. 354.

to subjective influences, propagandistic and otherwise. Usually he is made to feel poor even though he originally did not view his plane of living as falling within an objectively defined category of poverty. In the United States, many who were not aware of being poor have learned, after the manner of characters in a Molière play, that they had always been poor.

Third, a kind of ideological rationale for many kinds of public spending was canonized in the later 1930s as a result of the writings of Lord Keynes and his disciples. Arguments in support of public spending were not, of course, new, having long found utterance; but never before had so persuasive a case been made for the alleged social costlessness of a great deal of public spending. This rationale was to prove useful to both advocates of public welfare and their political spokesmen. Presumably, the progressive inflation to which these programs might give rise would not materialize until after the programs had become wedged into the essentially uncontrolled and uncontrollable bureaucratic structure of modern democratic governments. The rationale was useful also in that it had to do only with the elastic pecuniary dimension of welfare and not with its real dimension, which tends to be inelastic. For example, when Medicare was being developed, emphasis was on monetary support and not on increasing the supply of medical, paramedical, and service personnel in keeping with the necessarily augmented monetary demand for this personnel. As a result, many prices have risen notably, and the capacity of Medicare to support care of the aged has been reduced.*

The *real* conditions, of which six may be considered, are interrelated. First, historically, is the Great Depression, together with the resulting massive unemployment of the 1930s. Unemployment rose from 3.2 percent of the civilian labor force in 1929 to 8.7 percent in 1930. Thereafter, annual levels from 1931 to 1940 varied between 14.3 percent in 1937 and 24.9 percent in 1933. Moreover, not until after two years of defense spending and the country's entry into World War II did unem-

* On these issues, see Berry and Daugherty [2]. What is needed is careful economic analysis of the supply and allocation of medical services. Brackett [4] puts the annual cost of medical care of a couple with an annual income of around $4,000 at 7 to 8 percent of this income. In 1971 this cost slightly exceeded $600 in four-person families. Between 1950 and 1967, despite the prospect of Medicare, etc., physicians per 100,000 population increased only 6 percent [17, 23]. Between 1969 and 1971, physicians per 100,000 population increased from 163 to 174, compared with 149 in 1950.

ployment fall below the 5 percent level, in 1942. This long-continuing unemployment reduced the capacity of many households to make provision for their support after retirement. Moreover, such provision as was made underwent dissipation through inflation, with prices rising 71 percent between 1938 and 1948, 20 percent between 1948 and 1958, 60 percent between 1958 and 1974, and 238 percent over the whole period from 1938 to 1974.

Second, already by 1930 the number of aged persons was increasing more rapidly than the population, mainly because gross reproduction had been falling. Natality and the excess of births over deaths did not begin to rise until in the late 1930s and not notably until after the war and then only until the later 1950s, after which natality again fell. Those aged 65 and over formed only 5.3 percent of the population in 1929, but this fraction had risen to 9.6 percent by 1968 and may rise to about 11 percent by 1985 or earlier. It will rise significantly above 10 percent, however, only if gross reproduction falls appreciably, or if the expectation of life at birth rises notably above 70 years.

This aging trend gave greater visibility to the aged, even though it was not at first accompanied by a marked increase in their political power. Those of an age anticipatory of the advent of, say, age 65 are likely to have interests more in common with those aged 65 and over than with those aged 18 to 44 years, now that the population of voting age includes all aged 18 and over instead of those 21 and over. Suppose, at least for the sake of exposition, that we include in this anticipatory category persons aged 45 to 64 but without supposing their consciousness to be as intense as that of persons aged 65 and over. Not until recent years, however, did the aged, together with persons of similar interests, form close to a majority of the voting population. This near-preponderance has disappeared with the lowering of the voting age and will not reemerge until the next century. The aged can, however, improve their position through political means, since less than two-thirds of eligible voters normally vote.*

* Around 1930 the population 45 or more years old formed only four-tenths of the population of voting age, then 21 years and older. This fraction had risen to about 43 percent by 1950, 49 percent by 1960, and about 50 percent by 1968. With the expansion of the population of voting age to those 18 years and older, only about 46 percent of this population were 45 and over in 1972. In the text above it is supposed, though without establishing the fact for present and future, that

Third, a steady decrease in the number of persons living in rural areas had increased the number of persons exposed to economic disabilities of the sort to which older persons are especially prone (e.g., loss of job, inability to find employment, decrease in monetary income, large medical expenses). Today, of course, the risk of poverty, objectively defined, is greater in rural than in urban areas. In the past and often even today, however, a given plane of living is less expensive in rural than in urban areas. Moreover, the threshold of consciousness of being poor is associated with lower income levels in nonrural than in rural areas. Accordingly, as the nonrural population increased absolutely and relatively,* its increase must have been accompanied by an increase in the awareness of poverty, and in some measure also by an increase in demands for public assistance. After all, city populations probably are more collectivistically inclined, as a rule, than are rural populations.

Fourth, per capita real disposable income has been growing since 1940, by which time it had finally returned to the 1929 level from which it had declined with the advent of the Great Depression. Between 1940 and 1968, it grew about 2.5 percent per year. National income per capita grew at about the same rate. This steady increase in real income per capita, combined with the progressive nature of income-based tax revenue, suggested that use of the income-tax apparatus to redistribute income somewhat (in part to older persons) might be acceptable. The Social Security system also had a redistributive impact, especially after additional burdens were placed on it—justified, it was believed, by the lesser ability to pay of many of its beneficiaries. The steady increase in post-tax income must have made requests for some redistribution of income attractive to those who stood to benefit eventually, or were uncertain about their security in retirement, or both. It must also have fed

---

around age 45, people become concerned about retirement and begin to develop an identity of interests with those already retired.

* The farm population continued to decline after 1920 except for a temporary farmward movement in the economically depressed early 1930s. By 1950 the farm population formed only 15.3 percent of the total population—half what it had been in 1920. By 1966 it amounted to only 5.9 percent of the nation's population and by 1972, to only 4.6 percent. While the farm population has continued to decline, the rural population has not changed greatly in absolute size since 1910. It has, however, formed a declining fraction of the total population, falling from 54.3 percent in 1910 to 43.8 percent in 1930 and 40.4 percent in 1950. Currently, the rural fraction of the population is about one-fourth below what it was in 1950.

that "revolution of expectations" that for several or more decades has been causing the potential demands of many persons for goods and services to increase much faster than their post-tax earnings.

Fifth, with the development of poverty bench marks—albeit arbitrary and subject to variable definition—it was found that households headed by older persons predominated among those with incomes deemed below the poverty level. This condition reflected the inability of many persons to find steady and remunerative employment, as well as their earlier inability to accumulate adequate savings for old age. The incidence of unemployment has tended to be somewhat higher among workers over 55 years of age than among those aged 21 to 54; it would be higher still were not many older workers protected by rules of seniority. Indeed, unemployment among those aged 55 or over remains below the national level and compares favorably with that found among persons aged 21 to 54.* When older workers become unemployed, however, they find it much harder than younger workers to obtain new employment. They are sometimes handicapped, furthermore, by their being less mobile than younger workers.† It is not surprising, therefore, that the income status of the older population has been inferior to that of younger persons for a number of decades.‡

Sixth, older persons have become increasingly conscious of the income-eroding effects of inflation, effects that Congress has several times sought to counterbalance by increasing Social Security benefits. Periodic counterbalancing legislation on the part of Congress is an inferior means of offsetting the income-dissipating effects of inflation. It is preferable to prevent inflation altogether, or, failing in this, to attach an inflation-

---

* As late as 1968, between one-fifth and one-fourth of all families with heads over age 64 received incomes below the poverty level, whereas in 1963 two-thirds of those over age 64 and not in institutions were described as "subject to poverty" [30, 33, 45].
† The role of immobility probably is exaggerated (see Goldstein [19]).
‡ In 1949, for example, median income for white nonfarm males 65 years and over was only 40 percent as high as that for those aged 45 to 54; the corresponding percentage for nonwhite males was 38. The corresponding percentages in the farm population were 46 and 60. Even for those with a high school or a college education, median income after age 65 was very much lower than that for persons in the 45 to 54 age group [28]. In 1972 18.6 percent of all persons 65 and over were in the "below low-income level" compared with 11.9 percent of the population as a whole. In 1973, 16 percent of the recipients of Social Security benefits were living in poverty [11, pp. 161–176].

offsetting escalator clause to Social Security benefits as has now been accomplished. Inflation has, of course, long been under way. It is true that between 1930 and 1940 the Bureau of Labor Statistics consumer price index declined from 58.2 to 48.8. But thereafter it rose, to 83.8 by 1948, 100.7 by 1958, and 120.9 by 1968. It rose nearly 5 percent in 1968 and over 22 percent from 1960 to 1968, a period notable for the introduction by the Kennedy-Johnson administrations of the so-called New Economics. Today a consumer needs over $2.00 to buy what cost a dollar in 1949.

What has been said boils down to this: In and after the 1930s the demand for assistance to the aged and for measures suited to improve their situation increased markedly. This trend was reenforced by ideological changes. At the same time the capacity of the state to provide this assistance increased, especially after the late 1930s. Given these conditions, it was possible for political spokesmen for the aged to set up arrangements providing some income security in old age, together with relatively free access to medical care and related forms of assistance.

By 1974, moreover, the absolute as well as the relative position of the aged had improved. At the close of 1973, real per capita disposable income was about 54 percent above the 1959 level and about 21 percent above the 1967 level. The fraction of the population 65 years and over with incomes below a low-income level declined from 35.2 percent in 1959 to 24.6 percent in 1970 to 18.6 percent in 1972. Meanwhile, the corresponding fraction for those under 65 declined from 20.7 percent in 1959 to 11.3 percent in 1970 to 11.1 percent in 1972. Each age group thus experienced about the same relative decline in fraction of persons with incomes below a low-income level. This improvement in the relative position of the aged reflects improvement in Social Security (OASDHI) and other money transfer programs that "have dramatically decreased the measured relative inequality of family income" [11]. Thus the average monthly benefit for retired workers under Social Security rose from $74.04 in 1960 to $132.17 in 1971; this 78 percent increase in current dollars amounts to an increase of about 30 percent in 1972 dollars. Social Security benefits were increased by 20 percent across the board in October 1972 and by 7 and 4 percent respectively in March and June 1974. There is now provision also for increases in benefits related to the Consumer Price Index, the first of which is scheduled for

July 1, 1975. Allowance should be made also for Medicare benefits, which now cover 80 percent of specified costs for hospital care and post-hospital care and thus greatly reduce the burden of illness. But will recent trends persist? What does the future hold in store for the aged?

The Future of the Aged

While the lot of the younger aged in the United States should prove attractive in the near future, this future is not so attractive for most older-aged persons, especially not for those beyond their late seventies. After all, as Democritus wrote about 2½ millenia ago, "Old age is a general mutilation. It has all the limbs and organs, but they each lack something." The advent of this stage of aging may be put off for many, if not most, persons until late in the seventies, but it cannot be put off much longer, even under highly favorable circumstances. Even the supposedly salutary medication of King David of old loses its vaunted curative powers.* Given a more rational and less superstition-ridden view of life than now prevails, therefore, euthanasia may be given more serious consideration than at present. Otherwise, given further prolongation of life without corresponding prolongation of use of faculties, the lot of many aged could resemble that of mythological Tithonus, or that of residents in the Republic of the Half Dead portrayed in Kipling's *Strange Ride of Morrowbie Jukes,* or that of Jonathan Swift's Struldbrugs, whose very appearance weakened the appetite for living.†

Let us now consider some of the reasons that could make the emerging future of the aged bleak, certainly in a relative if not in an absolute sense. Notice will be taken mainly of real circumstances, though several ideological factors may be mentioned. The ideological factors differ from the real ones, of course, in that, being mental in character, they may be more susceptible of change.

It is highly probable that the society of the future, even more than

---

* "Let there be sought for my lord the king a young virgin; and let her stand before the king, and cherish him; and let her lie in thy bosom, that my lord the king may get heat . . . and the damsel . . . ministered to him; but the king knew her not." 1 Kings 1:2–4.

† "I am a hulk—only breathing and excreting," declared Sir Winston Churchill in 1953 as he watched himself becoming helpless and senile (*Time,* May 6, 1966). On the plight of the aged, also see Henry [24].

that of the present, will be a society of so-called secular values (in reality, often merely new superstitions in place of the old), one bereft of the beliefs and values that in the past have enabled an adaptive mankind to cushion the impact of hardship, even when in the guise of aging. In the past, when people were much less mobile than now, familial care reenforced whatever public care was conferred on the aged; and familial care was likely to include some love and affection—far less than was accorded to children, it is true—but much more than is likely to be bestowed even by kindly hirelings skilled at simulating affection. In one respect, however, the aged of today are better off: They lose fewer of their temporal associates. Writing in 1623, John Donne, the English poet, observed that when the bell tolls for friend or acquaintance, it also "tolls for thee"; for "no man is an Iland, entire of selfe," but one whose reality consists in his being part of the furniture of the minds of others. At that time, only about 84 in 1,000 females aged 20 reached the age of 80, whereas in 1900 about 194 in 1,000 white females aged 20 reached age 80. Today the corresponding figure is 489. We may say, therefore, that today the chances of an octogenarian's having surviving friends of his own age are twice as good as they were in 1900 and nearly six times as good as they were 1623. The chances are about one in three, moreover, that four generations of a family may coexist.

Ideology, or the content of people's minds, helps to determine the degree of support provided for the aged under given income conditions, for it affects the decisions of both legislatures and the public at large. How ideology will affect the future lot of the aged is not clear, however. It is not certain that secular ideological trends will continue in directions favorable to increasing and diversified support of measures designed to afford material aid to the aged. Should an upward trend continue, the impact of favorable material trends will be accentuated. Should a downward ideological trend develop, however, the impact of favorable material trends will be reduced somewhat.

With fertility in the neighborhood of the replacement level,* potential

---

* The overall ratio of departures to entries varies inversely with the gross reproduction rate; the ratio also varies greatly from industry to industry because of interindustry differences in growth of output, technology, and so on (see *The Aging of Populations and Its Economic and Social Implications* [43] and Jaffé and Froomkin [25].

productivity per capita will be higher than it has been for the past 25 years. For with net immigration negligible or at recent levels, the relative number of persons of working age (20 to 64 years old) in the population will rise above the 52 percent level prevailing around 1960 and 1970 to around 59 percent by the year 2000, only eventually to settle around 57 percent. Moreover, employment opportunities for older persons should remain relatively stable, since the number of persons entering the labor market will not be relatively large compared with the past 17 to 20 years' upsurges of births. Indicative of this stability is the behavior of the ratio of entries into the labor force to departures from it, here represented by the ratio of persons aged 15 to 19 to persons aged 60 to 69. With net immigration negligible, this ratio, which was 1.2 in 1970, will move to 1.1 in 1985 and 2000 and then decline to 0.7 in 2050, approximating 0.65 in a stationary population.

As was suggested earlier, the voting power of persons 45 and over was diluted by lowering the voting age everywhere to 18 in 1972. This action increased the number of persons of voting age under 45 by about 18 percent and increased from about 50 percent to about 54.2 percent the fraction that persons of voting age below 45 constituted of all persons should remain relatively stable, since the number of persons entering the labor market will not be relatively large compared with the past 17 to 20 years after upsurges of births. Indicative of this stability is the behavior of the ratio of entries into the labor force to departures from it, here represented by the ratio of persons aged 15 to 19 to persons aged 60 to 69. With net immigration negligible, this ratio, which was 1.2 in 1970, will move to 1.1 in 1985 and 2000 and then decline to 0.7 in 2050, approximating 0.65 in a stationary population.

The aged may continue to count on inflation to erode the purchasing power of their fixed incomes, whether these flow from pensions, government bonds, annuities, or other fixed sources. The economic disciplines formerly counted on to prevent both unwarranted price increases and a rising price level have disappeared along with the old prescription for curing a dog of killing sheep: "Cut off his tail, just behind the ears" [3]. Barriers to the upward movement of prices have been relaxed, with trade union and corporate czars increasing asked prices faster than warranted by increases in productivity and with the government standing by to increase the money supply commensurately if essential to prevent unemployment. An ideology in support of rising prices has come into being and infiltrated the minds of some economists, among others.

At least six specific forces may strengthen the upward drift of prices bearing on the aged. These will be discussed in the paragraphs that follow.

Outstanding is the decline in the relative political power of the aged, since, ultimately, whether or not we have inflation turns on whether congressmen who might acquiesce in inflation are permitted by the voters to endorse or pursue inflationary policies.

The amount of tax revenue slated to be collected by federal, state, and local governments is likely to exceed 40 percent of the national income, a ratio in excess of that which some believe compatible with the avoidance of inflation. The tendency toward inflation is intensified by the fact that so much of governmental expenditure is on objectives that amount to little more than governmental potlatch and that contribute little or nothing to man's welfare or to the progress of economic development.

Governmental and trade union wage policy contributes to inflation in several ways. On the one hand it causes unemployment by elevating wages to unemployment-fostering levels, thereby also increasing the cost of governmental support for the unemployed. On the other hand, trade union and business leaders, by agreeing to wage increases in excess of increases in productivity, not only prevent price decreases but also give rise to price increases and thereby strengthen inflation-generating forces. Even if wages in more productive industries merely keep pace with increases in output, their doing so fosters excessive wage and price increases in industries experiencing lower advances in output per manhour (e.g., in some of the service industries, the whole of which now employ more than two-thirds of the labor force).*

No "New Politics" has been brought into existence to complement the so-called New Economics. In other words, no new set of political institutions has been established to put the so-called new full-employment, growth-fostering fiscal policy into effect in such ways as to accomplish the objectives of this policy without at the same time generating continuing inflation. Hence, even as some economists warned years ago when they advised that the annual rate of growth of the national money sup-

* For a description of the price-increasing mechanism, see Spengler and Kreps [38]; on services, see Spengler [37].

ply be kept at the 3 or 4 percent level, inflation has become the hallmark of recent American administrations and is likely to remain so as long as a soft administration is combined with a prodigal Congress.*

It seems now to be assumed that when employment is less than full, deficit spending should be resorted to even though most unemployment is of short duration, at least two-fifths of households with an unemployed head have a breadwinner, and considerable unemployment is not imputable to a deficiency of aggregate demand. Moreover, if full employment is defined as equivalent to less than, say, 4 to 5 percent unemployment, inflation is assured, particularly when many of the unemployed lack the skills and experience that are in demand.† Should such a guideline be operative and produce inflation, the demand of the aged for assistance will be intensified.

Premature retirement also tends to strengthen the forces making for inflation, whether that retirement be voluntary or in effect imposed on a worker by a combination of trade union and corporate czars. For, as the ratio of a man's years in retirement to his years in the labor force increases, the ratio of his retirement income to his preretirement income diminishes proportionately.‡ This in turn leads to pressure on Congress to increase Social Security and other benefits, probably through recourse to general revenue or to deficit financing instead of to increase in Social Security "taxes."

Attention may be drawn to Clarence D. Long's theory of "creeping unemployment," a companion effect of the process that is set in motion by wage increases without corresponding increases in productivity. When all wages increase at the same pace as wages of the most productive workers, it becomes increasingly uneconomic to employ infra-average workers at these supra-average wage levels. The unemployment of infra-average workers therefore increases, and so does that of older workers, insofar as they are members of infra-average categories [27, pp. 397–398]. Here again, uneconomic arrangements price older and other work-

---

* On sources of inflation see Kreps [26], p. 228, Elson [15], *Studies by the Staff of the Cabinet Committee on Price Stability* [42], Cagan [7], and Harriss [21].
† On the original goal of the 1946 Employment Act see Nourse [29], Siegel [36], and Stahl [39].
‡ See reports in *U.S. News & World Report* [46]. Also see Faltermayer [16, p. 112]. A man's pension is reduced by something like 6 to 7 percent for each year he retires prior to his normal retirement age [16, p. 113]. See also Gordon [20].

ers out of the market and augment their need for public assistance and hence intensify inflation-generating forces.

The need for, as well as the demand of, the aged for greater assistance will be intensified by deterioration of the employment opportunities open to the aged, together with relatively early retirement imposed on older workers by trade union, corporate, and governmental bureaucracies. Given a relatively low ratio of years worked to years in retirement, a worker cannot earn enough to enjoy a comfortable income in retirement, nor can or will the federal government supplement retirement incomes enough to make them comfortable under prospective conditions. Yet this ratio has been falling even though most workers can continue in their employment until age 70, given good health and refresher training, the cost of which could be met by cutting down the cost of high school and college education, perhaps by one-fourth, as suggested by Machlup [27, pp. 133–134]. Indeed, the ratio could easily be kept at five or six work years to one year in retirement.*

One may divide the labor force in various ways, analytical or descriptive. For purposes of lay exposition one may divide it into *job makers* and *job takers*. One may also assume that the amount of employment of job takers depends very roughly on the number of job makers. If this be true, then whatever forces (e.g., excessive taxation) diminish the number or prevent the growth in number of job makers will affect job takers adversely, particularly job takers near the margin of employment, as a good many older workers are likely to be.

As Kreps has shown in Chapter 4, the average real income of older persons may increase over time but probably not fast enough to keep pace with the average real income of the population. A retired worker's income, being fixed, not only is not augmented by economic progress but also is subject to erosion through both inflation and the inability of many corporations to pay the pensions they are pledged to pay [48].

---

* Between 1900 and 1960 the number of years at work per year in retirement on relatively low retirement income fell from 14.1 to 6.1. Should a worker typically enter the labor force at age 20, retire at 60, and die at 80, he would work two years for every one in retirement. Within these two years he would have to earn enough to support himself comfortably and at the same time set aside enough to give rise to a comfortable retirement income. It would appear preferable under the assumed circumstances that he work at least 50 years to age 70 and thus raise the number of work years per retirement year at least to five (a ratio anticipated by the year 2000).

Not surprisingly, the incomes of many aged are below the poverty level and may be kept there if the poverty level is adjusted upward. Even so, given a prospective 2 percent per year increase in average output, the prospective need of the aged for governmental supplements can be met.*

The continuing employability of older workers, as shown elsewhere, depends on their meeting minimal health standards and hence, *inter alia,* on their having adequate access to medical and paramedical service, now in short supply because of the uneconomic manner in which medical service is produced and supplied [44]. Man's health problems are being intensified also, as René Dubos [13] points out, by the "slowly developing injurious effects" of man's "technological environment and the new ways of life." His whole environment is undergoing pollution—one might almost say that pollution is a form of entropy, a kind of perverse miracle of "loaves and fishes" wherein when man consumes x of something it gives rise to $3x$ of pollutants of one sort or another. To these conditions external to the worker must be added such body-weakening practices as overnutrition and the substitution of spectatorial for participative recreation. In sum, despite the improvements achieved in the field of medicine, the sum total of changes in the circumstances surrounding and animating man may eventually decrease man's employability in later years. After all, in the end, the functioning of a body may reflect adverse events much as a tree's rings reflect adverse seasons.

Contingencies

Uncertainty is a fellow traveler of man—especially of man in his later years—and thus conditions the shape of the future. Our assumptions regarding fertility have been borne out in that fertility has settled around the replacement level, with the average number of births currently *expected* per wife aged 20 to 24 very close to 2. Should this average persist, the population would become stationary in the 2030s at around 270 million in the absence of net immigration, with about 16 percent over age 64 and about 59 percent aged 18 to 64. Of course, given net immigration of 400,000 per year, population will have grown to 310 million or more by the 2030s. Given current class differences in morbidity and mortality, there is room for an increase in the life expectancy and the

* On some of the issues, see Brehm and Saving [5] and Conlisk [10].

length of the working life of those with lower incomes and educational attainment.

The financial prospect is not bright for three reasons. First, "stagflation" is wiping out paper assets of the aged and threatening Social Security payments by increasing unemployment and thus reducing the number of contributors to the Social Security system. Second, public claims on United States output have become so great, with government now absorbing about two-fifths of the national income, that government's share of the national income is not likely to increase very much in favor of older persons (e.g., for health insurance). Indeed, attempts to augment this share greatly will be increasingly resisted by employed members of the labor force out of whose incomes most tax revenue flows, directly or indirectly. Third, the current drive to reduce the normal age of retirement from 65 to between 55 and 60 may so much reduce the ratio of employed persons to persons dependent on Social Security and private pensions that the sources of income of persons in retirement will be threatened with shrinkage. After all, both Social Security and private pension systems rest essentially on a pay-as-you-go basis. For example, should everyone enter the labor force at 20 and withdraw at 55 instead of at 65, the ratio of contributors to these systems to retirees drawing on these systems would decline about 50 percent. The actual decline would be less, since not everyone of working age is gainfully employed, but it would still be great enough to undermine current Social Security and pension systems, since employed persons will resist paying taxes and sacrificing potential wage increases so that others can retire at, say, age 55. Intergenerational conflict will be intensified.

Conclusion

The need older people feel for public assistance will remain high in the future and will probably be intensified as well. On the one hand the purchasing power of their income streams will be gradually reduced by the inflationary pressures built into the American economy. On the other hand there will probably be increasing pressure to throw older workers out of the labor force as control of industry and access to employment becomes still more bureaucratized. Meanwhile, for at least several decades, the potential political power of the older members of the population is likely to be diminished. The prognosis, therefore, is for increasing public satisfaction of the material requirements of the aged but not in an amount sufficient to correct the current tendency toward increase in the relative deprivation of the aged. Only effective organization and leadership of the Townsend sort would be likely to reverse this tendency.

The older population's requirement of public assistance will turn in large part on the extent to which its disengagement from involvement in community socioeconomic activities parallels its physical and mental capacity for such involvement. Of overriding importance is its being kept engaged in economically gainful activity, since its involvement in other forms of activity depends largely on its remaining engaged in gainful activity. Such engagement depends in turn on the maintenance of physical and mental health at least into the early seventies and on the prevention of enforced disengagement of older persons either by trade union and corporate czars or by essentially autonomous bureaucrats. Flexibility and differentials in remuneration in keeping with differences in ability to perform are also essential. Some older persons may prefer disengagement. This they should be permitted, but with the right to reverse a decision to disengage within, say, 6 to 12 months should they find disengagement unsatisfying and be capable of reengagement [9].

References

1. Antipoverty Programs. *Law and Contemporary Problems* 31, No. 1, 1966.
2. Berry, W. F., and Daugherty, J. C. A closer look at rising medical costs. *Mon. Labor Rev.* 91:1, 1968.
3. Bleckman, B. M., et al. *Setting National Priorities: The 1975 Budget.* Washington, D.C.: Brookings Institution, 1974.
4. Brackett, J. C. A new budget for a retired couple. *Mon. Labor Rev.* 91:33, 1968.
5. Brehm, C. T., and Saving, T. R. The demand for general assistance payments. *Am. Econ. Rev.* 54:1002, 1964.
6. Brues, A. M., and Sacher, G. A. *Aging and Levels of Biological Organization.* Chicago: University of Chicago Press, 1965.
7. Cagan, P. *The Hydra-Headed Monster.* Washington, D.C.: American Enterprises Institute, 1964.
8. Canham, E. D. (Ed.). *The Concept of Poverty.* Washington, D.C.: U.S. Chamber of Commerce, 1965.
9. Clark, F. L. *Work, Age and Leisure.* London: Michael Joseph, 1966.
10. Conlisk, J. Simple dynamic effects in work-leisure choice: A skeptical comment on the static theory. *J. Hum. Resources* 3:324, 1968.

11. Council of Economic Advisors. *Annual Report.* Washington, D.C.: United States Government Printing Office, 1974.
12. Curtis, H. J. Biological mechanisms underlying the aging process. *Science* 141:686, 1963.
13. Dubos, R. *So Human an Animal.* New York: Scribner's, 1968.
14. Eastburn, D. P. Economic discipline and the middle generation. *Bus. Rev.* (Federal Reserve Bank of Philadelphia), January 1968.
15. Elson, R. T. How the old politics swamped the new economics. *Fortune,* September 1968. P. 75.
16. Faltermayer, E. K. The drift to early retirement. *Fortune,* May 1965.
17. Fein, R. *The Doctor Shortage: An Economic Diagnosis.* Washington, D.C.: Brookings Institution, 1967.
18. Future gains in longevity after age 65. *Stat. Bull. Metropol. Life Ins. Co.* 48:8, 1967.
19. Goldstein, S. Socio-economics and the migration differentials between the aged in the labor force and in the reserve. *Gerontologist* 7:37, 1967.
20. Gordon, M. S. National Retirement Policies and the Displaced Older Worker. In *Age with a Future.* Copenhagen: Munksgaard, 1964.
21. Harriss, C. L. (Ed.). Inflation: Long-term problems. *Proc. Am. Acad. Polit. Sci.* 31, 1975.
22. Hayflick, L. Human cells and aging. *Sci. Am.* 218:32, 1968.
23. *Health Resources Statistics.* Washington, D.C.: U.S. Department of Health, Education, and Welfare, December 1968. P. 123.
24. Henry, J. *Culture Against Man.* New York: Random House, 1963.
25. Jaffé, A. J., and Froomkin, J. *Technology and Jobs.* New York: Praeger, 1968.
26. Kreps, J. M. (Ed.). *Employment, Income, and Retirement Problems of the Aged.* Durham, N.C.: Duke University Press, 1963.
27. Machlup, F. *The Production and Distribution of Knowledge in the United States.* Princeton, N.J.: Princeton University Press, 1962.
28. Miller, H. P. *Income of the American People.* New York: Wiley, 1955. Chap. 6.
29. Nourse, E. G. Defining our employment goal under the 1946 Act. *Rev. Econ. Stat.* 38:193, 1956.
30. Orshansky, M. Counting the poor. *Soc. Sec. Bull.* 28:16, 1965.
31. Ott, D., et al. *Public Claims on U.S. Output.* Washington, D.C.: American Enterprise Institute, 1973.
32. Prehoda, R. W. *Extended Youth: The Promise of Gerontology.* New York: Putnam's, 1968.
33. Ryscavage, P. M., and Willacy, H. M. Employment of the nation's urban poor. *Mon. Labor Rev.* 91:15, 1968.
34. Seminar on Poverty. *Bull. Am. Acad. Sci.* 22:4, 1967.
35. Shock, N. W. The physiology of aging. *Sci. Am.* 206:100, 1962.
36. Siegel, I. H. Fuller employment with less inflation. Staff paper. Upjohn Institute, Kalamazoo, Michigan, January 1969.
37. Spengler, J. J. Services and the future of the American economy. *South. Atlantic Q.* 76:105, Winter 1967.
38. Spengler, J. J., and Kreps, J. M. Equity and Social Credit for the Re-

tired. In J. M. Kreps (Ed.), *Employment, Income, and Retirement Problems of the Aged.* Durham, N.C.: Duke University Press, 1963. Chap. 6 (especially pp. 213–219).

39. Stahl, S. W.   The Phillips curve: A dilemma for public policy—inflation versus unemployment. *Bus. Rev.* (Federal Reserve Bank of Philadelphia), January 1969. P. 11.

40. Strehler, B. L. (Ed.).   *Advances in Gerontological Research.* New York: Academic, 1964.

41. Strehler, B. L., and Mildvan, A. S.   General theory of mortality and aging. *Science* 132:14, 1960.

42. *Studies by the Staff of the Cabinet Committee on Price Stability.*   Washington, D.C.: Government Printing Office, January 1969. Chaps. 2 and 4.

43. *The Aging of Populations and Its Economic and Social Implications.* New York: United Nations, 1956. Pp. 55–59.

44. The plight of the U.S. patient.   *Time,* February 21, 1969. Pp. 53–58.

45. U.S. Bureau of the Census.   *Current Population Reports.* Series P-60, No. 55, August 1968.

46. *U.S. News & World Report,* October 16, (pp. 72–73); November 8 (pp. 99–100), 1965.

47. Valentine, C. A.   *Culture and Poverty.* Chicago: University of Chicago Press, 1968.

48. Wise, T. A.   Those uncertain actuaries. II. *Fortune,* January 1966. P. 164.

Index